A PEOPLE OF ONE BOOK: THE BIBLE AND THE VICTORIANS

A PEOPLE OF ONE BOOK

THE BIBLE AND THE VICTORIANS

TIMOTHY LARSEN

OXFORD
UNIVERSITY PRESS

OXFORD
UNIVERSITY PRESS

Great Clarendon Street, Oxford OX2 6DP

Oxford University Press is a department of the University of Oxford.

It furthers the University's objective of excellence in research, scholarship, and education by publishing worldwide in

Oxford New York

Auckland Cape Town Dar es Salaam Hong Kong Karachi
Kuala Lumpur Madrid Melbourne Mexico City Nairobi
New Delhi Shanghai Taipei Toronto

With offices in

Argentina Austria Brazil Chile Czech Republic France Greece
Guatemala Hungary Italy Japan Poland Portugal Singapore
South Korea Switzerland Thailand Turkey Ukraine Vietnam

Oxford is a registered trade mark of Oxford University Press
in the UK and in certain other countries

Published in the United States
by Oxford University Press Inc., New York

British Library Cataloguing in Publication Data

Data available

Library of Congress Cataloging in Publication Data

Data available

Typeset by SPI Publisher Services, Pondicherry, India
Printed in Great Britain
on acid-free paper by
MPG Books Group, Bodmin and King's Lynn

ISBN 978–0–19–957009–6

1 3 5 7 9 10 8 6 4 2

For Professor Boyd Hilton, F.B.A.
and *Trinity College, Cambridge*

Contents

Introduction

The eighteenth-century leader of the evangelical revival, John Wesley, famously described himself as 'a man of one book'.[1] He did not mean, of course, that he only read or valued one book—the Bible. Indeed, displaying his respect for classical learning, Wesley actually made his comment in Latin (*homo unius libri*), and he edited a series of fifty volumes of vital texts from across the centuries as a way of commending a starter library to his lay preachers. What Wesley meant was that one book—the Bible—was the Alpha and Omega of his life and thought—the foundation stone and the unrivalled pinnacle. In the same way, although the Victorians were awash in texts, the thesis of this volume is that they were a 'people of one book'—that the Bible loomed uniquely large in Victorian culture in fascinating and underexplored ways. The extent of the Bible's dominance, presence, and reach has to be encountered in the specifics of Victorian lives to be grasped fully, and thus this claim is supported by offering detailed, textured accounts of the lives, words, and thought of a range of Victorians from E. B. Pusey to Annie Besant, from Florence Nightingale to C. H. Spurgeon, from Catherine Booth to T. H. Huxley, from Grace Aguilar to Charles Bradlaugh, from Cardinal Wiseman to Elizabeth Fry, and more.

In short, this book explores the remarkable extent to which the Bible was a dominant presence in Victorian thought and culture. Numerous volumes—all mining different veins—could be written on the rich theme of the Bible and the Victorians. One approach would be to examine how the

---

[1] For a study of Wesley and Scripture, see Donald A. Bullen, *A Man of One Book? John Wesley's Interpretation of the Bible* (Milton Keynes: Paternoster, 2007).

Scriptures were the foundational textbook in schools and the main volume through which people gained basic literacy skills. For much of the nineteenth century many children learned to read at Sunday schools or at schools sponsored by churches or non-denominational religious organizations. The Scriptures were central in such contexts as a matter of course. Even in independent, working-class schools the Bible was still the standard book used 'for learning to read and for reading practice'.[2] This scriptural rite of passage to literacy was common for those educated at home as well. Even after universal state education was enacted in 1870 the Bible retained a fundamental place in schooling throughout the Victorian age. No less a figure than the polemical agnostic T. H. Huxley voted for the London School Board resolution on the core curriculum for elementary school children that named the Bible first, and only thereafter listed reading, writing, and arithmetic. Another approach would be to study the circulation of the Scriptures in the nineteenth century. Leslie Howsam, for example, has written an important study focused on the British and Foreign Bible Society.[3] Howsam's book takes the reader into a culture with organizations such as the Society for Reading Aloud the Word of God in Open Air—a title that it would be hard for even Charles Dickens to improve upon.[4]

Dickens serves to remind us that the centrality of the Bible in the Victorian age is amply revealed in its literature. The Scriptures were the common cultural currency of the Victorians. There are only two kinds of eminent Victorian authors—the kind who have had a whole book written about their use of Scripture and the kind who are ripe for such attention. The making of such books was begun by the Victorians themselves. For example, the influential art critic, John Ruskin, although he did not hold dogmatic religious views, nevertheless warranted a 303-page work entitled *The Bible References of John Ruskin* (1898).[5] Extraordinarily, this is an exploration of his work in the genre of a Bible dictionary. The first entry is 'Aaron, Death of' and the last one is 'Zedekiah'. An appendix arranges this

[2] Phil Gardner, *The Lost Elementary Schools of Victorian England: The People's Education* (London: Croom Helm, 1984), 177.

[3] Leslie Howsam, *Cheap Bibles: Nineteenth-Century Publishing and the British and Foreign Bible Society* (Cambridge: Cambridge University Press, 1991).

[4] Howsam, *Cheap Bibles*, 180.

[5] Mary and Ellen Gibbs, *The Bible References of John Ruskin* (London: George Allen, 1898).

material in canonical order by chapter from the fourteen references in Ruskin's works to Genesis chapter 1 to the nine references to Revelation chapter 22. Christina Rossetti is one of the most celebrated poets of the Victorian age. A scholar has produced a 256-page concordance of biblical allusions in her poetry.[6] A rather substantial such concordance could be compiled for any major Victorian poet, I suspect. The poet P. B. Shelley was one of the first public atheists in nineteenth-century elite culture. Irreligion and biblical illiteracy, however, do not correlate in this period and therefore there is an Oxford monograph entitled *Shelley and Scripture*.[7] Lord Byron is likewise not known for his piety or faith. One of his most famous poems is 'She walks in beauty', but few who admire it today are aware that it was originally published in a volume of his verse that had as its unifying theme the Old Testament, *Hebrew Melodies*. Many of the very titles of the poems in that collection are simply pure scriptural quotations.[8] Recently, my colleague Jeff Barbeau has published a book on the poet and philosopher S. T. Coleridge's use of Scripture.[9] The poet and critic Matthew Arnold's interest in Scripture is readily apparent. As Stefan Collini has observed: 'certainly no single text engaged his critical energies to anything like the same extent as did the Bible.'[10]

There is, of course, a book on the Bible and Dickens.[11] This premier Victorian novelist took his religion in his stride, disliked zealous and doctrinaire Christians, and left his wife for a mistress. Nevertheless, Dickens so assumed that every Victorian should know the contents of the Bible that he even created his own harmony of the Gospels as a tool for the education of his children.[12] In his last will, Dickens exhorted his offspring not to be bound by any dogmatic scheme but to take their rule of life directly from

---

[6] Nilda Jiménez (compiler), *The Bible and the Poetry of Christina Rossetti* (Westport, Connecticut: Greenwood Press, 1979). For a study of her handling of Scripture, see Timothy Larsen, 'Christina Rossetti, the Decalogue, and Biblical Interpretation', *Zeitschrift für Neuere Theologiegeschichte*, 16, 1 (2009), 21–36.

[7] Bryan Shelley, *Shelley and Scripture: The Interpreting Angel* (Oxford: Clarendon Press, 1994).

[8] Lord Byron, *Hebrew Melodies* (London: John Murray, 1815).

[9] Jeffrey W. Barbeau, *Coleridge, the Bible, and Religion* (New York: Palgrave Macmillan, 2008).

[10] Stefan Collini, 'Arnold, Matthew (1822–1888)', in H. C. G. Matthew and Brian Harrison (eds), *Oxford Dictionary of National Biography*, 60 vols (Oxford: Oxford University Press, 2004), 2, 487–94.

[11] Janet L. Larson, *Dickens and the Broken Scripture* (Athens, Georgia: University of Georgia Press, 1985). See also, Robert C. Hanna, *The Dickens Christian Reader: a collection of New Testament teachings and Biblical references from the works of Charles Dickens* (New York: AMS Press, 2000).

[12] Charles Dickens, *The Life of Our Lord* (London: Associated Newspapers Ltd, 1934).

the New Testament.[13] Pick up an annotated edition of any Victorian novel
and the notes will include biblical allusions that it never occurred to the
author would ever need explaining. The Bible provided an essential set of
metaphors and symbols. Scriptural knowledge is a required pre-requisite for
entering into a Victorian author's imaginative world; it is what Northrop
Frye called 'the great code' for understanding their works.[14] Literary scholars therefore have provided much of the scholarship that maps the vast
terrain of the Bible and the Victorians. A recent, useful introductory text on
nineteenth-century literature and religion, for example, is attuned to inter-
actions with Scripture, and numerous specialized monographs have been
published.[15] A particularly satisfying and stimulating volume which underlines that the Victorians were a people of one book is *Victorian Interpretation*.
In it, Suzy Anger uncovers how the interpretation of all texts in the
Victorian age was deeply indebted to scriptural hermeneutics and avers
that this genesis has left a permanent mark on literary studies.[16] Likewise,
this study, *A People of One Book*, reveals how the Bible provided an
irreplaceable linguistic register not only for novelists and poets, but for the
Victorians in general.

The content of the Scriptures also loomed large in nineteenth-century
visual arts. The older school of Academy painters was comprised of artists
who pursued biblical subjects as part of their work such as Charles Lock
Eastlake's *Hagar and Ishmael* or William Dyce's *Joash shooting the Arrow of
Deliverance*. The most significant new school of painting was the quintessentially Victorian art of the Pre-Raphaelites. Iconoclasts that they were in
other ways, the Pre-Raphaelites were even more scriptural than their pre-
decessors.[17] Not content with merely a biblical theme and title, Holman

[13] Rowland E. Prothero, *The Life and Correspondence of Arthur Penrhyn Stanley, D.D.*, 2 vols
(London: John Murray, 1894), II, 317. (Stanley read from Dickens's will in a memorial sermon for
the novelist at Westminster Abbey.)

[14] Northrop Frye, *The Great Code: The Bible and Literature* (New York: Harcourt Brace
Jovanovich, 1982).

[15] Mark Knight and Emma Mason, *Nineteenth-Century Religion and Literature: An Introduction*
(Oxford: Oxford University Press, 2006). A recent volume with a wider chronological sweep is
Rebecca Lemon, Emma Mason, Jonathan Roberts, and Christopher Rowland (eds), *The Blackwell
Companion to the Bible in English Literature* (Chichester: Wiley-Blackwell, 2009). As to the mono-
graphs see, for example, Sue Zemka, *Victorian Testaments: The Bible, Christology, and Literary
Authority in Early-Nineteenth-Century British Culture* (Stanford: Stanford University Press, 1997).

[16] Suzy Anger, *Victorian Interpretation* (Ithaca: Cornell University Press, 2005).

[17] Michaela Giebelhausen, *Painting the Bible: Representation and Belief in Mid-Victorian Britain*
(Aldershot: Ashgate, 2006).

Hunt even had the frames of his paintings inscribed with scriptural texts. *The Finding of the Saviour in the Temple* has Malachi 3: 1, 'And the Lord, whom ye seek, shall suddenly come to his Temple,' written out in the painting itself in both Hebrew and Latin, while the frame adds the New Testament reading, Luke 2: 48–9, in English. *The Scapegoat* has Isaiah 53: 4 written out on the top of the frame, balanced by Leviticus 16: 22 on the bottom. The third version of his most famous painting, *The Light of the World*, has Revelation 3: 20 in capital letters at its base: 'Behold, I stand at the door, and knock: if any man hear my voice, and open the door, I will come in to him, and will sup with him, and he with me.'[18] George P. Landow's classic study of the contours of Victorian biblical allusions combined both literature and the visual arts.[19]

Still other approaches would include examining the ordinary reader and the Bible, along the lines of Jonathan Rose's work, or the Victorian commitment to the Bible in relationship to race—as in the work of Colin Kidd—or to imperialism, as R. S. Sugirtharajah has done.[20] The approach taken in this study, however, is particularly in line with the emphasis on understanding the varieties of spiritual communities and schools of thought used by historians of religion. Moreover, it does not follow the well-trampled path of chronicling the Victorian encounter with modern biblical criticism. An early example, *The Bible in the Nineteenth Century*, was already being written before the Victorian age was over.[21] Willis B. Glover's mid-twentieth-century monograph is likewise typical of the scholarship that has come after it in that although he observes that 'the English became "the people of a book" to a degree that was rare in the rest of Christendom',

[18] For photographs of Hunt's frames, see Judith Bronkhurst, *William Holman Hunt: A Catalogue Raisonné*, 2 vols (New Haven: Yale University Press for the Paul Mellon Centre for Studies in British Art, 2006).

[19] George P. Landow, *Victorian Types, Victorian Shadows: Biblical Typology in Victorian Literature, Art and Thought* (Boston: Routledge & Kegan Paul, 1980).

[20] Jonathan Rose, *The Intellectual Life of the British Working Classes* (New Haven: Yale University Press, 2001); Colin Kidd, *The Forging of Races: Race and Scripture in the Protestant Atlantic World, 1600–2000* (Cambridge: Cambridge University Press, 2006); R. S. Sugirtharajah, *The Bible and Empire: Postcolonial Explorations* (Cambridge: Cambridge University Press, 2005). A recent cultural history with a wider chronological and geographical sweep is Lori Anne Ferrell, *The Bible and the People* (New Haven: Yale University Press, 2008).

[21] J. Estlin Carpenter, *The Bible in the Nineteenth Century* (London: Longmans, Green, and Co., 1903). (Carpenter wrote in the preface that he had began the project in 1900.)

his interest is not in displaying this Scripture-saturated culture, but rather in presenting the sources of its dissolution.[22]

Again, the unique and extraordinary centrality of this one book could be documented and explored in many ways. The structure of this volume is to show that it holds true across the religious and sceptical traditions. One book—the Bible alone, *sola Scriptura*—is a Protestant principle that, when the Victorian age is thought of, is particularly associated with evangelicalism in the minds of many. This study will indeed show what such a commitment looked like for nineteenth-century evangelical Protestants, but it will demonstrate furthermore that the Scriptures were also a preoccupation in the other varieties of belief and unbelief, and thus across the whole range of Victorian thought. Victorian atheists gave their best and most sustained labours to wrestling with Scripture; Victorian Unitarians commended their faith as more biblical than orthodox; Victorian Quakers experienced the inner light as a text prompter; Victorian liberal Anglicans weakened their doctrine of Scripture without loosening their grip on it; and so one could go on. This study will also bring back into view the Bible's place in marking the rhythm of life (most notably through morning and evening private and household devotions) and how it was the lens through which people saw their own experiences.

The aim of displaying the Victorians as a people of one book in this way is pursued through case studies of representative figures from the diverse traditions. As to the variety of traditions, the desire has been to be as comprehensive as possible within the limits of the space available. Therefore, it is hoped that this monograph will also serve as a useful tour of Victorian religion generally. While a common preoccupation with Scripture is a unifying theme, care is taken in each case study to show how this tradition thought about the nature of the Bible differently and pursued distinctive interpretative habits so that the diversity of Victorians' interactions with 'the book' is also underlined, elucidated, and explored. The common currency of the Bible is set in contrast to the distinctive theological views and practices of each tradition which are also carefully presented:

---

[22] Willis B. Glover, *Evangelical Nonconformists and Higher Criticism in the Nineteenth Century* (London: Independent Press, 1954), 16. John Rogerson has been a leading scholar in this field: see, for example, his *Old Testament Criticism in the Nineteenth Century: England and Germany* (London: SPCK, 1984). The Bible in the eighteenth century has likewise recently been rethought: Jonathan Sheehan, *The Enlightenment Bible: Translation, Scholarship, Culture* (Princeton: Princeton University Press, 2005).

many of the figures in this volume had such divergent views that they publicaly denounced one another as heretical, erroneous, or dangerous. Admittedly, the notion of an individual being 'representative' of a tradition is problematic and contestable. Nevertheless, an effort is made toward the start of each case study to commend the choice of this particular figure as defensible.

It is regrettable that accounts of religious history traditionally have so often focused overwhelmingly on men—and particularly so for studies of the Victorian age when we know that at most worship services a majority of those in attendance were women. Therefore, I committed from the beginning to design this volume so that at least half of the case-study figures would be women. Some readers might wonder if this goal has sometimes been a little in tension with the desire for a figure to be representative given that official representatives (bishops, for example) were more often—if not invariably—men in most traditions, but the author at any rate is satisfied that both aims have been sufficiently achieved. Moreover, choosing women subjects for many of the case studies has provided a deeper and richer connection to the lived experience of faith and doubt in the Victorian era and generated stimulating results that recast some set-piece assumptions and generalizations about various traditions in fruitful ways.

It should also be noted that the geographical scope of this study is confined to England due to the limitations of both space in the volume and stamina in the author (who felt able to have a go at Lake District peaks, but was daunted by Snowdon, let alone the Munros). The order of the chapters is simply the order in which they were researched, and this has no relationship to any internal logic of the subject matter, but rather was determined by external factors such as when I gained access to relevant sources. It seemed invidious to arrange the chapters—thereby asserting that certain traditions had particularly strong affinities with others—as the Victorians were so often concerned to dispel an outsider's assumption that their religious or sceptical group was similar in ilk to another one. The goal has been to allow each tradition to stand on its own and speak for itself rather than to colour the reader's perception by implying, for example, that a particular tradition was a weaker or strong version of another one.

Throughout this book I have followed my instincts about inserting biblical citations, trying to strike a *via media* in which the text did not become unduly cluttered, but readers are enabled to track down a crucial or quirky quotation or allusion and thereby assess or pursue the connection

themselves. The quotations densest with biblical allusions I particularly
tended to despair of and they therefore often end up with no citations at
all. It should also be kept in mind that the same, exact, distinctively
scriptural phrase can often recur in multiple places in the Bible, and the
reference I give might therefore be simply an arbitrarily chosen example
from among them. Citations in square brackets are always my addition and
not part of the quotation.

Scholars have too often ignored what Victorians wrote about the Bible
on the assumption that these are the least interesting of their works.
Moreover, when they have examined their comments on the Scriptures it
has often been in order to mine these sources for Victorian views on other
matters. In this volume I have sought to attend to what the Victorians
themselves were interested in rather than primarily to interrogate them
about our interests. When this is done, one finds a strong, consistent, and
pervasive preoccupation across the religious and sceptical spectrum with
engaging with the contents of one book—the Bible.

★★★

I have never before thought to acknowledge my editor and have sometimes
been bemused when I have read other authors doing so, but I now
understand fully: it has meant a great deal to me in recent years that
Tom Perridge at OUP has been so interested in my scholarly efforts. I am
so pleased to be able to work with him.

I am profoundly grateful for the help and friendship of many of my
colleagues, only a few of whom are named here. The intellectual nourishment I derive from the conversation of Alan Jacobs, Dan Treier, Brett
Foster, Rick Gibson, and the Café Padre crowd has been one of the greatest
benefits and joys of my professional life in recent years. Other colleagues
who have kindly shared their expert knowledge in the field of nineteenth-
century British studies with me include Christine Colón, Jeff Barbeau, and
Andy Tooley. John Walton is remarkably accessible for any random biblical
question I might have, and Dan Master has made a real mark on my
thinking. In a class of his own is another biblical studies colleague and
friend, Michael Graves, who read every chapter in draft as they were
researched and written each in turn, catching numerous minor errors, and
commenting insightfully on more substantial matters. Michael, I am deeply
grateful for your wide-ranging intellectual curiosity and generosity of
time and spirit. Postgraduate student research assistants who have helped

with this project and who are fine historians and scholars in their own right include Thomas Breimaier, Lindsey Eckberg, Amber Thomas, and Eric Brandt. The students in the autumn 2008 offering of my postgraduate seminar, 'The History of Evangelicalism', worked with zealous industry on transcribing Elizabeth Fry's Bible annotations. The Wheaton College administration—not least our Provost, Stan Jones—has also been very supportive of my work in numerous ways, including a generous Aldeen Grant to aid my sabbatical research in spring 2007. Jeff Greenman is not only a valued friend and a supportive Associate Dean, but he has even consistently allowed me to route our Reading the Bible through the Centuries series through Victorian Britain.

This project also benefited from a CCCU Scholarly Networking Grant. I am thankful for the insights of my primary collaborators, Stephen Alter, Sarah Miglio, and Tommy Kidd, and for those scholars we consulted who commented on my work: Bruce Kuklick, Stephen Shoemaker, and David Bebbington. Various scholars at other institutions have graciously answered questions or read a draft chapter of this work, including Pamela Walker, Roger Green, and Christian George. Numerous librarians and archives have helped to make this book possible, not least Mark Greenberg, Director, Special Collections Department, University of South Florida, and Richard Bernardy of that same department, and Katy Hooper, Special Collections and Archives, University of Liverpool Library.

This book began when I was on sabbatical in Cambridge. I am heartily thankful for the welcome I received from many members of the university, including Peter Mandler, David Gange, Michael Ledger-Lomas, Jeremy Morris, Mary Laven, Eugenio Biagini, David Thompson, Jon Parry, Michael Ward, and Jeremy Begbie. I take particular delight in the ongoing scholarly collaboration that has resulted from that time, especially with Peter Mandler, David Gange, and Michael Ledger-Lomas. Finally, and most of all, a word about the dedication: I have greatly admired Boyd Hilton's scholarship ever since I was a postgraduate student. I am still amazed that he sponsored me to be a Visiting Fellow, Trinity College, Cambridge, for the Lent and Easter terms 2007, and I am deeply grateful for this extraordinary act of assistance and thoughtfulness. Likewise, Trinity College was very supportive and generous and everyone there treated me with kindness. I hope that the dedication of this book—my project when I was at Trinity—serves as a token of my sincere gratitude.

I

Anglo-Catholics

E. B. Pusey and Holy Scripture

It is important to keep in mind how much E. B. Pusey (1800–82) was hated.[1] If there had been an annual opinion poll to identify the most notorious priest in the Church of England, it is probable that Oxford University's Regius Professor of Hebrew would have won it repeatedly, at the very least, in the period from the late 1840s through the 1850s. For others, of course, he was a true prophet and judge who had arisen in a time when the church needed to be set right, but whether he was despised or revered it was for the same reason—for endeavouring to move the Church of England, and therefore the English people, away from a Protestant identity and toward a Catholic one.

The Catholic revival in nineteenth-century Anglicanism goes by a range of names—'Tractarianism', 'the Oxford Movement', and 'Anglo-Catholicism' are three. It is a tribute to just how central Pusey was to this cause, however, that another prominent one during the mid-Victorian period was 'Puseyism'. Thus, when it came to pure vilification, we need look no further than to pamphlets with titles such as *Puseyism proved to be 'the number of the name' of the Apocalyptic Beast* (1843), *Puseyism, the School of the Infidels* (1865), and *Popery and Puseyism, Twin Demons with one soul, or, ritualism unmasked* (1867).[2] Indeed, a book with the title *Popery, Puseyism,*

[1] A longer version of this chapter has been published as Timothy Larsen, 'E. B. Pusey and Holy Scripture', *Journal of Theological Studies*, 60, 2 (October 2009), 490–526.

[2] Thomas Goodwin, *Puseyism proved to be 'the number of the name' of the apocalyptic beast* (Dublin: W. Curry, 1843); 'Layman of the Established Church', *Puseyism, the School of the Infidels* (London: A. Miall, 1865); R. M. Gurnell, *Popery and Puseyism, twin demons with one soul, or, ritualism unmasked* (London: Published at the Office of 'The Gospel Guide', 1867).

Jesuitism was published as late as 1903, that is, even after the Victorian age was over and Pusey himself had been dead for two decades.[3] John Keble, John Henry Newman, and Edward Bouverie Pusey are generally considered the three pre-eminent leaders of the Oxford Movement. Newman's conversion to Rome in 1845 means that only an early slice of his works could be used as representative of Anglo-Catholicism. Keble would have been a fitting case study for this chapter as well. Such a study might have featured an exploration of, among other of his writings, Keble's *The Psalter, or Psalms of David in English Verse* (1839).[4] Pusey certainly would have deferred to Keble as the true father and ongoing spiritual leader of the Oxford Movement. Nevertheless, Pusey was a much more active leader in a far more strategic post who survived the vicar of Hursley by over fifteen years. Keble himself boasted that he, notwithstanding being the older man, was 'a "Puseyite" of the very deepest dye'.[5] Brad Faught has recently observed that 'Dr Pusey was the visible head of Anglo-Catholicism.'[6] In short, it seems beyond all cavil to choose Pusey as a fitting representative of Victorian Anglo-Catholicism.[7]

This chapter is not the place to provide a comprehensive overview of Pusey's religious convictions and practices, but it would be useful to mention at least some aspects that distanced him from those who self-identified as Protestants. Pusey actively opposed Anglican cooperation with (other) Protestant groups. On the other hand, he earnestly set out

---

[3] Luigi Desanctis, *Popery, Puseyism, Jesuitism: described in a series of letters* (London: James, 1903). Admittedly, these letters were at least purportedly written in 1865 (in Italian), which would help to explain the dated term. On the other hand, presumably the publisher would have, at minimum, changed the title if he thought that readers would find it irrelevant. Moreover, the book even came out with the same title in a second edition in 1905.

[4] John Keble, *The Psalter, or Psalms of David in English Verse* (Oxford: J. H. Parker, 1839).

[5] Henry Parry Liddon, *Life of Edward Bouverie Pusey: Doctor of Divinity; Canon of Christ Church; Regius Professor of Hebrew in the University of Oxford*, ed. J. O. Johnston and Robert J. Wilson, third edition, 4 vols (London: Longmans, Green, and Co., 1893), vol. 4, 90. (Liddon died before he could complete this project and thus he is not solely responsible for its contents. For simplicity's sake, however, I will refer to Liddon and Liddon's *Life*.)

[6] C. Brad Faught, *The Oxford Movement: A Thematic History of the Tractarians and Their Times* (University Park, Pennsylvania: Pennsylvania State University Press, 2003), 27.

[7] Another option would have been a case study of Charles Gore (1853–1932), who was arguably the most prominent Anglo-Catholic of the late Victorian period, and who also was strikingly committed to writing biblical commentaries. One disadvantage of this option for the present volume, however, is that so much of Gore's work took place in the twentieth century. A suitable woman might have been Christina Rossetti, whose biblical faith I have explored elsewhere: Timothy Larsen, 'Christina Rossetti, the Decalogue, and Biblical Interpretation', *Zeitschrift für Neuere Theologiegeschichte*, 16, 1 (2009), 21–36.

proposals for working toward reunion with Rome. In his *Minor Prophets*, Pusey informed the reader that his aim was to incorporate throughout edifying or insightful quotations from 'those more thoughtful writers of all times'.[8] In practice, this meant not only the early church fathers and numerous medieval figures such as Bernard of Clairvaux and Thomas Aquinas, but also a very generous helping of a surprisingly wide range of authors belonging to the so-called 'Counter Reformation' including a clerical member of the Military Order of St James who attended the Council of Trent, Arias Montanus, and various Jesuits. In contrast, not only do later Protestant figures outside high church Anglicanism such as Puritan or Methodist divines never appear among the 'more thoughtful writers of all times', but even Luther and Calvin do not make it into this category. In terms of the sacraments, Pusey was a staunch defender of baptismal regeneration—the belief that salvation was bestowed at and through baptism. His doctrine of the Eucharist was deemed so unduly high and literal that an examination of it at Oxford in 1843 led to the extraordinary step of his being suspended for two years from university preaching. Pusey was the crucial figure in the restoration of auricular confession in Anglican circles, his own ministry as a father-confessor arousing much suspicion by those unsympathetic with the movement. Pusey's personal ascetic disciplines and penitential practices seemed bizarre and repulsive to most Protestants. Letters to Keble, for example, contain Pusey's concerns regarding what to do about the way that being physically ill was impeding his standard regime: 'I know not whether I am strong enough to resume the hair-cloth'; 'I have it on again, by God's mercy. I would try to get some sharper sort'; 'I cannot even smite on my breast much because the pressure of my lungs seems bad.'[9]

And then there was his very Catholic attitude toward celibacy. When expounding upon Jonah defying God's command by fleeing in the opposite direction, most Protestant commentators would never have considered as an apt application someone whom the Almighty calls to celibacy, but instead becomes engaged 'to marry forthwith'.[10] Likewise, from Pusey's reflections on a passage in Amos that refers to the Nazarites, one could easily forget that celibacy was no part of the Nazarite vow at all.[11] When Pusey

[8] E. B. Pusey, *The Minor Prophets, with a Commentary, Explanatory and Practical, and introductions to the several books*, 2 vols (New York: Funk & Wagnalls, 1885), I, p. viii.

[9] Liddon, *Pusey*, III, 99–108.

[10] Pusey, *Minor Prophets*, I, 397.   [11] Pusey, *Minor Prophets*, I, 267.

endowed St Saviour's Church, Leeds, and oversaw its establishment to reflect his ideal of an Anglo-Catholic parish, he made it clear that he wanted its spiritual leader to be a 'simple self-denying (unmarried) priest'.[12] Even more offensive to a typical Protestant sensibility, Pusey was a key figure in pioneering the establishing of convents for Anglican nuns.[13]

Low church Protestants view their strong commitment to the Bible as central to the *raison d'être* of their form of Christianity, and thus at least some of them seemed to long for a neat polarity in which Pusey would be unsound on this front. Alas for them, reality was not so obliging. John Morris's polemical tract, *Puseyism Unmasked! or, the Great Protestant Principle of the Right of Private Judgment Defended, against the arrogant assumptions of the advocates of Puseyism,* may serve to illustrate this point.[14] Morris, a Nonconformist minister of no or indeterminate denominational identity, asserted that Puseyites wanted 'to withhold the scriptures from the people', and concluded by informing his hearers that they should be grateful that, as Protestant Dissenters, they 'have the Bible, and may read it'.[15] This sharp divide was wishful thinking, however, which the rest of the pamphlet makes clear that even Morris himself did not believe. Indeed, so far was Morris from imagining that Pusey and his followers disdained the authority of the Bible that one of his complaints against them was 'their repudiation of our churches as unscriptural'.[16] Morris was much better at bald denunciation than coherent argument, but the title of his address did identify aright the real difference between himself and the Oxford professor: what was at stake was not the authority of the Bible itself but rather that of its interpreters.

Pusey believed that authoritative interpretation of Holy Scripture did not lie with private individuals today, but rather people today should be guided by the collective interpretation of the early church fathers. Individual fathers sometimes gave wrongheaded readings, but their consensus is a reliable guide, while the personal views of oneself or any given modern Christian are not. Pusey laid out this position when explaining the value of the *Library*

[12] Liddon, *Life*, III, 134.

[13] For how emotive an issue Catholic convents could be for a Victorian Anglican, see Walter L. Arnstein, *Protestant versus Catholic in Mid-Victorian England: Mr Newdegate and the Nuns* (Columbia, Missouri: University of Missouri Press, 1982).

[14] John Morris, *Puseyism Unmasked! or, the Great Protestant Principle of the Right of Private Judgment Defended, against the arrogant assumptions of the advocates of Puseyism: A Discourse,* third edition (London: Paternoster Row, 1842).

[15] Morris, *Puseyism,* 6, 14.   [16] Morris, *Puseyism,* 10.

of the Fathers (an edited series of volumes that tellingly was heavily weighted toward patristic works that were exegetical in nature):

> there is no semblance of 'contrasting Scripture and the Fathers, as coordinate authority'. Scripture is reverenced as paramount; the 'doctrine of the Old or New Testament' is the source; the 'Catholic Fathers and ancient Bishops' have but the office of 'collecting out of that same doctrine'; the Old and New Testaments are the fountain; the Catholic Fathers, the channel, through which it has flowed down to us. The contrast then in point of authority is not between Holy Scripture and the Fathers, but between the Fathers and *us*; not between the Book interpreted and the interpreters, but between one class of interpreters and another; between ancient Catholic truth and modern private opinions...[17]

In a letter he wrote in 1839 to the German biblical scholar Friedrich Tholuck, Pusey put the contrast this way:

> The Ultra-Protestants, on the other hand, deny this necessity of submission, and assert that to be truth which each individual himself derives from Holy Scripture...I believe the difference, when followed out, to be this: the Ultra-Protestant believes 'the good man', the individual, to be infallibly 'guided into all truth'; we, the Church Universal.... People can interpret Scripture as they please, in great measure, and therefore it often costs them no submission...[18]

In a punchy academic article, Colin Matthew argued that, although Pusey liked to imagine that he had more-or-less held to the same views throughout his life, there was a time when he was young at which he actually thought like a Broad Churchman (as this position would come to be termed).[19] Such a hidden discontinuity can be uncovered on the issue at hand. Although his Anglo-Catholic disciple and biographer, H. P. Liddon, omitted this portion of the letter (apologizing obliquely for its suppressed contents with the observation that Pusey had 'pronounced off-hand' on issues he had not really thought through yet),[20] the 28-year-old contender

[17] E. B. Pusey (trans.), *The Confessions of S. Augustine* (*Library of the Fathers* 1) (Oxford: John Henry Parker, 1853), p. v.

[18] Liddon, *Life*, II, 19.

[19] H. C. G. Matthew, 'Edward Bouverie Pusey: From Scholar to Tractarian', *Journal of Theological Studies*, n.s., 32, 1 (April 1981), 101–24. For Pusey's more sympathetic view of German theological liberalism as a young man, see also David Forrester, *Young Doctor Pusey: A Study in Development* (London: Mowbray, 1989), especially 32–50, 211–31.

[20] Liddon, *Life*, I, 185.

for the Regius professorship in Hebrew was once willing to reject the collective patristic exposition on a particular point:

> with regard the 'procession of the Holy Spirit'—I receive the words as they stand in Scripture, but I cannot but think that the speculations even in the Anti-Nicene [*sic*—i.e. Ante-Nicene] Church, made a higher mystery of this expression than is in Scripture, in that they considered it as describing some relation (so to speak) of God to Himself, whereas it seemed to me in Scripture only to relate to the Spirit coming, as the common gift of both, to man.[21]

Pusey's most concerted statement of his mature view on biblical interpretation was an articulation of the Anglican *via media*. In 1851 (presumably not coincidentally during the height of the so-called 'papal aggression' agitation), the Oxford professor preached a university sermon entitled 'The Rule of Faith'. Here he carefully explained that Scripture itself was the authoritative source, but the fathers collectively were the interpretative guide: 'not to supply any thing wanting to Holy Scripture, but to explain what is in it; not to add to our knowledge, but to prevent our misunderstanding it, or failing to understand the depth of the words which God the Holy Ghost spake.'[22] While Pusey does take a passing swipe at 'private judgment', his real target in this sermon is the Church of Rome, which the hearer is invited to observe has departed from the rule of faith on a range of issues, with particular attention being given to 'the cultus of the Blessed Virgin'.[23] In Pusey's view, Ultra-Catholics and Ultra-Protestants both needed to have their own views shaped and constrained more by those of the fathers.

Pusey was a Bible man his whole life. His intellectual life was focused upon the Scriptures from the outset. Again, while Pusey's retrospective claims that his youthful turn toward the Old Testament was apologetic in intent may have been a rewriting of his personal history, the basic fact of his immediate commitment to biblical studies is not in doubt. In 1823, the year after Pusey obtained his undergraduate degree, he was elected a Fellow of Oriel College, Oxford. It is both genuinely telling and fittingly symbolic

---

[21] Pusey House, Oxford, Pusey Collection, Liddon Bound Volumes (hereafter LBV), 108, Pusey to Bishop Lloyd, 6 October 1828. (LBV items are the copies that Liddon himself made of letters by Pusey. Liddon did this work meticulously and, as has been pointed out already, he chose to suppress this part of the letter.)

[22] E. B. Pusey, *The Rule of Faith as maintained by the Fathers, and the Church of England, A Sermon preached before the University on the fifth Sunday after Epiphany 1851*, third thousand (Oxford: James Parker, 1878), 14.

[23] Pusey, *Rule*, 5–6 (on private judgment), 47–59 (here 51).

that, as Alan Livesley has shown, the earliest record that can be recovered of Pusey's use of Oriel library is his having borrowed Graves's *Lectures on the Pentateuch*. Moreover, subsequent records for those first two years of his fellowship reveal 'a marked interest in Old Testament and oriental studies'.[24] John Henry Newman's assessment in May 1823 of this new addition to the Oriel common room was: 'How can I doubt his seriousness? His very eagerness to talk of the Scriptures seems to prove it.'[25] Then, Pusey spent over a year in Germany during the period 1825–7. His studies with scholars focused on the Bible and the languages useful for Old Testament study. During this period and upon his return to England, Pusey's scholarly schemes were biblical ones. The most ambitious one (a project that was embarked upon before *An Historical Enquiry*) was a plan to produce single-handedly a modern translation of the entire Old Testament.

Before pursuing the various works on scriptural themes that Pusey published throughout his lifetime, it would be helpful to look at the place of the Bible in his private life. Pusey came from a family and created one of his own in which the habitual study of Holy Scripture was a normal, expected part of personal piety. Of his mother, we are told: 'Her time was laid out by rule: a certain portion was always given to reading the Bible.'[26] In 1826 Pusey wrote from Bonn to his 16-year-old brother, William. His advice to him included that he read a chapter of the New Testament in Greek every day. While this can be set down partially to the fact that William had expressed an interest in becoming a clergyman, the way that it also reflects the values of the family more generally is illustrated by Pusey's additional suggestion that their sister could help William with his Hebrew.[27] When he was courting Maria Barker, the besotted lovers earnestly discussed various passages of Scripture that seemed problematic.[28] Moreover, Pusey

[24] Alan Livesley, 'Regius Professor of Hebrew', in Perry Butler (ed.), *Pusey Rediscovered* (London: SPCK, 1983), 71–118 (here 75–6).

[25] Liddon, *Life*, I, 61.

[26] Liddon, *Life*, I, 5.

[27] Liddon, *Life*, I, 109–10.

[28] R. William Franklin has pointed out that Liddon covered over the fact that Maria was expressing real doubts about the nature of Scripture: R. William Franklin, 'The Impact of Germany on the Anglican Catholic Revival in Nineteenth-Century Britain', *Anglican and Episcopal History*, 61, 4 (December 1992), 433–8 (here 438–9). The best source on the relationship between Pusey and Maria is Forrester. For the purpose at hand, see in particular her forthright comments on the epistle to the Romans: Forrester, *Young*, 60.

could write to her on the assumption that her personal habits were the same as those of his family: 'You will find in your daily reading of the Bible . . .'[29] As his wife, Maria's enthusiasm for the study of Scripture was so great, she undertook to write her own commentary on Matthew. Their frail son, Philip Edward, helped to translate into English Cyril of Alexandria's commentary on John's Gospel.[30] When Maria wanted her husband to understand just how ill she was, she explained that she was unable to perform even the most essential daily tasks: 'The Greek New Testament I have not opened to-day.'[31] It is perhaps unnecessary to add that daily Bible reading is a stereotypically Protestant form of devotion. More poignantly, Pusey throughout his life instinctively turned to Scripture for consolation when grieving the loss of a loved one.

Another way that 'more Catholic' versus 'more Protestant' forms of Christian life are often distinguished is to aver that high church worship exalts the altar at the expense of the pulpit, whilst low church worship privileges word at the expense of sacrament. This pattern is not borne out in Pusey's case. As extraordinarily deep as his sacramental faith was, it never nudged the exposition of Holy Scripture back in order to make more room. It is telling that Liddon routinely identified what Pusey preached on by giving a text rather than a theme. This holds true for even such a special address as the one the Regius professor gave at the opening of Keble College's chapel.[32] Indeed, Liddon's *Life* even includes an appendix listing Pusey's sermons, not chronologically, but rather 'in order of the texts' from a sermon on Genesis 3: 4–5 through some two hundred sermons sprinkled across the canon to one on Revelation 21: 6.[33] Even a Scottish Calvinist would have had to concede that when Pusey was the preacher, Scripture was given its due. Here, for example, is a typical report: 'I preached for an hour in the morning in Mr Dodsworth's chapel; then we administered the Communion to above a hundred people . . . preached for an hour in the evening.' The following month, he wrote again to his wife: 'My sermon was, I am told, an hour and a half. People were very attentive, and the dear little children very quiet and good.'[34] That seems to have been a special meeting,

---

[29] Liddon, *Life*, I, 125.
[30] St Cyril of Alexandria, *Commentary on the Gospel according to S. John*, trans. Philip Edward Pusey et al. (London: Rivingtons, 1874).
[31] Liddon, *Life*, II, 85.   [32] Liddon, *Life*, IV, 323.
[33] Liddon, *Life*, VI, 447–53.   [34] Liddon, *Life*, II, 22–3.

but over the years Pusey blessed quite a few ordinary Sunday morning congregations with a sermon lasting an hour and a half.

E. B. Pusey valued Holy Scripture so much that he perpetually worried that biblical literacy was on the wane. Already when he was just in his mid-twenties, he complained: 'of the contents, historical and doctrinal, of the Bible, and of any illustrations of them,—Eton boys are generally shamefully ignorant.'[35] Thirty years later, he imagined that the same was true of Oxford: 'The young men (our future Clergy) are ignorant, in the extreme, of the Bible.'[36] Pusey's letters are littered with apt quotations that bring the teaching of Scripture to bear on the subjects at hand. What is perhaps even more revealing is how often he turns to the Bible for language to express his own thoughts. Despairing over university politics, for example, he wrote to Keble: 'we are in the state of Israel under the Judges, when every one did that which was right in his own eyes.'[37] When thinking of what the founding of Keble College meant, his mind naturally gravitated to a rather obscure and involved biblical analogy:

> On higher authority, we know how Jeremiah while yet in prison, and with the certain knowledge that Jerusalem should be taken by the Chaldaeans, was taught of God to buy the inheritance of his uncle's son at Anathoth, and bury the title-deeds for many days. So now, be Oxford beleaguered as it may...[38]

This commitment arose, of course, from a deep conviction regarding biblical authority. It would be easy to imagine a certain kind of Victorian fleeing a crumbling biblical authority by seeking refuge in the authority of the church and tradition, but this is not at all what the Regius professor was doing. Pusey believed that 'all truth does indeed lie in Holy Scripture'.[39] He declaimed confidently from the pulpit that the 'source of faith is, beyond doubt, the Holy Scriptures', and that all matters of faith 'must be capable of being proved out of Holy Scripture'.[40] Many Protestants would refer to such statements as declarations of the principle of *sola Scriptura*. Throughout Pusey's writings, these convictions can be seen in operation. When he is asked to think about whether or not an idea or practice is appropriate, he

---

[35] Liddon, *Life*, I, 15.
[36] LBV, 104, Pusey to John Keble, n.d. (27 February 1856?).
[37] LBV, 106, Pusey to John Keble, St Mark's Day, 1863.
[38] Liddon, *Life*, VI, 205.   [39] Liddon, *Life*, III, 150.   [40] Pusey, *Rule*, 4, 36.

instinctively and habitually discusses those scriptural passages that he believes are germane. Thus, the issue, which had become a legislative question, of whether or not a man could marry his deceased wife's sister really did turn in Pusey's mind on the correct interpretation of Leviticus 18: 6. Pusey even had qualms about an organized, announced prayer meeting on the grounds that Matthew 6: 6 charges believers to pray secretly.[41] This is fascinating precisely because it is so quirky: it is stereotypically ultra-Protestants who generate hitherto unrecognized prohibitions on the basis of biblical texts. If all this seems paradoxical, it did not to the leader of the Anglo-Catholics who insisted that 'the most Tractarian book I ever open is the Bible' and 'Tractarianism, as it is called, or, as I believe it to be, the Catholic Faith, will survive in the Church of England while the Scriptures are reverenced.'[42] Catholic devotion and biblicist Christianity were not separate forms of spirituality in his mind: Dr Pusey wanted to beat himself as an act of penance—and recite Psalm 51 at the same time.[43]

Pusey's insistence that Tractarianism was simply the teaching of the Bible is exemplified in the Tracts for the Times themselves. Newman recalled regarding Pusey: 'His Tract *On Fasting* appeared as one of the series with the date December 21 [1833]. He was not, however, I think, fully associated in the Movement till 1835 and 1836, when he published his Tract *On Baptism* and started the *Library of the Fathers*. He at once gave us a position and a name.'[44] The name, of course, was 'Puseyites', and Newman is pointing out that the decisive factor identifying the Regius professor as the embodiment of the movement was Pusey's lengthy and rigorous treatment of baptismal regeneration in the *Tracts for the Times*. This contribution was not, however, entitled *On Baptism* (as Newman has it), but rather, significantly, *Scriptural Views of Holy Baptism*. And its true title was an accurate description of its contents, and one that reflected Pusey's deep and genuine commitment to the authority of Scripture. Tract 67 began:

> Every pious and well instructed member of our Church will in the abstract acknowledge, that in examining whether any doctrine be a portion

---

[41] Liddon, *Life*, II, 129.   [42] Liddon, *Life*, III, 149, 300.

[43] Liddon, *Life*, III, 108.

[44] John Henry Newman, *Apologia pro Vita Sua*, ed. Ian Ker (London: Penguin, 1994 [originally 1864]), 71.

of revealed truth, the one subject of inquiry must be, whether it be contained in Holy Scripture.[45]

The main body of *Scriptural Views of Holy Baptism* is hundreds of pages of careful exposition of Scripture. Indeed, this is so much the case that the table of contents is often just biblical references—to give just a few examples, the theme of pages 53–64 is 'Tit. iii. 5'; of pp. 124–33 is 'Col. ii. 10–13'; of pp. 200–5 is 'Eph. iv. 4', and so on.[46]

Although one would have a hard time realizing this by reading the existing studies, the exposition of Scripture was at the very heart of the mature Pusey's understanding of his own ministry. This can certainly be traced continuously from 1847. In that year, Pusey became exuberant about a scheme to parcel out the canon to various authors who would collectively create a 'Commentary for the unlearned' on the entire Bible. The Regius professor wrote to Henry Edward Manning trying to bully him up to his own level of commitment:

> It is a very important plan, but we want help. . . . Whom can we look to for doing any thing to draw out the meaning of the Gospel for the poor, if you do not? Must we own, things are so confused, that no one has leisure to study Holy Scripture or put down some of its meaning for others?[47]

Later that same month, February 1847, Pusey wrote to Keble: 'It is a very great work, but its very greatness seems to buoy me up and make me hope that it comes from God and that He wills it to be done.'[48]

In the end, all the other potential contributors fell by the wayside, but Pusey soldiered on as a lone expositor of Scripture along the lines of the original plan for the rest of his life. In 1860, the first part of his *The Minor Prophets, with a Commentary explanatory and practical and introductions to the several books*, appeared. In the introduction, he promised and predicted truthfully that this publication was not the end, but rather the beginning—that he would dedicate the rest of his life to this noble cause: 'To this employment, which I have had for many years at heart, but for which the various distresses of our times, and the duties which they have involved,

---

[45] E. B. Pusey, *Scriptural Views of Holy Baptism*, fourth edition, Tracts for the Times 67, Part 1 (London, Rivington, n.d. [original edition, 1835]), p. [1]. (I have accessed this from the following facsimile reprint of the *Tracts for the Times*: New York: AMS Press, 1969.)

[46] Pusey, *Scriptural Views*, 399–400 ('Contents').

[47] LBV, 108, Pusey to Henry Edward Manning, '1st Th. in Lent' [17 February 1847].

[48] LBV, 102, Pusey to John Keble, '2nd S[unday]. in Lent' [28 February], 1847.

have continually withheld me, I hope to consecrate the residue of the years and of the strength which God may give me.'[49] Such affirmations recur steadily from this point. Pusey wrote to the *Guardian* in the following year affirming again that his remaining years were reserved for biblical exposition.[50] In 1862, he wrote to Keble expressing his settled conviction that writing commentaries was the best way to foster the true faith and the right response to the times: 'I am sure that the development [i.e. elucidation] of Holy Scripture is, above all things, the way to meet heresy and Rationalism.'[51] By 1863, he was speaking of this identity retrospectively as well, implying that he consecrated his life to Old Testament studies at the age of 25 because his time in Germany had revealed to him that this was where the forces of orthodoxy need to marshal their troops for the coming battle.[52] It is often pointed out that the prompt for Pusey's *Daniel the Prophet* (1864) was his desire to counteract the influence of the theologically liberal *Essays and Reviews* (1860). What is not noticed, however, is that he was simply tempted to shift his focus from one biblical commentary project to another. *Daniel the Prophet* came precisely at the middle point of the *Minor Prophets* series with three parts already published and three still to come (the last arrived in 1877). In 1873, while in Italy, Pusey became seriously ill with pneumonia and almost died. Newman was naturally concerned about his friend's health. Pusey's reply reveals that this underlining of the fact that he was a frail, elderly man who had already outlived the biblically allotted lifespan of three score and ten, had only served to reinforce his self-understanding of his life's work:

> By God's blessing and mercy, I am able to work again, so, I have completed (as far as I could here) the Comm. On Haggai and (Zechariah being completed all but the Introd.) am within 8 verses of the close of Malachi. Now, being allowed to be in England early in May, I am leaving Genoa, though I feel doubtful whether my chest is strong enough to lecture yet. Still God allows me to go [on] with the Comm.y without hindrance, thanks be to His mercy.[53]

In the context of Pusey's hopes that others would have written commentaries in the series, Liddon reported: 'In later years Pusey bitterly lamented

[49] Pusey, *Minor Prophets*, I, p. vii (originally published in 1860).
[50] Pusey House Oxford, Pusey Collection, Pamphlet 11956a: *A Letter on the 'Essays and Reviews' By Dr Pusey. (Reprinted from 'The Guardian'.)*, dated 'Lent 1861'.
[51] LBV, 106, Pusey to John Keble, 12 October 1862.
[52] LBV, 133, Pusey to George Williams, 27 January 1863.
[53] LBV 122, Pusey to Newman, Genoa, 'Easter Tu.' [1873].

the failure of this—the most cherished project of his life.'[54] If all the scholars who have written about Pusey in the last fifty years had been asked, 'what was the most cherished project of his life?,' it is doubtful that a single one of them would have said the biblical commentaries.

Having finally completed the Minor Prophets in his late seventies, Pusey did not then embrace what for most people would have been seen as a much delayed retirement, but rather plunged into a commentary on the Psalms. It is worth quoting the Liddon biography on this:

> When he had completed his Commentary on the Minor Prophets in 1877, after eighteen years' persistent labour at every spare moment, he at once began a similar work on the Psalms. This was his last great plan for Hebrew study: he worked at it continually until his death. In Term time he lectured on these Psalms: in Vacation he increased his notes on them.[55]

Liddon's *Life* goes on to paint the ailing, octogenarian exegete's last movements before he was laid on his deathbed, not to rise again until (as he would have emphatically said) the Day of Judgment:

> During the morning of that day Pusey remained in his little bedroom reading the Hebrew Bible. He observed on coming out that he had spent a long time over a single botanical term without being able to satisfy himself as to its exact meaning. In his days of health, when he had come to the conclusion that the sense of a word was uncertain, he would have weighed the probabilities, decided, at any rate provisionally, in favour of one meaning, and gone on to something else. Now the word haunted him; he talked about it at luncheon to the kind friends who waited on him, and who, of course, did not understand Hebrew.[56]

Thus Pusey's lifelong quest to understand Holy Scripture continued to the very end.

Despite Pusey's biblical commentaries being his life's work, they have been unfairly ignored or dismissed. This treatment begins even at the beginning with Liddon's *Life*. As Pusey's Victorian biography was a mammoth four volumes, no one could reasonably wish that it was any longer. Nevertheless, the proportions are strange in this regard. While many slight and incidental works are given a great deal of attention, Pusey's *Minor Prophets* is never examined at all!—this despite the fact that it was the only

---

[54] Liddon, *Life*, III, 157.   [55] Liddon, *Life*, IV, 310.   [56] Liddon, *Life*, IV, 383.

fruit of what is conceded to have been 'the most cherished project of his life'. *Daniel the Prophet* receives just over three pages and reactions to the book are completely ignored. It would seem that by 1893 these works were embarrassing for Anglo-Catholics who had acquiesced in many modern theories of biblical criticism that Pusey had opposed. A leading figure in this transition toward a more liberal approach to biblical studies was Charles Gore, the first principal of Pusey House and one of Liddon's literary executors. After its brief discussion of *Daniel the Prophet*, the Liddon biography moves on to an apologetic paragraph which explains that Pusey wrote when critics were more hostile to the faith and when people did not think that the two could be reconciled.[57]

And that was Pusey in the hands of his disciples and friends. Since then, the dismissiveness has become much worse. The most egregious example is Colin Matthew's 1981 article. Its tendentious subtitle says it all: 'From Scholar to Tractarian'. Matthew sees it as a loss to scholarship that the Regius professor abandoned his youthful (on this reading of Pusey's life) Broad Church position. Matthew argues that, for the mature Pusey, 'his scholarship was subordinated to what was really a curious sort of statesman-ship'.[58] This sounds devastating until one wonders what it might actually mean—or even to whom it would not apply. It seems to mean no more than that Pusey came to his scholarly tasks with well-established views on a variety of germane issues, conscious that he was a leader within a group of likeminded people who were trying to influence society. I imagine a case for the same charge could be made for almost every major Broad Church leader as well: A. P. Stanley, Benjamin Jowett, John William Colenso, and so on. Indeed, Matthew's praise for Pusey's study of German theology, that it was 'a Broad Church manifesto', sounds suspiciously like Matthew celebrating statesmanship.[59] Matthew's main foil is Pusey's *Daniel*. Alas, it is apparent that Matthew never bothered to read this volume before denouncing and dismissing it. His citations from *Daniel the Prophet* are confined exclusively to the preface. Matthew claims that Pusey's slide down from the integrity of his Broad Church youth 'concluded with his response to Darwinism and theological liberalism in his notorious

---

[57] Liddon, *Life*, IV, 74.   [58] Matthew, 'Pusey', 101.

[59] Matthew, 'Pusey', 110. (I am merely playing with Matthew's language here. This comment is not intended to endorse the generally abandoned notion that there was such a thing as a Broad Church 'party'.)

commentary on the Book of Daniel in 1864'.[60] 'Notorious' is an effort to substitute an assertion that is as unfocused as it is prejudicial for a demonstration. Moreover, Pusey nowhere mentions Darwinism in the book and it is simply wrong to aver that he saw this study as in any way a response to Darwinism. Matthew must have thrown this in either as a guess regarding the contents of a book he had not read or as an easy (albeit erroneous) way to strengthen the impression that Pusey's book revealed him to be an obscurantist. The closest that Matthew gets to a substantive critique is condemning *Daniel the Prophet* on the grounds that Pusey's 'dogmatism was explicit'.[61] Matthew, it would seem, would have liked to imagine that Pusey had substituted dogmatic assertions for the hard work of grappling with the evidence but, in truth, *Daniel the Prophet* is as direct and thorough and learned an engagement with all the latest findings of biblical higher criticism as one could imagine. Thus Matthew absurdly accuses: 'rather than face the implications of his German scholarship, Pusey abjured them'; Pusey judged that modernism could not be beaten intellectually and so decided 'it must be defeated by piety' instead; and Pusey's approach was an 'attempt to answer modernism by ignoring it'.[62] Actually, it is Matthew who did not face the scholarship in Pusey's *Daniel* but rather evaded it; and Matthew who attempted to answer Pusey's learned efforts by ignoring them.[63]

More in line with the Liddon project, but somewhat cowed by Matthew's perspective, is the edited volume, *Pusey Rediscovered* (1983).[64] It contains fifteen essays—many of which carve out new areas of research in astute and fruitful ways. Nevertheless, the strange lacuna in Liddon's *Life* is perpetuated rather than redressed. The index has a section on Pusey's published works. In addition to his contributions to *Tracts for the Times* along with his university and other sermons, eleven specific titles are listed in the index including *Remarks on the Prospective and Past Benefits of Cathedral Institutions* (which is not only the theme of an entire essay, but also reappears

---

[60] Matthew, 'Pusey', 111.   [61] Matthew, 'Pusey', 115.

[62] Matthew, 'Pusey', 117–20. Admittedly, Matthew is addressing Pusey's views on university reform as well and his evidence (for what there is) really comes from that context.

[63] An insightful article by Franklin also belies the neat dichotomy that Matthew created by demonstrating that it was precisely the direct influence of leading German scholars during his time studying on the Continent that also fostered Pusey's growing interest in patristics. Franklin, 'Impact', especially 440–1.

[64] Butler, *Pusey*.

in other chapters), *The Proposed Statute for a Theological School*, *The Royal Supremacy not an Arbitrary Authority but limited by the Laws of the Church of which Kings are Members*, *The Royal and Parliamentary Ecclesiastical Commissions*, and, following Matthew's obsession, there are fifteen pages sprinkled throughout the volume that discuss Pusey's youthful *An Historical Enquiry into the Probable Causes of the Rationalist Character lately predominant in the Theology of Germany*. In contrast, there are no entries on either *Daniel the Prophet* or the *Minor Prophets*, despite biblical commentaries being Pusey's life's work (albeit there is a single page referring to them which the indexer presumably missed).[65] The one page is from Livesley's essay. He observes that *Daniel the Prophet* has 'become almost a byword in some quarters for an unscholarly and unbudging conservatism'. Livesley's attempt to moderate this harsh judgment is to own as 'fair' an assessment made in 1914: Pusey's *Minor Prophets* and *Daniel* 'were monuments of learning, but especially in the latter, of learning devoted to a dying, and now long-dead cause.' I shall argue below that this judgment might have seemed obvious in 1914 or even in 1983, but it was not in Pusey's own day. David Forrester's *Young Doctor Pusey* (1989) continued the obsession with Pusey's *An Historical Enquiry*—offering twenty additional pages analysing it—and ended before Pusey began writing biblical commentaries.[66]

Daniel the Prophet is essentially a monograph, the thesis of which is that the book of Daniel really was written in the sixth century BCE (the traditional view) and that, strictly on the basis of the evidence, the case that certain modern higher critics had made for a late dating (the second century BCE) could be shown to create more problems than it solved. By the end of the nineteenth century, most professional Old Testament scholars, even in Britain, had become convinced of the late dating and (outside certain conservative, confessional circles) the second-century theory has continued to be the standard one ever since. This subsequent history has tempted scholars to assume anachronistically that if Pusey had been a true scholar he would have agreed with the British scholarly consensus that emerged only after his death. Innumerable radical theories by nineteenth-century higher critics no longer hold sway either, but no one therefore tries to revoke their academic licenses retroactively. It is time to stop simply dismissing *Daniel the*

---

[65] Livesley, 'Regius Professor', 111.
[66] Forrester, *Young*, 211–31 (for the twenty pages).

Prophet as obscurantist because it was conservative and in support of a cause that is now widely considered lost, and instead actually to start examining its contents in context.

It will therefore be helpful to present an outline of the contents of the book before moving on to its reception. That this summary (even if it taxes the patience of readers) will nevertheless be inadequate only serves to further the point being made: Pusey's book, after all, is 668 pages of tightly packed, small-print erudition.[67] In the preface, Pusey explains that *Essays and Reviews* was the prompt for his study. The essayists had causally assumed that modern, liberal biblical scholarly theories had triumphed over traditional, conservative ones. Pusey decided to test this stance with a study of Daniel precisely because it was considered a patently obvious victory for higher criticism by those in favour of the new theories: 'True! Disbelief of Daniel had become an axiom in the unbelieving critical school. Only, they mistook the result of unbelief for the victory of criticism. . . . Disbelief had been the parent, not the offspring of their criticism.'[68] Pusey's goal in this book is 'to meet the pseudo-criticism on its own grounds'.[69] In other words, he will beat them at their own game with their acknowledged weapons; he will advance arguments that are built upon presuppositions or that employ methods which his opponents share. Pusey makes good on this promise. The volume also fully supports another boast: 'I have conscientiously read every thing which has been written against the book of Daniel, and have met every argument in those writings.'[70] He gives full disclosure on his own presuppositions. Pusey believed that the words of Jesus on Daniel as recorded in the Gospels settled the matter: his Christological convictions were such that Jesus Christ could not have said something erroneous. Thus, the very title of Pusey's work is actually a quotation from the canonical words of Christ (Matthew 24: 15), and thus a nod to this argument. A late dating of Daniel means that the book is a forgery containing no true prophecy and thus Jesus is falsely calling Daniel a prophet. Once again, however, Pusey does not offer this argument as a substitute for a scholarly shifting of the evidence. Instead, he goes on the attack. It is

---

[67] The contents of *Daniel the Prophet* are summarized in more detail in Larsen, 'Pusey'.

[68] E. B. Pusey, *Daniel the Prophet: Nine Lectures, delivered in the Divinity School of the University of Oxford, with copious notes*, third thousand (Oxford: John Henry and James Parker, 1864), p. vi.

[69] Pusey, *Daniel*, p. xii.   [70] Pusey, *Daniel*, pp. xiii–xiv.

actually the radical higher critics who have (in their case, undisclosed) presuppositions that have tempted them to rig the arguments. They do not believe that miracles or predictive prophecy are possible and therefore they are driven to date the book late in order to avoid acknowledging that these things happened. Pusey will argue throughout *Daniel the Prophet* that the pressure of these presuppositions prompts his opponents to advance arguments transparently not supported by the evidence.

Lecture One commences this line of attack: 'Those who use the argument call themselves "unprejudiced," simply because they are free from what they call *our* prejudices.'[71] Pusey promises (and, again, delivers on this promise in the book) to address every argument that has been advanced against a traditional view of Daniel. Pusey's great strength as a biblical scholar was undoubtedly as a linguist, and he persuasively advances philological arguments throughout this book. In a particularly compelling line of argument, Pusey demonstrates how when the Hebrew Scriptures were translated into Greek (the LXX) there were various terms in the book of Daniel that were so archaic that the translators found them unintelligible (sometimes despairing of hazarding a guess and just skipping over them altogether) even though, on the late date theory, the writer of Daniel would have been a near contemporary of the translators. Higher critics, he observed, had not satisfactorily dealt with this kind of evidence: 'Bleek had ignored the whole argument from language.'[72] And so it goes on: 'No opponent has ever ventured to look steadily at the facts of the correspondence of the language of Daniel and Ezra, and their difference from the language of the earliest Targums.'[73]

Lecture Two argues that even the late dating of Daniel does not solve the alleged problem of predictive prophecy as the last of the fourth empires is generally and persuasively seen to be the Roman one; it was still future and thus counts as evidence of foreknowledge. This line of thought continues in Lecture Three. Pusey ridicules the efforts of radical higher critics somehow to find an extra empire in order to end up with four by the second century (and so make the passage a commentary on current events): '1,1,1, and 0 have somehow to be made 4.... Every possible combination has been tried.'[74]

[71] Pusey, *Daniel*, 7.   [72] Pusey, *Daniel*, 42.
[73] Pusey, *Daniel*, 56.   [74] Pusey, *Daniel*, 100.

Lecture Four, in a similar vein, makes the case that the prophecy of the seventy weeks sets out a chronological period the only reasonable reading of which ends in Jesus of Nazareth. Once again, Pusey gleefully exposes the knots into which liberal critics twist themselves in order to attempt to evade this conclusion. Fascinatingly, he quotes approvingly Jowett's dictum from *Essays and Reviews* which was intended as a liberal one useful for exposing the contortions of conservatives: 'Such interpretations would soon cease, if people would "interpret Scripture like any other book."'[75] Here is the Regius professor on the desperation of one German critic: Karl Wieseler 'having first declared [Heinrich Corrodi's] solution "self-evidently arbitrary and at variance with the text," afterwards adopted it.'[76] Pusey tears into Johann Gottfried Eichhorn, whose lectures he had attended when he was in Germany: Eichhorn engaged in 'dishonest criticism'; Eichhorn 'well knew that he had falsified the text'; 'Eichhorn owned the unnaturalness of all this, and called it "cabbalistic"; but the fault was to be with the prophet, not with his own non-natural interpretation.'[77] Likewise the mathematical gymnastics of Cäsar von Lengerke are patiently chronicled.[78] This line of argument culminates in a detailed table showing the conflicting suggestions that a score of radical critics have hazarded regarding this reference (with several of these scholars who abandoned their earlier attempt for a new one being given double entries).[79]

Lecture Five emphasizes that the radical German higher critics have ruled out predictive prophecy a priori and therefore are forced to find alternative theories to evade finding an instance of it in the text. Here, for example, is Pusey's commentary on a quotation from Leonhard Bertholdt: 'In plain words, the object of the prophecy could not be Alexander, in whom it was exactly fulfilled, because then there would be prophecy. But no other account could be given of it, therefore we must imagine one.'[80] Lecture Six looks to the other parts of the canon and the Apocrypha and to the dating of the closing of the canon for clues in dating Daniel. Once again, the evidence from the Septuagint is impressive. Even a leading German higher critic, Wilhelm De Wette, had observed that Daniel must have been written long before the LXX translation (but, instead of presenting any evidence to refute it, had just quietly dropped this remark in a later edition).

---

[75] Pusey, *Daniel*, 183.   [76] Pusey, *Daniel*, 196.
[77] Pusey, *Daniel*, 199–201.   [78] Pusey, *Daniel*, 207.
[79] Pusey, *Daniel*, 215.   [80] Pusey, *Daniel*, 279.

Lecture Seven deals with a range of arguments made by radical critics alleging historical inaccuracies and implausible scenes in Daniel. It is illustrative of Pusey's thoroughness: he systematically works his way thorough every objection that has been made, facing them squarely one by one. One of the main arguments along these lines used to be that there was no such historical person as one of the characters in the book, the Babylonian king Belshazzar. This objection, however, had been exploded during the course of Pusey's own career by archaeological discoveries. Pusey asked his opponents to weigh the full import of this: 'But men might well ask themselves, which is the most likely to have known the name of Belshazzar, which remained unknown to Babylonian, Persian, or Greek historians, the prophet who lived in Babylon, or a Jew who is to have lived in Palestine nearly four centuries afterwards?'[81] Pusey's very systematic approach aids his effort to show that some of the radical critics so overplayed their hands as to indicate that they seemed positively to wish that the veracity of the book of Daniel was discredited. Both Lengerke and the English critic, Samuel Davidson, were determined to read the stone covering on the lion's den as indicating a physical impossibility: 'How did the animals live in a *cistern-like* den? Did an angel give them air to breathe, whose vitalising property could not be exhausted?' (Lengerke); other commentators 'forget that the lions too could not have held out in a hole, void of air, covered with stone. Over these no angel watched, as over Daniel (v. 21) and yet it were necessary to assume a 2nd miracle, to make their preservation, and so the miracle of the deliverance of Daniel, possible' (Davidson).[82] Apparently these critics either suspected that the Babylonians did not have the wit to create a viable enclosure for their captive animals or believed that it was incumbent upon the biblical writer to pause the story at its highest point of drama in order to discourse on engineering and ventilation. Pusey dismisses such cavils: 'to invent absurdities betrays the malus animus of the critic'.[83]

Lectures Eight and Nine dealt with theological assumptions and practices in Daniel which some critics had argued betrayed a later date, as well as with claims that some aspects of the book were derivative from Magism or other religious traditions. Once again, Pusey is at his best pursuing linguistic lines

---

[81] Pusey, *Daniel*, 403–4.   [82] Pusey, *Daniel*, 415.   [83] Pusey, *Daniel*, 417.

of argument. On the former charge, some of his best points are scored when he avers that radical critics had violated linguistic common sense in order to read certain doctrines out of older texts in other parts of the canon. As to comparative religion, his linguistic evidence was bolstered by personal information provided by Professor Max Müller. As Max Müller was a German-born and educated Oxford philologist widely respected by theological liberals, this was a clever tactic. Moreover, the book ends with six appendices, most of them providing the rough data of the linguistic evidence, the first of which, provided by Max Müller, is six, smaller print pages of analysis of the allegedly Aryan words in Daniel.

Although one would not come away from the existing secondary literature with this impression, *Daniel the Prophet* was so formidable that, in Britain at least, it was unanswerable. I have made a systematic effort to find every British review of the book. The vast majority of these turned out to be highly sympathetic treatments in religious publications. The leading journal of erudite freethought, the *Westminster Review*, did not review it at all. This journal, of course, would not have liked the thesis of Pusey's *Daniel*: it gloried in reviewing iconoclastic approaches to the Bible by figures such as Colenso, Strauss, and Renan. It seems reasonable to infer that the *Westminster Review* could not find a reviewer who could credibly challenge the mountain of evidence and the array of germane lines of argument presented by Oxford's Regius Professor of Hebrew. This speculation is further bolstered by the two negative reviews that have been found.

One, by the Broad Churchman and Old Testament scholar, J. J. Stewart Perowne, appeared in the very first issue of the *Contemporary Review*. Perowne acknowledged the greatness of Pusey's achievement:

> he has brought to bear upon this point a perfect encyclopedia of learning. He has cast into his volume the labour of a lifetime. It is by far the most complete work which has yet appeared, no Continental writer having handled the subject with anything like the same fullness or breadth of treatment. In England we need scarcely say it is unrivalled. Few men amongst us could have produced such a book.[84]

---

[84] *Contemporary Review*, I, 1 (January 1866); J. J. Stewart Perowne, 'Dr Pusey on Daniel the Prophet', 96–122 (here 96).

More than this, Perowne worked his way through Pusey's arguments, conceding reluctantly again and again that they are convincing. At one point he observes:

> The style of Daniel's Aramaic is no proof that the book was *not* written by a contemporary of Ezra in Babylon. And this we fear is, after all, the conclusion to be drawn from a consideration of the linguistic argument as a whole.[85]

The 'we fear' says it all—Perowne would rather that the traditional view had been overturned so that, as he saw it, progress could be made in theological thinking, but Pusey has swept away the arguments against an early dating of Daniel. Having judged that Pusey repeatedly wins on particular points in dispute—the reviewer even specifically declares that Pusey triumphs in his joust with Rowland Williams, an *Essays and Reviews* author—Perowne candidly admits that therefore the Tractarian scholar must be given the overall victory:

> we even admit the force of his arguments so far as to think that he has shown, and shown far more convincingly than any one who has yet made the attempt, that the Book of Daniel is not a late production of the Maccabaean age but belongs rightfully to the age to which it was for centuries commonly assigned.[86]

To admit this is to admit that Pusey has proved his thesis—what then is there left to say to make a review negative? Well, for Perowne, one thing is carping around the edges. Thus he spends a fair amount of space attacking a brief aside that Pusey had made on how geology and Genesis do not conflict. Perowne comes off sounding like he wants them to be irreconcilable and therefore is miffed that Pusey will not concede this. Perowne also engages in entirely appropriate and thoughtful challenges to Pusey's views on the dating of the Psalms, the closing of the canon, and the extent to which the fulfilment of prophecy may confidently be pinpointed. What primarily makes this review a hostile one, however, is a persistent attack on 'the general tone and temper' of *Daniel the Prophet* and the 'retrogressive' nature of Tractarian theology. Rhetoric along these lines takes up a great deal of space in Perowne's review, dominating its introduction and conclusion. Readers are told that Pusey has been breathing 'the pestilential miasma

---

[85] Perowne, 'Pusey', 112.   [86] Perowne, 'Pusey', 121–2.

which exhales from the fields of theological strife'; in contrast, the reviewer heralds 'a healthier tone, a broader theology' that will come and sweep Pusey's away.[87] Perowne does make one vague attempt to insinuate that Pusey's gloves-off assault on theological liberals ought somehow to count against him on the substantive argument: 'Instinctively we feel that such charges betray a weakness somewhere.'[88] Such a claim, however, would have been more forceful if Pusey had substituted denunciation for argument rather than having used it to garnish 668 pages of aptly marshalled evidence.

The most negative review that has been found is a two-part article by the Old Testament scholar Russell Martineau in the Unitarian journal, the *Theological Review*. Martineau strikes this pose: Pusey's acknowledgement of his own confessional convictions (conveniently) means that his arguments do not have to be considered at all. Pusey is *ipso facto* not scholarly; not competent. Rather, he is blind. Martineau even goes so far as to assert that the very fact that Pusey is an Anglican clergyman makes him unfit to enter this discussion (because he has subscribed to the Thirty-Nine Articles which prejudice the investigation by declaring Daniel to be canonical). With false bravado, Martineau dismisses *Daniel the Prophet* as 'a mere partizan pamphlet'.[89] He even speaks of 'this grasping at the desired end without much scruple as to the means', yet he does not illustrate this unjust charge but rather only assumes its logical necessity. Martineau literally does not even attempt to present, let alone answer, the main, linguistic arguments that make up the bulk of Pusey's *Daniel*. Instead, he argues that a well-known point of uncertainty regarding whether or not the right Hebrew king and/or date is given in the first verse of Daniel (a difficulty that Pusey had explicitly addressed, albeit not to Martineau's satisfaction), settles the issue and there is no need to inquire any further. In a fifty-seven-page review, Martineau returns to this again and again. His secondary clincher is the relationship between Nebuchadnezzar and Belshazzar. Recent archaeological evidence indicated that another king came between them in the succession, yet Daniel referred to Nebuchadnezzar as Belshazzar's father. Martineau, completely ignoring the fact that the archaeological evidence had also vindicated the historicity of Belshazzar, a point that had hitherto been denied by radical critics, also saw this discrepancy as sufficient to

---

[87] Perowne, 'Pusey', 99, 122.   [88] Perowne, 'Pusey', 97.
[89] *Theological Review*, II (1865): Russell Martineau, 'The Book of Daniel', 172–201; 'The Book of Daniel, No. II', 477–505 (here 173).

unravel the entire veracity of the book. Pusey had dealt with this objection at length, demonstrating patiently and convincingly that there was no word in any of the ancient Near Eastern languages for 'grandfather' and that 'father' was always used for this relationship as well. Martineau brushes this solution aside breezily on psychological grounds: 'it is rather too much to expect a careless and drunken grandson to be greatly worked upon by a reference to the grandfather.'[90]

Martineau does address the problem of the four empires. His theory is that there were only three empires (if you do not include the Roman one, as Martineau cannot on his theory), but to assert that the (late date) author of Daniel was probably so carried away by the mythological portent of the number four that he did not even notice he had got this wrong. Such a basic mistake might seem improbable to us, but one must keep in mind, Martineau helpfully explains, that ancient writers lacked 'common sense'.[91] As to this specific specimen—the book of Daniel—the allegories used are so bizarre as to make it 'difficult to imagine' that they were composed by 'a sane writer'.[92] Instead of engaging with Pusey's main linguistic arguments, Martineau runs the clock out by spending numerous pages of his review summarizing the contents of the book of Daniel! Martineau also veers off into such themes as Gospel criticism and the lesson of Galileo's case. He expresses his annoyance that Pusey had enlisted the help of Max Müller. It would seem, then and now, that it was easier just to condemn Pusey as obscurantist, than actually to try to grapple with his arguments.[93]

A review in the *Journal of Sacred Literature* might serve better to measure Pusey's achievement. Not agreeing with the author's viewpoint, the reviewer observes of Pusey as revealed in his *Daniel*: 'in his conservatism he goes beyond ourselves'.[94] Therefore, the reviewer claimed not to assent to some of Pusey's arguments in this volume. Nevertheless, the reviewer warned against underestimating the Regius professor:

> He has ranged over an immense field of ancient and of modern literature so successfully, that there seem to be very few matters of importance which he has overlooked. No candid critic can sneer down a work of this sort; if it is to

---

[90] Martineau, 'Daniel', 192.   [91] Martineau, 'Daniel', 499.

[92] Martineau, 'Daniel', 502.

[93] As to now, I am referring to the scholarship on Pusey. The current scholarship on the book of Daniel does, of course, take into account the evidence and arguments that Pusey marshalled.

[94] *Journal of Sacred Literature*, VI, n.s. (January 1865), 472–3.

be nullified, it must be refuted; and if it is to be refuted, it can only be less by starting new difficulties, than by driving our author from a very strong entrenchment of facts. On the whole, this is a most seasonable, serviceable, and important work, and one for which we desire a large measure of success.[95]

As long as Pusey lived, no consensus in favour of the late dating of Daniel emerged in Britain. His *Daniel* went through numerous editions in both Britain and America, including one in London as late as 1892, a full decade after Pusey's death.[96] A crucial figure in moving the British toward the second-century theory was Pusey's successor as Oxford's Regius Professor of Hebrew, Samuel Rolles Driver. Driver, a truly great Old Testament scholar, knew whereof he spoke on this subject and therefore he understood well that *Daniel the Prophet* could not be dismissed with a sneer. As late as 1912, he paid tribute to his predecessor's monograph as 'extremely learned and thorough'.[97]

Before leaving the reviews of *Daniel the Prophet*, it would also be useful to highlight the ones by Protestant authors who were forced by this book to rediscover Pusey for the Bible man that he was. Just as Pusey's achievement was passed over in silence by the *Westminster Review*, so also it was un-absorbable for the proudly Protestant world of Methodism. The *Wesleyan Methodist Magazine* did not review it, but rather ran a series of articles on Pusey's *Eirenicon*, a volume published in the following year that explored the possibility of an Anglican reunion with Rome.[98] Likewise, the *Primitive Methodist Magazine* did not review *Daniel*, but a couple of years later commended to its readers *Popery and Puseyism: Twin-Demons with One Soul*.[99] A good decade after its publication, however, Pusey's volume did receive favourable notice in a review essay discussing a collection of works

---

[95] *Journal of Sacred Literature*, VI, n.s. (January 1865), 473. For further appreciations of Pusey's book in this journal, see Franke Parker, '"Daniel the Prophet," by Dr Pusey', *Journal of Sacred Literature*, VI, n.s. (July 1865), 345–59 (although the real point of this article is for Parker to push a pet theory of his own); (October 1865), 218–21.

[96] E. B. Pusey, *Daniel the Prophet* (London: A. D. Innes, 1892).

[97] S. R. Driver, *The Book of Daniel, with introduction and notes* (Cambridge: Cambridge University Press, 1912), pp. ciii–civ. I have not seen the first edition of this book, which was published in 1900. Nevertheless, it was clearly revised for the 1912 edition. (The very same two pages as this quotation both have references in the main text to 1911 so, at the very least, Driver did not decide to change this judgment on Pusey's book when he went through this material again in 1911.)

[98] *Wesleyan Methodist Magazine*, 89 (1866): 'Dr Pusey's Eirenicon', 143–55; 'Mariolatry: Dr Pusey's Testimony Against Rome', 888–93; 'Glance at Public Occurrences', 167–8.

[99] *Primitive Methodist Magazine* (December 1867), 746–7.

on Daniel in the Wesleyan journal, the *London Quarterly Review* (albeit this review also informed its readers that the boastful little horn in Daniel's prophecy was the papacy).[100] On the other hand, both the *Baptist Magazine* and the *Eclectic and Congregational Review* gave *Daniel the Prophet* a favourable review without feeling a need to apologize to their evangelical Noncon-formist Protestant readers for recommending a book by the notorious Anglo-Catholic leader.[101] More telling, however, are the apologetic appre-ciations. The *Evangelical Magazine*, for example, began its review of *Daniel the Prophet*:

> In this volume we have a most valuable contribution toward the defence of the Bible against the attacks of modern unbelief. We hail the work with all the greater satisfaction that it comes from the pen of one from whom, on points both of doctrine and ecclesiastics, we have often very seriously differed. But these pages exhibit scarcely a trace of the religious system which has been so long identified with the name of Pusey. While replete throughout with the results of the richest scholarship, the tone of the work is eminently devout and Christian, and its sentiments thoroughly evangelical. We are glad of the indication thus afforded that, while his great contemporary and former coad-jutor, Dr. Newman, has been driven to seek a resting place in the Church of Rome, Dr. Pusey has found his in the Divine inspiration and authority of the Word of God.[102]

Likewise, the review in the evangelical Anglican *Christian Observer* reiter-ated its loathing of Tractarianism before heartily commending Pusey's work as a biblical commentator.[103] The journal praised the Regius professor all the more by contrasting him with his old co-religionist, Newman, whose *Apologia Pro Vita Sua* had also appeared in the same year as Pusey's lectures, observing waspishly that the convert to Rome's 'latest work is an exposition of himself, not of Holy Scripture.'[104] Not surprisingly, the high church Anglican organs, the *Ecclesiastic*, the *Christian Remembrancer*, and the *Guardian*, all gave Pusey's *Daniel* straightforwardly positive reviews which

---

[100] *London Quarterly Review*, 43, 86 (January 1875), 292–328.

[101] *Baptist Magazine*, 56 (December 1864), 812–16; 'Dr Pusey on Daniel', *Eclectic and Congrega-tional Review*, 9, n.s. (August 1865), 164–78.

[102] 'Daniel the Prophet', *Evangelical Magazine*, 43 (May 1865), 287–91.

[103] 'Dr Pusey's Lectures on the Prophet Daniel', *Christian Observer*, 64, 326 (Feb. 1865), 128–49 (here 128–9).

[104] *Christian Observer*, 64, 326 (Feb. 1865), 129.

declared that he had convincingly proved the traditional dating of Daniel to be correct.[105]

Finally, an exploration of Pusey's *Minor Prophets* is in order. It is hard to imagine why these volumes were passed over in Liddon's *Life*. Matthew dispenses with them along with *Daniel* and much else besides, saving Pusey's youthful book on German theology and his first *Eirenicon* as the only ones 'of his works whose influence and interest transcends its proximate cause'. The actual publication record does not bear out Matthew's judgment. *An Historical Enquiry* has never been republished—initially, of course, because Pusey suppressed it, but if the book has enduring interest one wonders why it has not been reprinted in the 125 years since his death. The *Eirenicon* barely outlived its author, receiving its last edition in 1885. Pusey's *Minor Prophets*, by contrast, has had extraordinary staying power. The original American publisher, Funk & Wagnall, brought out numerous reprints, the last one in 1907; likewise, a steady trail of British editions does not taper off until a reprint by J. Nisbet of London in 1907. Moreover, in 1950, *Minor Prophets* was reprinted in America by Baker Book House. Baker reprinted it several times during the 1950s, and then again in 1985, in 1998, and 2001 (and perhaps will continue to do so). Moreover, Baker has been successfully marketing Pusey's commentaries over all these decades to the ordinary, contemporary, intelligent reader, and not simply as period pieces. Indeed, Pusey's commitment to think about the contents of Scripture along with the voices of the great tradition of Christian thought is positively fashionable today. Eminent scholars and academic publishers are focusing on precisely this kind of work, further unsettling the assumption that Pusey was an obscurantist who drove into a dead end.

Explaining the idea of the original commentary series, Pusey told T. E. Morris in 1847: 'Our plan is to read all we can of the Fathers or old writers.'[106] Proving good on this, *Minor Prophets* serves as a catena of patristic and medieval exegesis. To take an extreme example, on Malachi's reference to the Elijah that is to come (Malachi 4: 5), in the main body of the text, Pusey quotes from the following authors: Justin Martyr; Tertullian; Origen; Hippolytus; Hilary; Hilary the Deacon; Gregory of Nyssa; Ambrose; St Jerome; John Chrysostom; Augustine of Hippo; Cyril

---

[105] 'Pusey on the Prophet Daniel', *Ecclesiastic*, 26 (November 1864), 489–503; *Christian Remembrancer*, 51, 127 (January 1865), 1–38; *Guardian* (28 December 1864), 1268.

[106] LBV 111, Pusey to the Rev. T. E. Morris, Thursday in 3rd week in Lent, 1847 [March 11].

of Alexandria; Theodoret; Theodore of Mopsuestia; 'The [5th century] African author of the work on the promises and predictions of God'; Isidore of Seville; Gregory the Great; John Damascene; and Bede.[107] Jerome is a particular favourite and he is a standard conversation partner throughout Pusey's commentaries on all twelve prophets. Such voices mean Pusey believed that allegorical readings were legitimate and profitable even for Victorians. Here, for example, is an excerpt from a passage by Gregory the Great on how the various locusts mentioned by the prophet Joel when referring to the plague can be read spiritually as types of the four chief passions of human beings: 'What is typified by the *cankerworm*, almost the whole of whose body is gathered into its belly, expect gluttony in eating?'[108] Not merely citing the spiritual readings of historic Christian thinkers, Pusey was not afraid to offer traditional allegorical reflections in his own commentary as well. Pusey explained, for example, that the dew mentioned in Micah 5: 7 can be viewed as 'a symbol of Divine doctrine'.[109]

This approach also means that Pusey is entirely comfortable finding embedded in the Hebrew Scriptures what is more clearly revealed or articulated in the New Testament and the Christian tradition. These commentaries are riddled with quotations from the New Testament. Hosea 2: 22, 'And the earth shall hear the corn, and the wine, and the oil; and they shall hear Jezreel', is, for Pusey, a symbolic reference to 'His highest gift, the Holy Eucharist.'[110] And the Regius professor could not stumble across a triad, however subtle, without discovering the Triune God hidden therein. A more sustained example of this comes in his commentary on Zephaniah chapter three.[111] Of Hosea 6: 2, we are told: 'The Resurrection of Christ, and our resurrection in Him and in His Resurrection, could not be more plainly foretold.'[112] Not only are Christians to read the Old Testament Christologically, but readers are informed that this was the

---

[107] Pusey, *Minor Prophets*, II, 472–502. Pusey also sprinkled the commentaries with references to Anglican resources, with Lancelot Andrewes being a favourite.

[108] Pusey, *Minor Prophets*, I, 160.

[109] Pusey, *Minor Prophets*, II, 76. He is not the first to say this, but it does stand as simply part of his commentary rather than as a quotation or citation. For Pusey on typology in the Hebrew Scriptures, see David Jasper, 'Pusey's "Lectures on Types and Prophecies of the Old Testament"', in Butler, *Pusey Rediscovered*, 51–70; Andrew Louth, 'The Oxford Movement, the Fathers and the Bible', *Sobornost*, 6, 1 (1984), 30–45.

[110] Pusey, *Minor Prophets*, I, 40.

[111] Pusey, *Minor Prophets*, II, 287–8.   [112] Pusey, *Minor Prophets*, I, 63.

original intention of its authors: 'Christ is ever the Hope as the End of prophecy, ever before the Prophets' mind.'[113]

This focus on historic Christian readings of Scripture, however, does not mean that Pusey ignores the modern discipline of biblical criticism. He is also interacting throughout *Minor Prophets* with German higher critics and other contemporary scholars. Much of this is citing approvingly modern conservative biblical scholars. A favourite source is Ernst Hengstenberg's *Christologie des Alten Testaments* (1829). Not surprisingly, Pusey also recurringly takes the time to attempt to refute various theories offered by radical critics. A discussion of the prophet Nahum, for example, prompts an attack on Heinrich Ewald.[114] Pusey would also use the conservative, apologetics argument from fulfilled prophecy.[115]

Nevertheless, it would be wrong to imagine that Pusey's engagement with modern, liberal, critical scholarship is entirely negative. He would also cite these authors approvingly, even ones as divergent ideologically from him as W. M. L. De Wette and A. P. Stanley.[116] This engagement with higher criticism can be extraordinarily thorough. On the prophet Zechariah, for example, Pusey argues that no issue of faith is at stake regarding its dating. Nevertheless, despite it being a matter of scholarly rather than devotional or theological interest, Pusey includes a table giving all the theories of its dating that have been offered. This table strikingly demonstrates that Pusey was familiar with all the existing critical scholarship. To mention just some of the more prominent names, Pusey's table includes the theories of Eichhorn, Henstenberg, De Wette, Keil, Hitzig, Stähelin, Bertholdt, Herzfeld, Baur, Ewald, Stanley, Bunsen, Gesenius, and Bleek.[117] Pusey also repeatedly cites the works of archaeologists, Assyriologists, and orientalists, notably A. H. Layard, Henry Rawlinson, and Edward Hincks, but even 'Miss Harris, the learned daughter of a learned Egyptologist'.[118] Travel writers are another staple, including Harriet Martineau's *Eastern Life, Past and Present* (1848). The urbane cover of information personally received from Max Müller is occasionally evoked as well. Joel's locusts prompt a

---

[113] Pusey, *Minor Prophets*, II, 23.   [114] Pusey, *Minor Prophets*, II, 111.

[115] For example, Pusey, *Minor Prophets*, II, 122.

[116] Pusey, *Minor Prophets*, I, 303, 125.   [117] Pusey, *Minor Prophets*, II, 335–8.

[118] Pusey, *Minor Prophets*, II, 153. For the role of archaeological discoveries in nineteenth-century biblical discussions, see Timothy Larsen, 'Austen Henry Layard's Nineveh: The Bible and Archaeology in Victorian Britain', *Journal of Religious History*, 33, 1 (March 2009), 66–81.

barrage of natural history sources as well as eye-witness narratives of insect plagues from parts of the world as far-flung as the Ukraine and Transylvania. Finally, Pusey repeatedly makes excursions into rabbinical reads of the text at hand. One footnote on Malachi, for example, cites Ibn Ezra, *Tanchuma*, Pesikta rabbathi, Midrash Shocher, Debarim rabba, Shir hashirim rabba, Kimchi, R. Abraham B. David, Abarbanel, and R. Tuanchum (from Maimonides).[119]

As to application, the twelve prophets give Pusey's lifelong obsession with divine judgment plenty of scope. He continually wants his readers to see biblical plagues as coming upon their land as well, perhaps in the form of potato blight or foot-and-mouth disease. When commenting on Amos chapter five, it is almost as if Pusey longs to be also among the prophets:

> We English know our own sins, many and grievous; we know of a vast reign of violence, murder, blasphemy, theft, uncleanness, covetousness, dishonest dealing, unrighteousness, and of the breach of every commandment of God: we know well now of an instrument in God's Hands, not far off, like the Assyrian, but within two hours of our coast . . . No one scarcely doubts that it will be. Yet who dare predict the issue? Will God permit that scourge to come? will he prevail? What would be the extent of our sufferings or loss? how would our commerce or our Empire be impaired? Would it be dismembered?[120]

More succinctly, 'In the judgments on the Jews, we may read our own national future.'[121] The overthrow of biblical cities is frequently an occasion for wondering when God's wrath will be poured out on London. The English metropolis is even directly equated with the archetypical sinful and doomed city, Babylon.[122] Pusey frequently attacks the current economic life and habits of the British as occasioning God's wrath:

> When for instance, wages are paid in necessaries priced exorbitantly, or when artizans are required to buy at a loss at their masters' shops, what is it but the union of deceit and oppression? The trading world is full of oppression, scarcely veiled by deceit . . . With the men of the world, with its politicians, in trade, it is the one decisive argument: "I was in the right, for I succeeded."[123]

---

[119] Pusey, *Minor Prophets*, II, 503, n. 3.   [120] Pusey, *Minor Prophets*, I, 304.
[121] Pusey, *Minor Prophets*, II, 44.   [122] Pusey, *Minor Prophets*, I, 414; II, 385.
[123] Pusey, *Minor Prophets*, I, 121.

Victorian prosperity needed to be examined from the perspective of the Righteous Judge:

> Truly we *build up Zion with blood*, when we cheapen luxuries and comforts at the price of souls, use Christian toil like brute strength, tempt men to dishonesty and women to other sin, to eke out the scanty wages which alone our selfish thirst for cheapness allows, heedless of every thing save of our individual gratification, or the commercial prosperity, which we have made our god.[124]

The staying of judgment in response to repentance revealed in Jonah, however, offers hope. This too has its contemporary manifestations: 'the first visitation of the Cholera was checked in its progress in England, upon one day's national fast and humiliation.'[125] According to this Anglo-Catholic divine, the Bible speaks today.

And so our task is at an end. Edward Bouverie Pusey had a deep love for Augustine's *Confessions*. He edited this text for publication and found surprisingly many opportunities to refer to it in his *Minor Prophets*. In his *Confessions*, the bishop of Hippo moves from autobiographical reflections to commentary on a specific portion of Scripture. In the same way, this chapter has moved from a discussion of Pusey's life and thought to an examination of his commentaries. The goal, however, is the same: to recover a picture of the Tractarian leader as a Bible man who lived an exegetical life. Commentaries exist for those who wish to attend to the contents of the Bible. Dr Pusey surveyed the challenges of the Victorian age and decided that the right response was to invite people to listen to Holy Scripture.

---

[124] Pusey, *Minor Prophets*, II, 44. For a secondary source exploring this theme, see Jane Garnett, 'Commercial ethics: a Victorian perspective on the practice of theory', in Roger Crisp and Christopher Cowton (eds), *Business Ethics: Perspectives on the Practice of Theory* (Oxford: Oxford University Press, 1998), 117–38.

[125] Pusey, *Minor Prophets*, I, 414.

2

Roman Catholics
Nicholas Wiseman and Sacred Scripture

T he first archbishop of Westminster, Nicholas Wiseman (1802–65), is
remembered by his co-religionists as the visionary and catalyst of the
revival of English Catholicism in the nineteenth century. Wiseman understood the times and he knew what to do. He was convinced while other
prominent Catholics were dismissive that the Oxford Movement would
lead on to conversions to Rome. When most English Catholics still assumed
that a policy of bland unobtrusiveness was the prudent course, Wiseman
believed that the English people were ready to hear reasoned arguments in
favour of Catholic beliefs, and that they could be persuaded by them. He led
his people from being a beleaguered, complacent, little flock, to becoming a
dynamic, well-organized, confident, and successful force in the land. This
theme has been the central and dominating one of all the biographies of
Cardinal Wiseman. 'The revival of English Catholic zeal by Wiseman' is
the overriding preoccupation of the standard Victorian life and letters
written by Wilfrid Ward.[1] The current, reigning modern critical biography
signals this theme in its very title, *Nicholas Wiseman and the Transformation of
English Catholicism*.[2] It superseded Brian Fotherhill's *Nicholas Wiseman*,
a book that proclaimed even more unabashedly on its cover as a kind
of unofficial subtitle, 'A Biography of the Great Nineteenth-Century
Churchman Who Restored a Vigorous Catholicism to England'.[3]

---

[1] Wilfrid Ward, *The Life and Times of Cardinal Wiseman*, 2 vols (London: Longmans, Green, and
Co., 1897), I, p. vii.
[2] Richard J. Schiefen, *Nicholas Wiseman and the Transformation of English Catholicism* (Shepherdtown, West Virginia: Patmos Press, 1984).
[3] Brian Fothergill, *Nicholas Wiseman* (New York: Doubleday, 1963).

In general histories of Britain, on the other hand, Wiseman is remembered for being the figure at the centre of the greatest outburst of anti-
Catholicism in the nineteenth century—indeed, it has not been equalled
since—the so-called 'Papal Aggression' agitation of 1850–1. In September
1850, Pope Pius IX implemented a plan that had been on the table for some
years to re-establish a regular ecclesiastical hierarchy in England. Henceforth, English bishops would not bear esoteric titles of defunct bishoprics
from other lands, but rather territorial titles arising from their actual loca-
tions. Under the old system, Wiseman, even though his district was, in fact,
London, had technically been bishop of Melipotamus *in partibus infidelium*.
The pope's action elevated him to the newly created position of archbishop
of Westminster. Wiseman's pastoral letter to the faithful announcing this
change was considered arrogant and usurping by many English Protestants,
and the cardinal found himself at the centre of the worst anti-Catholic storm
to hit those shores in seventy years.[4] In the story of England, this is Wiseman's moment of fame—or notoriety. The relevant volume in the Oxford
History of England, E. L. Woodward's *The Age of Reform: 1815–1870* (1938),
has one page number in the index for Wiseman and this directs the reader to
a discussion of the archbishop's pastoral letter and the 'sinister and aggressive
meaning' that was placed on its language.[5] A lot of things have changed
between that series and the New Oxford History of England sixty years on,
but this is not one of them. The relevant volume, K. Theodore Hoppen's
The Mid-Victorian Generation: 1846–1886 (1998), has one page number in the
index for the entry on Wiseman and this leads one to a reference to 'the
triumphalist tones' of his pastoral letter.[6] Although the rest of the story has
not been deemed to warrant a place in national histories, it is important to
keep in mind that Wiseman went on immediately to impress many Englishmen with his written response to this furore, *An Appeal to the Reason and
Good Feeling of the English People on the Subject of the Catholic Hierarchy*.[7] At his
death in 1865, he was celebrated throughout the English press as one of the
country's great men.

---

[4] For a scholarly treatment of this agitation and the wider context of anti-Catholicism in mid-
nineteenth-century Britain, see John Wolffe, *The Protestant Crusade in Great Britain, 1829–1860*
(Oxford: Clarendon Press, 1991).

[5] E. L. Woodward, *The Age of Reform: 1815–1870* (Oxford: Clarendon Press, 1938), 503.

[6] K. Theodore Hoppen, *The Mid-Victorian Generation: 1846–1886* (Oxford: Clarendon Press,
1998), 444.

[7] Nicholas Wiseman, *An Appeal to the Reason and Good Feeling of the English People on the Subject of
the Catholic Hierarchy* (London: Thomas Richardson and Son, 1850).

These two ways that Wiseman is remembered are interrelated. It is precisely because Protestants did foresee with fear the possibility that the cardinal was leading an English Catholic revival that the agitation had such force. Moreover, to move to the particular theme of this study, for polemical Protestants, a Catholic advance meant *ipso facto* a diminution of the place of the Bible in English life. This may be seen, for example, in the response of the British Society for Promoting the Religious Principles of the Reformation. It viewed the 'offensive and insulting' language of the pope and the archbishop as a call 'to arm Protestants against the assaults which Cardinal Wiseman has publicly announced are now to be made with redoubled energy to seduce Protestants from their scriptural faith'.[8] The back page of the pamphlet that contained these words presented a list of 'Books earnestly recommended to Roman Catholics'. It consists almost entirely of anti-Catholic tracts including *The Rule of Faith, and the Hostility of the Romish Church to God's Written Word* and *Are Roman Catholics forbidden to read the Holy Scriptures?*. However, this list began smugly: '1. THE HOLY SCRIPTURES'. The agitation predictably generated polemical works with titles such as *Popery: an Enemy of Scripture* (1850) and *Rome or the Bible—which?* (1850).[9] These two overriding themes—the Catholic revival and the agitation occasioned by the restored hierarchy—have meant that Wiseman's deep engagement with Sacred Scripture has been neglected, not only by militant Protestants who would prefer to imagine that Catholics ignore the Bible, but also by Catholics due to their desire to keep the focus on the main story of the cardinal's work as a reviver and ecclesiastical leader.

Before discussing Wiseman's study of and views regarding Holy Scripture, however, it would be helpful to recapitulate his biography. Although Nicholas Wiseman was at least partially of Irish descent and he was born in Spain, he consistently thought of himself as an Englishman. When speaking of Blanco White, who had become a well-known figure in Britain by parading his renunciation of his Catholic faith, Wiseman observed: 'Our parents were both English commercial settlers in Seville.'[10] Wiseman also

---

[8] *Apostolic Letter of Pope Pius IX; Pastoral Letter of Cardinal Wiseman; Lord John Russell's Letter to the Bishop of Durham* (London: British Society for Promoting the Religious Principles of the Reformation, 1850), 3. (It is telling that this society did not dare to reprint Wiseman's *Appeal* as well, even though the preface reveals that the editor had it before him.)

[9] Richard P. Blakeney et al., *Popery: an Enemy of Scripture* (London: British Society for Promoting the Religious Principles of the Reformation, 1850); Anon. [Benjamin Hall Kennedy], *Rome or the Bible—which?* (Shrewsbury: John Davies, 1850).

[10] Schiefen, *Wiseman*, 37.

referred to himself as 'an Englishman indeed by blood'.[11] While not having the ability or inclination to do DNA testing, at the very least one can say that Wiseman was culturally English due to his being educated in England from the age of eight, when he entered St Cuthbert's College, Ushaw, near Durham.[12] At the age of sixteen he went to Rome to continue his education and did not return permanently to England until he was thirty-eight, but even in Italy this identity was fostered as Wiseman was first a student at and ultimately the rector of the English College. Moreover, the English press and public, however much Protestant organs might attack him on other grounds, uniformly agreed that he was one of their own. The *Bath Chronicle*, for example, reported when Wiseman gave a lecture in town that 'he is thoroughly English in feature and in accent'.[13] Even the Nonconformist newspaper, the *Patriot*, which had let the anti-Catholic mood override its commitment to religious liberty during the 'Papal Aggression' agitation, declared in its obituary tribute to the cardinal that he had been 'a thorough Englishman . . . there was something in his English culture and full communion with English life, which tempered his Ultramontane zeal.'[14] The last part of this assessment might hint at how the Almighty had been pleased to turn the archbishop's weakness into strength. Nicholas Wiseman was fond of his food and had a girth that made this no secret. Such indulgence disappointed zealous Tractarians flush with the romance of neglected spiritual disciplines. Heroic Anglo-Catholics, who were surviving during Lent on herbs, bread, and water, were disconcerted to have the cardinal set before them a dinner consisting of four elegant fish courses. The Tractarian and eventually Catholic convert, F. W. Faber, quipped that Wiseman had a spiritual side and a 'lobster salad side'.[15] If this was deflating for those energetically being more Roman than Rome, it was endearing to many Englishmen and women. Catholic ascetics were widely viewed by Protestants as repulsive, inhuman creatures—a man who liked his joint of roast beef, however, was a man with whom you could get along. If Wiseman

---

[11] Ward, *Wiseman*, II, 282.

[12] For an assertion of Wiseman's blood lines as entirely Irish, see James E. McGee, *Lives of Irishmen's Sons and their Descendants* (New York: J. A. McGee, 1874), especially 157–8.

[13] Ward, *Wiseman*, II, 49.

[14] Ward, *Wiseman*, II, 521. For the *Patriot*'s position during the agitation, see Timothy Larsen, *Friends of Religious Equality: Nonconformist Politics in Mid-Victorian England* (Woodbridge, Suffolk: Boydell, 1999), 232.

[15] Ward, *Wiseman*, II, 189, 283–4.

was a saint, it was along the lines of the Victorian version of jolly old St Nick, a saint even English Protestants could admire. Wiseman himself delighted to tell the story of the poor woman who, meeting him for the first time, took one look at him and made the Freudian slip of altering the correct form of address for a cardinal so as to greet him with the words 'your Immense'.[16] Wiseman's selection as a representative figure for this study is a natural one. More than just accepted as a true Englishman, he was the formal head of the English Catholic community. Indeed, his influential place in British society was historic: he was unquestionably the most prominent leader of English Catholics since the Reformation.

The place of Sacred Scripture can now be integrated into Wiseman's biography. Although this aspect of his life has generally been given short shrift or ignored, Nicholas Wiseman first found his area of service in the church as a biblical scholar. Ward claims that the 'first thought of devoting himself to the Biblical studies' came when Wiseman was a fourteen-year-old schoolboy at Ushaw.[17] Making good on this early desire, when Wiseman's education in Rome progressed to where he could move beyond the general curriculum he immediately chose biblical studies as his own, particular field of research. At the age of twenty-two he reported in a letter that his personal library consisted almost entirely of works on the Bible.[18] Wiseman specialized in biblical languages and the adjacent languages that served to illuminate them, especially Syriac (the way to understand biblical Aramaic at that time). His extremely disciplined work in this field resulted in a monograph that was celebrated across Europe by scholars whose own expertise enabled them to appreciate it, *Horae Syriacae: seu commentationes et anecdota res vel litteras syriacas spectantia* (1828).[19] It consisted of three treatises. The first was in the service of the Catholic doctrine of the real presence of Christ in the Eucharist and thus more the work of an apologist or controversialist, albeit one formidably armed with original, technical expertise: philological treatise concerning objections derived from the Syriac language made against the literal sense of Matthew 26: 26, 28, and other biblical texts. Thereafter, came the material on which his reputation was primarily made: philological contributions to the history of the Syriac versions of the Old Testament, employing, in part, sources

---

[16] Ward, *Wiseman*, II, 174.   [17] Ward, *Wiseman*, I, 9.   [18] Ward, *Wiseman*, I, 50.
[19] Nicholas Wiseman, *Horae Syriacae: seu commentationes et anecdota res vel litteras syriacas spectantia* (Rome: Francisci Bourliè, 1828).

which, up to the present, have not been touched. First part: concerning the versions according to their species; and then, concerning the Peshitta. Second part: describing the now first recension of Karkaphensis.

Horae Syriacae not only demonstrated that Wiseman had been industrious and had notable linguistic expertise and abilities, but it was also a significant contribution to the field. He was the first scholar to explore the content of a key manuscript and his work advanced knowledge of the Syriac language, including adding a whole series of words and meanings to Syriac lexicons. Still in his early twenties and a priest working in Catholic institutions in Rome, Wiseman was highly respected as a biblical scholar and linguist in both Protestant England and Germany. A crucial admirer of his work in Germany was the Protestant biblical scholar Friedrich August Tholuck; in England his Protestant promoter was Thomas Burgess, bishop of St David's and then Salisbury. In Catholic circles, Wiseman gained the respect of figures such as J. M. A. Scholz, professor of exegesis at Bonn, and Leopold Ackermann, professor of exegesis at Vienna. On the strength of *Horae Syriacae*, he became a professor. Pope Leo XII appointed Wiseman to the chairs in Hebrew and Syro-Chaldaic (that is, the Aramaic that Jesus spoke) in the Roman University.[20] In other words, Wiseman could have quite easily ended up giving his whole life to biblical studies. The reason this did not happen had much more to do with the pressing need of the English Catholic church for leaders than his own inclinations.

It has become commonplace for scholars to lament Wiseman's change of direction as a cutting short of what could have been an unusually fruitful academic career. The English Protestant biblical scholar, F. H. A. Scrivener, who cited Wiseman's early scholarly works repeatedly, spoke of this loss incidentally more than two decades after the archbishop's death thus: 'Cardinal Wiseman, in the course of those youthful studies which gave such seemly, precocious, deceitful promise (Horae Syriacae, Rom. 1828)...'[21] For the purposes at hand, it is enough to recover the fact that biblical studies was the primary focus of Wiseman's early career. Moreover, in a way that is

---

[20] Leslie Stephen (ed.), *Dictionary of National Biography* (Oxford: Oxford University Press, 1912–21), XXI, 715. Schiefen (who also wrote the *Oxford DNB* entry on Wiseman) cites the old *DNB* on this as well in his biography, indicating that this level of precision on Wiseman's appointment has only been preserved in this source: Schiefen, *Wiseman*, 344, n. 44.

[21] F. H. A. Scrivener, *A Plain Introduction to the Criticism of the New Testament*, ed. Revd Edward Miller, M.A., fourth edition, 2 vols (London: George Bell & Sons, 1894), I, 34.

a stereotypically Protestant story from the nineteenth century, Wiseman's immersion in the critical study of the Bible even provoked a period of struggling with religious doubts.[22] The standard telling of Wiseman's life story—including his own autobiographical version—emphasizes his being called out of his specialized, academic pursuits to teach and lead the faithful and defend the faith in more general, public, and popular ways. The pope prodded him to develop these skills and instincts by requiring him, against his natural inclination, to embark upon a regular preaching ministry. Father Ignatius Spencer who, as an early English convert to Rome, understood what the times called for, arrested Wiseman with the observation 'that he should apply his mind to something more practical than Syrian MSS'.[23] Wiseman himself claimed that a turning point came in 1833 when earnest Oxford Movement figures, Hurrell Froude and John Henry Newman, visited him in Rome, and he grasped that these were propitious times for a revival of the English Catholic church: 'From that moment it took the uppermost place in my thoughts, and became the object of their intensest interest.'[24]

In 1835, Wiseman returned to England for an extended visit. True to his newfound convictions, he embarked upon aggressive work designed to foster conversions to Rome. His main effort was a series of addresses, subsequently published, that were designed to dispel Protestant misconceptions regarding Catholic beliefs, *Lectures on the Principal Doctrines and Practices of the Catholic Church* (1836).[25] David Lewis who, at the time of these addresses, was a student at Oxford, recalled later: '[Wiseman] had come to England with a very considerable reputation for learning and ability; and this took many to the Sardinian Chapel. The lectures more than sustained his reputation, and produced an immense sensation. I date from their delivery the beginning of a serious revival of Catholicism in England.'[26] Wiseman himself judged that the popularity of these lectures had proved that the 'close hermeneutical examination, and the strict methods of philological criticism' he had followed in his lectures at the English College could be simplified so as to be effective when addressing ordinary people from a

---

[22] Ward, *Wiseman*, I, 64–5.   [23] Ward, *Wiseman*, I, 101.

[24] Nicholas Wiseman, *Essays on Various Subjects*, 3 vols (London: Charles Dolman, 1853), II, pp. vi–vii.

[25] Nicholas Wiseman, *Lectures on the Principal Doctrines and Practices of the Catholic Church, delivered at St Mary's Moorfields, during the Lent of 1836*, 2 vols (London: Joseph Booker, 1836).

[26] Ward, *Wiseman*, I, 235.

pulpit.[27] These lectures are deeply attentive to Holy Scripture. Indeed, Wiseman understood that, if he wanted to appeal to Victorian Protestants, he needed to begin with the doctrine of Scripture and, as has been shown, this was no mere ploy, but rather fully in line with his own inclinations, interests, and training. The first seven lectures are formally about the rule of faith. This theme, however, is employed in order to address the question of the nature, extent, and uniqueness of the Bible as an authority in Christian thought. Nicholas Wiseman was so keen to convince Protestants that Catholics had a sound doctrine of Scripture that he ended up, as apologists are wont to do, unsettling some of his co-religionists. He acknowledged in the preface to the published lectures:

> There is one passage on which several of my friends have favoured me with their remarks: from which I conclude that there must be an unintentional ambiguity in the phrase. I allude to Vol. I, p. 60, where the following words occur: 'We believe, then, in the first place, that there is no ground-work whatever for faith, except the written word of God.' This expression has been considered inaccurate, as seeming to exclude Church authority, and making the Bible the only rule of faith. . . . In fact, it will be obvious that the meaning of my words simply is, that the first step in the order of argument or demonstration, is the Scripture, which contains all the evidence that we require to establish Church authority.[28]

The lectures all have a biblical text given at their head as if they are sermons. They are also filled with references to specific additional scriptural texts. Wiseman sets out to demolish any suspicion that Protestants might have that Catholics do not sufficiently value the Bible:

> We are told that the Catholic loves not the Scriptures; that his Church esteems not the word of God: that it wishes to suppress it, to put the light of God under a bushel, and so extinguish it. The Catholic Church not love and esteem the word of God! Is there any other Church that places a heavier stake on the authority of the Scriptures, than the Catholic? Is there any other Church that pretends to base so much of rule over men, on the words of that book? Is there any one, consequently, that has a greater interest in maintaining, preserving, and exhibiting the Word? For those who have been educated in that religion know, that when the Church claims authority, it is on the holy Scriptures that she grounds it . . . Has she not commanded it to be studied in

---

[27] Ushaw College Archives, Ushaw College, Durham, Nicholas Wiseman Papers, 801, Nicholas Wiseman to William Tandy, 11 December 1835.
[28] Wiseman, *Lectures on Principal Doctrines*, I, p. viii.

every religious house, in every university, in every ecclesiastical college, and expounded to the faithful, in every place, and at all times? Has she not produced, in every age, learned and holy men, who have dedicated themselves to its illustration, by erudite commentaries, and popular expositions?...But not only, do I say, that the Catholic Church has been always foremost in the task of translating the Scriptures, but also in placing them in the hands of the faithful.[29]

This was an appeal that the Victorians could understand.

Carefully, Wiseman distinguishes between Catholic and Protestant views of authority. Catholics believe that God has provided an infallible church as an essential guide. The infallibility of the church, far from being a rival authority to the Bible, is a guarantee that the church's teaching is biblical:

> The Catholic, too, will say that the Church *cannot* require anything to be believed that is contrary to God's written word; but then the word which I pronounced emphatically is taken by us literally: the Church *cannot* teach any such doctrine, because God's word is pledged that she shall not. The superior control exists in the guidance of the Holy Spirit. But if the Church, not being infallible, may teach things contrary to Scripture, who shall judge it, and decide between it and those whose obedience its exacts? 'If the salt lose its savour, with what shall *it* be salted?' [Matthew 5: 13][30]

God's promise to keep the church from error, besides being grounded in more standard verses from the New Testament, in Wiseman's presentation also finds a proof text in Isaiah 59: 21. The Protestant error is the notion of the right (indeed, duty) of private judgment. This places on ordinary people—every individual—the impossible burden of proving the entire faith for themselves from scratch. On strict Protestant thinking, every factory worker or parlour maid should establish the canonicity of every book of the Bible for his or her self as there is no infallible church whose guidance they may rely on in this matter. The area of missions provides another *reductio ad absurdum* of this Protestant principle: 'suppose a missionary arriving in a foreign country, where the name of Christ was not known, and advancing as his fundamental rule, that it was necessary for all men to read the Bible, and for each one to satisfy his own mind, on all that he should believe.'[31] There was a sense, however, in which the Catholic

[29] Wiseman, *Lectures on Principal Doctrines*, I, 49–51.
[30] Wiseman, *Lectures on Principal Doctrines*, I, 30.
[31] Wiseman, *Lectures on Principal Doctrines*, I, 132.

church was not in favour of disseminating Bibles as widely as possible—
'indiscriminately' as they would put it. As vast amounts of Protestant
resources were being mobilized in Victorian Britain to do just this, some
explanation of this reticence was needed. The Catholic view was that the
Bible should be read with the church and that to thrust it into the hands of
unsuitable recipients devoid of her guidance was to tempt them to become
heretics or scoffers. Cleverly, Wiseman gave biblical reasons for this reserve
that Protestants assumed betrayed a fear of biblical truth:

> It is supposed to have been grounded on several passages of Scripture,
> such as where our Saviour warns his Apostles 'not to throw pearls before
> swine,' . . . Several hints, too, of such a system are thrown out in the Epistles of
> St Paul, where he speaks of some doctrines as being food for the strong, while
> others are compared to milk . . . [32]

An example of Wiseman's modelling a commitment to Scripture is an
elaborate exposition he gives of a rather obscure chapter of the Bible,
Deuteronomy 31.[33] This is the kind of teaching, when it happened in-
house, that Protestants delighted in. In short, Nicholas Wiseman began his
campaign to revive English Catholicism by tackling head-on the question of
the place and authority of the Bible.

In the very same year that these lectures were delivered and published,
1836, Wiseman also published another volume which presented at much
greater length the biblical support of one of the doctrines that most often
was cited as a significant point of difference between Catholics and Protestants, *The Real Presence of the Body and Blood of Our Lord Jesus Christ in the
Blessed Eucharist, Proved From Scripture*. Wiseman stated explicitly that he was
continuing the work he had begun in the *Lectures on the Principal Doctrines
and Practices of the Catholic Church*.[34] The first parts of the book are an
exposition of John 6: 26–71, and Wiseman's desire to address English
Protestants on what they perceived to be their own ground is illustrated

---

[32] Wiseman, *Lectures on Principal Doctrines*, I, 135. The first reference is to Matthew 7: 6. The
second is to 1 Corinthians 3: 2 and Hebrews 5: 12–13 (reflecting the traditional view that the
apostle Paul wrote the epistle to the Hebrews).

[33] Wiseman, *Lectures on Principal Doctrines*, I, 58–9.

[34] Nicholas Wiseman, *The Real Presence of the Body and Blood of Our Lord Jesus Christ in the Blessed
Eucharist, Proved From Scripture*, new edition (Dublin: James Duffy and Co., n.d.), p. iv. (The first
edition was in 1836; this is a posthumous one, indicating the perceived, continuing usefulness of
biblical reasoning on this matter.)

by his setting out the whole of this long passage of Scripture in both the Greek original and the English of the (Protestant) Authorized Version (as well as in the Latin of the Vulgate). He states unabashedly that his aim is to lead people to 'the true faith' by 'satisfying their minds' on this arch difference between Protestants and Catholics.[35] Throughout this book, Wiseman drives home principles of hermeneutics that are stereotypically Protestant:

> The true meaning of a word or phrase is that which was attached to it at the time when the person whom we interpret wrote or spoke. . . . We shall simply have to ask the question, Could the hearers of Christ, or the readers of St Paul, have understood him in that manner? If not, we shall be authorized to conclude, that such interpretations are of no value whatsoever.[36]

No value whatsoever? This is to attempt to beat Protestants at their own game with a vengeance. Is there really no hidden allegorical or mystical meanings, no *sensus plenior*, no possibility that the Holy Spirit has embedded truths which the original hearers or readers could not possibly perceive? (It is a tribute to how much Wiseman was focused on speaking to Protestants that such objections do not seem to have even occurred to him. If asked them by a Catholic, one suspects he would have said that the allegorical does not erase the literal and that the literal interpretation needs to be established first and accepted, but Protestants are evading it.) Wiseman even goes so far as to commend the German Protestant scholar, 'the learned' Karl Keil, for having convincingly established that 'the historico-grammatical interpreta-tion' is the correct one.[37] Wiseman then brings a sustained barrage of learning, including philological arguments from Hebrew, Arabic, Chaldaic, and Syriac, material on the cultural contexts of the time period, and inter-actions with a wide range of contemporary scholars including the eminent Protestant liberal critical scholar, W. M. L. De Wette. Protestants are hoisted with their own petard; they are not being biblical enough; they are not submitting to the authority of Scripture. Here, for example, is his attack on the interpretation given that same year in the inaugural lecture of the Regius Professor of Divinity at the University of Oxford, R. D. Hampden: 'Where in Scripture is this nice distinction drawn between

[35] Wiseman, *Real Presence*, 14.   [36] Wiseman, *Real Presence*, 25, 39.
[37] Wiseman, *Real Presence*, 37.

a real, vital presence, and a corporal presence?'[38] Or, more generally, of the divide between the two groups:

> 'This is my body,' says our Lord; 'I believe it to be thy body,' replies the Catholic: 'This is my blood,' repeats our Redeemer; 'I believe it to be the *figure* of thy blood,' rejoins the Protestant. Whose speech is here *yea, yea?* Who saith *amen* to the teaching of Christ?[39]

Wiseman sifts all the relevant biblical material thoroughly and systemically, addressing, for example, every text in which it is agreed that Christ was speaking metaphorically rather than literally (such as 'I am the vine' in John 15: 5), and patiently explains the consistent traits that enable one to distinguish between these two modes of speech.

The Real Presence also enabled Wiseman to disseminate more widely and in a more popular form the findings of the first treatise in his *Horae Syriacae*. The English Methodist scholar, Adam Clarke, had argued that Jesus' native language (which at the time was referred to as Syro-Chaldaic, but now is called Aramaic) did not have a verb which expressed that one was speaking figuratively and thus the fact that Christ's words sound literal to us ('This *is* my body' rather than something like 'represents' or 'signifies') is simply a reflection of the limitations of language. Through his Syriac research Wiseman had demonstrated triumphantly that there were 'FORTY-FIVE words which our Saviour could have used!'[40] The fact that even Protestants knew that Wiseman had won this round was indicated by T. H. Horne's removal of Clarke's argument from the seventh edition of his influential *Introduction to the Critical Study and Knowledge of the Holy Scriptures* (1834). The third section of Wiseman's *Real Presence* was 'On the Doctrine of St Paul Regarding the Eucharist'. One issue that Wiseman deals with here is the Protestant argument that the apostle Paul still referred to the consecrated host as 'bread' (1 Corinthians 11: 26–8), thereby refuting the Catholic doctrine of transubstantiation which declares that there is no longer any bread. Wiseman replies with proof-texting that would make an evangelical Protestant proud in order to show that such reasoning is too pedantic for scriptural language: to wit, a man whose sight Christ had restored is still identified after this transformation as 'the blind man' (John 9: 17) and Aaron's rod is still referred to as such even after 'it became a serpent' (Exodus 7: 10, 12).

---

[38] Wiseman, *Real Presence*, 180.   [39] Wiseman, *Real Presence*, 196–7.
[40] Wiseman, *Real Presence*, 291.

This is a sufficient survey of the contents of *Real Presence*, but it is worth underlining how far from self-evident the entire project was. Presumably, in Catholic thought, there was no need to prove the real presence of Christ in the Eucharist from Scripture. The fact that such a belief was part of the unwritten traditions of the church would surely suffice. The suitability of this book as a work to speak to the Bible-steeped Victorians was not lost on Wiseman's contemporaries. The English Catholic priest, Frederick Husenbeth, wrote to Wiseman to enthuse about *The Real Presence* and the exposition of the evidence for this doctrine that it contains:

> you have certainly treated it in a new manner, I think, with marked success, and have found some novel corroborating arguments of great value. I have sent a copy to the famous Quaker J. J. Gurney, a noted Hebrew and Biblical scholar; for I think it is a disquisition so philological and purely scriptural, that it must attract him, and ought to convince him.[41]

Underlining Wiseman's own identity as a serious biblical scholar, Husenbeth's main criticism was that the book was too learned for 'ordinary readers'. Likewise, an American priest, Peter Richard Kenrick, who would go on to become the first archbishop of St Louis, wrote:

> to express my satisfaction at the philosophic and powerful 'lectures on the Catholic Church[']; which, I trust, ere long will appear at this side of the Atlantic in a book form. Your lectures on the Scripture proofs of the Holy Eucharist make me anxiously expect the forthcoming volume of that work. I regret that the multiplied quotations from the oriental writers will render this work less likely to be soon reprinted here, as the catholics of this country are not generally prepared to profit by the profound erudition it unveils. I must candidly tell you that the reading of your various writings has revived a desire I once was possessed of—of acquiring an acquaintance with oriental literature, and of using my little influence to have Hebrew, at least, taught in our Seminaries.[42]

The greatest tribute to the effectiveness of Wiseman's *The Real Presence* was how much it rattled Protestants. No less a personage than the Regius Professor of Divinity at the University of Cambridge was exercised sufficiently by it to write a 356-page reply: Thomas Turton, *The Roman Catholic*

---

[41] Ushaw College Archives, Ushaw College, Durham, Nicholas Wiseman Papers, 806, Frederick C. Husenbeth to Nicholas Wiseman, 13 November 1836 (post stamp: 15 Nov. 1836, addressed to Wiseman at the English College, Rome).

[42] Ushaw College Archives, Ushaw College, Durham, Nicholas Wiseman Papers, 292, Peter Richard Kenrick to Nicholas Wiseman, 30 July 1837.

Doctrine of the Eucharist considered in reply to Dr Wiseman's Argument from Scripture (1837). Turton admitted that Wiseman was right to expect such an appeal to tempt Protestants to convert to Rome as it was 'on the authority of Scripture—an authority common to both parties'.[43] Wiseman grumbled in private that it might be his duty, against his standard policy, to answer this attack, but Turton had written at such length that an adequate reply would be prohibitive: 'This I could afford neither time nor money for. The English Catholics have not yet a reading public of their own sufficient to remunerate an author.'[44]

Wiseman was a Bible man his whole life. There was much work on many different fronts to be done to make English Catholics the force in the land that he longed for them to be, but Wiseman consistently insisted that increased attentiveness to the study of Holy Scripture was a priority. He pushed for biblical studies to be strengthened in the training programmes of the English seminaries, including requiring Hebrew for everyone preparing for the priesthood.[45] The cardinal also repeatedly called for a new, approved, Catholic English translation of the Bible. He carefully explained why it was insufficient for a new translation to be made simply from the Latin Vulgate, but rather it was essential that it be undertaken with 'constant recourse to the original Hebrew and Greek texts'.[46] There was a scheme for John Henry Newman to oversee this project, and a decree of the Second Synod of Westminster (1855) approved it, but the press of other commitments meant that adequate provision and ongoing support was not made to implement this plan at that time.[47] Wiseman also repeatedly lamented that the English Catholic community did not have scholars who were publishing significant works in the field of biblical studies. (He also added on one occasion that the English Protestant community was also lagging behind continental scholarship, lest anyone should overread his comment as saying

[43] Thomas Turton, *The Roman Catholic Doctrine of the Eucharist considered in reply to Dr Wiseman's Argument from Scripture* (Cambridge: Deighton, 1837), 332.
[44] Ushaw College Archives, Ushaw College, Durham, Nicholas Wiseman Papers, 815. Letter by Wiseman dated Rome, 17 July 1837. This is probably only a draft that Wiseman saved, and the recipient is not mentioned, but it is clear from references in the letter that it is Frederick Husenbeth.
[45] Schiefen, *Wiseman*, 208, 287.
[46] Nicholas Wiseman, *Essays on Various Subjects*, 3 vols (London: Charles Dolman, 1853), I, 79. This is an essay entitled 'Catholic Versions of Scripture', which was originally published in 1837 in the *Dublin Review*.
[47] Schiefen, *Wiseman*, 242.

something about Catholic values.)[48] Another expression of regret regarding the dearth of critical biblical scholarship by English Catholics prompted a Catholic paper to intimate that modern criticism was sufficiently barren that it was perhaps better left alone. Wiseman, far from being cowed by this response, took it on defiantly. The 'critical study of the Bible' was, in truth, 'graceful' and 'noble', cultivating an 'appreciation of the real beauties of the divine writings' and uncovering 'many hidden treasures'.[49] If one were to put in the hard work, and through perseverance make it through the tedious first stage of mastering the languages, then it would become 'a pleasant and gratifying pursuit' thereafter.[50] With these aspirations in mind, it is little wonder that Wiseman was thrilled when J. B. Morris, a Fellow of Exeter College, Oxford, who lectured on Hebrew, converted to Rome in 1846. The archbishop enthused in a letter that Morris was 'a great scholar, and a Syrian scholar, which I much value. He will join us here.'[51]

Wiseman repeatedly testified to his own, personal devotion to Sacred Scripture. Here is one instance:

> As for ourselves, we refuse to yield to any Protestant, in love and reverence for God's written word. It has been the Book of our predilection from earliest youth...It has been the study of years; nor have we accounted pains, or trouble, or time, as anything, if they could help us to know it, and to profit by it. Days and nights have been passed by us, in collecting knowledge subservient to it; and we have read and written not a little, to assist our imperfect power, in defending, illustrating, and applying it.[52]

Wiseman's preaching was one way that he modelled this commitment. His sermons (indeed, his lectures) all had a text at their head and additional passages of Scripture cited throughout: it is a rare sermon that does not have a reference to another biblical text already in the opening paragraph. No perfunctory homilies, Wiseman standardly preached for a full hour. Well over a hundred of his sermons were published. He once observed that he was on schedule to preach about ninety one-hour sermons during a

---

[48] Wiseman, 'Catholic Versions', *Various Subjects*, I, 74.

[49] Wiseman, 'The Miracles of the New Testament', *Various Subjects*, I, 169 (originally published in 1849 in the *Dublin Review*).

[50] Wiseman, 'The Miracles of the New Testament', *Various Subjects*, I, 172.

[51] Ward, *Wiseman*, I, 445.

[52] Nicholas Wiseman, *The Catholic Doctrine on the Use of the Bible, being a review of His Grace Archbishop Dixon's 'Catholic Introduction to Scripture'* (London: Richardson and Son, 1853), 32 (an earlier version of this essay was published in 1852 in the *Dublin Review*).

six-week period (that is, an average of more than two hours a day seven days a week).[53] Wiseman instinctively reached for biblical language and imagery to express his own thoughts. Even away from the press of the conflict with English Protestants, here is the archbishop's way of telling the Catholics of Ireland that he was excited to be in their midst:

> And then this, our common joy, like the waters which the prophet Ezechiel saw first collected in the temple and then issue through its gates overflowing, will go forth from these most sacred precincts, a swelling flood, to mingle with the exultation of the multitudes outside.[54]

When he asked the faithful to pray for him, he did so by appropriating the words of 1 Corinthians 9: 27.[55] Even his notorious Pastoral Letter had the actual citation of a biblical passage in the very first paragraph ('2 Cor. vi. 2'), and his *Appeal*, despite its emphasis on reason rather than revelation, was sprinkled with embedded biblical quotations (1 Peter 2: 23, 2 Chronicles 32: 8, Luke 4: 14/Romans 15: 9, and 1 Peter 3: 9). As has been said, Wiseman's engagement with Holy Scripture was no preoccupation of his biographer, Wilfrid Ward. Ward, however, included a humorous anecdote relayed by Bishop Patterson which—although Ward does not remark on this—incidentally reveals the cardinal's astonishing knowledge of Scripture. It is worth quoting it to gain the full effect:

> Once in a great function, when he was sitting on his throne, the celebrant of the High Mass was a dignitary distinguished by great learning and a very singular congeries of personal defects—small and deformed, comically plain in features, and unkempt and untidy in garb, who was clad in a gorgeous and ample medieval vestment and a long stole, which had got entangled with his feet, so that he could scarcely move. When thus accoutred he advanced to make his homage to the Cardinal. He made a sign to me to come near, and said *sotto voce* and with great gravity, 'Quis est iste qui venit de Edom, tinctis vestibus de Bosra, iste formosus gradiens in stola sua?'[56]

The quotation is from Isaiah 63: 1, which, in the Roman Catholic Douay-Rheims Version, says: 'Who is this that cometh from Edom, with dyed garments from Bosra, this beautiful one in his robe, walking in the greatness

---

[53] Ward, *Wiseman*, I, 311.   [54] Ward, *Wiseman*, II, 297.

[55] Wiseman, *Various Subjects*, II, p. x. Wiseman's request for prayer concludes: 'that he who has here presumed to preach to others may not, through neglected graces, himself become a castaway.'

[56] Ward, *Wiseman*, II, 192–3.

of his strength'? This is hardly one of the more familiar texts of the Bible. Wiseman's ability to think of it and quote it simply as banter reveals a knowledge of Scripture that could hold its own with the most biblicist Protestants.

It remains in this chapter to explore Wiseman's other main writings on Sacred Scripture. Again, no scholar has ever before analysed Wiseman's biblical essays. Several years after *Horae Syriacae* Wiseman published a second scholarly monograph in the discipline of biblical studies, *Two Letters on Some Parts of the Controversy concerning the genuineness of 1 John v. 7., containing also an inquiry into the origin of the first Latin version of Scripture, commonly called 'The Itala'.*[57] This is a careful, learned work, showing a deep knowledge of the relevant ancient languages and manuscripts, as well as contemporary scholarship in multiple languages. Wiseman made a convincing case for the African origins of the old Latin version of the Bible. This work therefore continued to be cited favourably by biblical scholars well after his death. The English Protestant scholar, F. H. A. Scrivener, wrote in 1883:

> On the ground of *internal* evidence, however, Wiseman made out a case which all who have followed him, Lachmann, Tischendorf, Davidson, Tregelles, accept as irresistible; indeed it is not easy to draw any other conclusion from his elaborate comparison of the words, the phrases, and grammatical constructions of the Latin version of Holy Scripture, with the parallel instances by which they can be illustrated from African writers, and from them only.[58]

The purpose of this monograph was to defend the authenticity of 1 John 5: 7 which, in the Authorized Version, says: 'For there are three that bear record in heaven, the Father, the Word, and the Holy Ghost; and these three are one.' Most ancient manuscripts do not have this, indicating that it was a later addition or gloss and not therefore divinely inspired, apostolic teaching, the Word of God written.[59] If it were genuine, however, it would be the clearest, simplest, fullest, most straightforward statement of the orthodox

---

[57] It originally appeared in the *Catholic Magazine* in 1832–3, and then was published as a separate item in Rome in 1835. I am using the republication in Wiseman, *Various Subjects*.

[58] Scrivener, *Plain Introduction*, 44.

[59] The argument of Wiseman's monograph is as follows: (1) everyone agrees that it is the African manuscripts that include 1 John 5: 7; (2) he can demonstrate that the old Latin translations of the Bible were first produced in Africa, not Italy; (3) hence, the African version is the older and more reliable and therefore the verse is authentic: 'if the Italian Fathers had it not, it was from its having been lost in their recension' (Wiseman, 'Two Letters', *Various Subjects*, I, 66).

doctrine of the Trinity to be found in the whole of Holy Scripture, so its loss
was felt deeply by those defending this doctrine. Once again, however, it
strikes one that this is a stereotypically Protestant concern. As apt biblical
passages are the only warrant for a doctrine that Protestants generally
recognize, the absence of 1 John 5: 7 should indeed cause orthodox
Protestants wishing to defend Trinitarian thought to sigh. Catholics, however, have the authority of the church, the councils, the creeds, the
tradition, and the pope for guidance—all of which affirm the doctrine of
the Trinity unequivocally—and therefore they should presumably be able
to take the decommissioning of one biblical text more in their stride. Once
again, Wiseman's profound commitment to scriptural reasoning is on display in his desire to research and write an entire monograph on this point.

Two companion articles on the New Testament of Wiseman's, originally
published in 1849 in the *Dublin Review*, were 'The Parables of the New
Testament as illustrating Catholic doctrine' and 'The Miracles of the
New Testament as illustrating Catholic doctrine'. The first one was ostensibly prompted by *The Four Gospels* by F. P. Kenrick, the brother of
Wiseman's correspondent P. R. Kenrick. F. P. Kenrick would be elevated
to an archbishopric a year after Wiseman (in his case, that of Baltimore).
Nevertheless, 'The Parables of the New Testament', rather than a review,
was really a constructive piece in which Wiseman boldly stood the standard
charge against Catholics on its head by arguing that it is actually Protestants
who ignore much of the content and teaching of the Bible:

> Then what can a Protestant do with the evangelical counsels, poverty and
> chastity, and renouncing of all possessions; with the apostles, sent without
> scrip or staff to preach to heathens; with celibacy and virginity; with fasting
> and watching; with the forgiveness of sins, and the eating of Christ's Body;
> with miracles and wonders to be wrought by the Church?...Only the
> Catholic can fully and lovingly enter into the heart of God's word, and feel
> its whole truth and perfect reality.[60]

Wiseman then went on to a close reading of many of Christ's parables in
order to demonstrate that they fully make sense only if one believes in
Catholic distinctives. The kingdom of God as a tree accords with the
Catholic system of the visible unity of the church and not Protestant

---

[60] Wiseman, 'The Parables of the New Testament', *Various Subjects*, I, 107 (originally published
in 1849 in the *Dublin Review*).

denominationalism. The kingdom of God as a feast corresponds to Catholic worship which is centred around the Eucharist:

> The Church is not merely a teaching, but a feast-place: not a lecture-room, but a banqueting-hall. And which Church exclusively is this? Enter the Catholic church (the type of the Church in the abstract), and you find not only always a table, but if one may speak in so homely a way, a table with the cloth spread, which tells you that to-day there has been already a feast, and to-morrow there will be another, and the day after, as there was yesterday. . . . Where else is this to be found? In the meeting-house, we trow, the pulpit reminds one not of feasts.[61]

Wiseman pays particular attention to the parable of the Good Samaritan, arguing that the truths expressed in many of its details are indiscernible outside of Catholic thought (for example, 'what is the oil, which has ceased to have all meaning in the Protestant system?').[62]

'The Miracles of the New Testament' continues the same line of argument with another set of biblical passages. Wiseman cleverly connects details of healings in the New Testament with those of the Catholic baptismal service (the former being a sign illustrating the more important, spiritual realities bestowed in the latter). Protestants have sometimes found it difficult to explain why, on one occasion, Jesus seemed to need a second attempt to perform a healing of a blind man completely. Wiseman elucidates from a Catholic perspective:

> '. . . laying His hand upon him, He asked him if he saw anything. And looking up, he said: I see men, as it were trees walking. After that, again He laid his hands upon his eyes, and he began to see and was restored, so that he saw all things clearly.' [Mark 8: 23–5] Now we have seen how just twice, in the administration of baptism, the priest places his hand upon the child, with a prayer for the removal of blindness at the first, and for the granting of light at the second time.[63]

The paralytic who is pronounced by Jesus to be forgiven and then healed is a story which demonstrates that priestly absolution is 'not declaratory but efficacious': Jesus was obviously not merely observing that the man was healed but rather his words made it so, the same is true for the paralleled

---

[61] Wiseman, 'The Parables of the New Testament', *Various Subjects*, I, 140.
[62] Wiseman, 'The Parables of the New Testament', *Various Subjects*, I, 156.
[63] Wiseman, 'The Miracles of the New Testament', *Various Subjects*, I, 201–2.

words of absolution.[64] The resurrection of Lazarus is interpreted as teaching the authority of priests to bind and loose: '"And presently he that had been dead came forth, *bound* feet and hands with winding-bands, and his face was *bound* about with a napkin. Jesus said to them: *Loose* him, and let him go." [John 11: 44] He did not do so Himself, but He commissioned others.'[65] Christ's transforming of water into wine teaches the doctrine of transubstantiation. Wiseman the academic biblical scholar longed to find a way to express that side of himself in this article in discussions of linguistic and manuscript points. In the version reprinted in his collected essays, he even added four pages of philological notes, heavily sprinkled with Hebrew, Greek, and Arabic, as a kind of appendix.

Wiseman decided that this duo of articles should really be a triad and therefore explicitly carried on the discussion in 'The Actions of the New Testament'. This is the most aggressive and punchy of the three in its persistent insistence that Catholics are more biblical than Protestants. Here is an opening salvo:

> And we cannot forbear remarking, how, in every Catholic community, the presence of Christ instructing His disciples, at their common table, is imitated by the reading of Scripture during meals; a practice, we believe, confined to our 'unscriptural' and 'Scripture-hating' Church.[66]

Catholics can also match the most conservative evangelical Protestant commitment to biblical inerrancy, affirming that the Holy Spirit had super-intended the writing of the canonical books so as to prevent the 'smallest error'.[67] Wiseman proceeds into a discussion of what is recorded in the New Testament regarding the Blessed Virgin Mary in order to demonstrate that Catholics have not overstated her significance, but rather Protestants have overlooked or suppressed it. For example, the first miracle of Christ—the revealing of his power—came through the agency of Mary at whose request it was performed. Tellingly, Wiseman argues that Catholic devotional practices (he was an enthusiast for spiritual retreats on the model of Loyola) allowed Catholics to find meanings in Scripture that Protestants

---

[64] Wiseman, 'The Parables of the New Testament', *Various Subjects*, I, 212.

[65] Wiseman, 'The Miracles of the New Testament', *Various Subjects*, I, 222.

[66] Wiseman, 'The Actions of the New Testament', *Various Subjects*, I, 585 (originally published in 1851 in the *Dublin Review*).

[67] Wiseman, 'The Actions of the New Testament', *Various Subjects*, I, 586.

passed over: 'Catholic meditation will go deeper than this.'[68] Wiseman goes on to likewise make a biblical case for the greater significance of the apostle Peter than that espoused by Protestants. A close reading of several passages reveals that there were two boats available—one was Peter's and the other belonged to the sons of Zebedee—and that Jesus chose the former. As this detail is carefully recorded it must be for some purpose and the reason is to teach that the church, which even Protestants speak of as a ship, is piloted by Peter. Protestants will dismiss the fact that it was Peter's boat as devoid of portent, but that only reveals once again that Catholics take Scripture more seriously than them: the Catholic 'discovers a purpose in every detail, in every word'.[69]

Having defended from Holy Scripture Catholic views of Mary and Peter, Wiseman then attacks the British, Protestant view of the Sabbath. To begin with, he observes that Protestants continually condemn Catholics for accepting beliefs and practices on the authority merely of tradition, but the conviction that the Christian day of rest is Sunday rather than the Jewish one of Saturday is exclusively derived from tradition. Moreover, Catholics never refer to Sunday as 'the Sabbath': 'What makes this strange infatuation still more amazing is, that in the New Testament, it is so clearly attributed, as a characteristic, to the Pharisee. A simple-minded reader of the Gospel would naturally ask, who defended Sabbatarian strictness, our Lord, or His enemies?'[70] Christ defiantly healed on the Sabbath precisely in order to inculcate a new viewpoint, but Protestants refuse to submit to the teaching of these numerous texts of the New Testament: 'Had our Lord said, in these cases: "To-morrow come and I will heal you, for this is the Sabbath," He would have spoken words with which Exeter Hall would have rung, and given a text to be stereotyped by tract-dealers, and engraved for children's copies.'[71] In what was probably a particularly delicious return of a standard charge against Catholics, Wiseman argued that the Protestant attitude toward the Sabbath was superstitious.

[68] Wiseman, 'The Actions of the New Testament', *Various Subjects*, I, 601.

[69] Wiseman, 'The Actions of the New Testament', *Various Subjects*, I, 626.

[70] Wiseman, 'The Actions of the New Testament', *Various Subjects*, I, 630–1.

[71] Wiseman, 'The Actions of the New Testament', *Various Subjects*, I, 636. Exeter Hall was the standard venue used for the annual meetings of evangelical societies and the Lord's Day Observance Society even had an office there: John Wigley, *The Rise and Fall of the Victorian Sunday* (Manchester: Manchester University Press, 1980), 35.

One final work by Wiseman is worth highlighting: *The Catholic Doctrine on the Use of the Bible, being a review of His Grace Archbishop Dixon's 'Catholic Introduction to Scripture'*. Having long complained that Catholics were not producing works in the field of biblical studies, the publication of Dixon's textbook was an occasion to celebrate. Once again, Wiseman's emphasis was on belying Protestant assumptions:

> Some consternation, indeed, this valuable work will cast into the enemy's camp. 'What! Is the Bible allowed to be read in Maynooth? Is there a course of reading, and a chair, of Scripture there? Why, this is more than we have in our universities!' . . . nor can it possibly have occurred to the minds of readers on this lately absorbing topic, that after all is said and done, Scripture is there read, Scripture is studied, Scripture is expounded. Now, if Scripture be the very essential of education, here it is; as full, as extensive, as palpable as in Oxford, or at Trinity College.[72]

Wiseman used his review to help British Catholics think about the relationship of their community to the practice of Bible reading. He was well aware that ordinary Catholics were often flummoxed by Protestant accusations that their church opposed the dissemination of copies of the Bible and discouraged the masses from reading it. As ever, Wiseman responded with a counter-attack. By way of context, he made comments that, for the purposes of this study, underline the extent to which the Victorians were a Bible people to an unprecedented extent:

> It is true that the abstract principle of the 'Bible alone,' as expressed boldly by the apostate Chillingworth, has been an axiom of Protestantism; but it is only within our own generation that its practical working has been tried. Two means were previously wanting. The great bulk of the working classes could not read, and there were no Bible-readers, to supply the deficiency. And the Bible was not brought within the reach of the population by gratuitous distribution, till societies for that purpose had sprung up. It is, therefore, only now, that the experiment is being tried on a great scale, of what the indiscriminate reading of the Bible will make a people.[73]

The fatal flaw of the Protestant scheme was that it left it to the masses to prove to themselves that the Bible was inspired and to interpret its contents. The Bible alone had already led to rapid unorthodoxy in Protestant Germany.

---

[72] Wiseman, *Catholic Doctrine*, 7–8. Joseph Dixon held the chair of Sacred Scripture and Hebrew at Maynooth College, the main Irish Catholic seminary.

[73] Wiseman, *Catholic Doctrine*, 15.

The fruit of this method in England was becoming more and more apparent: the Bible was held up for ridicule in publications such as the Secularist newspaper, the *Reasoner*. Or, on the opposite front, new religious movements such as the Irvingites were springing up that justified their wrong-headed beliefs and practices through 'Protestant biblical fanaticism'.[74] Turning the tables again, Wiseman advances the counter-thesis that the authority of Scripture is only upheld unwaveringly in the Catholic church. He observed that the bishop of London in his charge for 1850 had warned his clergy that they must not speak against the inspiration of the Bible: 'Let any Catholic, of whatever country, be asked, if he should think it possible that a Bishop of his Church, addressing his clergy, should have cautioned them— priests already—against denying the inspiration of Holy Scripture?'[75] The Protestant principle of the right of private judgment was, in effect, to make one's own personal pride one's final authority. The true love of Scripture is to be found in the true church: Catholics cherish Holy Scripture as a 'gift of insuperable value'.[76]

In conclusion, if the thesis of this volume is correct, it is not surprising that the mid-Victorian face of Catholicism, the first archbishop of Westminster, and the most prominent leader of English Catholics since the Reformation, was also a Bible man through and through.

---

[74] Wiseman, *Catholic Doctrine*, 18.   [75] Wiseman, *Catholic Doctrine*, 19.
[76] Wiseman, *Catholic Doctrine*, 21.

3

Atheists

Charles Bradlaugh, Annie Besant, and 'this indictable book'

Annie Besant first met Charles Bradlaugh on 2 August 1874. Early in his public freethinking career, Bradlaugh had adopted the pugnacious *nom de plume*, 'Iconoclast'. Overcoming her initial assumption that he was too 'rough' a speaker for her more refined tastes, Besant had come to hear him lecture in London's freethinking stronghold, the Hall of Science.[1] His address over, Bradlaugh was distributing membership certificates to those in attendance who had recently joined the National Secular Society. Besant was one of these new members. Bradlaugh engaged her in conversation, advancing the argument that she was really an atheist already who was not admitting this to herself because of the unpleasant associations and misconceptions she had regarding that label. Annie Besant (1847–1933) had been impressed with his lecture that night. It had been on 'The ancestry and birth of Jesus'.[2] In other words, it was essentially an anti-Bible lecture. If the biblical nature of the contents of this address is not self-evident from its title, it is from Bradlaugh's extant writings.[3] It is not just a happy coincidence for

---

[1] Annie Besant, *Autobiographical Sketches* (London: Freethought Publishing Company, 1885), 86.
[2] Besant, *Autobiographical Sketches*, 89.
[3] Bishopsgate Institute, Bishopsgate Library, London, Bradlaugh Papers, 19, 'Examination of the four Gospels according to Matthew, Mark, Luke, and John with Remarks on the life and death of the meek & lowly Jesus', handwritten manuscript dated May 1850; (slightly) revised June 1854. This early anti-Bible effort has an index listing eighteen themes covered in it. One is the genealogy of Jesus, another is the birth of Jesus, and another is a comparison of Chrishna (Krishna) and Jesus, a subject that Besant mentions that Bradlaugh had included in his address.

the theme of this chapter that Bradlaugh's subject when Besant first heard him speak was a biblical one. The odds were distinctly in favour of this. It would have been more surprising if Besant had happened to come to the Hall of Science on one of the rarer occasions when Bradlaugh's oration was not a denunciation of the contents of the Bible.

At the time of this initial meeting with Besant, Charles Bradlaugh (1833–1891) was already the most eminent leader of organized atheism in Britain. He was the editor of the nation's leading atheistic newspaper, the *National Reformer*, and had been at its founding in 1860. In 1866, he had become the founding president of the National Secular Society and he would be its animating spirit until his final illness in 1890. Iconoclast also toured the country giving freethinking addresses and, by 1874, he was widely considered the most popular speaker in the Secularist movement. His reputation would continue to grow thereafter, not least through his long and eventually successful campaign to sit in Parliament as an avowed atheist.[4] Whether they admired him or detested him, if asked to identify an atheist leader, most Britons for much of the second half of the nineteenth century would have named Bradlaugh. Charles Bradlaugh is the most obvious and defensible choice for an example figure to represent Victorian atheism.

Bradlaugh was born in 1833 and grew up in Bethnal Green, London. His father was a solicitor's clerk and, in regards to his financial position, Bradlaugh was content to say flatly that he was poor.[5] Bradlaugh's formal schooling, begun when he was seven years old, ended before he reached his eleventh birthday. This education was steeped in Scripture. Indeed, extraordinarily, everything that has survived of his school work is explicitly biblical, although these works were clearly retained merely as examples of his achievements rather than because of their theme. They are samples of his developing handwriting sent home as Christmas pieces. These school projects started with a pre-printed page. Each of these pages has as its theme a biblical narrative and the top and both sides have biblical texts accompanied by illustrations printed on them. In the middle of the page, there was blank space in which the

[4] For this campaign, see Timothy Larsen, 'Charles Bradlaugh, Militant Unbelief, and the Civil Rights of Atheists', in Caroline Litzenberger and Eileen Groth Lyon (eds), *The Human Tradition in Modern Britain* (Lanham, Maryland: Rowman and Littlefield, 2006), 127–38; Walter L. Arnstein, *The Bradlaugh Case: Atheism, Sex, and Politics among the Late Victorians* (Columbia, Missouri: University of Missouri Press, 1983).

[5] Charles Bradlaugh, *The Autobiography of Mr Bradlaugh. A Page of his Life* (London: Austin and Co., 1873).

schoolboy has dutifully written. The first one, produced when Bradlaugh was just aged seven, is on 'The Life of Samuel'. His main writing sample is the words of 1 Samuel 3: 3–4, written out in cursive.[6] The second one, from when he was nine years old, is on 'The Death of Ahab', and his writing sample is a standard piece of sampler advice about not being a bad example (presumably, the connection being, as Ahab was).[7] The final one, when he was aged ten and thus toward the end of his formal education, is on the 'Death of Absalom'. For it, Bradlaugh's main writing sample is 2 Samuel 18: 14–15. This is all we have from his formal education. His day schooling completed, Bradlaugh continued to attend Sunday school and eventually became a Sunday school teacher—a context that, if possible, would have presumably been even more immersed in the Bible than his day school had been.

The turning point in Bradlaugh's life came when he was around fifteen years old. In good Anglican, coming-of-age manner, the bishop of London was scheduled to visit the area in order to confirm a group of candidates, of which Bradlaugh was one. His own local clergyman, John Graham Packer, incumbent of the Church of St Peter's, Hackney Road, instructed Bradlaugh to prepare himself to make an impression as a bright, well-informed lad. Perhaps going beyond the call of duty, Bradlaugh began studying the gospels. This research resulted in his being unsettled by the apparently irreconcilable discrepancies he found there.[8] Bradlaugh wrote to Packer asking for his explanations for these conundrums. Packer responded by banning him from teaching Sunday school and informing his father that Bradlaugh was becoming an atheist. This became a kind of self-fulfilling prophecy. No longer involved in the Sunday school, Bradlaugh used that time to listen to and join the open debating and speechifying in Bonner's Fields. He held to Christian orthodoxy initially, but abandoned it, tellingly, after being bested in a debate on 'The Inspiration of the Bible'.[9] Bradlaugh's father responded by adorning the house with apt biblical quotations. The most prominent one, hung so as to be directly in front of Bradlaugh whenever he sat down to a meal, was: 'The fool hath said in his heart, There

---

[6] Bishopsgate Institute, Bishopsgate Library, London, Bradlaugh Papers, 18/B, 'The Life of Samuel', 1840.

[7] Bishopsgate Institute, Bishopsgate Library, London, Bradlaugh Papers, 8/C, 'The Death of Ahab', 1842.

[8] Hypatia Bradlaugh Bonner, *Charles Bradlaugh: His Life and Work*, 2 vols, second edition (London: T. Fisher Unwin, 1895), I, 8.

[9] Bonner, *Bradlaugh*, I, 12.

is no God' (Psalms 14: 1; 53: 1). This biblical text seems to have haunted
Bradlaugh for the rest of his life. As a self-avowed atheist, he was always
careful to clarify that he did not assert that there was no God and therefore
he did not fall under this text's censure. Here is an example of Iconoclast's
standard definition of his atheism in which he makes the connection with
this passage of Scripture explicit:

> I do not stand here to prove that there is no God. If I should undertake to
> prove such a proposition, I should deserve the ill words of the oft-quoted
> psalmist applied to those who say there is no God. I do not say there is no God,
> but I am an Atheist without God. To me the word God conveys no idea . . . [10]

On another occasion, he put it this way: 'He did not deny that there was
"a God," because to deny that which is unknown was as absurd as to affirm
it. As an Atheist he denied the God of the Bible'.[11]

His resolute freethinking stance and the resulting clash with his father
prompted Bradlaugh to leave home at the age of sixteen. Also in his
sixteenth year, Charles Bradlaugh wrote his first substantial composition as
a freethinker. It was an explicitly anti-Bible work: 'Examination of the four
Gospels according to Matthew, Mark, Luke, and John with Remarks on the
life and death of the meek & lowly Jesus'.[12] Bradlaugh added a few marginal
notes to this manuscript in 1854 when he was twenty years old. The later
additions are easily distinguishable, and they show that he had grown more
radical in his views. Most notably, Bradlaugh inserted a note observing
that he would no longer concede that Jesus of Nazareth even existed. In
other words, when what was untenable in the gospels was stripped away,
there might be no historical residue left at all. Bradlaugh's fundamentally
scriptural frame of mind was such that—in good Protestant, biblicist fashion—his manuscript includes a proof-text justifying his project on the title

---

[10] *Discussion between Mr Thomas Cooper and Mr C. Bradlaugh* [in 1864] (London: Freethinking
Publishing Company, 1888), 9.

[11] This is from an 1859 debate. It was standard practice at that time to change reported speech
from the first person to the second person: Bonner, *Bradlaugh*, I, 87. Bradlaugh added that he also
denied the God of 'the Koran, of the Vedas', but this did not preoccupy his thinking, while the
God of the Bible most certainly did. As John M. Robertson put it, in his sympathetic, official
review of Bradlaugh's life: 'Bradlaugh did not go about lecturing against witch-burning or the
Koran. He attacked an aggressive and endowed superstition'. Bonner, *Bradlaugh*, II, 147.

[12] Bishopsgate Institute, Bishopsgate Library, London, Bradlaugh Papers, 19, 'Examination of
the four Gospels according to Matthew, Mark, Luke, and John with Remarks on the life and death
of the meek & lowly Jesus'. Marked: 'Written May/50 at the age of 16 years 7½ months Altered &
Amended, June 54/at the age of 20 yrs 9 months'.

page: '"Prove all things & hold fast that which is true."—"Paul"' (1 Thessalonians 5: 21). Even more strikingly, the genre of Bradlaugh's first freethinking work is that of a biblical commentary. He actual wrote out by hand in full
numerous passages of Scripture as the text upon which to comment. His
standard approach is to put related texts from the four gospels side by side in
four parallel columns, thus a whole page might be taken up with just
Scripture. After this, he would provide a section entitled 'observations',
that is, the commentary. His intent, however, is to discredit the veracity of
the gospels. As Bradlaugh acknowledges in the preface, the manuscript also
includes lengthy quotations from popular British freethinkers: 'I have quoted
largely from Revd R. Taylor & Thomas Paine as well as from Thomas
Cooper.' Robert Taylor was an ordained Anglican priest who had left the
church and become a freethinking lecturer. Bradlaugh frequently quotes
from Taylor's *The Diegesis: being a discovery of the origin, evidences, and early
history of Christianity, never yet before or elsewhere so fully and faithfully set forth*
(1829).[13] Taylor argued that the gospels were not historical but rather an
expression of ideas borrowed from the religious traditions of other places,
notably Egypt and India. Thomas Paine's influential *Age of Reason* (1795),
its grand title notwithstanding, was actually an (anti-)biblical commentary
that worked its way breezily through the whole canon denouncing the
contents of each book or section of the Bible in turn. Thomas Cooper is
particularly interesting as his series of articles entitled 'Critical Exegesis of
Gospel History, on the basis of Strauss's "Leben Jesu"' had only begun to
appear in January 1850 and it was still in progress when Bradlaugh wrote his
manuscript in May 1850.[14]

Bradlaugh declared in the preface what his approach would be: 'I will
demonstrate to any one that the 4 Gospels as we have them are a jumble of
nonsense & contradiction.' He asserts repeatedly that orthodox Christians
think that they must believe that every detail of the Bible is truth or
that 'they'll be damned'. Therefore, to show even a trivial discrepancy is,
in his reckoning, to demolish the Christian religion—a high view of
Scripture indeed. Occasionally, his malice is palpable. Not content to
deny the Virgin Birth, he asserts that 'Mary had a number of gallants'.

---

[13] Robert Taylor, *The Diegesis: being a discovery of the origin, evidences, and early history of
Christianity, never yet before or elsewhere so fully and faithfully set forth* (London: R. Carlile, 1829).
[14] For an examination of these articles by Cooper, see Timothy Larsen, *Contested Christianity:
The Political and Social Contexts of Victorian Theology* (Waco, Texas: Baylor University Press), 43–58.

Drawing on Taylor, he develops the theory that Jesus was trained in Egypt as a therapeutan monk. This theory seems to have been especially attractive to Bradlaugh as having the double punch of reducing Christianity to borrowed paganism and labelling Jesus as a monk, a pejorative term for most Victorians. Nevertheless, the basic structure of a gospels commentary must be kept in view. The headings of Bradlaugh's sections such as 'Healing the Sick', 'Raising the Dead', 'The Death', and 'The Resurrection' would serve equally well in an orthodox volume.

The fact that Iconoclast's lecturing was primarily on anti-Bible themes may be illustrated by a handwritten list of his which records every time— twenty-four in total—he spoke at the Hall of Science, London, in 1865.[15] The first occasion was fittingly 'A Review of the Last Year. Our progress— church progress—scientific progress'. The theme is not clear for two items listed—one was apparently a reply to something Joseph Barker had said in a lecture, the other is just recorded as 'Short address at a Soirée'. Another was a benefit for a widow. There was one truly secular subject in the sense of not on a religious theme at all. Delightfully, it was a lecture given in reply to the question: 'Why do men shave?' A few of the rest were on generally theological or anti-Christian themes such as 'Atonement' and 'Supposed effects of Christianity on the World'. The overwhelming category, how- ever, is explicitly (anti-)biblical addresses. For example, 'Prophecies before Jesus & by Jesus, the morality & concord of the four Gospels', 'Woman & the Bible', 'The child Jeremiah & his lamentations', and 'Bible account of Creation tested by itself & Science'. When the freethinking faithful assem- bled on New Year's Eve they were treated to an address by Bradlaugh on 'The Twelve tribes in the desert'. The one debate that Bradlaugh held at the Hall of Science that year was with a Christian minister and on the theme of 'Bible History of Creation'. Indeed, the list is so biblical that, reminiscent of Christian sermons, lectures are repeatedly identified simply by a text: for example, 'St Paul's Epistle to the Romans', 'St Paul's Epistle to the Corinthians', and 'Revelation of St John the Divine'. The one occasion listed where Bradlaugh was not the speaker, change did not extend to the subject matter. For July 2, Bradlaugh records that he was the chair. The speaker was Harriet Law and her theme is reported as 'On Bible'. This list provides a thorough and convenient snapshot, but it is not atypical. The consistent preoccupation of Bradlaugh with biblical themes across his

---

[15] Bishopsgate Institute, Bishopsgate Library, London, Bradlaugh Papers, 142.

lecturing life is amply confirmed by paging through the titles of his addresses as noticed in the *National Reformer*. To give just one additional example, when in 1861 Bradlaugh attempted to give an outdoor lecture under the auspices of the Plymouth and Devonport Secular Society the animus of local authorities prevented it. The only words he had managed to speak before he was arrested were: 'Friends, I am about to address you on the Bible'.[16]

After that first meeting in 1874, the relationship between Besant and Bradlaugh quickly ripened into a close friendship. When she promptly followed up by writing to Iconoclast inviting him to her house, he did not initially accept, but rather warned her that a friendship with a notorious atheist such as himself would do her considerable damage in society. She replied, echoing biblical teaching, that she 'had counted the cost' (Luke 14: 28).[17] The risk proved to be mutual. In Bradlaugh's fight to take his seat in Parliament, Sir Henry Tyler offered this objection: 'The fact was that Mr Bradlaugh could not come into the House without bringing Annie Besant with him.' Another speaker in the debate, implying that it was Besant who was the bad influence, referred to 'Bradlaugh's Besantine doctrines of morality or avowed Atheism'.[18] (Ironically, when in 1886 Bradlaugh did finally take his seat in Parliament he did so by taking the standard oath which included the act of kissing the Bible.) Both Bradlaugh and Besant were already married when they met, but separated from their spouses—she because of religious incompatibility (her husband was a clergyman), he because his wife was an alcoholic. Even Bradlaugh's daughter, who did not like Besant, admitted that the couple would have undoubtedly married if they had both been free.[19] In fact, for years they saw more of each other than most married couples. On a typical weekday, he would come to her house in the morning and they would do their work in each other's company. He would take all his meals at her house save breakfast, and not go home until 10 p.m.[20] They also went on holidays together and lecturing tours.

Besant's rise in the Secularist world was fast. Having gone to the Hall of Science for the first time, met Bradlaugh, and received her certificate of membership in the National Secular Society on 2 August 1874, she was

---

[16] Bradlaugh, *Autobiography*, 14–15.
[17] Annie Besant, *An Autobiography* (London: T. Fisher Unwin, 1908), 177.
[18] *Hansard's Parliamentary Debates*, Third Series, Vol. CCLIII (1880), columns 593, 1296.
[19] Bonner, *Bradlaugh*, II, 13.   [20] Besant, *Autobiography*, 178.

hired as a staff writer for the *National Reformer* before the month was out. By January, she had dedicated herself to being a Secularist lecturer. In May came her first opportunity to attend the annual conference of the National Secular Society and there Bradlaugh was elected president and she was elected a vice president. They would both continue to hold those offices until 1890. In 1877, they founded the influential Freethought Publishing Company. Remarkably, her name came first: 'The partners in the Freethought Publishing Company are Annie Besant and Charles Bradlaugh' (with their names again signed in that order at that the end of this announcement).[21] Besant also became co-editor and co-proprietor with Bradlaugh of the *National Reformer*. In other words, almost anywhere Bradlaugh's name was in the world of organized atheism, Besant's was there beside it. Added to this, they invited notoriety in 1877 by defiantly repub-lishing Charles Knowlton's *The Fruits of Philosophy*, a birth-control manual that had already been condemned as obscene. The attention-grabbing trial which they successfully provoked further linked their names together in the public mind. Besant was highly popular in the Secularist movement as both a speaker and a writer. She had certainly become the leading woman in the Secularist movement and a case could be made that she was the second most important figure in the movement beside Bradlaugh himself. Moreover, Bradlaugh's wing of the Secularist movement was the largest and the most visible and influential and she was certainly the most important leader in it beside him. Moreover, her position should not be misconstrued as simply a gift from Bradlaugh. It was just as much a reflection of her extraordinary talents and personality. This is amply illustrated by the way that she rose to the top of other movements as well, notably becoming the president of the Theosophical Society. Annie Besant even became the president of the Indian National Congress party just four years after she had joined it. Her Zelig-like qualities even extended to being the one who conferred on Gandhi the honorary title 'Mahatma'.[22] For the purposes at hand, certainly in the late 1870s and the first half of the 1880s, whether they liked it or not, no one would have denied that Besant was one of the chief leaders of organized atheism.

Annie Wood, to give her maiden name, was from a family that was notably higher up in the social scale from that of Bradlaugh's. Her great

---

[21] Besant, *Autobiographical Sketches*, 117.
[22] Anne Taylor, *Annie Besant: A Biography* (Oxford: Oxford University Press, 1992), 315.

uncle's career included Lord Mayor of London, MP for the City, and a baronetcy. Her father, who died when she was five years old, had studied at Trinity College, Dublin. Her only surviving sibling, her older brother, Henry, went to Harrow and Cambridge and was eventually knighted. Her father had been a religious sceptic, but her mother was an easy-going Anglican who was pleased with Broad Church articulations of the faith. When Annie was nine years old, her mother sent her away to Dorsetshire to be educated by Ellen Marryat. A thoroughgoing evangelical, Marryat ensured that Annie received a biblical education. Marryat's idea of a game was a Bible quiz—thus the girls gained scriptural knowledge even while playing. If that sounds oppressive it was not experienced that way by Besant who, even as an atheist, had nothing but enthusiastic praise for her old evangelical schoolmistress. Marryat valued biblical memorization and Annie, who was a quick study and hungry for honour, pursued it precociously. She even learned by heart the entire Epistle of James. Besant recalled that 'the dignified cadences' of the Bible 'pleased my ear'.[23] In her mid-teens, Annie Wood became a zealous Tractarian. In 1867, at the age of twenty, she married Frank Besant, a clergyman. The couple had a son and a daughter.

Annie Besant recalled as an atheist that her 'first doubt' came during Lent 1866. It concerned 'the historical accuracy of the Bible'.[24] As a devotional exercise, she wanted to meditate during Holy Week on the events that happened to Christ on each of those days of the week, as recorded in the gospels. She began creating a table for this purpose, but she discovered that she could not get the chronological statements spread across the four gospels to harmonize. This story should not be accepted uncritically. First, by the time Besant wrote it, she had long been under the influence of Bradlaugh, and her story is suspiciously similar to his own one of stumbling upon discrepancies in the four gospels while pursuing a religious task in good faith (and then he listed them in a table in his first manuscript). Second, Besant printed her table for the benefit of her readers. She also acknowledged, however, that she had quickly thrown down her pen, repented of her project, and done penance by fasting. For the next three years, she was again a devout Christian not plagued by sceptical thoughts. She was even writing pious literature for the *Family Herald*. If Besant really thought that her table had been a temptation to sin that needed to be purged by fasting and had been wholehearted in her repentance, then she would have

[23] Besant, *Autobiographical Sketches*, 19.   [24] Besant, *Autobiographical Sketches*, 31.

certainly destroyed it. A not much more plausible alternative to her having kept her table is that she was able to reproduce it from memory eighteen years later. Even if this story is unreliable, however, it would be no less telling. At the very least, it would still reveal that Besant thought that a narrative of a journey to atheism should begin with an anti-Bible prompt. Moreover, it seems reasonable to assume that the basic story is true, even if the table is merely a later reconstruction aimed at putting ammunition in the hands of atheists.

Besant's Christian identity was rattled again in 1871. Her infant daughter, Mabel, endured a life-threatening illness, leading Besant to begin questioning God and her religious beliefs. She began reading Broad Church and sceptical works. Steadily, she abandoned various orthodox Christian beliefs. In 1872, she wrote her first sceptical work. Its theme was the inspiration of the Bible. It was not the first one she published and it was revised before it eventually was published. The printed version emphasizes scriptural contradictions.[25] Besant whimsically recounted her first 'lecture' as taking place in 1873. Alone in the church building where her husband was the priest, she entered the pulpit and the words poured out. Her theme was 'the Inspiration of the Bible'.[26] Her early freethinking essays were published beginning in 1873 by a committed patron of liberal and sceptical religious thought, Thomas Scott. Besant later collected them and published them unaltered in the order in which they had originally appeared under the telling title, *My Path to Atheism* (1885). In the preface, she observed:

> Most inquirers who begin to study by themselves, before they have read any heretical works, or heard controversies, will have been awakened to thought by the discrepancies and inconsistencies of the Bible itself. A thorough knowledge of the Bible is the groundwork of heresy.[27]

She recalled that her own early doubts had included scepticism about atonement and eternal punishment, but these where symptomatic 'while the doctrine of Inspiration of Scripture underlay everything, and was the very foundation of Christianity'.[28] Her first published essay she had initially

---

[25] Annie Besant, *My Path to Atheism* (London: Freethinking Publishing Company, 1885), 77–91.

[26] Besant, *Autobiography*, 116.

[27] Besant, *My Path*, pp. v–vi.

[28] Besant, *My Path*, pp. vi–vii. Since I wrote this chapter, a germane source has appeared, Christiana de Groot, 'Annie Besant: An Adversarial Interpreter of Scripture', in Christiana de Groot and Marion Ann Taylor (eds), *Recovering Nineteenth-Century Women Interpreters of the Bible*

given a biblical title, 'What think ye of Christ?' (Matthew 22: 42), but this was thought by others to be heavy-handed so this text was left as the opening quotation of the essay and the title was changed to 'On the Deity of Jesus of Nazareth'.[29] Even more explicitly biblical criticism, her second published essay was 'A Comparison between the Fourth Gospel and the Three Synoptics'. Indeed, the biblicism of these essays is remarkable. Although Besant no longer believed in the authority of the Bible, when there was a biblical text that made her point, like a pious evangelical, she found it irresistible to quote her proof-text triumphantly. Thus, statements by Christ about his own identity cannot be used to bolster an argument for his divinity because he had said: 'If I bear witness of myself, my witness is not true' (John 5: 31). Freethinkers do not need to have all the answers provided in advance by revelation, because they 'walk by faith, not by sight' (2 Corinthians 5: 7).[30] And so it goes on. When attacking Christianity and the Bible, Besant continually reaches for biblical language that would sound esoteric to many today. She can observe, for example, that she has 'written Tekel on the Christian faith' (Daniel 5: 27). She even condemns the God of the Bible as 'a blood-craving Moloch' (cf. Leviticus 20: 1–5).[31] Her love of biblical cadences was such that she delighted to employ them in order to attempt to make her own rhetoric more dignified, important, and persuasive. For example, her essay 'On the Religious Education of Children' ends on a high by the linguistic trick of employing the structure of 1 Corinthians 13: 8:

> Morality never faileth; but, whether there be dogmas, they shall fail; whether they be creeds, they shall cease; whether there be churches, they shall crumble away; but morality shall abide for evermore and endure as long as the endless circle of Nature revolves around the Eternal Throne.[32]

Annie Besant spoke the truth when she observed that her childhood education 'made me very familiar with the Bible and very apt with its phrases'.[33]

(Atlanta: Society of Biblical Literature, 2007), 201–15. It complements this chapter well in that it explores only two works of Besant and neither of them are addressed here, namely *Woman's Position according to the Bible* (1885) and *God's Views on Marriage* (1890).

[29] Taylor, *Besant*, 55.   [30] Besant, *My Path*, 2, 114.
[31] Besant, *My Path*, 93, 58.   [32] Besant, *My Path*, 100.
[33] Besant, *Autobiography*, 44.

This habit extended to her correspondence. In a particularly remarkable example, it is on display in a series of private letters she wrote in 1887–8 to the well-known journalist, W. T. Stead. Bradlaugh rejected socialism and therefore Besant's growing commitment to that cause meant that the Freethought Publishing Company partners were not as close as they had been. Besant was clearly besotted with Stead.[34] Her pet name for the crusading journalist—as literally romantic as one could imagine—was 'Sir Galahad'. As Stead was not separated from his wife, he was naturally more cautious about this relationship, but even he admitted to her that they had a 'political & spiritual marriage'.[35] Nevertheless, despite the seemingly unpropitious context of a *sub rosa* flirtation, Besant's prose in these letters is infused with biblical language. For example, she reflected in this way on her deflated suspicion that her political work might be in vain:

> But, my dear Sir Galahad, the power of darkness has only his hour [Luke 22: 53], & the underlying belief remains. Do you know, I have always fancied that the real blackness of Gethsemane & of the 'Eli, Eli' on Calvary [Matthew 27: 46], was the <u>doubt</u> if, after all, the life's ideal were a delusion.[36]

At times, Besant seems almost unable or unwilling to express a single thought without recourse to Scripture. Here she is on their efforts to build a diverse coalition to help labouring men who had been imprisoned for participating in lawful political protests:

> I think it would have met the rebuke 'Ye know not what manner of spirit ye are of' [Luke 9: 55]. I feel no resentment against a hesitation which springs from real love to an ideal which I am thought to have insulted; but it is sad that after 19 centuries the lesson of brotherhood with all who are willing to work for 'the least of these my brethren,' [Matthew 25: 40] is not yet learned. Well, well, it may be. Any how, ours is the more excellent way [1 Corinthians 12: 31]. I was inclined to say, 'thy money perish with thee' [Acts 8: 20].[37]

[34] For Anne Taylor's account of this relationship, see Taylor, *Besant*, 195–202.

[35] W. T. Stead Papers, Churchill Archives Centre, Churchill College, Cambridge, Stead 1/6, Annie Besant to W. T. Stead, 4 March 1888.

[36] W. T. Stead Papers, Churchill Archives Centre, Churchill College, Cambridge, Stead 1/6, Annie Besant to W. T. Stead, 19 January 1888.

[37] W. T. Stead Papers, Churchill Archives Centre, Churchill College, Cambridge, Stead 1/6, Annie Besant to W. T. Stead, 13 February 1888.

When Stead continues to elicit resources, she refers to 'your widow's cruse' (1 Kings 17).[38] And so it goes on.

Before developing this theme any further, it is essential to grasp that Besant's substantive view as an atheist of the contents of the Bible was that it was a dangerous and despicable book. Already in her early essays she was asserting that the Bible was not a safe book to give to children, or even a sixteen-year-old.[39] In Besant's own parenting, she did not find even the New Testament a fit book for her daughter to read. She gave this way of thinking free and forceful expression in a tract published in 1877 or 1878, *Is the Bible Indictable?*.[40] Annie Besant wrote it in response to the Lord Chief Justice's condemnation of Knowlton's *The Fruits of Philosophy*. Her argument is that the same charges he made against that book apply to the Bible. Besant did not shrink from venting her objection to the Scriptures in unmeasured language: 'Surely if any book be indictable for obscenity, the Bible should be the first to be prosecuted. I know of no other book in which is to be found such utterly unredeemed coarseness.'[41] She even strikes the pose that parts of the Bible are so filthy that it would be inappropriate, if not downright immoral, even to cite them:

> The difficulty of dealing with this question is that many of the quotations necessary to prove that the Bible comes under the ruling of the Lord Chief Justice are of such an extremely coarse and disgusting character, that it is really impossible to reproduce them without intensifying the evil which they are calculated to do. While I see no indecency in a plain statement of physiological facts, written for people's instruction, I do see indecency in coarse and indelicate stories, the reading of which can do no good to any human being, and can have no effect save that of corrupting the mind and suggesting unclean ideas. I therefore refuse to soil my pages with quotations...[42]

[38] W. T. Stead Papers, Churchill Archives Centre, Churchill College, Cambridge, Stead 1/6, Annie Besant to W. T. Stead, 24 January 1888.

[39] Besant, *My Path*, 85.

[40] Annie Besant, *Is the Bible Indictable? Being an enquiry whether the Bible comes within the ruling of the Lord Chief Justice as to Obscene Literature* (London: Freethought Publishing Company, n.d. (c. 1877–8)).

[41] Besant, *Is the Bible Indictable?*, 12–13.

[42] Besant, *Is the Bible Indictable?*, 8.

Reminiscent of Paine's *Age of Reason*, she systematically marches her way through the canon, pointing out where obscenity hunters should go to find particularly vulgar parts of 'this indictable book'.[43]

In the light of this strong objection to the Scriptures, it is all the more remarkable to see the compulsive way that Annie Besant quotes from the Bible in her autobiographies. The first one, *Autobiographical Sketches* (1885), is written at the height of her atheist identity and issued by her and Bradlaugh's Freethought Publishing Company. The second one, *An Autobiography*, was initially published in 1893, and a revised edition appeared in 1908, both versions being when she was a pre-eminent Theosophist. *An Autobiography* is fuller and better written and even more biblical, so it will sometimes be the one cited from, but it must be borne in mind that it essentially incorporates *Autobiographical Sketches* and then carries on the story and therefore many of the biblical quotations were already present in the Freethought Publishing Company version, as will be indicated in the footnotes.

It would be tedious to catalogue the numerous biblical allusions in Besant's autobiographies and therefore only a sampling will be given here, but it is startling to witness the entire collection. To take a random example, when she introduces her early freethinking patron, Thomas Scott, because he had once spent a few months living with Native Americans, Besant quotes the statement in Genesis 10: 9 about Nimrod being a mighty hunter.[44] It is hard to imagine a more gratuitous circling back to Scripture. In an address she published in the *National Reformer* that she wrote to rally support to fight the condemnation of Knowlton's book, Besant warned Secularists that they must be careful not to make any legal blunders 'for they may be sure that such sins will find them out' (Numbers 32: 23).[45] More substantively, Besant seems to reach for Scripture instinctively whenever she wants to give weight and dignity to an important event in her life. Only the most striking examples of this tendency will be presented here. She was a public, freethinking non-Christian when her mother died, and she wrote about this terrible event in her life as an atheist. Nevertheless, Besant reached for the Bible to give words to her loss: 'Truly, my "house was

---

[43] Besant, *Is the Bible Indictable?*, 14. Her own position seems to have been that no book written with good motives should be indictable, and that would include both Knowlton and the Bible, even though the contents of the former are useful to people while the latter are harmful.

[44] Besant, *Autobiographical Sketches*, 68.

[45] Besant, *Autobiographical Sketches*, 149–50.

left unto me desolate"' (Matthew 23: 38).[46] When in 1875 Bradlaugh was severely ill and it was feared that he would die, Besant tells us that 'he walked down the valley of the shadow of death' (Psalm 23: 4).[47] Most extraordinary is the way that Besant expressed her decision to commit herself to being an atheist lecturer:

> I knew that an Atheist was outside the law . . . I seemed to hear the voice of Truth ringing over the battlefield: 'Who will go? Who will speak for me?' And I sprang forward with passionate enthusiasm, with the resolute cry: 'Here am I, send me!' [Isaiah 6: 8] . . . No weightier responsibility can any take, no more sacred charge. . . . I have not given to my mistress Truth that 'which hath cost me nothing' [2 Samuel 24: 24].

Not only does this present her decision as a call to ministry lifted word for word from Isaiah's call to be a prophet, but the importance of this is underlined with another biblical word, 'sacred', and rounded off with an additional, explicit biblical quotation.[48]

Annie Besant quoted Scripture to express her own thoughts eloquently as an atheist right to the end. Her parting speech as a Secularist declared that her commitment to 'Truth' was such that she could say: 'though she slay me, yet will I trust in her' (Job 13: 15).[49] While this book has not chosen to allot a separate case study to Theosophists, as the president of the Theosophical Society, Besant would be a fitting subject of such a study, and the quotations given from her *An Autobiography* amply prove that her thought patterns continued to be steeped in the Bible in that period of her life as well. A particularly remarkable example of this is a moment that she undoubtedly viewed as one of the most important speeches of her life, her presidential address in 1917 at the annual meeting of the Indian National Congress. Bizarrely, given both her own religious identity and the predominant ones in her audience—but well in keeping with her lifelong instinct that biblical language added weight to a pronouncement—her peroration was: 'India the Crucified among Nations now stands on this her Resurrection morning . . . as the Light and Blessing of the World.'[50] The speech was not a success.

---

[46] Besant, *Autobiography*, 126–7; Besant, *Autobiographical Sketches*, 84.

[47] Besant, *Autobiography*, 201.

[48] Besant, *Autobiography*, 188–9; Besant, *Autobiographical Sketches*, 96–7. (The earlier version lacks the Isaiah motif, but includes the word 'sacred' and the quotation from 2 Samuel 24: 24.)

[49] Besant, *Autobiography*, 358.   [50] Taylor, *Besant*, 312.

While Besant's energies were diverted into Theosophy from 1889 onwards, Bradlaugh remained committed to the cause of atheism to the end. It is worth highlighting some of his other various works on the Bible and briefly noticing the wider context of Victorian organized atheism and the Bible, before moving on to examining Bradlaugh's most ambitious literary project. When Bradlaugh became the editor of the *Investigator* in 1858, he declared that its mission included the necessity 'to destroy Bible influence'.[51] One of the ways that he did this was through a series discrediting biblical heroes. These were also printed separately, and later kept in circulation by the Freethought Publishing Company. Titles included *New Life of Abraham*, *New Life of Jacob*, *New Life of Moses*, *New Life of David*, and *New Life of Jonah*.[52] The Bible was also a favourite subject of debate for Bradlaugh, and thus one can track a succession of encounters with Christian ministers across the decades with the subject being a biblical one.[53]

While Bradlaugh is indisputably the most prominent leader of Victorian organized atheism, and Annie Besant was his most important colleague, it is worth underlying that their heavy orientation toward Scripture was typical of the movement as a whole. To give an example, a key leader in the movement in the generation before Bradlaugh was Robert Cooper (1818–68), who founded the atheistic paper that Bradlaugh would later edit, the *Investigator*. Cooper's main publications were *The 'Holy Scriptures' analyzed, or Extracts from the Bible shewing its contradictions, absurdities and immoralities* (1832), *The Infidel's Text-Book, being the substance of thirteen lectures on the Bible* (1846), and *The Bible and its evidences* (1858).[54] When the *Investigator* failed, and the *National Reformer* was founded as an atheistic paper, Bradlaugh's original co-editor was Joseph Barker (1806–75). Barker was not only the most popular Secularist in the north of England—if not the whole country—at that time, but he was also, if anything, even more

---

[51] Bonner, *Bradlaugh*, I, 80.

[52] For some of the more entertaining passages from this series, see Larsen, *Contested Christianity*, 107–8.

[53] For example, *Is the Bible divine? A six nights' discussion between Mr Charles Bradlaugh . . . and Mr Robert Roberts* (London: F. Pitman, 1876); *God, Man, and the Bible. Three Nights' Discussion between Rev. Joseph Baylee, D.D., and Mr C. Bradlaugh [then debating as 'Iconoclast'], on the 27th, 28th, and 29th June, 1860, at the Teutonic Hall, Liverpool* (London: Freethought Publishing Company, n.d.).

[54] For Robert Cooper, see Edward Royle, *Victorian Infidels: The Origins of the British Secularist Movement, 1791–1866* (Manchester: Manchester University Press, 1974).

preoccupied with Scripture than Bradlaugh.[55] The most prominent Secularist in the generation after Bradlaugh was George William Foote (1850–1915), who succeeded Bradlaugh in 1890 as the president of the National Secular Society. Foote rose to the top of the movement due to his trial and prison sentence for blasphemy. Foote's offence had been to publish a series of 'Comic Bible' sketches. These were parodies of the kind of illustrations that had accompanied Bradlaugh's schoolboy writing samples, that is, they were irreverent cartoons accompanied by a text of Scripture written out as a caption.[56] Foote's numerous works on the Bible stretch across the late Victorian period and beyond. As late as 1912, just a few years before his death, Foote published with his own Pioneer Press his *Bible and Beer* and his *The Bible Handbook for freethinkers and inquiring Christians*.[57] Susan Budd, in her analysis of the life stories of freethinkers, discovered that when Secularists mentioned books as influential in their loss of faith, as they often did, they most often named the Bible itself or Paine's anti-Bible work, *The Age of Reason*.[58] The Bible loomed large for Victorian atheists.

Bradlaugh's modern biographer, David Tribe, was sympathetic to his subject and wrote as a Secularist insider. Indeed, when his biography was published, Tribe was serving as president of the National Secular Society, and thus was standing in a succession that had Bradlaugh as its esteemed founding father—a point he underlined by giving his subject the designation 'President' in the book's title. Tribe observed that Bradlaugh's *The Bible: What It Is* was the president's '*magnum opus*'.[59] Charles Bradlaugh embarked upon this project in 1857, intending it to become a commentary on the entire Bible ('from Genesis to Revelation').[60] The initial version made it through to Isaiah. It was hampered by his parting ways with his eminent Secularist publisher, G. J. Holyoake, who decided that it was 'an

---

[55] For this, see Timothy Larsen, 'Joseph Barker and Popular Biblical Criticism in the Nineteenth Century, *Bulletin of the John Rylands University Library of Manchester*, 82, 1 (Spring 2000), 115–34 (reprinted as 'Biblical Criticism and Anti-Christian Rhetoric: Joseph Barker and the Case against the Bible' in Larsen, *Contested Christianity*, 79–95).

[56] David Nash, *Blasphemy in Modern Britain: 1789 to the Present* (Aldershot: Ashgate, 1999), 107–66.

[57] G. W. Foote, *Bible and Beer* (London: Pioneer Press, 1912); G. W. Foote, *The Bible Handbook for freethinkers and inquiring Christians* (London: Pioneer Press, 1912).

[58] Susan Budd, *Varieties of Unbelief: Atheists and Agnostics in English Society, 1850–1960* (London: Heinemann, 1977), 107.

[59] David Tribe, *President Charles Bradlaugh, M.P.* (London: Elek Books, 1971), 50.

[60] Bonner, *Bradlaugh*, I, 63.

obscene book'.[61] Bradlaugh determined to start over and go about the task more thoroughly. This resulted in a new version of *The Bible: What It Is* in 1870. This time it was 434 pages long and confined to the Pentateuch. Once again he started over and in 1882 just the section on Genesis—now expanded to 346 pages—appeared separately.[62] In other words, not only was Bradlaugh's first manuscript a gospels commentary, but the great literary work of Bradlaugh's mature life—a project which he laboured over for a quarter of a century, if not longer—was a biblical commentary.

Bradlaugh was so focused on Scripture, and so conscientious in his Old Testament criticism, that he even took the trouble to learn Hebrew. In one public debate he was challenged without warning to prove this, and he passed this impromptu linguistic examination to the satisfaction of the hostile Christian ministers present.[63] In *The Bible: What It Is* (the 1870 edition is being analysed here) discussions of the Hebrew language mainly arise in order to make the point that the inability of scholars to determine the meaning of various Hebrew words ought to lead to the conclusion that this is an ill-fitting way for a divine revelation to be communicated. Here is a typical example of this sentiment: 'It is useless to do more in this place than regret that there should be so much room for difference as to the meaning of Hebrew words, when our salvation is said to depend on the rightly understanding their signification.'[64] As with his early gospels manuscript, Bradlaugh quotes heavily from other works in *The Bible: What It Is*. Once again, he draws on freethinkers such as Thomas Paine and Robert Taylor. Nevertheless, he had by this time moved into more scholarly literature as well. A particular favourite is the criticism of the Pentateuch offered by John William Colenso, bishop of Natal, from whom he repeatedly provides extracts that are several pages long.[65] Overwhelmingly, any German biblical criticism comes into the commentary through the medium of Colenso, not least because Bradlaugh himself did not know German, but occasionally

---

[61] Tribe, *President*, 54.

[62] Charles Bradlaugh, *Genesis: Its Authorship and Authenticity*, third edition (London: Freethought Publishing Company, 1882).

[63] Bonner, *Bradlaugh*, I, 73.

[64] Charles Bradlaugh, *The Bible: What It Is* (London: Austin & Co., 1870), 61. The idea that salvation is at issue is merely a rhetorical heightening of the stakes by Bradlaugh.

[65] See, for this, Larsen, *Contested Christianity*, ch. 5, 'Biblical Criticism and the Desire for Reform: Bishop Colenso on the Pentateuch', 59–77.

Bradlaugh does cite the English or French translation of a leading German scholar, notably W. M. L. De Wette.[66]

The Bible: What It Is examines the Pentateuch in canonical order with the section on each biblical book subtitled as an exploration of 'Its Authorship & Authenticity'. The first section states in the preface that it is 'a commentary on Genesis, written for the purpose of demonstrating that the book is not a perfect and infallible revelation specially given from an all-wise and infinite Deity, Creator, and Ruler of all worlds.'[67] After various introductory remarks, Bradlaugh announces accurately: 'I shall now take each chapter and verse in its Biblical order.'[68] In other words, it is not a mere rhetorical flourish to speak of this book as a commentary. Bradlaugh himself calls it a commentary without irony and he makes good on that claim by following the conventions of the genre faithfully.

Iconoclast's animating purpose is to discredit the Bible in every possible way. This animus often tempts him into making pedantic points. For example, on Numbers 3: 39, he objects to the round figure 22,000 being used for the number of the Levites when the actual calculation is 22,300, even though he derived that more precise number by adding together all the figures provided for the Levite clans (as the reader is obviously being invited to do by the biblical author), which are themselves clearly round numbers.[69] The statement in Exodus 32: 20 that Moses ground the golden calf into powder, put it in water, and made the Israelites drink it, prompts this cavil:

> Unless a chloride of gold had been formed by the use of chlorine and nitro-muriatic acid, and of which we have no account, or unless some analogous chemical process had been pursued, the gold would not be soluble in water, but would sink to the bottom, leaving the water entirely unaffected.[70]

No indeterminacy in the precise meaning of some biblical word is too small to ignore. The reader is apparently meant to be concerned, for example, that: 'One version says the glory appeared "in" the tabernacle; the Douay says that it appeared "over" the tabernacle.'[71] Bradlaugh even discredits Numbers 19: 13, 'The dead body of any man that is dead', on the grounds of literary style.[72] This pedantic tendency was furthered by a wooden literalism. Jacob's vision, for example, must be communicating something about

---

[66] For example, see Bradlaugh, *The Bible*, 55, 334, 426.
[67] Bradlaugh, *The Bible*, p. v.   [68] Bradlaugh, *The Bible*, 6.
[69] Bradlaugh, *The Bible*, 339.   [70] Bradlaugh, *The Bible*, 287.
[71] Bradlaugh, *The Bible*, 350.   [72] Bradlaugh, *The Bible*, 354.

furniture and locomotion: 'The writer of Genesis evidently conceived a ladder necessary to enable the angels of God to get up to heaven, in the same style in which you or I might ascend to the roof of a house.'[73]

Bradlaugh's determinedly critical stance also led to an inconsistent approach to the question of historicity. In general, his tendency is to deny historicity in thoroughgoing, sweeping ways. He posits, for example, that Abraham is not a historical figure at all, and will not concede that even the bare fact of the 'departure of the Jews from Egypt' is a genuine historical residue in the story.[74] On the other hand, when Bradlaugh decides that certain actions are morally suspect, then suddenly he writes as if he is speaking of historical events that are accurately recorded. Thus, to take the two examples just given, Abraham (who now does exist) did indeed accept cattle as compensation for the affront to his wife, and the Israelites did 'borrow' jewellery from the Egyptians when they departed (which they now did indeed do)—as these events are judged by Bradlaugh to have been morally improper actions.[75] To continue with the moral critique, Iconoclast also steadfastly expresses outrage that the Bible contains sexually frank material. Indeed, Bradlaugh is so prudish—this from a man who fought in court for the right to publish a birth-control manual so that ordinary people would have access to sexual facts—that the mere mention of testicles in the Bible prompts him to switch the discussion into French and Latin.[76] Bradlaugh repeatedly claims that decent parents should not want their daughters to read the Bible.

As Genesis teaches the monogenesis of the human race, Bradlaugh presented polygenesis as the truly scientific view, despite the fact that Darwinists were also committed to monogenesis.[77] This move tempted Iconoclast into a racist account of what he believed were the three, separately originating stocks of human beings. Here is the last phrase of his descriptions of each of these: the Mongolian is in 'stature rather low, trunk long, extremities rather short, wrists and ankles weak'; the Ethiopian 'emits a strong offensive odour, especially under exposure to the sun'; while the Caucasian possesses 'muscular strength, energy, and endurance generally

---

[73] Bradlaugh, *The Bible*, 122.   [74] Bradlaugh, *The Bible*, 86, 159.
[75] Bradlaugh, *The Bible*, 89, 288.   [76] Bradlaugh, *The Bible*, 416.
[77] For the wider context of this discussion see Colin Kidd, *The Forging of the Races: Race and Scripture in the Protestant Atlantic World, 1600–2000* (Cambridge: Cambridge University Press, 2006).

considerable—in many superior'.[78] Thus one ends up with the key adjectives for the three races being 'weak' (the people of Asia), 'offensive' (the people of Africa), and 'superior' (the people of Europe).

One of the most surprising features of *The Bible: What It Is* comes when Bradlaugh arrives at Exodus 20: 7: 'Thou shalt not take the name of the Lord thy God in vain.' This occasions a long section decrying the requirements of British law to swear oaths in the name of God. Quite literally, it is a sermon with a text. Bradlaugh is not trying to undermine the meaning of Exodus 20: 7, nor deploy it ironically, he is rather preaching from it. This goes on for seventeen pages, making it the longest sustained argument in the entire book.[79] There are other ways in which Bradlaugh's commentary is unwittingly extraordinarily conservative, especially by the standards of our day rather than his. For example, Bradlaugh assumes uncritically that the apostle Paul wrote the Epistle to the Hebrews, a traditional view that even conservative evangelical scholars do not hold today.[80] A major way that Bradlaugh attempts to discredit the notion that the Bible is a divine revelation is to argue that Hebrew religion was borrowed from the so-called heathen cultures around them. His choice for this influence is Egypt, and he asserts that a whole catalogue of aspects of the religious life of the Israelites are copied from this source. The scholarly consensus is now the complete inverse, namely, that connections with Egypt are suspiciously hard to find. Bradlaugh, however, is so enthusiastic about this pay-off that he is even willing to affirm that Moses was indeed 'reared at the Court of Pharaoh' in order to underline it.[81]

Even if he occasionally overplayed his hand, Bradlaugh's commentary was surely effective at prodding readers into seeing familiar texts in a new light. It must have been jarring to some readers to be invited again and again to see the supernatural elements in the Pentateuch as no different in kind from the magical elements in the Arabian Nights. Or to have Moses' burning bush recast as a mere 'pyrotechnic juggle', unworthy of a serious purpose.[82] Here is Iconoclast on another passage: 'Can any sane person imagine that the infinite Creator presented on Sinai to the gaze of Moses heaven-made samples of golden candlesticks?'[83] For Bradlaugh, the Deluge account tells a story of a God who is so bloodthirsty that after having killed

[78] Bradlaugh, *The Bible*, 28–34.   [79] Bradlaugh, *The Bible*, 222–39.
[80] Bradlaugh, *The Bible*, 357.   [81] Bradlaugh, *The Bible*, 336.
[82] Bradlaugh, *The Bible*, 168.   [83] Bradlaugh, *The Bible*, 344.

all the animals in the world except for the ones in the ark, he then demands that some of them be sacrificed. Leviticus, in particular, also gave Charles Bradlaugh plenty of scope to expound on the point of view that religious regulations are often self-serving priestly plots. Iconoclast is on particularly good form when he observes that ministers today set aside the Pentateuchal rule that priests are not to have land of their own, but instead allow the Lord to be their inheritance, while insisting that the regulations regarding people tithing to them are still in force.[84] And so Victorian Britain's pre-eminent atheist leader went on, struggling with Scripture to the end.

[84] Bradlaugh, The Bible, 354.

Methodist and Holiness

Catherine Booth, William Cooke, and the Scriptures

Catherine Mumford (1829–90), who became well known under her married name of Booth, was raised as a Wesleyan Methodist. For a time her father was even a Wesleyan local preacher. The family was living in London when Catherine had a dramatic evangelical conversion experience at the age of sixteen. Soon thereafter she became a member in her own right of the Wesleyan chapel in Brixton. Roger Green, her modern biographer, has insisted that in order to understand Booth aright she needs to be put back into 'her Wesleyan framework'.[1] As will be shown, she subsequently made her spiritual home in a couple of other Methodist denominations, and then went on to found a new Holiness denomination with its own distinctives, the Salvation Army. That is to say, Booth can serve as a representative figure for Methodist and Holiness Christians because her own spiritual formation was in the context of its largest denomination, Wesleyan Methodism, and she passed through some others on her way to founding the most significant new Holiness group in Britain in the second half of the nineteenth century. When Booth died in 1890 the Wesleyan newspaper, the *Methodist Times*, edited by the influential Wesleyan minister, Hugh Price Hughes, declared that she was 'the greatest Methodist woman of this generation'.[2]

---

[1] Roger J. Green, *Catherine Booth: A Biography of the Cofounder of The Salvation Army* (Grand Rapids: Baker, 1996), 15.
[2] *Methodist Times* (9 October 1890), 1.

Catherine did not receive any formal schooling until she had reached the age of twelve and, even then, it was all over within two years. Nevertheless, it would be a mistake to imagine that she was not learning much of anything at home. Her self-education was centred on the Bible. She was already reading it by the age of five. Before she reached the age of twelve and was sent off to school, she had already 'read the sacred Book from cover to cover eight times through'.[3] Keep in mind that this was done with no other intention than general piety and learning. Her parents had no schemes for her to become a minister, nor did she harbour any such aspirations. In fact, by her own subsequent reckoning, she was not even converted yet. This continuous, energetic, systematic study of Scripture represents simply a normal course that the education of a precocious evangelical child might take in Victorian Britain. Nor did her voracious consumption of the Bible slacken as Catherine progressed through her teenage years. Here is her primary New Year's resolution for 1848 when she was eighteen years old:

> above all, I am determined to search the Scriptures more attentively, for in them I have eternal life. I have read my Bible through twice during the last sixteen months, but I must read it with more prayer for light and understanding. Oh, may it be my meat and drink! May I meditate on it day and night! And then I shall 'bring forth fruit in season, my leaf also shall not wither, and whatsoever I do shall prosper.' [Psalm 1: 2–3][4]

The result, not unexpectedly, was that Catherine routinely thought, spoke, and wrote in biblical language and patterns of thought. To take a telling example, even when describing seaside Brighton as a teenager on holiday, she reached eccentrically to the Old Testament to evoke the scene: 'I have just returned from the beach. It is a lovely morning, but very rough and cold. The sea looks sublime. I never saw it so troubled. Its waters "cast up mire and dirt" [Isaiah 57: 20], and lash the shore with great violence'.[5]

Wesleyan Methodism was having considerable internal turmoil at mid-century and Catherine sided with the Wesleyan Reformers who were expelled from the main body.[6] William Booth likewise had been converted

---

[3] F. de L. Booth-Tucker, *The Life of Catherine Booth: The Mother of The Salvation Army*, 2 vols, third edition (London: Salvationist Publishing, 1924), I, 15.

[4] Booth-Tucker, *Life*, I, 52–3.

[5] Booth-Tucker, *Life*, I, 48.

[6] For the Wesleyan Reformers, see Rupert Davies, A. Raymond George, and Gordon Rupp (eds), *A History of the Methodist Church in Great Britain*, Vol. II (London: Epworth Press, 1978); Robert Currie, *Methodism Divided: A Study in the Sociology of Ecumenicalism* (London: Faber and Faber, 1968).

in a Wesleyan context, and he had begun his preaching ministry as a Wesleyan. He joined the Wesleyan Reformers in 1851. That same year, he came to preach at the congregation where Catherine was worshipping. William and Catherine Booth are one of the great couples in the whole of modern church history. They loved each other passionately from soon after their first meeting until her death in 1890. It is indicative of the place of the Bible in Catherine's life that the one thing that she always remembered about her first encounter with the man who swept her off her feet was his biblical text (John 4: 42).[7] They became formally engaged on 15 May 1852. He continued to serve in Wesleyan Reformer circles in 1853, but as it became clear that reconciliation with the main body was not possible and the future of the Reformers as a separate body looked uncertain, William and Catherine began to look around for a new denominational setting. They decided on the Methodist New Connexion, the oldest breakaway group from the Wesleyans.[8] It was therefore agreed that William would undertake six months of ministerial instruction in 1854 from the Methodist New Connexion minister, William Cooke, as preparation for his ordination as a Methodist New Connexion minister. Before offering an exposition of Catherine Booth's mature engagement with Scripture, it will be useful to explore Cooke's thought as a way of adding another significant Methodist voice.

William Cooke (1806–84) may certainly be allowed to represent his denomination. Indeed, extraordinarily, he was elected president of the Methodist New Connexion conference three times (1843, 1859, and 1869). Moreover, he can also fittingly stand as an example of the Methodist community as a whole. Cooke himself thought that there was much more that the various Methodist groups had in common than that separated them. He actively worked for Methodist reunion. During his last presidency Cooke worked hard on concrete negotiations for the Methodist New Connexion to merge with another Methodist group, the Bible Christians.[9] He was also well respected by the largest breakaway group, the Primitive Methodists, including being invited to write on Methodist reunion for the

---

[7] Booth-Tucker, *Life*, I, 58.

[8] For an account of the Methodist New Connexion and its relationship to other Methodist bodies, see Timothy Larsen, *Contested Christianity: The Political and Social Contexts of Victorian Theology* (Waco, Texas: Baylor University Press, 2004), ch. 9, 'Free Church Ecclesiology: Lay Representation and the Methodist New Connexion', 133–43.

[9] Methodist New Connexion Magazine (December 1869), 729–41, 'Address by the president of the Conference, William Cooke, on union with the Bible Christians'.

Primitive Methodist Quarterly Review.[10] Many people thought that the main hindrance to English Methodism in the early and mid-Victorian periods was the stiffly conservative and autocratic Wesleyan leader and frequent conference president, Jabez Bunting. Cooke, however, would send him copies of his publications and write him flattering letters. He appealed to their common Methodist identity, rejected explicitly the calumny that Bunting was 'a tyrant', and praised him for his 'enlightened judgment & candor, as well as your Christian courtesy and kindness of heart'. On the one issue that formally divided their two Methodist denominations—whether or not lay people should be represented in the conference—Cooke loyally asserted that his denomination's allowance of this was the practice that had 'New Testament sanction'.[11] When the first Ecumenical Methodist Conference was convened in 1881 it was natural that William Cooke was invited to give the opening address. When he visited Canada in 1872, Cooke received significant invitations from all the major Methodist bodies. As a distinguished, invited guest at the Wesleyan Methodist Conference in Canada, he was honoured by the president, the eminent English Wesleyan preacher, William Morley Punshon, who would serve as the president of the Wesleyan Conference in England in a couple of years' time. Here is Cooke's report of that event:

> The Rev. Dr Punshon was in the chair. He heartily greeted us, and in presenting to us a congratulatory resolution singled me out, and said he should, in the name of the Conference, address himself specially to me, inasmuch as Dr Cooke, he said, belonged not merely to the Methodist New Connexion, but to the world of Methodism, and all Christendom was indebted to me for my writings and my defence of Christianity.[12]

Moreover, the differences between Methodist bodies were focused on issues of church government, the use of power by church leaders, and ministerial and evangelistic strategies and techniques and did not extent to the doctrine or use of Scripture.

---

[10] Samuel Hulme, *Memoir of the Rev. William Cooke, D.D., Author of 'The Deity,' 'Christian Theology,' 'Shekinah,' &c.* (London: C. D. Ward, 1886), 364.
[11] John Rylands University Library of Manchester, Methodist Archives, William Cooke Papers, William Cooke to Jabez Bunting, 2 February 1847. (There are several other letters from Cooke to Bunting in this collection which also reinforce the general point that he is treating him more as an esteemed co-religionist than as a religious 'other'.)
[12] Hulme, *Cooke*, 227.

William Cooke has also been chosen because he is a prime example of a Victorian Methodist theologian. As other evangelicals in this book were primarily preachers or social reformers, this is an opportunity to investigate the handling of Scripture in more rigorously and explicitly doctrinal discussions. Cooke's reputation, especially beyond Methodist New Connexion circles, was first and foremost as a theologian. In *Methodist Worthies*, a Victorian work that spanned the various Methodist denominations, Cooke's contribution is described thus: 'his several works on theology are now standard text-books in Colleges and Universities, both in England and America; and Dr William Cooke is now recognised as a standard classic in theology.'[13] When he is identified as an author it is always his theological works that are named as his most significant publications, as indeed they were.

Cooke's most widely disseminated substantial work was his *Christian Theology*. First published in 1863, within two decades six editions and 17,000 copies had been printed in England. It was used as a key textbook in Cooke's own 'domestic "school of the prophets"'—the ministerial training that he provided in his own home.[14] William Booth studied there before it was published, but it is likely that he encountered at least some of this material as lectures, discussions, or notes. *Christian Theology* is intended as a systematic theology, that is, that it will cover all the main doctrines of the Christian faith each in turn in a coherent way. In the historic Christian tradition, the classic way to pursue this task is to begin with the doctrine of God. Cooke reveals his biblicism from the outset by choosing to begin instead with the doctrine of Scripture. Thus, chapter one is entitled 'The Holy Scriptures: Their Divine Authority', and chapter two is 'The Holy Scriptures: Their Infallible Inspiration'. It is only in chapter three, 'The Holy Trinity', that the reader begins to learn about this God who has made the Bible into the paramount book through bestowing divine authority and inspiration upon it.[15] Chapter one is standard apologetics. Orthodox Christian claims for the Bible are verified by the fulfilment of prophecy and archaeological discoveries. The Bible has been attacked so forcefully for so long, Cooke avers, that its triumphant

[13] George John Stevenson, *Methodist Worthies: Characteristic Sketches of Methodist Preachers of the Several Denominations* (London: Thomas C. Jack, 1885), IV, 609.

[14] Hulme, *Cooke*, 98, 100.

[15] William Cooke, *Christian Theology: Its Doctrines and Ordinances Explained and Defended* (London: Hamilton, Adams, and Co., 1869).

survival demonstrates its authenticity. Chapter two insists that only the highest doctrine of Scripture is adequate and correct. The Bible was created through 'plenary inspiration' or 'verbal inspiration'.[16] This means that the writers were preserved 'from all error' and thus 'the records of Holy Scripture are unmixed and infallible truth'.[17] Many orthodox Victorian theologians and thinkers—even fellow-evangelical ones—would not have wished to nail things down quite so tightly. Cooke also takes a breezy march through the canon, defending each part of it in turn as belonging in the Bible. The sensual Song of Solomon causes a momentary slow down ('True, there may be a difficulty in rightly explaining and applying the allegorical imagery of this ancient book') and the letter to the Hebrews gets in on the grounds that this anonymous document was clearly written by the apostle Paul, or so Cooke asserts at any rate.[18] The transmission of the text through the centuries, it is conceded, cannot be said to have been an infallible process, but such pedantic concerns are never raised when discussing the works of ancient authors such as Homer or Virgil so they can be set aside in the case of the Bible as well. The implication of all this teaching for one's personal life is clear: 'If you have time to read no book but one, let it be the Book of God!'[19] There is, however, no record of any of Cooke's readers feeling it necessary to cast aside his *Christian Theology* on the strength of this admonition. Having time for both was a yet more perfect way. When Cooke wrote to a widow, Mrs Lowe, in 1881, he imagined her life with her daughter as one in which they would read aloud to one another in their 'cheerful room', alternating between 'some sweet portion of God's Word' and his own theological treatises.[20]

Cooke started his *Christian Theology* as he meant to go on. Every doctrine is addressed by expounding the Scriptures that support his view and challenging the interpretation of texts that have been used by the proponents of an alternative theological position. The book is filled with passages of Scripture written out in full: the inserted Bible quotation portion of Cooke's volume surely comprises a significant percentage of the

---

[16] Cooke, *Christian Theology*, 41, 56.   [17] Cooke, *Christian Theology*, 54, 59.
[18] Cooke, *Christian Theology*, 46, 51.   [19] Cooke, *Christian Theology*, 66.
[20] Cooke, *Christian Theology*, 309. His treatment of the Scriptures in this textbook was so valued that his publisher had it printed as a separate publication: William Cooke, *The Bible: Its Trials, and its Triumphs* (London: Hamilton, Adams, & Co., n.d.).

whole work. The doctrine of the Trinity is often viewed as more clearly expounded by the early church councils and the Christian tradition than in the Bible, but Cooke ostensibly accepts no aid from such quarters: 'the Holy Scriptures alone are the source of authoritative and infallible teaching on this great subject'.[21] Instead, he offers a compelling exposition of the Holy Trinity that arises from Matthew 28: 19: 'baptizing them in the name of the Father, and of the Son, and of the Holy Ghost'. Coyly refuting the suggestion that this phrase might not have been part of the original document, Cooke observes that even Unitarian Bible translations include it. Nevertheless, Unitarians refuse to understand its plain meaning: 'hence the Sabellian and Unitarian heresies imply that "baptism is to be administered in the Name of the Father, and of a creature, and of an attribute"'.[22] Throughout *Christian Theology*, Cooke freely makes arguments on the basis of the meaning of a text in the original Hebrew or Greek and in this discussion he finds in the Old Testament, unbeknownst to the Jewish community, the doctrine of the Trinity latent in Hebrew grammar: 'Elohim [a divine name], though *plural*, is construed with verbs and pronouns in the *singular*' (hence witness is borne to God as three-in-one).[23]

So it is with all the doctrines Cooke addresses. He is always careful to tackle the texts used by his opponents. This is particularly strong in chapter fifteen, 'The Doctrine of Purgatory Proved to Be Unscriptural', which is broken into sections based on the biblical passage examined therein. As a good Methodist, Cooke also examines all the parts of the Bible used by Calvinists to defend limited atonement and unconditional reprobation and to deny the possibility of entire sanctification in this lifetime. On the mode of baptism, however, the Baptists seem to have outflanked him. In a very Victorian manner, his objection to immersion is that its practice in a mixed assembly does not 'comport with English notions of propriety', a standard which if used to support a position with which he did not agree he would have presumably pounced upon as deflecting from the Bible alone.[24] Cooke's strong commitment to Scripture occasionally leaps out of *Christian Theology* in odd ways. He avers, 'The fire, then, that will try every soul of man on the day of judgment will be the fire of God's holy, searching, and inflexible word', which reads as if the Bible is the Protestant purgatory.[25]

---

[21] Cooke, *Christian Theology*, 67.
[22] Cooke, *Christian Theology*, 71.
[23] Cooke, *Christian Theology*, 76.
[24] Cooke, *Christian Theology*, 596.
[25] Cooke, *Christian Theology*, 482.

On the vexing question of discerning whether or not a person is truly regenerate, Cooke puts forward love of the Bible as a key distinguishing mark.[26] Finally, there is his definition of adoption, an idea that has theological import regarding the believer's relationship to God the Father: 'It is the act of a person taking a child into his family, and treating him in all respects as his own. Thus Moses was adopted by Pharaoh's daughter, and Esther by Mordecai.'[27] Only a compulsive biblicist would imagine that such a commonplace idea as adoption would be clarified for the uninitiated by a reference to the relationship that reputedly existed between two people in ancient Egypt or Persia.

Cooke's commitment to approach doctrine biblically is also on display in his *A Catechism: embracing the most important doctrines of Christianity. Designed for the use of schools, families, and Bible classes* (1860).[28] A catechism is a kind of every believer's systematic theology, designed to cover, in a question-and-answer format, all the major doctrines in a way that a youth can comprehend and master. For this work, Cooke does not defy convention, but rather acquiesces to the standard practice of beginning with a section on 'God and His Attributes'. Nevertheless, the work is scrupulously biblical. Cooke even claims that its very goal is 'to stimulate to the study of the Sacred Volume'.[29] To this end, answers in the catechism standardly come with a list of references to biblical texts as proof of their correctness. Moreover, numerous questions have as their answers direct quotations from Scripture, thus cleverly weaving Bible memorization into the exercise. Numerous questions exist as prompts for this such as 'Do you remember any passages in Holy Scripture which declare God to be eternal?', 'Can you mention any passage of Holy Scripture which directly teaches this doctrine?', 'Repeat the passage of Scripture in which the command of God on this point is given', and numerous others of the same ilk. Even the teaching that it is incorrect to think that God is revealed 'solely on the testimony of Holy Scripture' is ironically established exclusively by a quotation from the Bible (Romans 1: 20).[30] As to the doctrine of Scripture itself: the Bible

---

[26] Cooke, *Christian Theology*, 377.

[27] Cooke, *Christian Theology*, 342.

[28] William Cooke, *A Catechism: embracing the most important doctrines of Christianity. Designed for the use of schools, families, and Bible classes* (London: Methodist New Connexion Book Room, new and enlarged edition, 1860).

[29] Cooke, *Catechism*, from the 'preface to the new edition' printed on the back cover.

[30] Cooke, *Catechism*, 6.

teaches 'truth unmixed with error'. The answer to the question 'Is there any other standard of religious truth but the Holy Scriptures?' is: 'There is not any other, because no other can claim to be infallible.'[31] Cooke even smuggles some retorts to modern biblical critics into his catechism, prompting students to affirm that the Pentateuch was written by Moses and that the documents of the New Testament, in contrast to the theories of the Tübingen school, 'were all written within seventy years after our Lord's crucifixion'.[32] The Christian life, the catechism affirms, is one marked by the practice of daily Bible reading.

To turn to the life of this theologian is to witness the abiding presence of Scripture. William Cooke was a serious student of the Bible from a young age, greedily mastering Hebrew and Greek to this end. After five years as an ordinary ordained Methodist New Connexion minister in England, William Cooke's first placement as a superintendent was to Ireland. His practice there was to visit the poor in their homes and induce these Catholic folk to accept a copy of the Bible. So grateful were the Irish members of his denomination that, when his placement there came to an end, they presented him with Bagster's *Polyglot Bible* (the Scriptures in ten different languages). Clearly great minds think alike: the gift of the Newcastle upon Tyne circuit a few years later was Bagster's *Comprehensive Bible*. Cooke having bagged his Bagster's Bible early in life, the Methodist faithful appear to have assumed that a theologian would thereby have all he could need or want to go about his task triumphantly and gave up on giving him gifts thereafter. Early in life, and earlier in the century than most evangelicals, Cooke became a resolute and public teetotaler, and even published a lecture defending this cause. Nevertheless, when he realized that some teetotal advocates were handling the Bible cavalierly, he felt duty bound to write against them as well. He later recollected:

> I felt constrained to oppose their views, and, in doing so, examined every Hebrew word in the Old Testament, every Greek word in the New Testament, and their contexts, in order to ascertain the meaning of the same.[33]

---

[31] Cooke, *Catechism*, 75–6.
[32] Cooke, *Catechism*, 75. [33] Hulme, *Cooke*, 125–6.

Cooke took the right understanding of Scripture too seriously to let pass convenient assumptions such as that the wine Christ miraculously produced for the wedding at Cana was really grape juice. It would not serve to belabour the point: a couple more illustrations from Cooke's life will suffice. When William Cooke wrote to an older minister in their denomination, despite the fact that the man had just defended the faith triumphantly in a book, Cooke felt obliged to express this biblically charged wish: 'I hope God is still your strength and consolation, as he will assuredly be your great and everlasting reward.'[34] In a letter to the widow of a Methodist minister, Cooke naturally wanted to comfort her with the thought that her husband's life had been effective. He proved this decisively by observing that—all these years later—he could still recall the biblical texts that her husband had used for his sermons.[35]

It would be unfair to paint William Cooke as a narrowly conservative religious thinker and highlight only those views of his which correspond to such a picture. For example, in *Christian Theology* Cooke affirms that 'many heathens' who have never heard of Christ are saved eternally, as well as 'all who died in infancy'.[36] Nevertheless, Cooke did hold a goodly number of archly conservative views and these serve well both to illustrate his handling of and commitment to Scripture and to allow him to represent a wing of Victorian religious thought distinct from many other chapters in this volume. Very much in defiance of the tide of Victorian learning, Cooke insisted that the whole of human history had to be limited to the literalist approach to biblical chronology as calculated by Bishop Ussher, that is, around 6,000 years. He championed this quixotic cause in *The Fallacies of the Alleged Antiquity of Man Proved, and the Theory shown to be a Mere Speculation* (1872).[37] He insisted that both the notion of tracing the human race back tens of thousands of years and applying Darwinian evolution to human beings were incompatible with the Bible and therefore must be rejected. In another book, Cooke is happy to contemplate the miracle of the sun standing still during the time of Joshua as having been accomplished by

---

[34] John Rylands University Library of Manchester, Methodist Archives, William Cooke Papers, William Cooke to Thomas Allin, 14 March 1865.
[35] Hulme, *Cooke*, 358.
[36] Cooke, *Christian Theology*, 213–14.
[37] William Cooke, *The Fallacies of the Alleged Antiquity of Man Proved, and the Theory shown to be a Mere Speculation* (London: Hamilton, Adams, and Co., 1872).

'an arrest of the earth's rotation on its axis'.[38] Cooke spent many years as the editor of the Methodist New Connexion publications, one of which, aimed at Sunday school students and their teachers, was entitled the *Juvenile Instructor*. In it, he ran an enormously popular column in which he answered readers' questions about biblical passages that confused them. These were collected into a volume entitled *Explanations of Difficult Portions of Holy Scripture, &c., in 565 Queries and Answers* (1866).[39] This material reveals that, although William Cooke was primarily a theologian, he had given considerable study and thought to the contents of the entire Bible.

In this work, Cooke is most comfortable as defender of the literal truthfulness of Scripture. His young readers are repeatedly reassured that all is well. The old saw of where Cain's wife came from, for example, meets the confident reply: 'The question admits a very easy solution.'[40] As to biblical criticism, Cooke is so unwaveringly traditional that he even insists that Moses wrote Genesis 36: 31 ('before there reigned any king over the children of Israel') rather than allowing that it was added by way of explanation once Israel actually had become a monarchy. Cooke does draw the line, however, at requiring Moses to have recorded his own death, taking the next most conservative position possible, that this account was in all likelihood inserted by Joshua.

Cooke also prides himself on taking passages literally. He rejects smugly the suggestion that the account of Christ's temptation by the devil might best be read figuratively: 'I take the Word of God with the simplicity of a little child, and believe that the narrative is a literal record of a real transaction'.[41] Likewise, it is 'a blot' on Albert Barnes's commentary that he naturalizes the angel who systematically makes efficacious a local therapeutic pool (John 5: 4).[42] As to the number of the beast, 666, Cooke provides the code-breaking calculations to demonstrate that it is a reference to the pope. Ironically in all likelihood deflating confidence by over-proving his point, Cooke gives four different papal phrases from 'the

---

[38] William Cooke, *A Survey of the Unity, Harmony, and Growing Evidence of Sacred Truth* (London: Hamilton and Adams, 1874), 225.

[39] William Cooke, *Explanations of Difficult Portions of Holy Scripture, &c., in 565 Queries and Answers* (London: Henry Webber, 1866).

[40] Cooke, *Explanations*, 29.   [41] Cooke, *Explanations*, 244.

[42] Cooke, *Explanations*, 264.

Latin man' to the 'general vicar of Christ' which he can crunch the numbers to make fit.[43] Such an approach is an invitation for his interlocutors to outflank him on the right. Children are great literalists and thus Cooke rather wearily had to explain in numerous answers that a wide range of texts should not be read too woodenly. Given the last point on 666, the one with the most theological import is the words of institution at the Last Supper: 'This is my body'.

Cooke insists that daily Bible reading is a Christian requirement. In one of the more extreme examples of his biblicist orientation, Cooke confirmed to an inquirer that a statement he had made in a speech should indeed be taken literally: the theologian anticipated life in heaven being occupied with an eternal Bible study.[44] If one is especially busy on a particular day, the duty to read Scripture cannot be cut: the time can be made up by sleeping or eating less. Not least striking in Cooke's answers is his methodistical disapproval of entertainment. He concedes that youths may play cricket for exercise, but sport 'is beneath the dignity and gravity of adult Christians'.[45] Novels are banned but, in another generous concession, the best poetry is occasionally permissible. After that, there was no more ground to give. Children, you must not go to the circus: you might die there. Would you dare go straight from such frivolity to final judgment? Secular music on Sundays is forbidden. The Bible, in Cooke's reading, demands a total ban on joking. The answer to the question, 'May I go to the theatre?', certainly cannot be accused of being equivocal: 'Certainly not if you wish to go to heaven.'[46] Finally, to move from secular entertainment to Christian ministry, Cooke pronounces flatly against women preachers: 'If I am to take Jesus Christ, the Apostle Paul, and New Testament usage for my guide, I must conclude that female preaching is not ordained of God.'[47]

Catherine Booth found her public voice by opposing such a view. Biblicist that she was, Catherine also appealed to the Scriptures in order to challenge traditional restrictions on women in ministry. Already when she was still just engaged to William, she wrote to him in defence of her unconventional conviction on this matter:

[43] Cooke, *Explanations*, 355.   [44] Cooke, *Explanations*, 419–20.
[45] Cooke, *Explanations*, 413.   [46] Cooke, *Explanations*, 463.
[47] Cooke, *Explanations*, 410–11.

I have searched the Word of God through & through, I have tried to deal honestly with every passage on the subject . . . I solemnly assert that the more I think & read on the subject, the more satisfied I become of the true & scriptural character of my own views. . . . Oh for a few more Adam Clarkes to dispel the ignorance of the Church . . . [48]

Adam Clarke was a famous Wesleyan biblical commentator from earlier in the century. It is telling that her idea of a champion of women's rights is a good biblical scholar. In the end, Booth was provoked into taking on the task herself. In 1859, the prominent American Methodist Holiness preacher, Phoebe Palmer, was ministering in England. An English Congregational minister, A. A. Rees, responded by delivering a lecture in which he argued that it was unscriptural for women to preach. Booth wrote a tract in reply, *Female Teaching: or, the Rev. A. A. Rees versus Mrs Palmer* (1859).[49] It was a *tour de force*. She acknowledged that if the Bible affirms what Rees claims it does then this teaching deserves her 'immediate acquiescence', but she set out to demonstrate that it does not.[50] Rees, and evangelicals generally who held his view, rested their case primarily on two passages which appear to set a prohibition on women in ministry: 1 Corinthians 14: 34–5 and 1 Timothy 2: 11–12. Drawing on the original Greek, Booth argues these are not prohibitions on women speaking in church per se, but only on their doing so in a confrontational manner:

they were to refrain from such questionings, dogmatical assertions, and disputations, as would bring them into collision with the men—as would ruffle their tempers, and occasion an unamiable volubility of speech. This kind of speaking, and this alone, as it appears to me, was forbidden by the apostle in the passage before us.[51]

The bulk of the tract, however, consists of highlighting all the texts which support women in ministry: Joel 2, Acts 2, Galatians 3: 28, and much more. The risen Christ himself commanded Mary Magdalene to teach the apostles. Even the Old Testament contains a whole string of concrete cases. For example, she writes on Micah 6: 4:

---

[48] British Library, London, Booth Papers, Ms. 64,802, Catherine Mumford to William Booth, 9 April 1855.

[49] Catherine Booth (as 'Mrs Booth'), *Female Teaching: or, the Rev. A. A. Rees versus Mrs Palmer*, second edition, enlarged (London: G. J. Stevenson, 1861). No copy of the original, 1859 edition has apparently survived.

[50] Booth, *Female Teaching*, 7.

[51] Booth, *Female Teaching*, 12.

God here classes Miriam with Moses and Aaron, and declares that *He* sent her before his people. Had Mr Rees been a man of Israel at that time, we presume he would have disputed such a leadership.[52]

A male bias has hindered the right understanding of God's word, Booth continued. Although the original Greek reveals that Phoebe was a deacon, the translators rendered this as 'servant' so as not to suggest that women were permitted in the Christian ministry. Repeatedly, she goes on the counter-attack, charging Rees with being the one who is twisting some texts and ignoring others. Booth also gives a swift, feminist puncture to his patronizing praise:

> 'Nay, I hold,' says Mr R., 'that a good woman is the best thing in the world.' We do not for a moment doubt the truth of this assertion; *a thing*, and not a *being*, is what Mr Rees has been labouring to make a woman appear all the way through his remarks . . .[53]

In addition to a comprehensive sifting of the biblical evidence, Booth's rhetoric also finds power in the language of Scripture: Rees apparently thinks that women are only fit for 'the hewing of wood and the drawing of water' (Joshua 9: 23) and he wants gifted women (Harriet Beecher Stowe is named as an example) to hide their light 'under a bushel' (Matthew 5: 15–16).[54] If the mainstream evangelical community wanted Catherine Booth to believe that the Bible forbids women's preaching, then they should not have allowed her to study it so thoroughly.

As early as 1857 Booth herself had begun public speaking in connection with temperance work. She wrote enthusiastically to her mother: 'I felt quite at home on the <u>Platform</u>—far more so than I do in the <u>Kitchen</u>!!'[55] Nevertheless, deeply formative in her own life story was her long struggle to overcome her fears and respond to a divine call to preach that she sensed. One Sunday morning in 1860 she submitted to this call by standing up after William had preached. After he had conceded to her request to speak, she gave an impromptu confession that she had been resisting the Spirit on this matter. As she later retold this incident, the devil tried to stop her by suggesting that she would make a fool of herself. Satan had forgotten, however, the extent to which what Booth thought, heard, or saw sparked

[52] Booth, *Female Teaching*, 18.   [53] Booth, *Female Teaching*, 23.
[54] Booth, *Female Teaching*, 25, 4.   [55] Green, *Booth*, p. 134.

biblical allusions in her mind. Catherine's counterintuitive response was that then she must go forward as this would be an opportunity to become 'a fool for Christ' (I Corinthians 4: 10).[56] She recalled saying: 'I have come to tell you this, and to promise the Lord that I will be obedient to the Heavenly vision.' (Acts 26: 19) It is telling that she in this way identified her own call with that of the apostle Paul. William joyfully insisted that she preach a proper sermon at the service that very night. We are told she 'took for her subject, "Filled With the Spirit"', and it is typical of her biblicism that the subject, the title, and text (Ephesians 5: 18) of her sermon are identical.[57] From then on, Catherine Booth had an effective, well-received, and demanding preaching ministry. Her standard practice was to preach for over an hour. On one occasion she was so ill that she sent a message to William, who was away, to return and preach in her place. He did come, but she summoned all her willpower and decided to give the sermon herself: although in pain throughout, she still preached for an hour and a quarter.

It also must be kept in mind that preparing sermons was not Booth's only responsibility in life. When she began her regular preaching ministry she had four children, the oldest being only four years and three months old! Catherine and William eventually had eight biological children (five girls and three boys) and one adopted son. Catherine used the same heavily biblical, largely home-based educational model for her own children that her mother had used for her. The oldest, William Bramwell, was destined to lead the Salvation Army after his parents had been promoted to glory. His very name—a tribute to a fervent Wesleyan preacher—reveals the Booths' Methodist identity. When William Bramwell was only three years and two months old, Catherine could already report progress: 'He loves to listen to stories about Joseph, Moses, Daniel, and the Saviour. Indeed, he can "p'each," as he calls it, very nicely.'[58] By the time he was thirteen, he was writing to his mother the kind of biblically charged letters home that she herself wrote to her mother at that age: 'my soul has prospered this last week. [3 John 2] The Lord has led me beside the still waters and in the paths of righteousness for His Name's sake. [Psalm 23: 2–3]'[59] One daugh-ter—her name is discreetly concealed so that her temptation by the world

---

[56] Catherine Booth, *Papers on Aggressive Christianity* (London: The Salvation Army, 1891), 138.

[57] Booth-Tucker, *Life*, I, 186. A sermon of hers with this same text, title, and subject, was published in Booth, *Papers*, 145–59.

[58] Booth-Tucker, *Life*, I, 167.

[59] Booth-Tucker, *Life*, II, 7.

should not be exposed—was offered free tuition at a lady's college by an evangelical well-wisher. The formal education was entirely religiously sound by Booth's standards, but she nevertheless could not allow it because of the dangerous nature of the overall atmosphere as revealed by some of the girls' fashionable apparel. The daughter pleaded her case by arguing that her brother Herbert had gone to a proper school for a while and this had led on to his becoming 'a mighty man in God's Israel' (playing on a stock scriptural phrase). This was an amateur effort at biblical reasoning, however. Her mother decided the matter with the rhetorical question: 'What hast thou to do in the way of Egypt to drink the waters of Sihor?' (Jeremiah 2: 18).[60]

Although this is not a denominational history, this is perhaps an appropriate point briefly to fill in developments on that front. William and Catherine increasingly envisioned for themselves a free-ranging evangelistic preaching ministry. This desire chafed against the circuit placement structure and duties of the Methodist New Connexion. They left that denomination in 1861 and struck out on an independent revivalist ministry, initially accepting an invitation to do a series of meetings in methodistic Cornwall. In 1865, they decided to tackle that great modern Babylon, London. The official history of the Salvation Army begins with that year.[61] This metropolitan work coalesced into what they initially called the 'East London Christian Mission', as it was focused on the East End, the disreputable, working-class section of the city. This was then organized as simply the 'Christian Mission' in 1870. In 1877, the mission was restructured on a so-called military basis, that is, with centralized, strong command from the top. The first War Congress (annual conference) was held in 1878 and the necessary legal changes were made, and thus that year is considered when the Salvation Army proper was founded. The 'Salvation Army' was an informal name for the Christian Mission which, once it was coined, quickly supplanted the official one.

Catherine Booth's doctrine of Scripture was no less high and absolutist than that of William Cooke. Here, for example, is her articulation of the same version of the Bible's infallibility held by her husband's theologian-mentor: 'the darkness is in our own poor, blind, puny brains, and not in

---

[60] Booth-Tucker, *Life*, II, 59–62.

[61] Robert Sandall, *The History of the Salvation Army*, 5 vols, Vol. 1: 1865–1878 (London: Thomas Nelson and Sons, 1947). The best social history of the movement is Pamela J. Walker, *Pulling the Devil's Kingdom Down: The Salvation Army in Victorian Britain* (Berkeley: University of California Press, 2001).

God or in His Book. In His Book, rightly interpreted, there is no contradiction whatsoever.'[62] Booth was so committed to the Bible as the final authority by which all things stand or fall, that she would often evoke this measuring rod in odd ways. To take an extreme example, she once remarked on the proper way to preach a sermon:

> Not to *deliver* it. I wish the word had never been coined in connexion with Christian work. 'Deliver' it, indeed—*that* is not in the Bible. No, no; not deliver it; but drive it home—send it in—make it felt.[63]

This is telling precisely because, as an argument, it is nonsensical. Booth would not have insisted as a matter of principle that all phrases used about ministry needed to come from Scripture and, in any event, the suggestions she offered for substitutes did not either! It is simply that she felt there was something amiss and her doctrine of Scripture was so strong that she instinctively assumed that anything wrong was *ipso facto* unbiblical. Again, outflanked by the so-called Plymouth Brethren, Booth could write absurdly on their teaching regarding 'Jesus Only' (Matthew 17: 8) that she objected 'to the phrase as unscriptural'.[64] She goes on with more coherence to claim that the teaching attached to this biblical phrase by them cannot be derived from it, but clearly she would have been more comfortable in an argument where the scriptural resonances were all on her side. According to Booth, the Salvation Army, in its uncompromising radicalism, was the Christian group that would really live up to the doctrine of *sola Scriptura*:

> Now, here it seems to me that the Church—I speak universally—has made a grand mistake, the same old mistake which we are so prone to fall into, of exalting the traditions of the elders into the same importance and authority as the Word of God, as the clearly laid down principles of the New Testament.[65]

The place of the Bible in the Salvation Army generally will be returned to below: Booth's use of Scripture shall be examined first. The Bible was central to her public ministry. Not only did her sermons have a text, and not only were they filled with additional scriptural quotations and references, but they were also preceded by numerous Bible readings. For example, before her sermon, 'A Pure Gospel'—which had as its official

[62] Booth, *Papers*, 128.   [63] Booth-Tucker, *Life*, I, 132.
[64] Booth-Tucker, *Life*, II, 105.   [65] Booth, *Papers*, 52–3.

text Acts 26: 15–20—Booth had no less than nine different passages read.[66]
Her remarkable biblical literacy is underlined by the fact that these sermons,
which were taken down by a shorthand writer for publication, were given,
on principle, extemporaneously without notes. Therefore, the numerous
biblical quotations in them from other parts of Scripture were all done from
memory. This context explains a habit she had of introducing additional
scriptural quotations in her sermons with a fairly vague phrase such as, 'the
Apostle says', which saved her the effort of thinking up a more precise
reference in mid-flight. This must have been the case often in her letter
writing as well. For example, she cited from memory to one of her sons:
'Son, remember! Thou in thy lifetime hadst thy good things, but Lazarus
evil things; now he is comforted, but thou art tormented.' (Luke 16: 25)
'Perhaps I have not quoted the exact words', she wrote apologetically, but
the minor variations between her memory and the Authorized Version
are certainly not worth quibbling over.[67] Moreover, as has already been
indicated, these sermons were often so biblical that the title, text, and
subject were identical. This is true, for example, of four sermons in her
collection, *Life and Death*. The strongest example is 'Quench Not the Spirit'
(1 Thessalonians 5: 19), a sermon that had its very title in quotation marks in
order to underline its biblical derivation.[68] Likewise, when in 1868 she
became the founding editor of the mission's gospel newspaper, the *East
London Evangelist*, the first articles she wrote herself all had texts for their
titles.[69]

Catherine Booth first took up a hallmark form of Salvation Army
ministry—unsolicited direct gospel appeals to working-class people in
their own neighbourhoods and homes—in the late 1850s. She answered
this divine prompt with trepidation. The first woman she approached had a
wretched life because of her husband's drink problem. Conquering any fear,
Booth immediately tackled the inebriated spouse himself. Her approach was
to read an apt portion of the Bible aloud to him, which duly sobered him
up. Booth went rapidly on to reclaim other local drunks and then gathered
them together into a weekly meeting 'for reading the Scriptures' in order to

[66] Booth, *Papers*, 28.
[67] Booth-Tucker, *Life*, II, 101–2.
[68] Catherine Booth (as 'Mrs Booth of The Salvation Army'), *Life and Death. Being reports of addresses delivered in London* (London: The Salvation Army, 1889). 'Quench Not the Spirit' is pp. 98–108.
[69] Booth-Tucker, *Life*, I, 333.

make sure the cure did not wear off.[70] Nor was she the kind of physician of souls who does not take her own advice. Booth could write to her best friend, Mrs Billups, a mature, faithful Christian and a co-labourer in the Salvation Army work, after listing a barrage of biblical texts, an exhortation to herself as well as her correspondent: 'Bless the Lord for these psalms. My dear friend, be determined to get more time to read the Word. With our shattered nerves we must have retirement if we are to maintain our spiritual life.'[71] Her letters to friends and family members recur with testimonies that she had been blessed by specific, named texts read that day in her devotions. A few general examples of her biblical way of speaking and writing will suffice. Those converted under her ministry needed to start as she meant them to go on. Her sinner's prayer could include words that would surely sound rather odd to someone unaccustomed to scriptural resonances: 'I will put my neck under Thy yoke for ever'.[72] Booth wrote to her husband about the spiritual progress of one person who prayed such a prayer: 'The man whom I told you about as having been brought in a month ago under "Be ye reconciled" [2 Corinthians 5: 20], prayed last night with power.'[73] Here is a man identified between the two of them, not by his name, but rather by a biblical text! Catherine Booth could also dismiss a complainer with the question: 'Is there no balm in Gilead?' (Jeremiah 8: 22).[74]

Booth's scriptural way of thinking was so ingrained that she habitually transposed her own life, and those of her followers, into biblical narratives. This is perhaps the most striking trait in her use of Scripture. The Salvation Army must strive to find its way into the biblical story: 'God is with us, and out of this movement He is going to resuscitate the Acts of the Apostles. We see the pillar of cloud, and after it we must go.'[75] She herself strongly identified with the life of the apostle Paul and she hoped for no less for her followers: 'Then you will, like the Apostles, be willing to push your limbs into a basket, and so be let down by the wall, if need be, or suffer shipwreck, hunger, peril, nakedness, fire, or sword'.[76] One should read the New Testament as the story of one's own life (or potentially so) and not as if 'God intended such experiences and visions only for Paul and the Apostles'.[77] The Day of Pentecost is now, she insists to fellow Salvationists,

[70] Booth-Tucker, *Life*, I, 170–1.   [71] Booth-Tucker, *Life*, II, 75.
[72] Booth, *Papers*, 38.   [73] Booth-Tucker, *Life*, I, 191.
[74] Booth-Tucker, *Life*, II, 104.   [75] Booth-Tucker, *Life*, II, 118.
[76] Booth, *Papers*, 19.   [77] Booth, *Papers*, 158.

and you are receiving the baptism in the Holy Ghost and being transformed into prophets and prophetesses. Identifying with Christ is, of course, standard Christian spirituality. Booth, however, recommends reading his story as our story to such an extent that her followers would even become 'saviours of men'.[78] She was well aware that this way of thinking is too bold for some, but defends it nonetheless as a faithful reading of oneself into the narrative. It would not be profitable to attempt to chronicle the innumerable times when Booth can be seen transferring her own experiences into the frame of biblical accounts. Here is a random example of this persistent way of thinking and speaking: 'I have been half the week, I think, with Elijah under the juniper tree.'[79] It was not always clear to her, however, which scriptural story applied. When dealing with some unpleasant circumstances, Booth candidly reflected that she was not sure if she should view them through the lens of Christ in the wilderness as an attack of the devil to be repulsed or through the biblical account of the apostle Paul's thorn in the flesh as a necessary trial that must be accepted.[80] Catherine Booth understood her own life by situating it inside the stories of the Scriptures.

The very fact that the Bible was highly valued by Victorians across a wide religious spectrum invited awareness that some additional decisive factor needed to be identified. This added component would help to account for why a commitment to Scripture had not kept one's theological opponents from their errors. For Pusey, the formula was Holy Scripture plus patristic patterns of interpretation; for Nicholas Wiseman it was Sacred Scripture plus the authority of the church hierarchy. Catherine Booth faced the same dilemma. Her solution was the Scriptures plus the Spirit. As one might be able to predict, even her critique of the limits of the Bible was expressed through scriptural thoughts and words. She found it in the Pauline distinction between letter and spirit. This enabled her to understand why a Bible-soaked, church-going culture was so far away from the sound spiritual state that she believed God expected. When Salvationists were attacked by some 'Lancashire roughs', Booth was told that these lads were known for their Sunday school attendance (and therefore they had studied the Bible). Her response was: 'So much for teaching the *letter without the spirit!*'[81] She shared

---

[78] Booth-Tucker, *Life*, II, 316–17.   [79] Booth, *Papers*, 152.
[80] Booth-Tucker, *Life*, II, 182.   [81] Booth-Tucker, *Life*, II, 131.

this insight in a letter to her son Bramwell: 'The longer I live the more I believe in the study of the Bible *with the Spirit*; it is dead without it.'[82] She struggled to communicate this truth effectively in her ministry. On the one hand, she did not want to say anything that would indicate the slightest downgrading of the significance, authority, and place that the Bible ought to have in the lives of believers. On the other, however, she had a spiritual duty to attempt to awaken unconverted people whose deep knowledge of the Scriptures and formal acceptance of their teaching gave them a false sense of security about their spiritual state:

> Use your Heavenly Father's letter to find your way up to Him. It is not the letter you are to rest in: it is the God who wrote it. Use the letter to get at the Spirit, for the letter will not save you—it is the Spirit that saves you. Hug this volume to your heart as the expression of your Father's will and the record through which you are to believe on His Son, but it is the Son who is to save you.[83]

And again in another sermon:

> They think they believe because they receive into their minds the written record that God has given of His Son; but they have not believed and rested on the promise in such a way as to bring the witness of the *Spirit*. They have stopped short of that. They have been satisfied with the *letter*. Now, do not think, friends, that I underestimate the *letter*. Perhaps few of you, if any, value this word more than I do ... Take the blessed record to your heart, but do not rest in the letter.[84]

The Salvation Army was perhaps the most significant new religious movement to emerge in Victorian Britain. Nevertheless, this fresh spiritual effort was in no way a departure from the deep attachment to the Bible which marked many existing denominations. Booth boasted that Salvationists were the ones who were effectively getting the Bible to the masses:

> Oh, they are dying for lack of knowledge—they are, friends; thousands, are dying for the lack of knowledge. It is quite common thing for us to get people into our services who say, 'I never knew there was anything so pretty as that in the Bible. I didn't know you were reading from the Bible. We never heard anything like that before.'[85]

---

[82] Booth-Tucker, *Life*, II, 101.   [83] Booth, *Papers*, 79.
[84] Booth, *Papers*, 83–4.   [85] Booth, *Papers*, 59.

The Army viewed Elijah Cadman, an erstwhile working-class rough, as an archetypal Salvationist convert. Cadman's response to his new life was to carry his Bible around with him everywhere he went and to sleep with it under his pillow even though he was so illiterate that he did not know if it was right side up or upside down! He soon learned to read under the specific motivation of Bible devotion. Scripture reading was such a strong expectation that the Army had for its followers that it even produced its own lectionary. The very title of this volume clearly reveals that the normative model being set out for the faithful was reading the Bible daily in both the morning and the evening, with additional short readings at midday.[86] The Army chose to identify their full-time Christian workers through the title 'Captain' rather than 'Reverend' on the grounds that the former was a biblical word. More substantively, the Salvation Army's original doctrinal statement, which was adopted in 1878 and has never been superseded, like William Cooke's *Christian Theology*, departs from Christian tradition by expressing a deeper biblicism through beginning with the doctrine of Scripture. Its first point is: 'We believe that the Scriptures of Old and New Testaments were given by inspiration of God and that they only constitute the Divine rule of Christian faith and practice.'[87] It is only with that paramount doctrine clearly in place that the statement goes on in its second point to establish monotheism.

In 1888, Booth learned that she had breast cancer. Although bedridden and in great pain for many months, she lived on for longer than anyone expected, not dying until October 1890. In the classic Victorian way, this period gave tremendous scope for meaning-laden deathbed scenes. In the nineteenth century, famous ministers were not exempt from the need to make a final confession of faith in order to reassure everyone that they had died believing. Extraordinarily, Booth's son-in-law and official Salvationist biographer felt a need to confirm her faith to the last not only in God and the gospel but also in the Bible:

> To the end of life, Catherine maintained this intense love and reverence for the Scriptures, and her last and most valued gift to each member of her family, from the very banks of the Jordan, was that of a Bible, into which, with the

---

[86] *The Salvation Soldiers' Guide: Being a Bible Chapter for the Morning and Evening of Every Day in the Year, with Fragments for Mid-day Reading* (London: The Salvation Army, 1883).
[87] Sandall, *History*, I, 288.

greatest pain and difficulty, she traced her name, as 'the last token of a mother's love'.[88]

When she gathered her family together for the official parting scene, Booth characteristically recast the moment inside a biblical narrative: 'I want you to promise me, as we stand in the middle of this Jordan, there are no stones that we can set up as an altar, but you can set up a memorial in your hearts . . .'[89] Even after she was so far gone that she was no longer able to speak, the biblical resonances continued. At one point, Booth communicated by dramatically gesturing at a wall-hanging that presented a text: 'My grace is sufficient for thee' (2 Corinthians 12: 9). By this stage she knew which scriptural story was unfolding: it was not the devil but rather a fatal thorn in the flesh. The inscription on her coffin was confined simply to her name, her identity as 'The Mother of the Salvation Army', and a biblical phrase, 'More than conqueror' (Romans 8: 37). On top of the coffin they placed Catherine Booth's Army uniform and her well-worn Bible.[90]

[88] Booth-Tucker, *Life*, I, 15–16.
[89] Booth-Tucker, *Life*, II, 366.
[90] Bramwell Booth, *On the Banks of the River; being a brief history of the last days on earth of Mrs General Booth*, second edition (London: The Salvation Army, 1900), 116.

5

Liberal Anglicans

Florence Nightingale and the Bible

Having become a national hero through her leadership at the head of an experimental unit of nurses during the Crimean War, Florence Nightingale (1820–1910) settled down to a long life in which she was highly productive and influential in reforming causes ranging from the design of hospital buildings to the irrigation of India despite also becoming within a few years of her return from the war a permanent invalid and a recluse. A lifelong Anglican, in 1862 Nightingale solved the problem of how to communicate as a shut-in by inviting a leading Broad Church clergyman, Benjamin Jowett, to come to her home and administer the sacrament to her and a few others in her immediate circle. Jowett, a Fellow of Balliol College, Oxford, wrote to the bishop of London, in whose diocese Nightingale resided, to gain permission to fulfil this request, adding by way of full disclosure: 'I ought perhaps to tell you also that she is not what some persons would call orthodox.'[1]

Jowett himself was by that time a notorious case of an Anglican who was considered by many Victorians to be unorthodox, not least because of his chapter 'On the Interpretation of Scripture' in *Essays and Reviews*, an edited volume which generated a heated public controversy due to its alleged heretical drift.[2] Jowett was a liberal Anglican, that is, a member of

---

[1] Benjamin Jowett to A. C. Tait, 12 October 1862: Lynn McDonald (ed.), *Florence Nightingale's Theology: Essays, Letters and Journal Notes*, The Collected Works of Florence Nightingale Vol. 3 (Waterloo, Ontario: Wilfrid Laurier University Press, 2002) [hereafter *Collected Works* 3], 523.

[2] Victor Shea and William Whitla (eds), *'Essays and Reviews': The 1860 Text and Its Reading* (Charlottesville, Virginia: University of Virginia Press, 2000). For a study of Jowett's beliefs, see Peter Hinchliff, *Benjamin Jowett and the Christian Religion* (Oxford: Clarendon Press, 1987).

the Church of England who believed that various doctrinal positions which had long been considered essential to the Christian faith needed to be modified or even abandoned in the light of modern thought. He was also a Broad Churchman, which is to say someone who believed that the Church of England should not enforce precise and rigid boundaries on matters of belief, but rather seek to be as inclusive as possible within what were deemed to be reasonable limits, with some even going so far as to envision Unitarians as members of the national church in good standing.[3] Florence Nightingale, who became one of Jowett's closest friends and who regularly received the sacrament from him in her own home for the rest of his life, is the most obvious woman to represent the liberal or Broad Church variety of Victorian Anglicanism. Moreover, the men who are usually named as representative of this way of being Anglican were generally ordained—one thinks of Thomas Arnold, A. P. Stanley, J. W. Colenso, F. D. Maurice, and Jowett himself—and therefore restrained by clerical subscription and ministerial propriety and effectiveness from being too bold in their speculations and pronouncements. Nightingale, on the other hand, having no official position and largely writing for the private eyes of herself and her friends and relations, was able to articulate new theological positions in a much more thoroughgoing and forthright way. Indeed, her critiques of many traditional Christian doctrines were in advance of all those men, making her an extreme, and therefore all the more telling, example of how a rejection of traditional doctrines, including doctrines on Scripture, among liberal Anglicans did not result in a lessening of engagement with the Bible. Furthermore, the pressure to ensure that a figure is representative is lessened for the Broad Church precisely because it was so clearly pre-occupied with Scripture, undercutting any suspicion that a figure has been chosen whose attentiveness to the Bible is exceptional. Indeed, all the male figures named as representative actually wrote a biblical commentary—save for Thomas Arnold whose premature death came when he was in the midst of creating a series on the Pauline epistles.[4]

---

[3] For a recent study of this variety of nineteenth-century Anglicanism, see Tod E. Jones, *The Broad Church: A Biography of a Movement* (Lanham, Maryland: Lexington Books, 2003).

[4] Arthur Penrhyn Stanley, *The Life and Correspondence of Thomas Arnold, D.D.* (New York: Charles Scribner's Sons, n.d. [originally 1844]), I, 193. I have already, in a sense, done the more traditional, male version of this chapter in my writings on J. W. Colenso in which I explore both his Broad Church identity and his biblical commentaries: Timothy Larsen, 'John William Colenso', in Jeffrey P. Greenman and Timothy Larsen (eds), *Reading Romans through the Centuries: From the Early Church to Karl Barth* (Grand Rapids: Brazos Press, 2005), 187–204; Timothy Larsen,

Unorthodoxy was part of Florence Nightingale's birthright. Her parents' families were Unitarian on both sides. Her maternal grandfather was one of the most famous Unitarians of his generation, the political and social reformer William Smith, M.P. Her father, William Nightingale, studied at Trinity College, Cambridge, but his Dissenting identity meant that he was ineligible for a degree. Her mother, Frances Smith (to use her maiden name), also continued to identify with Unitarianism as a young woman. The decision of Nightingale's parents to conform to the Church of England and raise their two children as Anglicans co-existed easily with an ongoing appreciation of Dissent, especially Unitarianism. William Nightingale was more sceptical of religious beliefs than the other members of the immediate family and he was delighted with Florence's unorthodox theological reflections as an adult. Even her mother, who was more traditionally devout, clearly wanted the family to maintain some continuity with its religious roots, even going so far as trying to secure a Unitarian governess for Florence and her elder sister, Parthenope.[5] The family read aloud Unitarian works. In her late teens, the American Unitarian William Ellery Channing became one of Nightingale's favourite authors. A dominant influence on Nightingale was her Aunt Mai (Mary Shore Smith, eventually a double aunt as she was her father's sister who married her mother's brother). Nightingale once even claimed that her aunt's influence upon her was greater than that of her own mother. Mai was without question a major sharper of Nightingale's unorthodox views as an adult. Aunt Mai sat under the ministry of the most prominent Victorian Unitarian minister, James Martineau—a theological mind whose own ideas were considered advanced even within the denomination.

Florence Nightingale's childhood was also steeped in Scripture. Frances Nightingale read the Bible aloud to her daughters first thing every morning. Letters that Nightingale wrote when she was away from her mother at various times when she was aged seven through nine are preoccupied with

---

Contested Christianity: The Political and Social Contexts of Victorian Theology (Waco, Texas: Baylor University Press, 2004), ch. 5, 'Biblical Criticism and the Desire for Reform: Bishop Colenso on the Pentateuch', 59–77. The only other obvious name for a representative liberal Anglican often offered is that of S. T. Coleridge. For his extensive engagement with Scripture, see Jeffrey W. Barbeau, Coleridge, the Bible, and Religion (Basingstoke: Palgrave Macmillan, 2008).

[5] Mark Bostridge, Florence Nightingale: The Making of An Icon (New York: Farrar, Straus and Giroux, 2008), 53.

reporting that she is reading the Scriptures, often naming the specific chapter covered that day. Here, for example, is a portion of a letter written in 1829: 'read in the Bible the seventeenth chapter of the 1 Kings (about Elijah being fed by ravens and being supported by the Sareptan woman, and raising her son to life again) and the fourth chapter of the 2 Kings (about Elisha).'[6] Around this time Nightingale also corresponded with a cousin. The earliest surviving of these letters, apparently written when she was around eight years old, launches straight into matters biblical: 'My dear cousin and friend Bon, I have been reading the 121st psalm. We think it very beautiful and we think you would like it.'[7] The only other surviving letter to this cousin, again when Nightingale was probably eight or nine, proudly lists the books she personally owns, beginning with *Goody Two Shoes* and culminating in *An Abstract of the History of the Bible*.[8] Another book from her girlhood was entitled *Scripture Riddles*.[9] Also around the age of eight, Nightingale reported on the lessons she had with a tutor: mathematics, music, Latin, and 'making maps of Palestine (and such like about the Bible)'.[10] At the age of nine she began a diary which was entitled, 'Journal of Flo, Embley', and began: 'The Lord is with thee wherever thou art' (cf. Joshua 1: 9).[11] In 1830, when Nightingale was nine, her New Year's resolutions included to read her Bible twice daily.[12] A few years on, her confidant was another cousin, Hilary Bonham Carter. Here is Nightingale's teenage notion of how to wish her friend a happy birthday:

> You cease, I do indeed believe, to feel the weariness of life, for such naturally inherit the blessings given to that divine 'poverty of spirit.' And such too *receive* the promise, that they shall hunger no more, for they are fed with the same meat (which Christ found all-sufficient for him) to do the will of

---

[6] Florence Nightingale to her mother, n.d. [1829], Lynn McDonald (ed.), *Florence Nightingale: An Introduction to Her Life and Family*, The Collected Works of Florence Nightingale, Vol. 1 (Waterloo, Ontario: Wilfrid Laurier University Press, 2001 [hereafter *Collected Works* 1]), 107.

[7] 'Bon' stands for the surname Bonham Carter. The cousin's first name is not known apparently, and the letter was not dated: *Collected Works* 1, 425.

[8] *Collected Works* 1, 426.

[9] Bostridge, *Nightingale*, 35.

[10] Bostridge, *Nightingale*, 36.

[11] Edward Cook, *The Life of Florence Nightingale*, 2 vols (London: Macmillan, 1913), I, 11. Embley means she is at their home in Hampshire, Embley Park, as opposed to the family seat in Derbyshire, Lea Hurst.

[12] *Collected Works* 1, 109.

Him that sent them, for what is duty or conscience but the will of God for the particular dutist? Therefore, my dearest, I can truly and sincerely say joy, joy, on thy birthday.[13]

Nightingale's nickname for Hilary was 'brother Jonathan', biblical code for the deepest of friendships (2 Samuel 1: 26).[14]

One example will serve to demonstrate how biblically charged her mind had become by the end of her teens. In 1839, Parthenope was away when Nightingale and their parents returned to their house at Embley after alterations had been done on it. Nightingale reported to her sister on their adventures upon arrival: 'Rain has been almost incessant ever since we came. Our mattresses, on which we are to sleep, have just gone down and will probably soon have become the pool of Siloam' (John 9: 7).[15] This is telling precisely because it is so odd. There is nothing that connects this incident with that Scripture other than that both contain a collection of water: in other words, when Nightingale thinks of something as mundane as a pool she does not think of anything she has actually experienced firsthand but rather of a biblical text. Moreover, if biblical literacy was the water that most Victorians lived in, Nightingale was self-aware enough to notice it, writing when she was nineteen: 'Mama and I read the newspaper and the Bible and my phraseology, as my ideas, are equal parts of both.'[16] By her twenties, Nightingale was teaching her own Bible class on Sunday after-noons. She also became interested in the subject of angels and did a serious study of what the biblical writers actually thought on the matter. She sometimes used this material for playful effect, writing to Julia Ward Howe, who would achieve fame as the author of 'The Battle Hymn of the Republic' and whom she had met when the Howes honeymooned in Britain: 'How do your little cherubim do? Though, as upon consulting the "Hebrew Greek," we find cherubim to mean knowing ones or fullness of knowledge, it may be doubted whether your cherub (big one or little one) according to strict etymology, is entitled to the term'.[17]

We can take the year 1850 as the end of the beginning of Nightingale's formation. Seeing her life through a biblical lens, Nightingale herself

[13] Collected Works 1, 426. (This passage is dense with biblical allusions, primarily to the Beatitudes in Matthew chapter 5.)

[14] Cook, Nightingale, I, 99.

[15] Collected Works 1, 292.

[16] Collected Works 1, 230.

[17] Collected Works 1, 721. This letter, which is undated as to year, was almost certainly written in 1846.

thought this, writing on her birthday: 'Today I am thirty, the age Christ began his mission. Now no more childish things, no more vain things, no more love, no more marriage. Now, Lord, let me only think of Thy will'.[18] She had been taught to read the New Testament in the Greek original as part of her childhood education, but in that year she determined to learn Hebrew as well in order to pursue the meaning of the Old Testament more thoroughly. The year 1850 also marks the beginning of the record of 'the voice', messages she received the rest of her life that she believed were from Almighty God. Even this personal God spoke through scriptural language: 'All the afternoon a voice was saying to me, *"If thou knowest the gift of God and who it is that saith unto thee, Give me to drink, thou wouldest have asked him and he would give thee living water"'* (John 4: 10).[19] There is also an extraordinary document from that year in which she records the Christian counsel and discipleship she offered to a girl named Louise. Nightingale had been alarmed to learn that the girl had unpleasant associations with the Bible because she had been forced to memorize it. She was thrilled to be able to guide Louise into loving the Scriptures. She also taught the girl how to use the Bible as a comfort during life's trials. Here is but a small portion of a barrage of texts that she offered her as applicable to an assortment of different named trials:

> Yes, she said, I know my stepfather is a light-minded man, and he drinks and if he does not care for me and grudges me my bread, what am I to do? Why, I said, open your Bible, and it will tell you what you are to do, and I showed her a place, Psalm 27: 10, Isaiah 49. And, I said, if people speak bad words of you or want to quarrel with you, what will you do? I wanted to prepare her, you know, and I showed her in the Bible Ephesians 5: 1–2, John 13: 36 . . .[20]

In the struggle of life, Nightingale valued the sword of the Spirit which is the word of God.

At the start of 1853, Florence Nightingale reported in her diary that in the previous year she had 'remodeled my whole religious belief from beginning to end.'[21] The fruit of this was her *Suggestions for Thought*, the first draft of which was completed in 1852. Later, Nightingale vastly expanded it and

---

[18] *Collected Works* 3, 373.

[19] Lynn McDonald (ed.), *Florence Nightingale's Spiritual Journey: Biblical Annotations, Sermons and Journal Notes*, The Collected Works of Florence Nightingale, Vol. 2 (Waterloo, Ontario: Wilfrid Laurier University Press, 2001 [hereafter *Collected Works* 2]), 377 (20 May 1850).

[20] *Collected Works* 3, 374.

[21] Cook, *Nightingale*, I, 469.

privately printed a three-volume version in 1860 in order to circulate it for comment among a handful of key thinkers. Arthur Hugh Clough, who was married to a cousin of Nightingale's, sent a copy to Benjamin Jowett, and thus began their close and enduring friendship.

Suggestions for Thought reveals the full extent of Nightingale's theological liberalism. The basic contours of its viewpoint she would hold the rest of her life, and she held most of these unorthodox views in a less systematic form before 1852 as well. Nevertheless, two motivations must be kept in mind in order to appraise it aright. First, Nightingale was writing apologetics. The full title of the first volume made this explicit: *Suggestions for Thought to the Searchers After Truth Among the Artizans of England.* She wanted to demonstrate to those who had come to the conclusion that orthodoxy was incredible that atheism was not the only alternative. It is telling that she also sent a copy to the unbelieving philosopher John Stuart Mill: she clearly hoped to present a reasoned defence of religion to minds which thought that faith was irrational. This is important because apologetic writings often do not present all that the writer believes, but are rather tailored to be winsome for the target audience. In Nightingale's case her rich devotional and mystical inner spiritual life is not prominent in *Suggestions for Thought.* Secondly, Nightingale hoped to present a systematic theological scheme. She thought that the influence of the prominent liberal Anglican thinkers was limited because they failed to do this. Once again, the relevance of this is that parts of Nightingale's spirituality were therefore obscured in her effort to present a tidy, coherent system of religious thought.

Nightingale's scheme went something like this: we discern in the natural world laws and therefore we may infer a lawgiver. This is God. God is perfect and God's laws are perfect and therefore are inviolable, even for the Almighty. She often sounded like a Deist when affirming this point. As she expounded it to Jowett, a deity who intervened in the regular running of the universe according to fixed laws would be 'a capricious stupid god'.[22] God's plan is for human beings to reach perfection through discovering God's laws and thereby learning not to live against their grain. Understanding this, resolves the problem of evil. Evil is merely the marker that we have not yet done this, it is simply our ignorance and mistakes, but as these are necessary on a free path of discovery towards perfection, God's character is vindicated as perfect, both almighty and good. Nature's laws reflect the

---

[22] *Collected Works* 3, 180.

mind of God and therefore God himself is to be discovered through investigation and experience. To discover how the universe is ordered is to know the Almighty and to hear divine thoughts. The task of theologians should be collating and interpreting what human beings are progressively learning about the nature of God through their explorations of the world and personal experience.

In terms of the implications for a doctrine of Scripture, Nightingale argues unequivocally that there is no such thing as special or supernatural revelation. She explicitly ruled out the notion that the Bible is a divine revelation:

> There have been three parties—those who have said that there was a revelation through the book; those who have said that there was a revelation through the Church, or through the book and the Church; and those who have said that there was no revelation at all. Now we say that there is a revelation to everyone, through the exercise of his own nature—that God is always revealing Himself.[23]

In the very dedication page of the first volume, Nightingale averred that although Moses and Paul presented their teaching as 'miraculously revealed truth', they were simply wrong about this: everything we know of God we know by discovery and experience.[24] Those who believe that the Bible is a special revelation she dismisses as 'bibliolaters'.[25] In order to drive home that the Scriptures have no such status, Nightingale repeatedly claims that specific texts are wrongheaded. Far from highlighting only trivial discrepancies, Nightingale attacks the most cherished portions of the Bible in the most uncompromising of language. The Psalms present such an unworthy portrait of the Almighty that, in our age, only a lunatic should be able to recite them as expressing their own convictions: 'Is it as extraordinary that a man should think himself a teapot as that we should think God like this?'[26] The Ten Commandments are full of mistakes. Nor are these structural flaws confined to the Hebrew Scriptures: 'in the few times when God is said to have spoken in the New Testament, it does not appear that He said anything

---

[23] Michael D. Calabria and Janet A. Macrae (eds), *'Suggestions for Thought' by Florence Nightingale: Selections and Commentaries* (Philadelphia: University of Pennsylvania Press, 1994, [hereafter *Suggestions*]), 24–5. (At the time of writing, the volume in the *Collected Works* that contains *Suggestions for Thought* had not been published.)

[24] *Suggestions*, [4].   [25] *Suggestions*, 29.   [26] *Suggestions*, 9.

very inspiring.'[27] The God of the epistles calls on people to submit to oppression, but we now know that the Almighty would have us struggle for freedom. Even the heart of Christ's teaching, the Sermon on the Mount, is often misguided: it is certainly bad advice to take no thought for tomorrow. As for the Lord's Prayer, 'there is hardly a word of exact truth' in it.[28] While many theological liberals would concede that the Bible was wrong on history and science, they usually defended as truthful its portrait of God: in 1859, however, Nightingale argued that a fundamental mistake about the nature of God 'reigns throughout the whole Bible'.[29] Still, the Bible is not to be scorned. It is one of a number of books that we have which contain 'man's noble attempts (up to the present time) in the course of his development, to understand God'.[30] Therefore: 'Much is to be learnt from the Bible, and probably from all books which have been accepted by large portions of mankind as inspired; but man's capabilities of observation, thought, and feeling exercised on the universe, past, present, and to come, are the source of religious knowledge.'[31]

Year after year, Nightingale enthused about this scheme. While her advisers convinced her that *Suggestions for Thought* was in too repetitive, disorganized, and elusive a form to be published without substantial editing and revision (for which task she lacked the will), in 1873 Nightingale was able to put a *précis* of it before the public in two articles in *Fraser's Magazine*.[32] Her ongoing conversation with Jowett returned again and again to her desire that the Oxford don would take up the task of offering a theological system himself. Nightingale repeatedly complains that the preachers and theologians of her day are not investigating the nature of God, by which she means making progress by concentrating on what can be learned by natural revelation. She insists that studying such mundane matters as the prevention of diseases, mechanical principles of locomotion, and irrigation will generate the mind of God. This theological monomania is vital for the subject under consideration, as whenever Nightingale is speaking in this mode the obvious implication is that the Bible has no vital or clear place in the search for God and his ways. Jowett gently tried

---

[27] *Suggestions*, 14.   [28] *Suggestions*, 85.
[29] *Collected Works* 3, 363.   [30] *Suggestions*, 22.
[31] *Suggestions*, 126.
[32] These can be found in *Collected Works* 3, 9–55.

to indicate that he was not sure that the road from observation of nature to Nightingale's theological convictions was as smooth as she imagined:

> When you admit that a part of the witness of the character of God is to be sought for in nature, how do you distinguish between the true and false witness of nature? For we cannot deny that physical good is sometimes at variance with moral—*e.g.* in marriage the sole or chief principle ought to be health and strength in the parents whether with or without a marriage ceremony—in other words Plato's Republic: I mean on physical principles. Or again the laws of physical improvement would require that we should get rid of sickly and deformed infants. And if, as Huxley would say, you reconstruct the world on a physical basis, you have to go to war with received principles of morality.[33]

Nightingale replied that she was 'quite scandalized' by his 'materialism' and reminded him that human beings have immortal souls.[34] This was to beg the question: Jowett's point was that he was not convinced that a study of nature would unambiguously reveal that human beings had souls and therefore perhaps she was too sanguine about this method. Jowett's concern is underlined by the fact that in her first *Fraser's Magazine* article Nightingale gave a rare and unfortunate example of what she meant: 'contagion' (that is, germ theory) cannot be true as it would reveal that God is not a God of love.[35] It was fashionable in the mid-Victorian period to argue that the religious argument had reached the point at which people had to believe either less or more: that a deistic view was discredited and therefore people needed to move on to more thoroughgoing positions on the poles such as atheism or Roman Catholicism. In such a climate, one can perhaps see Florence Nightingale as the last latitudinarian.[36]

Nightingale's scheme and own convictions also entailed the sweeping away or radical reinterpretation of numerous traditional Christian beliefs. There is no such thing as miracles—that would be God breaking his own laws. Likewise, there is no place for petitionary prayer—God's laws will unfold what is for the best without deviation and without being at the whim of whether or not someone asks for something. The Almighty does not

---

[33] Benjamin Jowett to Florence Nightingale, 29 September 1871: Cook, *Nightingale*, II, 223.

[34] Florence Nightingale to Benjamin Jowett, 3 October 1871: Cook, *Nightingale*, II, 224.

[35] *Collected Works* 3, 25.

[36] On the other hand, an attempt has been made to see Nightingale as a liberation theologian before her time and to appropriate her religious thought for today: Val Webb, *Florence Nightingale: the Making of a Radical Theologian* (St Louis: Chalice Press, 2002).

intervene to offer special providences or judgments: 'God does *not* send me a toothache to punish me for telling a lie.'[37] Indeed, when Nightingale really had the bit between her teeth she even averred that God does not forgive or show mercy as both of these are a kind of tinkering with the orderly unfolding of law by muting its effects. There is no eternal punishment—God's plan is ultimately to bring everyone to perfection (in other words, she was a Universalist). In 1856, Nightingale observed that the current theological debate about everlasting punishment was in a muddle because it was centred on the question, 'is it in the Bible?', when people ought to be asking whether or not it was compatible with the nature of God.[38] Throughout her adult life, Nightingale returned to her insight that hell is a name for things that are experienced in this life, not the next.

Nor did she believe in a traditional doctrine of the deity of Christ: 'We too think him divine as all men are divine'.[39] Indeed, not only was Jesus not God proper, but he even had a wrong view of the Almighty: 'Certainly Christ's was not the God of Law.'[40] Nightingale recognized that her Christology was lower than that of even the standard Unitarian view in her day which affirmed that Jesus was a 'perfect man'.[41] The most expansive claim she could make for him was that Jesus was 'the greatest genius in spiritual things that ever was'.[42] The term 'genius' is significant. On another occasion, her tribute was that 'Christ was as great a discoverer as Newton'.[43] A scientist does not get the final word on their area of study, but they can make more progress in the advance of knowledge than anyone else has ever done in a single life. Jesus is the same in the spiritual realm: his religious thoughts are not always correct, let alone the last word on who God is, but one can still recognize that no other life ever advanced human knowledge in this field as much as his did. At a different time, Nightingale was less definitive: Christ 'probably knew God, felt God, that is, understood more, or rather *felt* more of the character of God, than any person who has ever lived.'[44] The word 'probably' speaks volumes regarding how

---

[37] *Collected Works* 3, 375.   [38] *Collected Works* 3, 356.
[39] *Suggestions*, 30.   [40] *Suggestions*, 53.
[41] *Suggestions*, 131–2.   [42] *Collected Works* 3, 172–3.
[43] *Collected Works* 3, 362.   [44] *Collected Works* 2, 337.

differently her thoughts about Christology were from those of most Victorian Christians, whatever their denominational stripe. Nightingale's rejection of miracles also meant a view of the life of Jesus that removed
everything miraculous from the Virgin Birth onwards. His alleged bodily
resurrection is not even worth serious contemplation: 'It is such a poor tale,
so evidently put together afterwards.'[45] In the same way that Nightingale
continued to allow language about the divinity of Christ as it expressed a
general truth about all human nature, so she tolerated Trinitarian language
as bearing witness to the reality that human beings and the Almighty are
interrelated. Here is an attempt to articulate what Nightingale appears to
have believed about the Trinity: the 'Father' is a name we use to refer to
God proper; the 'Son' is a name we use in recognition of the divine quality
in other human beings; and the 'Holy Spirit' is a name we can give to the
divine impulses we discern within ourselves.

Florence Nightingale was a theological liberal rather than a religious
sceptic for three reasons. First, she had clear, unwavering, lifelong religious
convictions, notably regarding the existence of a good, perfect, Almighty
God and the reality of a future life after death. Secondly, her focus was on
proclaiming religious truth rather than debunking religious error and she
therefore viewed the iconoclasm of offering concerted attacks on traditional
ideas such as a belief in miracles as misspent energy. Thirdly, her own
instinct was to level up rather than down. This can be witnessed in her
handling of a wide range of beliefs. For example, a rejection of the traditional doctrine of the incarnation did not mean for her (as it would a
religious sceptic) that there is no such thing, but rather that 'God is incarnate
in *every* man.'[46] Nightingale rejected the doctrine of substitutionary atonement, but affirmed the truth of Christ's work on the cross in the sense that
'*God* does hang on the cross *every day* in *every one* of us.'[47] Most germane,
already in 1847 she was making this move with her doctrine of Scripture,
reflecting on the spiritual insights offered by Michelangelo's paintings in the
Sistine Chapel: 'I feel these things to be part of the word of God, of the
ladder to Heaven. The word of God is all by which He reveals His thought,
all by which He makes a manifestation of Himself to men. It is not to be
narrowed and confined to one book.'[48]

---

[45] *Collected Works* 3, 189.   [46] *Suggestions*, 13.
[47] *Collected Works* 3, 369.   [48] Cook, *Nightingale*, I, 72.

In addition to being a theological liberal, Nightingale also held Broad Church convictions. Again and again she was vexed by attempts to force advanced thinkers out of the Church of England. She became so inflamed in 1853 by the attacks on F. D. Maurice's right to hold his views as a clergyman that she wrote, and almost submitted to the *Westminster Review*, an article defending his position, but pulled back in the end: 'I reflected that it was only dragging truth out of her hiding place to betray her (to people who could not understand her)'.[49] Given their budding friendship, it is perhaps not surprising that she contributed her money (but not her name) to the Jowett defence fund. More tellingly, she did the same for Colenso, despite disliking his iconoclastic approach. Jesus, she insisted, would have taken the Broad Church view of the matter: 'For certainly Christ would not have . . . excommunicated Bishop Colenso'.[50] Theological liberals must not imagine that the honourable course was for them to leave the Church of England. Her advice was: 'Stick to the church till you are turned out.'[51] If liberals were to decide they could not stay in, this would just doom the Church to never make any progress: 'Would it not be a higher thing to do, if they endeavoured to "educate" the national church, that is to stretch and modify her "creeds," "formularies" and forms of worship and bring them up to the thoughts of the day?'[52] Liberals should not see this as a dishonest position: no one believes everything in the Prayer Book so it would make just as much sense for the liberals to demand that high church or evangelical Anglicans leave the church as the other way around. Nightingale, of course, set a good example by never leaving the church herself.

As the reader will suspect—if a play on a double meaning may be forgiven—although Nightingale took the Bible out of her system, she could not get it out of her system. To back track a bit, it is worth observing her road to nursing. Nightingale's family was wealthy and socially well connected. She first felt the desire to be a nurse as a girl, but her family was opposed to her pursuing what was then widely perceived to be an unsuitable vocation for a lady. Nightingale's twenties were wasted years in which family opposition thwarted her calling. At least in retrospect, Nightingale came to understand this struggle through the lens of Jesus'

[49] *Collected Works* 3, 357.   [50] *Collected Works* 3, 352.
[51] *Collected Works* 3, 235.   [52] *Collected Works* 3, 621.

need to pursue his God-given work: 'Christ's whole life was a war against the family. From a child, *he* said he must be about his Father's business' (Luke 2: 49).[53] In *Suggestions for Thought*, Nightingale becomes a narrative preacher expounding another text to make this same point:

> Christ was saying something to the people one day, which interested Him very much, and interested them very much; and Mary and his brothers came in the middle of it, and wanted to interrupt Him, and take Him home to dinner, very likely—(how natural that story is! does it not speak more home than any historic evidences of the Gospel's reality?), and He, instead of being angry with their interruption of Him in such an important work for some trifling thing, answers, 'Who is my mother? And who are my brethren? Whosoever shall do the will of my Father which is in heaven, the same is my brother and sister and mother.'[54]

Nightingale was able to spend some time at a Protestant experiment in nursing at Kaiserwerth in 1850 (a scheme that included Bible classes in its training programme). Finally, her parents agreed that she could take a nursing position and in 1853 Florence Nightingale became the superintendent of the Institute for Sick Governesses in Distressed Circumstances in London. In the following year came the Crimean War. Sidney Herbert, whom Nightingale had met on a trip to Rome, was the secretary at war. He asked her to organize a group of nurses to tend to soldiers who were ill or wounded. Nightingale became not only a ministering angel to the troops, but also a whirlwind of organization and advocacy in the face of bureaucratic inefficiency and incompetence. Although her religious system was already formulated, Nightingale could not help but view these momentous times through biblical narratives. Less than two weeks after she arrived, she reported in a letter: 'in the midst of this appalling Horror (we are steeped up to our necks in blood) there is good, and I can truly say, like St Peter, "It is good for us to be here"' (Matthew 17: 4).[55] After she had been with the military hospital for a year, she was seeing herself and people around her as manifestations of biblical types: 'War makes Deborahs and Absaloms and Achitophels'.[56] Notes that Nightingale apparently wrote shortly after the war continually draw on Scripture to express the depths of her reactions:

---

[53] *Collected Works* 3, 147. (From an unpublished essay or sermon dated 31 December 1870.)
[54] *Suggestions*, 30. (Her text may be found in Matthew 12 or Mark 3.)
[55] Florence Nightingale to Dr Bowman, 14 November 1854: Cook, *Nightingale*, I, 184.
[56] Florence Nightingale to Charles Bracebridge, 4 November 1855: Cook, *Nightingale*, I, 306.

Surely this is the age of cant. . . . Is not this the most hopeless state of all, the sin against the Holy Ghost? [Matthew 12: 31] . . . We are tired of hearing of the Crimean catastrophe. . . . Our men were 'led as sheep to the slaughter and as a lamb before her shearers is dumb, so they opened not their mouths.' [Isaiah 53: 7] . . . Christ has shown, in strong language, the state of the scribes and Pharisees. . . . Moses arose to lead an enslaved race, but we have had no Moses. . . . two or three 'have borne the griefs and carried the sorrows of all and the Lord has laid upon them the iniquity of all.' [Isaiah 53: 4, 6] . . . If no one is found, will not the decline of this nation begin? My God, my God, why hast Thou forsaken us? [Mark 15: 34][57]

Looking back on her Crimean days, Nightingale would recall the incompetent care given to the wounded under the supervision of another party of nurses: 'The patients were grimed with dirt, infected with vermin, with bed sores like Lazarus' (Luke 16: 20).[58] In 1871, she recollected in a letter to Jowett: 'I have seen a crisis in a campaign, when 30,000 men were dying like flies for want of necessaries of life. And it was not known whether tomorrow this exhausted host would not be like the Assyrians, all "dead men," and not from the stroke of the enemy' (cf. 2 Kings 19: 35).[59]

A few general examples will suffice of how Nightingale spouted biblical texts in the most gratuitous of ways. In an article published in *Good Words* in 1879 she reminisced about the splendour of an Egyptian sunset, comparing it to 'the gold and jewels and precious stones of the Revelations' (Revelation 21).[60] When Nightingale's mother died in 1880, she quoted Ezekiel 24: 18, a rather obscure corner of the Bible, in order to understand her situation.[61] On the other hand, the death of Crown Prince Rudolf of Austria in 1889 seems a little too remote from Nightingale's own life to have prompted her citation of Lamentations 1: 12.[62] Arthur Clough's death in 1861 warranted a use of the Jonathan biblical reference that she had used as a child to express the depth of her friendship with her cousin. When her sister was ill in 1888, Nightingale wrote her a letter of consolation which was essentially a sermon or sustained commentary on the text Joshua 1: 9.[63] When the *Tasmania* was shipwrecked with a party of nurses on board in

[57] *Collected Works* 2, 391–5.
[58] Bostridge, *Nightingale*, 296.
[59] Florence Nightingale to Benjamin Jowett, 7 August 1871: *Collected Works* 3, 537.
[60] Cook, *Nightingale*, I, 87.
[61] Cook, *Nightingale*, II, 323.
[62] Florence Nightingale to her sister, 3 February 1889: *Collected Works* 2, 391–5.
[63] Florence Nightingale to her sister, 21 October 1888: *Collected Works* 1, 388–90.

1887, Nightingale saw the whole adventure through the template of the apostle Paul's experience in Acts 27–8.[64] Nightingale's nickname for vegetarians was 'Nebuchadnezzars', after the scriptural account of the king of Babylon who went mad and ate grass like an ox (Daniel 4: 33). In 1892, this is how Nightingale described her harried life to her nephew: 'What with Bishop, Board of Guardians, County Council, Privy Council, we are compassed round with wild bulls of Bashan' (Psalm 22: 12).[65] In that same year, she had this rather eccentric and forceful response to Princess Christian's support for the registration of nurses, a scheme that Nightingale opposed: 'She is made a tool of by two or three people. "Lift up your heads, ye gates, and the King of Glory shall come in. Who is the King of Glory? The Lord strong in battle"' (Psalm 24: 7–8).[66]

More substantively, Nightingale was an inveterate proof-texter. That is to say, if a Scripture verse expressed the view she was advocating she would quote it triumphantly. This practice sits uneasily with her insistence that the Bible is not an authority. Here are but a few of the numerous examples from even the least likely place, *Suggestions for Thought*, of this habit. Her assumption that the Almighty does not intervene in the orderly unfolding of natural laws is bolstered by the description of God in James 1: 17 as 'the Father of lights, with whom is no variableness nor shadow of turning' and of Jesus Christ as the same 'yesterday, today, and forever' (Hebrews 13: 8).[67] The fact that we discover God through the steady witness of nature rather than miraculous interventions is indicated by Elijah's learning that God was not to be found in dramatic events such as an earthquake but rather as a 'still small voice' (1 Kings 19: 12).[68] The biblical title for the Almighty as 'the most high God' Nightingale cites as warrant for rejecting any view of God (even one presented in the Bible) which is not deemed worthy of a perfect being.[69] Nightingale continued this practice throughout her life. Here is a random example:

> There is nothing very inspiring in denying the miracles; there is nothing very inspiring in denying the resurrection; there is nothing very inspiring in pooh-poohing the first chapter of Genesis. Let all that settle itself: 'let the dead

[64] *Collected Works* 3, 220.
[65] Florence Nightingale to Edmund Verney, 27 November 1892: *Collected Works* 3, 507.
[66] Cook, *Nightingale*, II, 363.
[67] *Suggestions*, 42, 56.
[68] *Suggestions*, 49.   [69] *Suggestions*, 49.

past bury its dead' [Matthew 8: 22]. Let us teach first the perfect God and 'all these things will be added unto' [Matthew 6: 33] us, that is, will be made plain of themselves.[70]

At times, she seems to forget her scheme enough to imagine that biblical data is a trump card. In 1871, she wrote: ' "Resignation" disappears as equally untrue in word and in feeling. N.B. It is a word never used in the Bible.'[71] In 1889, Nightingale offered this argument against the claims of Roman Catholic ecclesiology: 'In the New Testament, in the epistles of St Paul, the word translated church is simply, in the meaning it there bears, properly translated congregation.'[72]

As a theological liberal, Florence Nightingale also wrote sermons. Not only did she assume that a sermon should be an exposition of a biblical text (though her scheme would seem to call this into question) but, in good biblicist fashion, she often took the very title of the sermon from the text. 'Be Ye Perfect' (Matthew 5: 48) and 'Lord, to Whom Shall We Go' (John 6: 68) being two examples. This habit even spilt into her secular discourses. Nightingale entitled her defence of Lord Ripon's Bengal Land Tenure Bill, *The Dumb shall speak, and the Deaf shall hear* (Mark 7: 37). A particularly eccentric example is when she lectured her nurses on the proper way to dress for work by giving a four-point exposition from the text in which Christ admonishes his hearers to consider how God clothes the flowers of the field (Matthew 6: 28). Nightingale's homily perhaps has to be read to be believed, but a fragment might evoke it: 'Even when our clothes are getting rather old we may imitate the flower: for we may make them look as fresh as a daisy.'[73]

In a note written in 1894 Nightingale reflected that her scheme had been procrustean and apparently blamed this on the influence of Aunt Mai: 'She took away religion and gave me nothing but logic instead. She took away prayer and gave me nothing but *law* instead. Religion is not logic (M Mohl).'[74] This correction must not be overread either: it is primarily devotional rather than doctrinal. Nightingale continued to hold throughout her life her critiques of traditional views on miracles, the deity of Christ, the resurrection, the authority of Scripture, and the like. Nevertheless, her rich

---

[70] *Collected Works* 2, p. 345.   [71] *Collected Works* 2, p. 341.
[72] *Collected Works* 3, pp. 328–9.   [73] Cook, *Nightingale*, II, p. 267.
[74] *Collected Works* 2, p. 537.

and fervent inner, spiritual life was given more freedom to be itself. She had always had an undeistic sense that she was hearing specific, personal words from the Lord. She returned to the practice of petitionary prayer. She also cried out to the Lord day and night without worrying about pedantic notions regarding the inappropriateness of forgiveness and mercy.

This less schematized stance also seems to have sat better with her lifelong, deep, experiential appreciation of the power of the Bible to offer comfort, guidance, insight, and edification. In a particularly striking continuity in her life, her letters to her brother-in-law, Sir Harry Verney, when she was 68 years old, are reminiscent of her juvenile missives which also launched rather promptly and abruptly into biblical discussions. A letter to Sir Harry on 18 January 1889 began: 'Your letters are very precious to me. How often I think of those first two verses of Romans 12'; another a few weeks later opened thus: 'I hope you are very good. I am so fond of the last half of Jude'.[75] There were a handful of scriptural texts that Nightingale built her own life upon: she quoted them to herself and others in season and out of season decade after decade. The most important of these was Luke 1: 38. Christiana de Groot, in a recent study of Nightingale's annotated Bible, claims that 'Nightingale never identifies with the female characters in Scripture...Joseph is the only character in Scripture with whom she identifies.'[76] This observation does not hold true once a larger primary source base is brought into view. In fact, Nightingale identified profoundly with the Virgin Mary from when she was a teenager onwards. Florence Nightingale testified for the rest of her life to a divine call to service she received on 7 February 1837. It would seem that her immediate response was that of Mary: 'Behold the handmaid of the Lord; be it unto me according to thy word.' (Luke 1: 38) Certainly, this text quickly became identified with her call. In 1846, she confessed that she recited this text every morning as a prayer of dedication.[77] Nightingale quotes it during her Crimean work, when explaining the vocation of nursing, and in numerous other contexts. She commemorated the anniversary of her call by citing this text in her journal. The last journal entry dated 7 February which has

[75] Florence Nightingale to Sir Harry Verney, 18 January 1889, 3 February 1889: *Collected Works* 3, 415, 417.

[76] Christiana de Groot, 'Florence Nightingale: A Mother to Many', in Christiana de Groot and Marion Ann Taylor (eds), *Recovering Nineteenth-Century Women Interpreters of the Bible* (Atlanta: Society of Biblical Literature, 2007), 117–33 (here 130–1).

[77] Florence Nightingale to Hannah Nicholson, 24 September 1846: *Collected Works* 3, 349.

survived is from 1892 (Nightingale's 72nd year) and it contains the words, 'Behold the handmaid of the Lord'.[78] Florence Nightingale found a spiritual meaning in the notion of the Virgin Birth. In this reading, it refers to the truth that celibates can have more influence over people for good than their natural parents. Therefore, Nightingale was fond of having the appellation 'mother' applied to herself: in her levelling-up sort of way, she was the Blessed Virgin.[79]

It was Nightingale's custom throughout her adult life to read her Bible on a daily basis in private. As the head of her own household, she also gathered her servants together and read a passage from the Bible to them every day at morning prayers.[80] She often gave away Bibles as gifts, valued her father's Greek New Testament when he died, praised Catherine Marsh, who distributed Bibles to the soldiers in the Crimea, and the work of Bible women, and donated money to the British Army Scripture Readers. While some other nursing programmes at the time did not, Nightingale even required Bible classes as a part of her nurses' training. Progress reports were required on each probationer's Scripture reading.[81] Nightingale had some-times taught these Bible classes personally and was pleased to report that the women accepted them whatever their denominational identity.[82] It is worth emphasizing how at odds these practices are with her formal theological scheme. In that mode, she would ridicule the place the Bible had in many Christians' thinking by asking them to imagine a scientist treating a book written in his or her discipline in the same way: when Aristotle's writings on mechanics were read as the final word on the subject all progress ended.[83] Again, this argument is belied by her devotional practices. Precisely because scientists do not think this way, they therefore do not dutifully read selections from Aristotle every morning.

Nightingale read with interest modern biblical criticism and formally accepted its findings: 'Long since, the German philologists have proved that we have not a line of Hebrew of the time of Moses, that the Pentateuch was written partly by a priest in the time of Solomon, partly later.'[84] She

---

[78] *Collected Works* 2, 516.
[79] *Collected Works* 3, 526–7.
[80] *Collected Works* 1, 703.
[81] Cook, *Nightingale*, II, 249.
[82] *Collected Works* 3, 337.
[83] *Suggestions*, 126.
[84] *Collected Works* 3, 368.

seemed to pride herself in not flinching at any of this. When he father asked
her in 1865, 'Where are the words of Christ to be found?', she replied rather
breezily 'nowhere', as if she could not imagine someone making a fuss about
this realization.[85] On the other hand, she continued to assert that Christ had
said something and then quote from the Gospels—and someone else tam-
pering with a text she cherished could rattle her. When the revised English
translation of the Bible excised a line she often used as a prayer her
devotional self trumped her critical self: 'in St Paul's conversion, they
have omitted those memorable words which have saved so many: "Lord,
what wilt Thou have me to do?"' (Acts 9: 6).[86]

Florence Nightingale's varied response to the contents of the Bible—
from contemptuous dismissal of some passages to clinging tenaciously to
others as sources of comfort and insight—was put on display in 1871 when
Jowett asked for her advice on the editing of *The School and Children's Bible*.
This was essentially a plan for a bowdlerized Bible. Nightingale responded
to a rough draft and thereby worked her way through the canon commenting on whether biblical passages should be removed, retained, or reinstated.
Her comments are informed by the latest theories in German biblical
criticism. She repeatedly refers to the work of a contemporary who was a
leading Old Testament scholar, Heinrich Ewald. Nightingale's handling of
Isaiah is a particularly dramatic example of this influence. The latest critical
theory was that it was not the work of a single author, but rather it was a
combination of material from more than one time period. Nightingale
found this insight so important that she ideally wanted Isaiah chapters
40–66 to be broken off from the rest and placed further down the list of
books where it would be surrounded by other post-exilic documents.
Recognizing that this was probably too radical a plan, her compromise
was that it be clearly set off under a separate heading announcing the new
context (a change that was indeed included in the published volume).[87]
Nightingale's recommended omissions are often motivated by a flat disapproval, with her conviction that the Bible should not be singled out as a
superior book in the library of human achievements to the fore:

> The story of Achilles and his horses is far more fit for children than that of
> Balaam and his ass, which is only fit to be told to asses . . . Yet we give all these

[85] Florence Nightingale to her father, 3 January 1865: *Collected Works* 3, 376.
[86] Florence Nightingale to Edmund Verney, 10 March 1897: *Collected Works* 1, 697.
[87] *Collected Works* 3, 557.

stories to children as 'Holy Writ'. There are some things in Homer we might better call '*holy*' writ, many many in Sophocles and Aeschylus. The stories about Andromache and Antigone are worth all the women in the Old Testament put together, nay, almost all the women in the Bible.[88]

Nightingale calls for numerous specific passages to be excised with pithy rationales such as 'nasty story', 'nothing moral in it', and 'not very edifying'.

On the other hand, Nightingale wanted passages reinstated when a spiritualized reading of them had given her inner strength, even when they contained miraculous elements which probably would have made them doomed to go in the eyes of most deists. She recommends (unsuccessfully) that Numbers 9: 15–23, which describes how the Israelites were supernaturally guided in the wilderness, be reinstated. In her twenties, Nightingale can be witnessed gaining spiritual nourishment from this text: 'in the night He always shines a brighter fire, while in the prosperous day he appears to us often only as a cloud, *now* as He did of old.'[89] Jonah had been removed as well and Nightingale also failed to have it restored. She wanted the whole book back, but for readers to view it as 'a prophetic saga'.

Perhaps the best source for understanding Florence Nightingale's varied reactions to the content of the Scriptures is her own Bible, which she was in the habit of annotating. Indeed, it was an edition especially designed for this purpose with blank sheets interspersed between the pages of text. It was not her standard practice to date a comment, but she occasionally did so if prompted by a connection between the text and the events of her life. These dates range from 1844 through 1875. Another Bible, given to her in 1892, has a note dated 1895. These notes are written in seven different languages: English, German, French, Italian, Latin, Greek, and Hebrew. Some of Nightingale's remarks reflect her acceptance of critical scholarship. For example, her banner comment on the book of Daniel is: 'Bears traces of the ages of Antiochus Epiphanes.'[90] She is willing to reject texts as well, approving of Luke 11: 29–30, for instance, at the expense of Matthew's version, which foreshadows the resurrection:

> Entirely spoiled by Matthew 12: 40. Here he says, when required to work a miracle to show his divine mission (what seems almost too bold even for the nineteenth century), 'Does this perverse generation ask for a sign? No other

---

[88] *Collected Works* 3, 557.
[89] Florence Nightingale to Hilary Bonham Carter, 14 August 1846: *Collected Works* 1, 438.
[90] *Collected Works* 2, 223.

sign shall be given it than that of Jonah. As Jonah (by his preaching) has been a sign to Nineveh, so the Son of Man shall be a sign (by his preaching) to men of this generation.' This last phrase is suppressed by Matthew and a contradiction substituted.[91]

More of her comments, however, revolve around her finding biblical warrant for her liberal theological convictions. Psalm 18: 5, in which (according to the inscription) King David describes a troubled time in his life with the words, 'the sorrows of hell compassed me about', delighting her as confirming her own naturalized view, and she observed: 'This world is hell. 27 October 1862'.[92] Recurringly, her comments provide a naturalized interpretation for texts which traditionally have been read as making a supernatural claim. For example, at Acts 2: 22, she wrote: 'Miracles considered in the New Testament merely as *signs*.'[93] The most sustained intellectual pursuit of Nightingale's in the notes is an attempt to discover who Christ is—or (not necessarily the same thing for her) who various biblical authors thought him to be. She was deeply interested in what titles used for the Almighty or angelic beings in the Hebrew Scriptures were also applied to the Christ by Old Testament prophets or New Testament writers. Here is one of numerous such remarks, this one at Isaiah 25: 'Does it appear then that Christ was the Adon, Adonai Jehovah and Adonai Elohim?'[94]

Most of Nightingale's Bible notes, however, are devotional ones. A typical response is one of pious application, such as this remark on the psalmist's promise that he will seek the Lord: 'Ah! Strive to be able to say this.'[95] At 2 Kings 6: 12 she exhorted:

> How few, with confidence carry to the throne of Grace the little events of every hour. Yet He who could make Elisha acquainted with every word spoken by the King of Syria in his bedchamber must hear every prayer from ours.[96]

It is possible, of course, that she wrote that before she had worked out her theological scheme, but it is clear that the devotional and critical notes cannot be segregated into separate periods of her life. Indeed, far from these being merely the traces of a naïve youthful spirituality, Nightingale's 1892

---

[91] *Collected Works* 2, 255.   [92] *Collected Works* 2, 255.
[93] *Collected Works* 2, 255.   [94] *Collected Works* 2, 178.
[95] *Collected Works* 2, 141.   [96] *Collected Works* 2, 127.

Bible also includes pious notes of personal application. Perhaps Nightingale's Bible offers a truer picture of the relationship that theological liberal Victorians had with the Bible than the standard published works of the period that usually are the focus of analysis. Published books tend to concentrate on being either critical or devotional, tempting scholars to imagine that these are separate groups of people rather than modes of engagement. For many, the Victorian way was to hold on to the one without letting go of the other.

In conclusion, it is worth observing that Nightingale was herself willing to give the Bible the final word. She wrote to her father in 1870:

> it strikes me that all truth lies between these two: man saying to God, as Samuel did, Lord, here am I [1 Samuel 3: 4], and God saying to man as Christ did, in the storm, Lo it is I, be not afraid. [Matthew 14: 27] ... You see, so far from disliking the biblical language, as you do, I always fall into it. The Bible puts into four words of one syllable what whole sermons cannot say so well. The whole of religion is in God's Lo, it is I, and man's Here am I, Lord.[97]

Nightingale commissioned wall-hangings to be made of various biblical texts and, as a shut-in who spent most of her life in her bedroom, the one that she stared at day after day until her death was one of the divine side of this summary of all religion, Matthew 14: 17. In 1889, Nightingale wrote to Jowett that her entire approach to spirituality was 'the mystical or spiritual religion, as laid down by John's gospel'.[98] Nightingale's religiosity was not orthodox, let alone conventional, but this chapter should serve to prove how wrong F. B. Smith was to assert that it was 'non-Biblical'.[99]

---

[97] Florence Nightingale to her father, 7 May 1870: *Collected Works* 3, 390. (Matthew 14: 27 actually says 'be of good cheer' rather than 'lo' in the Authorized Version. Nightingale was presumably conflating it with Matthew 28: 20 in which Christ says, 'lo, I am with you always'.)

[98] *Collected Works* 3, 330.

[99] F. B. Smith, *Florence Nightingale: Reputation and Power* (New York: St Martin's Press, 1982), 21.

6

Unitarians

Mary Carpenter and the Sacred Writings

Mary Carpenter's wider Victorian reputation rested on her prominent work as a social reformer. The primary focus of these endeavours was the education and care of deprived or delinquent children or youths. She began in the ragged school movement before adding to her chief areas of activity and concern reformatory schools for juvenile delinquents, and then also what she called 'industrial feeding schools'—institutions for children so neglected or deprived that they needed to be given meals in order to make educating them a viable proposition. Carpenter personally founded, direct-ed, and taught in all three types of institutions in Bristol, where she lived. She also came to take a very active interest in education and reform on the subcontinent, and went on four fact-finding tours of India. These frontline experiences both at home and abroad gave her credibility and a national, indeed international, voice as an expert. In the 1850s, her views influenced parliamentary legislation on education and juvenile offenders. In 1867, she even had an interview with the Queen about her work and ideas.[1] Car-penter's views were eagerly sought out by reformers and officials on her tours of Canada and America, as well as India.

Mary Carpenter (1807–77) finds her place in this book as a representative Unitarian, a Dissenting Protestant tradition that rejected the doctrine of the Trinity and the claim that Jesus Christ is God and therefore was considered unorthodox by almost all other Christian bodies. To secure Carpenter's

---

[1] J. Estlin Carpenter, *The Life and Work of Mary Carpenter* (London: Macmillan and Co., 1881), 281.

place as representative, however, requires an excursus on nineteenth-century Unitarianism as there is a lot of fuzziness that needs to be clarified to make good on it. There seems to be a general tendency to assume that the Unitarians are an exception to all general disapprobation applied to the Victorians. One repeatedly runs into sentences along the lines of: except for the Unitarians, people in nineteenth-century Britain did not generally floss their teeth. This is particularly true when it comes to critiques of conservative approaches to the Bible as a few rogue Unitarian laymen who advocated radical views in the 1840s are often inaccurately portrayed as representative.[2] Scholars who have attended to British Unitarianism, however, have uniformly agreed that the tradition was entirely biblicist well into the nineteenth century. Nevertheless, biblical Unitarianism is persistently marginalized, ignored, underrepresented, or minimized because scholars have found it uninteresting, if not an embarrassment.[3] Actually, biblical Unitarianism was the exclusive tradition for over a third of the century and the dominant one for most of the nineteenth century, indeed for most of the Victorian age. A prime example of the obscuring of this reality is Dennis G. Wigmore-Beddoes's monograph *Yesterday's Radicals: A study of the affinity between Unitarianism and Broad Church Anglicanism in the nineteenth century*.[4] Wigmore-Beddoes admitted that there came to be two traditions within nineteenth-century British Unitarianism, a liberal one that emerged in the 1830s while the biblicist one continued, and declared that his book is only interested in tracing the newer, liberal one.[5] Nevertheless, having acknowledged this, he quickly slid into presenting the views of these liberals as simply the position of the Unitarians.[6] Moreover, the relative weighing of these two groups is obscured by a vague, teleological chronology:

---

[2] For example, L. E. Elliott-Binns has an entire section on 'the Unitarian attack' in which the reader is left to assume that the views of Charles Hennell, Charles Bray, and F. W. Newman were representative of 1840s English Unitarian attitudes to the Bible: L. E. Elliott-Binns, *Religion in the Victorian Era* (London: Lutterworth Press, 1946), 151–2.

[3] Throughout this chapter I will follow the standard terminology in the existing, scholarly literature and refer to this wing as 'biblical Unitarianism'. This usage, however, is not intended to imply that liberal Unitarianism was non-biblical. For a source that uses this terminology which is not elsewhere cited in this chapter see, Horton Davies, *Worship and Theology in England: From Watts and Wesley to Martineau, 1690–1990*, vol. 4 (Grand Rapids, Michigan: Eerdmans, 1996 (originally 1961)), 264. (This volume is book two in a three-book series. Book two consists of volumes three and four.)

[4] Dennis G. Wigmore-Beddoes, *Yesterday's Radicals: A study of the affinity between Unitarianism and Broad Church Anglicanism in the Nineteenth Century* (Cambridge: James Clarke, 1971).

[5] Wigmore-Beddoes, *Yesterday's Radicals*, 27.

[6] See, for example, Wigmore-Beddoes, *Yesterday's Radicals*, 49.

At the beginning of the century Unitarians accepted the traditional belief in miracles, the latter being received as an important authentication of the teaching of Jesus. Later, under the influence of Biblical criticism and the knowledge of scientific discoveries, belief in miracles weakened among them, and in spite of some opposition from the less important Biblically-based wing of Unitarianism, finally disappeared by the end of the century.[7]

In order to understand who can best represent nineteenth-century English Unitarianism one needs to know when 'later' is and at what point before 'finally' it emerged as the stronger wing. Again, the answer is, for most of the century, biblical Unitarianism was the more important not the less important wing.

All scholars of English Unitarianism acknowledge that this religious group began the nineteenth century uniformly biblicist. Moreover, they agree in dating the start of the liberal wing to the publication in 1836 of James Martineau's *The Rationale of Religious Inquiry*. Well into the second half of the century, biblical Unitarianism continued to dominate the denominational machinery, most Unitarian journals and newspapers, and most of the local churches. E. M. Wilbur concedes in passing that the *Inquirer* became the one organ expressing the liberal perspective, while the biblicist approach was advanced in the *Christian Reformer*, as well as two journals that did not even appear until the second half of the century, the *Unitarian Herald* (founded in 1861), and the *Christian Life* (founded in 1876).[8] R. K. Webb is a rare scholar who has cared to pinpoint the chronology. He has accurately observed: 'As in the Church of England, the crucial turning came in the 1880s.'[9] In other words, Unitarianism was in line with most of the other major denominations which also accepted in the 1880s, but not before, that the findings of biblical criticism necessitated significant changes to their convictions regarding the Scriptures.[10] While it lost its dominant position in the 1880s, biblical Unitarianism continued even in the last decade of the century. Robert Spears, for example, was a

---

[7] Wigmore-Beddoes, *Yesterday's Radicals*, 57.

[8] Earl Morse Wilbur, *A History of Unitarianism: In Transylvania, England, and America* (Boston: Beacon Press, 1945), 369.

[9] R. K. Webb, 'The Limits of Religious Liberty: Theology and Criticism in Nineteenth-Century England', in Richard J. Helmstadter (ed.), *Freedom and Religion in the Nineteenth Century* (Stanford: Stanford University Press, 1997), 120–49 (here 143).

[10] Willis Glover documents this chronology for Dissent and confirms that at mid-century most Unitarians still rejected modern biblical criticism: Willis B. Glover, *Evangelical Nonconformists and Higher Criticism in the Nineteenth Century* (London: Independent Press, 1954), 43.

prominent Unitarian editor and denominational leader who was still an active influence holding to the biblicist position at his death in 1899.[11]

A focus on biblical Unitarianism arguably would be justifiable simply on the grounds that this is the first work of scholarship to show an interest in this wing of the movement, while the liberal one is highlighted in all the existing secondary sources which purport to treat English Unitarianism generally. It is certainly justifiable on the grounds that biblical Unitarianism was the dominant wing for most of the nineteenth century. Nevertheless, Mary Carpenter is particularly representative as she transcended the biblical-liberal divide, valuing the friendship and writings of ministers on both sides and, in turn, being honoured by them. If forced to choose between the two wings, it is right to identify Carpenter with biblical Unitarianism which was, after all, the dominant tradition throughout her entire lifetime. Her father, Lant Carpenter, LL.D. (1780–1840), was from the generation before the divide. The minister of one of the wealthiest, largest, and most influential Dissenting congregations of his day, Lewin Mead Chapel, Bristol, he had a leading position among Unitarians already at the early date of 1826 as indicated by his being given the honour of delivering the very first anniversary sermon for the British and Foreign Unitarian Association, the new, central, unifying body for Unitarian congregations.[12] Dr Carpenter was a leading champion of Unitarianism and therefore a major articulator of the biblicist perspective. Mary Carpenter revered her father and throughout her entire life was always proud to present her own religious identity as the faith of her father living still. This has led to a mistaken impression that her religious views were old-fashioned in her own day when actually they were typical.

A particular contributing factor to this distorted impression is that a key commentator on Mary Carpenter's life and thought was her friend, Frances Power Cobbe. Cobbe's own religious position was so advanced that she no longer considered herself a Christian, but rather simply a 'Theist'. From this perspective, she found Mary's religious identity too conservative but, of course, this was her view of all Unitarians whether liberal or biblicist. Cobbe clearly hoped to guide Carpenter into becoming a freethinking Theist like herself and, when unsuccessful, she could not resist attributing

---

[11] *Memorials of Robert Spears, 1825–1899* (Belfast: Ulster Unitarian Christian Association, 1903).
[12] Russell Lant Carpenter, *Memoirs of the Life of the Rev. Lant Carpenter, LL.D.* (Bristol: Philip and Evans, 1842), 294.

Mary's continued confidence in her Unitarian Christian faith as a stubborn clinging to an outmoded theological system. In truth, it is readily apparent that Carpenter was not being a conservative obscurantist but rather that she, and not Cobbe, was the true liberal of the two—graciously deflecting the annoying proselytizing of her friend. It is only after having told Cobbe politely in several different ways over the course of many months that she did not want to debate these controversial religious issues with her, that Mary Carpenter was finally reduced to telling her dismissively: 'My views you will find in my Meditations & in my Uncle's Prayer book as well as in my Father's works.'[13] Cobbe therefore hinted that Carpenter's religious thought was a generation behind. The Theist could also be more accurate, however, reporting rightly that Mary's theology was 'a little out of date as representing Free Thought at this end of the century'.[14] As Mary was a Unitarian and not a freethinker and she was born in 1807 and died in 1877, this hardly impinges on her representative status here.

All sources agree that the leading figure in the liberal wing of nineteenth-century English Unitarianism was James Martineau. Lant Carpenter was his schoolmaster and Mary Carpenter and James Martineau were classmates. When Dr Carpenter was ill in 1828, he secured Martineau's help as his assistant, and he offered to make the arrangement a permanent partnership (and therefore establish Martineau as his successor), but the young man decided to make his start elsewhere.[15] A letter has survived from that time in which Mary thanks Martineau for 'your kind & constant endeavours to promote the welfare of our family'.[16] E. M. Wilbur claims that Martineau's *Rationale* (1836) prompted the established biblical Unitarians to regard him as 'a dangerous heretic', but he does not offer any evidence in support of this claim.[17] There is no indication that Lant Carpenter expressed any disappointment or disapproval. Martineau, in turn, throughout his life honoured Dr Carpenter as a wise and effective educator, a serious biblical scholar, and

[13] The Huntington Library, San Marino, California, Frances Power Cobbe Papers, Mary Carpenter to Frances Power Cobbe, 12 September 1859. For the polite refusals, see Mary Carpenter to Frances Power Cobbe, 17 March 1859 and 12 August 1859.

[14] Frances Power Cobbe, 'Personal Recollections of Mary Carpenter', *Modern Review*, 19, 2 (April 1880), 279–300 (here 295–6). This material was reprinted in her autobiography: Frances Power Cobbe, *Life of Frances Power Cobbe, By Herself*, 2 vols (Boston: Houghton, Mifflin and Company, 1894), I, 250–75.

[15] Carpenter, *Lant Carpenter*, 318–19.

[16] Harris Manchester College, Oxford, Carpenter Papers, Mary Carpenter (on behalf of her sisters as well) to James Martineau, 17 June 1828.

[17] Wilbur, *History*, 370.

a leading and able Unitarian thinker and defender. As for Mary Carpenter herself, throughout her life she leaned on James Martineau as the one English Unitarian minister whose religious opinions she valued more than any others beside the members of her own family. They had an unbroken friendship across her entire adult life. When she compiled her devotional book, *Morning and Evening Meditations*, in 1844 (eight years after his *Rationale*), Mary Carpenter successfully solicited material from Martineau, including a specially written piece as well as existing items, and sought his advice on the entire manuscript.[18] When therefore she told Cobbe that her views were contained in her *Meditations* she was referring to a volume that was vetted by the premier liberal Unitarian in England and that included contributions by both biblical and liberal Unitarians (including the colourful and controversial Blanco White). Mary Carpenter and James Martineau continued to write to each other and to arrange to meet as the decades rolled by. When she died, her family naturally chose him to write the inscription for her memorial in Bristol Cathedral.[19] Her favourite nephew, J. Estlin Carpenter, wrote both her reverent Victorian life and letters and an admiring biography of Martineau.[20]

Mary Carpenter's position as someone who belonged to Unitarianism as a whole is underlined by the striking way that she was admired across the Unitarian spectrum in America. Her father had an ongoing pen friendship with the eminent American Unitarian minister, William Ellery Channing, and Mary was deeply impressed with Channing's writings and thought. She wrote to an American friend four years after Channing's death:

> Dr Channing did more than I think any one has done in showing the bearing of [Christianity] on great moral & political questions: but when have the prophets spoken & been heard? But his spirit still breathes in his writings, & will, as it has done awaken many. I have myself seen a new force & truth, & beauty in many of the discourses of our Saviour since my mind has been dwelling much on this subject.[21]

Carpenter had close friendships with a range of American Unitarian ministers, most notably Joseph Tuckerman of Boston and S. J. May of

---

[18] Jo Manton, *Mary Carpenter and the Children of the Streets* (London: Heinemann, 1976), 69.
[19] Carpenter, *Mary Carpenter*, 388.
[20] J. Estlin Carpenter, *James Martineau: Theologian and Teacher* (London: Philip Green, 1905).
[21] Boston Public Library, Boston, Massachusetts, Mary Carpenter Papers, Ms. A.9.2, Vol. 22, No. 107, Mary Carpenter to Mrs Maria (Weston) Chapman, Boston, 31 October 1846.

Syracuse. Most extraordinary for the theme at hand is her admiration of Theodore Parker, a liberal Unitarian notably more advanced than Martineau whom many American Unitarian ministers disowned as a heretic. In 1876 (over fifteen years after Parker's death and the year before Carpenter's own death), the English biblical Unitarian Robert Spears resigned his post with the British and Foreign Unitarian Association because of a plan to republish Parker's works.[22] Mary Carpenter's response to Parker was markedly different. She and Parker carried on a friendly and sympathetic correspondence and the American theologian even had hanging in his study a drawing that Carpenter had done of the garden of Gethsemane.[23] In 1865, while in the midst of reading a life of the late Theodore Parker, Carpenter wrote a letter in which she enthusiastically praised him. She acknowledged in passing that she did not happen to agree with his distinctive advanced religious views, but this was not the germane issue in her mind: 'He was a noble being!'[24] She confessed that, even five years on, thinking of his death still made her 'quite upset', and she could not understand why God would have allowed such a loss to humanity. An 1852 letter of hers to Parker is written from the perspective of one theological liberal to another, looking for sympathy regarding the resistance to her reforming ideas which was rooted in 'the popular theology' that they both rejected.[25] In 1859, she wrote to him: 'You, my dear sir, have carried religion into the dark places of the earth, and have shed its light on the great social evils which others pass by or ignore.'[26] Nor did she admire only his good deeds to the exclusion of his thought and writings. Carpenter was so struck by Parker's sermons on the 'Perishing Classes' and the 'Dangerous Classes', for example, that she incorporated these terms into the very title of one of her most important and influential books, *Reformatory Schools for the Children of the Perishing and Dangerous Classes and for Juvenile Offenders* (1851).[27]

In fact, there is no evidence that Mary Carpenter was ever shocked or offended by anyone's radical religious (or irreligious) opinions. Biblical Unitarians are standardly portrayed as denouncing liberal Unitarians and

---

[22] Webb, 'Limits', 142.

[23] Carpenter, *Mary Carpenter*, 74.

[24] The Huntington Library, San Marino, California, Frances Power Cobbe Papers, Mary Carpenter to Frances Power Cobbe, 15 January 1865.

[25] Carpenter, *Mary Carpenter*, 132.

[26] Carpenter, *Mary Carpenter*, 207.

[27] For the sermons, see Dean Grodzins, *American Heretic: Theodore Parker and Transcendentalism* (Chapel Hill, North Carolina: University of North Carolina Press, 2002), 498.

trying to thwart their influence, but this was certainly not Carpenter's approach. She was not browbeaten into renouncing her religious convictions, but neither was she alarmed or threatened by more liberal ones than her own. This is true not only in her response to more liberal Unitarians, but also freethinkers. Her lifelong friendship with Frances Power Cobbe is itself evidence of this. Likewise, she had an enduring friendship with the American anti-slavery campaigner, William Lloyd Garrison, his freethinking approach to religion notwithstanding. Indeed, her very last letter—written on the day of her death—was to Garrison: she was arranging a reception for him.[28] Far from denouncing him as an enemy of the gospel, in 1848 Carpenter wrote of Garrison: 'I greatly value his friendship, & esteem it a privilege to be personally acquainted with so devoted & earnest a servant of his Lord.'[29] Mary Carpenter even maintained a lifelong friendship with her old classmate, the writer Harriet Martineau, despite Harriet's own brother, the leading liberal Unitarian, James Martineau, of all people, permanently snubbing her because of Harriet's move into freethought.

While this chapter will go on to explore at length the biblical Unitarianism of Mary Carpenter and her father, it is worth demonstrating upfront that this stance did not lead her to denounce or even reject *in toto* the radical findings of modern biblical criticism—assertions to the contrary notwithstanding. Carpenter would have had every reason to see D. F. Strauss's *Leben Jesu* as a direct attack on the stance taken in her father's magnum opus, *An Apostolic Harmony of the Gospels* (second edition, 1838). Instead, when in Schaffhausen in 1842, she reported a view that strikes well the kind of pose that she herself tended to take when it came to such issues: 'This minister thinks that Strauss has done rather more good than harm to religion; for he was merely the echo of a party, and the public expression of what had long been received in private led to much beneficial investigation of the subject.'[30] In 1848, Carpenter even recommended F. W. Newman's radical work, *History of the Hebrew Monarchy*, acknowledging that 'the freest principles of criticism and historical research are applied to the Bible' in it.[31] In

---

[28] [Mary Carpenter], *Voices of the Spirit and Spirit Pictures*, 'For Private Circulation Only' (Bristol: I. Arrowsmith, 1877), pp. xxii–xxiii.

[29] Boston Public Library, Boston, Massachusetts, Mary Carpenter Papers, Ms. A.9.2, Vol. 24, No. 50, Mary Carpenter to Mrs Maria (Weston) Chapman, Boston, 19 March 1848.

[30] Carpenter, *Mary Carpenter*, 59. For English Unitarians and Strauss's *Leben Jesu*, see Timothy Larsen, *Contested Christianity: The Political and Social Contexts of Victorian Theology* (Waco, Texas: Baylor University Press, 2004), 43–58.

[31] Carpenter, *Mary Carpenter*, 97.

particular, Carpenter held to the findings of modern science at the expense of a literal view of the early chapters of the book of Genesis. Here is a conversation with a local man which she reported in a letter in 1847:

> at last he asked me what I thought of the apple with which Eve was tempted. I was sorely perplexed, having the fear of Mr Kenrick, whose *Essay on Primeval History* we are reading, before my eyes; so, fortunately, the bright idea occurred to me to tell him that the whole thing is a sort of parable, to show that in those early times, as now, disobedience was punished by God, and that we can only be happy, now as then, while obedient to God's commands. The good man was quite satisfied.[32]

Kenrick's *Essay* unequivocally declares that it is impossible to find an interpretation of Genesis 1–11 that will square these texts with what modern science has discovered. He consoles his readers with the thought that their faith does not depend on 'the correctness of the opinions which prevailed among the Hebrew people, respecting cosmogony and primaeval history'.[33] In 1865, Carpenter even spoke positively of the highly controversial and widely condemned biblical criticism of John William Colenso, bishop of Natal:

> Dr Colenso has sent me his fifth Part in return for the *Convicts*, I am delighted with the preface and conclusion. I do not mind about the Creation being cut up, and I think in general the light he throws helps one out of difficulties and contradictions which I have felt as well as the Zulus; but I do not mean to read anything against the exquisite narrative of Joseph. I had an hour's chat at Miss Cobbe's with the Bishop, and was *much* delighted with him and his work, to which I am glad he is returning.[34]

This comment so clearly supported Wigmore-Bebboes's championing of the liberal Unitarian position that Mary Carpenter's approval of Colenso's work is the only reference to her in his monograph.[35]

Which, of course, leaves out her primary identity as a biblical Unitarian. It is that which now needs to be uncovered. As Lant Carpenter was a leading spokesperson for this religious identity, and as Mary claimed that her own views could be found in her father's writings, it is worth first taking

---

[32] Carpenter, *Mary Carpenter*, 96.

[33] John Kenrick, *An Essay on Primaeval History* (London: B. Fellowes, 1846).

[34] Carpenter, *Mary Carpenter*, 243. For the controversy over Colenso on the Pentateuch, see Larsen, *Contested Christianity*, 59–77.

[35] Wigmore-Beddoes, *Yesterday's Radicals*, 105.

time to explore his thought. As with Mary, however, before presenting some decidedly conservative views that Dr Carpenter held, it is useful to put on record his liberal impulses, lest the main story be overread. Lant Carpenter recurringly found himself in Unitarian contexts in which he was considered the liberal. At the age of seventeen, he entered Northampton Academy. Here, Arianism was taught (the belief that Jesus was the incarnation of a pre-existent, exalted being who is, nevertheless, not God proper). Lant Carpenter, however, was identified as 'a determined Socinian' (in this context, the germane point of this position is that he believed that Jesus was simply and exclusively a human being who, like all others, did not exist before his earthly life).[36] This conviction was so radical that the trustees eventually took the drastic step of shutting Northampton Academy down for a period in order to keep the liberal, Socinian virus from infecting more students. Likewise, when Lant Carpenter became a minister at the Unitarian chapel in Exeter his pre-existing (if the pun, can be forgiven) co-pastor was 'a moderate Arian', and this was the ethos of the whole congregation, meaning that once again he was the one in advance of the Unitarian pack he was running with.[37]

Moreover, Lant Carpenter's radical views extended even into his beliefs regarding Scripture. Specifically, especially as a young man, he was not convinced of the authority of the Old Testament. He observed in 1801 that the balance of the evidence was against 'the credibility of many of the Pentateuchal narratives.'[38] When in 1807 he published *An Introduction to the Geography of the New Testament*, Carpenter deliberately excluded the Hebrew Scriptures from this work because he was not certain that the historical passages in the Old Testament could be taken as reliable.[39] When he wrote a catechism for Sunday school children in 1812, the answer to the question, 'What book teaches us how to please God?', was: 'The Bible, (and especially the New Testament,) teaches us everything needful about God, and how to please Him.'[40] As this catechism was meant to be the simplest possible text (Carpenter even suggested it was a suitable book to use when teaching a child to read), the perceived need parenthetically to qualify 'the Bible' as too crude an answer is striking. Moreover, while he

---

[36] Carpenter, *Lant Carpenter*, 31.   [37] Carpenter, *Lant Carpenter*, 154.
[38] Carpenter, *Lant Carpenter*, 65.   [39] Carpenter, *Lant Carpenter*, 163.
[40] Lant Carpenter, *An Introductory Catechism* (Boston: Christian Register Office, 1828), 6. (The preface is dated 1812.)

became more confident in the Old Testament as he became older, Lant Carpenter actually became more radical as the years passed when it came to the New Testament canon. In his 1823 work *Unitarianism, the Doctrine of the Gospel*, Dr Carpenter rejected the authority of the anonymous epistle to the Hebrews on the grounds that he did not believe it was written by an apostle.[41] The Gospels were the absolute core of his canon, as will be shown, but even they are not immune to such iconoclastic paring down. In particular, Lant Carpenter claimed that the birth narrative in Matthew's Gospel was not a part of the original, apostolic document and therefore it must be set aside.[42]

Having said all that, Dr Carpenter would not have conceded to any person in nineteenth-century England, whatever their denomination might have been, that they were more biblical than him. Many considered his *magnum opus* to be *An Apostolic Harmony of the Gospels*. He intended it to be, not a work of Unitarian polemics, but rather a volume of use to all (biblical) Christians. In a notable coup for making this claim, Lant Carpenter gained permission from Queen Victoria to dedicate the second edition, published in 1838, to her majesty. A standard challenge to the truthfulness of the gospels is the so-called synoptic problem, that is, apparent discrepancies between parallel accounts in different gospels. A radical response to these discrepancies is to attempt to deny the veracity of even the most basic and prominent events in the story of Jesus' life. A moderate response is to argue that the gospels include trivial inaccuracies, but that these do not overturn the fundamental truthfulness of the events described. Dr Carpenter, however, was pursuing the conservative approach of harmonizing in which one attempts to show that there are no real discrepancies but rather that all the details of the various texts can be retained as part of a unified, meticulously truthful whole. He asserted that his careful scholarship demonstrated 'the reality of it all'.[43] The subject of his book is 'our Saviour's Ministry', which allows him to sidestep the problem of the birth narratives, but the miracles, Jesus' resurrection, and his ascension are all confidently affirmed to be

---

[41] Lant Carpenter, *Unitarianism the Doctrine of the Gospel. A View of the Scriptural Grounds of Unitarianism; with an examination of all the expressions in the New Testament which are generally considered as supporting opposite doctrines*, third edition (Bristol: Parsons and Browne, 1823; facsimile by Kessinger Publishing's Legacy Reprints Series), 424.

[42] Carpenter, *Unitarianism*, 20.

[43] Lant Carpenter, *An Apostolic Harmony of the Gospels*, second edition (London: Longman, Orme, Brown, Green, and Longmans, 1838), p. i.

literal, historical events. Indeed, belying any assumption that Unitarians are the exception to such practices, in a manner reminiscent of Bishop Ussher, Lant Carpenter dates these events in a way that would strike many today as comic in its precision. For example, while one of the first steps towards a critical view would be to argue that the feeding of the 5,000 and the feeding of the 4,000 are actually varying reports of the same event, Lant Carpenter informed his readers that the former happened on 4 March A.D. 30, while the latter happened a week and half later, on 14 March. Moreover, lest anyone should try a naturalizing explanation for what actually happened on these two, distinct occasions, the Unitarian divine explicitly identifies these events as miracles.[44] Conservative readers were particularly grateful for the masterly way in which Dr Carpenter directed traffic at the empty tomb. The ascension took place on 18 May A.D. 30. This might sound so quirky as to lead one to imagine that Dr Carpenter was a Unitarian minority of one, but actually his harmony was widely accepted. The American Unitarian minister and divinity professor at Harvard, John Gorham Palfrey, was so excited about Dr Carpenter's harmony that he used it (with full acknowledgement) as the basis of his own similar publication.[45] Likewise, the eminent Harvard Unitarian divinity professor, Henry Ware, Jr, used Carpenter's harmony as the structure for his *Life of the Saviour*, declaring: 'I have seen cause to vary from it very little. It commends itself by its simplicity and ingenuity.'[46] Moreover, far from Unitarians quickly becoming embarrassed by this, the American Unitarian Association continued to defend the propriety of coming out with new editions of Ware's work that maintained this scheme intact, with the eighth edition of *The Life of the Saviour* appearing as late as 1892.

Most of Lant Carpenter's other works were efforts to defend and expound Unitarian beliefs. The very titles of most of these works betray their thoroughgoing biblicism, including such volumes as *Comparative View of the Scriptural Evidence for Unitarianism and Trinitarianism*; *Unitarianism the Doctrine of the Gospel: A View of the Scriptural Grounds of Unitarianism*; *Proof from Scripture, that God, even the Father, is the only true God, and the only proper*

---

[44] Carpenter, *Apostolic Harmony*, p. clxii.

[45] John Gorham Palfrey, *Harmony of the Gospels* (Boston: Gray and Bowen, 1831).

[46] Henry Ware, Jr, *The Life of the Saviour*, seventh edition (Boston: American Unitarian Association, 1873), 44.

object of Religious Worship; and *The Scripture Doctrine of Redemption, or of Reconciliation, through our Lord Jesus Christ*. Again, far from this being an eccentric approach, Dr Carpenter was walking in a well-established, beloved path exemplified by classic texts cherished by English Unitarians such as Samuel Clarke's *The Scripture Doctrine of the Trinity* (1712) and John Taylor's *The Scripture-doctrine of original sin* (1740).[47]

It is important to emphasize that this was not merely an apologetic tack in which Dr Carpenter was trying to hoist orthodox, conservative Christians with their own petard: he sincerely believed that the Bible was *the* authority for revealed truth—and, as such, that it had to be submitted to rather than evaded even if it said things he would rather not hear. This was how his own, personal belief system worked. Already in 1803, he wrote to a confidant that he was trying to make up his mind regarding an intermediate state for souls after death by weighing the 'Scriptural arguments' as 'others will have little weight with me'.[48] In 1810, Dr Carpenter preached the annual sermon for an organization that gave institutional unity to the denomination, the Unitarian Fund for Promoting Unitarianism. In it, he expressed his conviction that 'the best foundation for Unitarianism is that which is laid on the Scriptures'.[49] A keynote text for Lant Carpenter's ministry was Acts 17: 11 in which the Bereans are praised because they 'searched the scriptures daily, whether those things were so'. A student from his catechism class recalled that 'search the Scriptures' was Dr Carpenter's continuing admonition to them and, indeed, his catechism classes were often pure Bible studies in which scriptural texts were systematically expounded *ad seriatim*. His congregation was also nurtured this way, complete with a sermon 'On the Bereans', and canonically ordered sermon series.[50] This was Lant Carpenter's approach in personal pastoral care as well. One anecdote tells of how when he read Joshua 1: 9 in the course of daily morning household devotions he was struck by how apt this text was for a parishioner who was currently in the midst of some trying circumstances. The minister acted on this impulse and the verse so went home to her that not only did she cherish it the rest of her life, thanking him

---

[47] Samuel Clarke, *The Scripture Doctrine of the Trinity* (London: James Knapton, 1712); John Taylor, *The Scripture-doctrine of original sin proposed to free and candid examination* (London: J. Wilson, 1740).

[48] Carpenter, *Lant Carpenter*, 114.   [49] Carpenter, *Lant Carpenter*, 188.

[50] Carpenter, *Lant Carpenter*, 264–5.

repeatedly for this intervention, but even sent him a message from her deathbed testifying that Joshua 1: 9 was helping her to the very end.[51] Another tells of Dr Carpenter's ministry to a poor Irish (presumably Catholic) woman. He presented her with a New Testament inscribed like a medicine bottle with the following instructions: 'Read or hear daily'.[52]

Nowhere, however, is this approach to spiritual formation more poignant than in his pastoral care for his own eldest child, Mary Carpenter. As a young adult, she confessed to her father that she was tempted by the orthodox Protestant view of the atonement. By this she meant a belief that Jesus died in one's stead in order to pay the price for one's sins and therefore, if appropriated by faith, one was made completely righteous and forgiven in the sight of God on the basis of what Jesus had achieved. Carpenter had a sensitive conscience and longed for such a clean slate. The Unitarian view, however, as articulated by her father, was that the death of Christ was not a payment or substitution. Christ came to declare something that was equally true before his death: namely, that God is merciful. In this scheme, one simply repented and determined to live a future life in which one did not engage in sinful practices and then a merciful God allowed one to go forward in the expectation that this resolve would prove good. Dr Carpenter never denied the allure of the orthodox view; he merely doused it with biblicism:

> I would have you beware of founding any doctrinal opinion on strength of emotion, or on deep conviction of your own unworthiness. The Scriptures are our only guide. . . . If ever you feel such tendencies, my dear child, read Luke I. 77–79. Tit. III. 3., &c. Is. LV. 6–9. Ps. CIII. LI. 17, &c., &c . . . . Keep close to the Scriptures, my child, and they will be a light that will become brighter and brighter unto the perfect day.[53]

Mary Carpenter, of course, was able to resist this temptation and reaffirm biblical Unitarianism: 'I am sorry that my attention has been turned to the doctrine of Atonement, for now when reading the Scriptures I find so many texts strongly against it, that I do not think I can ever again embrace such a doctrine while I keep to the Scriptures.'[54]

---

[51] Carpenter, *Lant Carpenter*, 477–8.
[52] Carpenter, *Lant Carpenter*, 289.
[53] Carpenter, *Lant Carpenter*, 337–8.
[54] Carpenter, *Mary Carpenter*, 14–15.

Indeed, Lant Carpenter was so biblicist that he endearingly confessed that he used to assume as a young man that Trinitarians simply did not take the Scriptures seriously—so obvious was it to him that the Bible teaches Unitarianism—but he came to realize that many orthodox Christians were also biblicists after their fashion.[55] Thus the problem many figures in the nineteenth century faced of accounting for theological diversity despite widespread unity on the authority of Scripture. If Wiseman advocated reading the Bible with the church and Pusey reading it with the church fathers, Dr Carpenter offered the hyper-biblicist solution that the Bible needed to be read *without* the influence of creeds, councils, and church authorities. For example, after quoting part of the second article from the Anglican Thirty-Nine Articles of Religion in which the divine nature of Christ is affirmed, he remarks: 'I look in vain for this doctrine in the Scriptures; and I believe that most others would too, if they had never learnt it from human Creeds and Articles'.[56] In his *Comparative View of the Scriptural Evidence for Unitarianism and Trinitarianism*, parallel columns are set out in which the Unitarian view of various doctrinal questions is pointedly presented purely and exclusively by quoting Scripture, while the orthodox view is presented by quoting creeds.[57] In summing up Lant Carpenter's whole religious life, his biographer-son declared that his father had 'clung to' Unitarianism across the years because it 'seemed the only faith supported by Scripture, unencumbered with tradition'.[58] In this light, Dr Carpenter's rejection of portions of the traditional canon on authorial grounds (most notably the epistle to the Hebrews) actually reveals him being more biblicist, not less. It is precisely because he could not go outside the Bible to another authority that he could not take the canon of Scripture as given but, in good Berean fashion, must search and decide for himself whether or not it really is so. Anglicans, on the other hand, had the canon of biblical books authoritatively listed for them in Article VI.

Once he determined that a text in an epistle or Gospel was really written by an apostle, however, Lant Carpenter believed it was authoritative and he was not free to reject it. This habit can be witnessed throughout his life and writings, but it was put systematically on display in his *Unitarianism, the*

---

[55] Carpenter, *Lant Carpenter*, 56.

[56] Carpenter, *Unitarianism*, 52.

[57] Lant Carpenter, *Comparative View of the Scriptural Evidence for Unitarianism and Trinitarianism*, third edition (London: Rowland Hunter, 1823), 4.

[58] Carpenter, *Lant Carpenter*, 459.

Doctrine of the Gospel, the telling subtitle of which was *A View of the Scriptural Grounds of Unitarianism; with an examination of all the expressions in the New Testament which are generally considered as supporting opposite doctrines*. Dr Carpenter made good on this promise by marching through the New Testament material thoroughly and unflinchingly. A few additional inconvenient texts could be dismissed as interpolations rather than apostolic, but numerous texts remained that were widely read as teaching doctrines that Unitarians rejected. He faced these squarely and patiently and without allowing himself the option of saying the biblical author was in error on this point. For example, he retained the birth narrative from Luke's gospel. He thought it might be read in a way that did not teach the Virgin Birth but argued that it was possible for Unitarians to accept that doctrine, if the Bible told them so, while still maintaining Christ's exclusive humanity. He conceded that the apostle Thomas really did address the risen Jesus with the title 'God', but averred: 'Employing the Jewish idiom, Jesus *was* God, as being a representative of God'.[59] Likewise, he acknowledged the authority of the prologue to John's gospel, and even that 'the Word' is a reference to Jesus, but rather than conceding the traditional, orthodox interpretation in which it is therefore a statement of Christ's pre-existence, he suggested it meant that Christ was there at the beginning as the creator, not of the physical world, but rather of 'this new age'.[60] If some of this sounds like special pleading, Dr Carpenter replied cogently that most texts, taken in their plain sense, support Unitarian doctrine and therefore it is orthodox exegetes who have to generate complicated interpretations for the bulk of the relevant passages. If errors were taught on the grounds that they were scriptural, the solution to this problem, in classic people-of-one-book fashion, was more Bible, not less: 'WE have reason to be thankful, that though men, by a perversion of the language of the Scriptures, have derived these doctrines from them, yet that the same source supplies the antidote also.'[61]

With the various nuances of Dr Carpenter's approach now laid out, it simply remains to present the general principles upon which he based his religious thought. In *Unitarianism, the Doctrine of the Gospel*, he enumerated them thus:

---

[59] Carpenter, *Unitarianism*, 73.   [60] Carpenter, *Unitarianism*, 61–2.
[61] Carpenter, *Unitarianism*, 395.

1. Revealed truth can be found ONLY in the records of Revelation contained in the Scriptures.
2. Revealed truths can never be *inconsistent* with the general tenor of the Scriptures, with each other, or with any truths which can be *proved* from the light of reason.[62]

Likewise Lant Carpenter's *Comparative View of the Scriptural Evidence for Unitarianism and Trinitarianism* concluded with this summative statement:

> Such, in the plain language of Scripture, is the Unitarian's belief. He can admit nothing in opposition to it, because Revelation cannot contradict itself. . . . And he keeps close to the great principle, *The Bible, and the Bible only, is the religion of Protestants.*[63]

In short, Dr Carpenter gloried in Unitarian thought being even more thoroughly biblical than that of other Protestant bodies.

This then is the Unitarian faith that Mary Carpenter received from her father and to which she was proudly faithful unto death. Having expounded the teaching revealed in her father's writings, the obvious work to attend to next is Carpenter's own *Morning and Evening Meditations, For Every Day in A Month,* which she herself commended to Frances Power Cobbe as the way to discover her personal religious views. Indeed, as late as 1872, Carpenter referred to this volume as best revealing her inner spiritual life: 'I do not often like to allude to religion in public, or to those whose spirit I do not know, lest it should be misunderstood; but you will gather from each of my books, especially the *Meditations*, that this has been the moving spring of my life.'[64] Carpenter was the head of her own home for most of her adult life and, as had happened before that in her father's house, everyone gathered together in both the morning and evening for household devotions at which the Bible was read aloud. Among other sources, Cobbe incidentally reveals this in her reminiscences, and even though she emphasized that Carpenter was so busy that she 'did the work of three people'—and sometimes literally did not have time to eat—yet even this freethinking Theist did not question this twice daily priority give to Scripture.[65] Of an

---

[62] Carpenter, *Unitarianism*, 126.

[63] Lant Carpenter, *Comparative View of the Scriptural Evidence for Unitarianism and Trinitarianism*, third edition (London: Rowland Hunter, 1823), 39–40.

[64] Carpenter, *Mary Carpenter*, 311.

[65] Cobbe, 'Recollections', 282–3, 292.

eminent, non-Christian house guest from India, Keshub Chunder Sen, on the other hand, we are told: 'He was most surprised at finding that servants and all assembled before breakfast for morning prayer and reading'.[66] Nevertheless, Carpenter's *Meditations* were not an aid to household worship. Rather, this book was designed for the practice of twice daily personal devotions: 'To assist in the private meditation on the Scriptures... which is the best preparation for secret prayer'.[67] The volume sets out biblical texts with reflections for every morning and evening in a month, including Sundays. In other words, her normative expectation was that a person would read or hear Scripture at least four times a day—even if they never left the house. To this minimum, of course, typically would be added the weekly rhythm of a life of congregational worship, and the reading of Scripture at numerous other public occasions such as weddings and funerals.

Carpenter compiled this volume in 1844, when she was 37 years old. This was four years after the death of her father, to whom it is dedicated.[68] Published anonymously in 1845, *Morning and Evening Meditations, For Every Day in A Month*, to Carpenter's surprise and delight, sold out within a few months. It was published in America and was received even more enthusiastically there. It eventually went through six editions. It is essentially a compilation and Carpenter was primarily an editor. Each entry consists of a biblical text, followed by a reflection, and then an apt poem. Carpenter prided herself on having created an ecumenical devotional manual by including some reflections written by orthodox Christians, but the overwhelming majority of them were written by Unitarians. Indeed, a decisive majority of them were written by Unitarians who were also family members (her father, her brothers Russell Lant and Philip Pearsall Carpenter, and her aunt 'Mrs S. Bache') and her personal friends or friends of the family (most notably, Martineau, Channing, and Tuckerman). Carpenter herself contributed two poems. One of them ends with a poetic rendition of a blend of 1 Corinthians 15: 43 and Romans 8: 17:

---

[66] Carpenter, *Mary Carpenter*, 298.

[67] [Mary Carpenter], *Morning and Evening Meditations, For Every Day in A Month* (Boston: Wm. Crosby and H. P. Nichols, 1847), p. vi (hereafter *Meditations*).

[68] Jo Manton, Mary Carpenter's sole modern or academic biographer, wrongly inferred from the relevant passage in the life by Carpenter's nephew that she had only dedicated it to her father 'secretly' in her journal. This assumption indicates that Manton never even looked at a copy of the *Meditations*. This is a telling example of how the religious thought and writings of such figures has been ignored. Manton, *Carpenter*, 70.

> But *there* the mortal seeds, in weakness sown,
> Shall rise in power and glory, heirs with Christ,
> Glorious partakers with the sons of God![69]

The whole volume is fundamentally biblical. Indeed, there are no titles, but only texts. Thus, 'Index of Prose Meditations' lists them all in their monthly order on the basis of the text from 'Let us search and try our ways.—Lam. iii.40' starting on page 1 (for Sunday morning of the first week) through to 'A cloud received him out of their sight.—Acts i.9' starting on page 212 (for the Saturday evening of the fourth month). Beyond that came various additional material, including texts and reflections for special days ranging from Ascension Day ('He was parted from them, &c.—Luke xxiv.51') to New Year's Eve ('What is your life?—James iv.14'). The texts range across both Testaments and even include one from the epistle to the Hebrews, so its devotional use was retained even if her father questioned its doctrinal authority. Mary Carpenter explained in the preface that the goal of the volume was to allow people's hearts and minds to dwell 'on a short passage of the sacred writings'.[70] (As James Martineau was also in the habit of using the phrase 'the sacred writings' it seemed a suitable one to use in the title of this chapter on Unitarians.)[71] While readers ultimately must make such elusive judgments for themselves, it seems fair to say that these meditations stick closely to their biblical texts and depend upon them for their emotional power. A good example of this is Lant Carpenter's reflection on Psalm 42: 11 which simply builds to heighten the impact of asking the question which is the text: 'Why, then, are thou cast down, O my soul, and why art thou disquieted within me?'[72] Moreover, the biblicism of the meditations is rich in other ways. A reflection on Revelation 21: 4 by the Methodist Richard Watson offers a classic example of the quaint, biblicist habit of proving from the Scriptures what people already know from their own experience. In this case, a range of biblical passages are quoted to support the claim that 'tears are the visible and affecting expressions of distress'.[73] The Harvard theologian, Henry Ware, Jr, reflected on 'The Saviour's Promise' in Matthew 28: 20: 'Lo, I am with

---

[69] Carpenter, *Meditations*, 58.
[70] Carpenter, *Meditations*, p. iii.
[71] For an example of Martineau using this phrase, see James Martineau, *Essays, Philosophical and Theological* (Boston: William V. Spencer, 1860), 362.
[72] Carpenter, *Meditations*, 30–2.
[73] Carpenter, *Meditations*, 102–3.

you always, even unto the end of the world.' A traditional, orthodox reading of this text is that it is a reference to the work of the Holy Spirit, the third person of the Trinity. As a Unitarian, Ware does not interpret it thus, but what is striking about his meditation is that he makes the Bible itself the fulfilment of this promise:

> Yet, through the abundant goodness of our Heavenly Father, who, in ways so marvellous, has preserved for us the record of that holy revelation, and made it now accessible to every heart, we, of this remote clime, and in this distant period, hear the blessed words as if they were sounded in our ears ... How near is my Saviour to me when I read records of his life ... [74]

Finally, James Martineau himself pays homage to the Bible in Carpenter's *Meditations*: 'We reverently read those ancient Scriptures, which have gathered around them the trust, and procured the heartfelt repose, of so many tribes and periods, since prophets and apostles first gave them forth.'[75]

Moving to Mary Carpenter's thought and writings more generally, themes already introduced in her father's works recur. She also could de-emphasize the Hebrew Scriptures on occasion. She could even go so far as to play the New Testament off against the Old: in an address at the Church of the Messiah, Montreal, Carpenter observed that in the Old Testament: 'little is written of the way whereby sinners can be reclaimed, and nothing (that I remember) of our duty to try to reform them. In the New Testament, it is otherwise.'[76] More fundamental to a biblical Unitarian identity, Mary Carpenter also believed that deep human needs would be best met by the Scriptures unencumbered by creeds. This is most often made explicit in her interaction with Indians whom she repeatedly presented as a kind of control group who had not been raised with the standard religious views inculcated into most Britons and who, when they encountered this material as adults, proved to be impressed by the Bible, but not orthodox dogmas. Here is a typical example: 'When I gave Subrayatu, the secretary of the Veda Somaj, a copy of Russell's *Combined Gospels*, he said

---

[74] Carpenter, *Meditations*, 261–2.

[75] Carpenter, *Meditations*, 164.

[76] Mary Carpenter, *The Duty of Society to the Criminal Classes; An Address delivered in the Church of the Messiah, Montreal, on Sunday, July 6, 1873* (Montreal: Daniel Rose, 1873), 3. See also Mary Carpenter, *Our Convicts*, 2 vols (London: Longman, Green, Longman, Roberts & Green, 1864), I, 87.

he should be very glad of it. They did not object to Christianity as Christ taught it, only to the creeds added to it.'[77]

Carpenter's work as a social reformer and her advocacy writing in the field of education and the care of youths was immersed in Scripture. In these writings, she advanced schemes that included a heavy dose of Bible instruction and reading and she commended them through biblical quotations. Her first major advocacy book, *Reformatory Schools for the Children of the Perishing and Dangerous Classes and for Juvenile Offenders* (1851), strongly emphasized Bible teaching. As one would expect given the book's theme, this was hardly a novel approach in Victorian Britain. She therefore distinguished her work from other existing institutions of which she disapproved by a section in which she made the case for really making the Scriptures comprehensible and interesting to children. Others, she claimed, merely forced children to read or memorize the Bible, while allowing them to remain 'quite ignorant of the sense of the passage'.[78] What is particularly striking about *Reformatory Schools*, however, is the sermonic way in which the advocacy is advanced by barrages of biblical quotations. The preface crescendos to these concluding lines:

> Then let every one go forth to do what he can in this great cause;—all may find a way;—and what they do, let them 'do quickly'—the hour is fully come; the harvest is ripe;—may the Lord send many labourers to gather it in faithfully.[79]

The last three phrases are a kind of biblical, missionary appeal (see, for one key text, Luke 10: 2), indicating that she thought the most persuasive appeal possible was a scriptural one. 'Do quickly' (John 13: 27) is just plain odd, however: these are Jesus' words to Judas in which he intimates that since he has decided to betray him, he should get on with it. Such a random, infelicitous biblical fragment betrays (if the pun may be forgiven) a compulsive habit of thinking, speaking, and therefore writing in biblical language.

---

[77] Carpenter, *Mary Carpenter*, 260. The book was her brother's continuation of their father's efforts to solve the synoptic problem: Russell Lant Carpenter, *A Monotessaron: or, the gospel record of the life of Christ, combined into one narrative, on the basis of Dr Carpenter's apostolic harmony* (London: E. T. Whitfield, 1851). For another example of Carpenter presenting an Indian in this way, see Mary Carpenter, *The Last Days in England of the Rajah Rammohun Roy* (London: Trübner & Co., 1866), 48.

[78] Mary Carpenter, *Reformatory Schools for the Children of the Perishing and Dangerous Classes and for Juvenile Offenders* (London: G. Gilpin, 1851; facsimile reprint: London: Woburn Press, 1968), 78.

[79] Carpenter, *Reformatory Schools*, p. vii.

One more such Scripture-saturated, sermonic passage from this book will suffice:

> If we impiously exclaim, 'Am I my brother's keeper?'—the Lord will reply, in a voice we shall be compelled to hear, 'The voice of thy brother's blood crieth unto me from the ground.' A fearful retribution will come upon us, which we shall find increasingly heavy to bear, the longer we delay to fulfil towards these 'little ones' the commands of that Saviour, whose words cannot pass away, though Heaven and earth should be removed.[80]

As to the content of her teaching, this excerpt from her diary is provided:

> Gethsemane:—I let my class read in each Gospel the narrative of the events, making them remark the additional incidents recorded by each evangelist, afterwards reading to them one connected narration from the four. They quite entered into the spirit of it . . .[81]

One might see this as apostolic harmonizing for roughs.

Carpenter's second major advocacy book was *Juvenile Delinquents: Their Condition and Treatment* (1853). Once again, in addition to making Bible study a core part of the plan for reforming juvenile delinquents, this book sets a scriptural, homiletic tone. The preface defines her goal: 'May this volume stimulate some to work in this sacred cause,—sacred, for it is the work of the Redeemer, "to seek and to save them that are lost." [Luke 19: 10]'[82] Indeed, for Mary Carpenter, the recipients of these efforts all find their dignity in and through Scripture. Thus the first chapter begins with a rapid-fire, biblical rationale for why one should be concerned about the care of other people's offspring:

> For we are speaking of children,—of young beings but recently come from the hands of their Maker, of whom the Saviour has said, that 'of such is the Kingdom of Heaven,' and that unless we be converted and become as such, we can in no wise enter therein;—Children of whom he declared, 'Whosoever shall receive one of such in my name receiveth me,' and the care of whom as his 'lambs' he committed with twice repeated injunctions to that apostle whom he appointed to be the rock on which his church should be built.[83]

---

[80] Carpenter, *Reformatory Schools*, 57.
[81] Carpenter, *Reformatory Schools*, 98.
[82] Mary Carpenter, *Juvenile Delinquents: Their Condition and Treatment* (Montclair, New Jersey: Patterson Smith, 1970; reprint of 1853 edition), p. xxxix.
[83] Carpenter, *Juvenile Delinquents*, 15.

Likewise, the chapter on girls grounded their worth in scriptural narratives: 'as the Saviour first revealed himself in an undying form to a woman, and confided to her the first message of his approaching glorification, so to woman are the blessed messages of the Gospel still intrusted'.[84]

For an account of Mary Carpenter's principles being implemented in a specific institution under her direction, one turns to her *Red Lodge Girls' Reformatory School, Bristol: Its History, Principles and Working* (1875), a text which, given its late date, also has the advantage of showing how deep her biblicism remained to the end of her life. Carpenter was the founder of Red Lodge and it was completely under her control. A central point of this book is to reveal that her methods could be implemented successfully and had proven their rightness in practice. And these methods were literally first and foremost biblical. The section on *Means Employed for the Carrying Out of These Principles* begins: 'Daily reading and inculcation of the Scriptures with prayer, and other direct religious and moral instruction'.[85] Likewise, the section on *Religious Instruction* begins: 'The great object of the religious instruction of these children will be to give them accurate and rational acquaintance with the Holy Scripture'.[86] The list of rules optimistically incorporated by way of presupposition the entire corpus of biblical injunctions: 'In addition to the laws of God which are contained in His Holy Word, every girl is required to attend strictly to the following rules . . .'[87] A day in the life of Red Lodge began with the reading of Scripture to the girls in household devotions before breakfast, including the study of Scripture as part of their school work in the heart of the day, and—we are invited to believe—ended thus: 'At eight the gas is lighted; the school girls come cheerfully in with the Matron, gently take their places, sweetly sing their evening hymn, listen with reverence to some words of Holy Writ, and join in supplications at the Throne of Grace.'[88] Carpenter herself came in once a week 'to read some more difficult portions of Scripture with the older girls

---

[84] Carpenter, *Juvenile Delinquents*, 82.

[85] [Mary Carpenter], *Red Lodge Girls' Reformatory School, Bristol: Its History, Principles and Working* (Bristol: Arrowsmith, 1875), 4.

[86] Carpenter, *Red Lodge*, 4. 'Rational', of course, is a characteristically Unitarian concern. It has not been emphasized as much in this chapter as might be expected, however, because it provides less of a distinctive trait than readers might imagine. On the one hand, orthodox Christians also often insisted that their religious beliefs were rational and, on the other, more radical thinkers would have disallowed Carpenter's conviction that the miracles, resurrection, and ascension of Christ were rational doctrines.

[87] Carpenter, *Red Lodge*, 7.

[88] Carpenter, *Red Lodge*, 41.

alone.'[89] The girls, we are told, eagerly saved up their earnings in order to be able to buy their own copy of the Bible. The walls of Red Lodge's rooms were covered with illuminated biblical texts. Government inspectors continually reported that the scriptural knowledge of the girls was impressive. In 1859, for example, the inspector observed that the school children 'answered my questions very intelligently, on scriptural subjects especially'.[90] As with hostile views of Anglo-Catholics, certain opponents of Unitarianism were apt erroneously to imagine that they did not value the Scriptures—wishing to have a neat correlation between their own doctrinal positions and devotion to the sacred writings. Carpenter observed wearily: 'Some people seem addicted to breaking the Ninth Commandment. The report is disseminated in quarters fit to receive such, that the Bible is not used in Red Lodge.'[91] The truth, of course, was not that Unitarians, as a general rule, did not want the Bible, but rather that biblicist, orthodox Christians often did not want the Unitarians. In a private letter to a friend in America, Carpenter complained bitterly: 'Shut out, as we Unitarians have been, even from Bible Society'.[92]

Nor should it be suspected that Mary Carpenter insisted on Bible reading and bolstered her reforming recommendations with scriptural quotations merely as a way of placating the views of others such as evangelical Protestants. Her biographer–nephew reported regarding her ragged school efforts:

> Into all her work she threw a weight of character which belonged only to few; but her Scripture lessons allowed all tenderness of her soul to flow freely forth without the checks of scholastic necessity. Morning and evening on Sundays, and on many a week night besides, she was found in the school with the little band of youths around her, to whom she delighted to unfold the truths of the Gospel story. Many of them were Catholics, and had never seen Bibles or Testaments . . .[93]

[89] Carpenter, *Red Lodge*, 41.

[90] Manton, *Carpenter*, 135.

[91] Carpenter, *Mary Carpenter*, 219.

[92] Boston Public Library, Boston, Massachusetts, Mary Carpenter Papers, Ms. A.9.2, Vol. 22, No. 107, Mary Carpenter to Mrs Maria (Weston) Chapman, Boston, 31 October 1846. (In 1831, the Trinitarian Bible Society was founded as a way to carry on the work of distributing the Scriptures without allowing Unitarians to cooperate in it, as was the case in the older British and Foreign Bible Society: Leslie Howsam, *Cheap Bibles: Nineteenth-Century Publishing and the British and Foreign Bible Society* (Cambridge: Cambridge University Press, 1991), 16.)

[93] Carpenter, *Mary Carpenter*, 219.

In 1856, she confided to her diary: 'I have continued to give my lessons as usual, and have increasing satisfaction in them...The Scripture lessons especially give me most pleasure.'[94] She delighted in her pedagogical technique of teaching the Bible with the aid of pictures, maps, and objects gathered from the Holy Land. Belying the scholarly assumption today that Victorian Unitarians were promoters of a critical approach to the Old Testament, when Carpenter taught the Genesis stories about Joseph and the students 'all found a difficulty in realizing that this had really occurred' she saw this as a sign of ignorance rather than critical awareness: 'I showed them engravings of Egyptian buildings, being desirous of giving reality to the Scripture histories as a ground for their faith.'[95] She made sketches of scenes from the Holy Land by copying illustrations from a book and had travellers collect curiosities for her such as a stone from the Sea of Galilee. When, in 1854, Sir John Bowring passed through biblical lands on his way to his new appointment as governor of Hong Kong and took the trouble to write to her what he saw, Carpenter was overjoyed: 'That Red Sea letter has given very great pleasure to numerous hearers, both high and low; indeed, it gave me a more vivid conception than I have ever had before of that most deeply interesting part of the world.'[96] In 1860, Mary Carpenter identified 'the Scriptures' alongside slavery and education as the three great subjects that always had, and that continued to, deeply occupy her mind.[97]

Readers of Carpenter's *Our Convicts* (1864) were repeatedly presented with substantial quotations from not only reports on prison conditions but also, less predictably, the liberal Anglican F. W. Robertson's *Expository Lectures on St Paul's Epistles to the Corinthians*.[98] Even Carpenter's *Six Months in India* (1868) is sprinkled with references to the Bible. Many of these are testimonies of Indians having favourable encounters with the Christian Scriptures. Others are accounts of events such as portions of the Bible read aloud, the texts of sermons she heard, the production of Bibles, and the training of indigenous ministers in the Greek New Testament. Moreover, as Carpenter encounters people and events in India, texts of the Bible sometimes spring into her mind. Religious activities that seemed to her to have the whiff of idolatry, for example, prompted this outburst: 'I could

---

[94] Carpenter, *Mary Carpenter*, 178.   [95] Carpenter, *Reformatory Schools*, 96–7.
[96] Carpenter, *Mary Carpenter*, 162–3.   [97] Carpenter, *Mary Carpenter*, 217.
[98] Carpenter, *Our Convicts*, I, 88, 108–9, 110–11. F. W. Robertson, *Expository Lectures on St Paul's Epistle to the Corinthians* (London: Smith, Elder and Co., 1859).

now fully sympathise with the prophet of old, who indignantly exclaimed, "Your new moons and your appointed feasts my soul hateth: they are a trouble unto me; I am weary to bear them."' (Isaiah 1: 14)[99]

It would be redundant at this point to observe that Carpenter's own entire education and upbringing was steeped in Scripture, but it is worth making the specific observation that every child in her father's school studied the New Testament in Greek (while only bright students such as herself and James Martineau could add to this essential core less necessary subjects such as mathematics).[100] Far from this being part of the childish things that she later was glad to leave behind, Carpenter occupied herself on a voyage to India in 1866 by teaching New Testament Greek to a young lady who expressed an interest.[101] Even the only scholar to pursue a book-length, academic study of Mary Carpenter, Jo Manton, is hampered by ill-founded expectations of Unitarian exceptionalism. For example, Manton writes: 'While literal-minded Bible readers of church and chapel denounced the use of chloroform in childbirth as contrary to God's will, Unitarians welcomed it as an example of "knowledge and improvement".'[102] This contrast is meaningless as there were no literal-minded Bible readers opposing chloroform—this is simply an urban legend.[103] Most bizarrely, Manton claims that Carpenter 'had a fastidious dislike for the habit of interlarding conversation with biblical texts, and rarely quoted from the Bible.'[104] This is not only simply wrong—it is well-nigh inexplicable. Either Manton did not recognize as such the biblical quotations that litter everything that Carpenter wrote—as well as her reported speech—or Manton so wanted to be able to commend Carpenter as a cut above Victorian biblicists that she imagined it was so. Without putting too fine a point on it, here (in the footnote) is a haphazardly compiled (and no doubt incomplete) list of scores of pages of her Victorian biography in which Carpenter is recorded quoting Scripture.[105] It is also telling that in Frances Power Cobbe's personal sketch

[99] Mary Carpenter, *Six Months in India* (London: Longmans, Green, and Co., 1868), 74.

[100] Carpenter, *Mary Carpenter*, 7.

[101] Carpenter, *Mary Carpenter*, 252.

[102] Manton, *Carpenter*, 28.

[103] Rennie B. Schoepflin, 'Myth 14. That the Church Denounced Anesthesia in Childbirth on Biblical Grounds', in Ronald L. Numbers (ed.), *Galileo Goes to Jail and Other Myths about Science and Religion* (Cambridge, MA: Harvard University Press, 2009).

[104] Manton, *Carpenter*, 212.

[105] Carpenter, *Mary Carpenter*, 16, 25–6, 33, 36, 37, 42, 44, 45, 56, 61, 64, 77, 81, 83, 84, 95, 98, 99, 116, 120, 126, 130, 131, 135, 167, 177, 183, 197, 203, 211, 220, 221, 248, 262, 272, 278, 284–5, 290, 292, 294, 302, 310, 311, 351, 360, 375, 379, 384, 387.

of Mary Carpenter almost all of the reported speech is centred on direct biblical quotations. It might be fair to somewhat discount this result by wondering if Cobbe has done this in order to highlight Carpenter's more conservative religious identity than her own. Nevertheless, most of these verbatim flashes are clearly included to enliven the essay with humour. Carpenter explains playfully when she made a kind invitation to someone who had been annoying her that she was 'heaping coals of fire on his head' (Romans 12: 20). During the period in which she lived with her, Cobbe found it a trial to conform to the austere way of life that Carpenter followed, and therefore teased her about the only luxury which Carpenter appeared to allow herself—a modest cushion on her chair. The Unitarian social reformer retorted: 'Yes, indeed! I am sorry to say that since my illness I have been obliged to have recourse to *these indulgences* (!). I used to try, like St Paul, to "endure hardness."' (2 Timothy 2: 3)[106]

Carpenter often advanced her positions on social issues by citing biblical proof-texts. 2 Corinthians 3: 17 demonstrated that slavery was anti-Christian—as was the orthodox attitude to Unitarians: 'Where is the spirit of Xt [Christ], there is freedom, & where there is not freedom, it does not appear to me that there can be the Spirit of Christ.'[107] She was warranted to think optimistically about God's attitude toward enlightened Indian Hindus by Christ's words in John 10: 16: 'And other sheep I have, which are not of this fold'.[108] A few proof-texts recur often as they—in her deployment of them—touched so directly on the heart of her work. Carpenter spent her whole working life tirelessly advocating for a reforming rather than punitive approach to delinquents and criminals, and frequently fired off Romans 12: 19 in defence of this stance: 'Vengeance is mine, I will repay, saith the Lord.'[109] Those who worked with difficult youths needed to learn how to overcome evil with good (Romans 12: 21).[110] Her conviction that every child should receive an education was repeatedly advanced through Hosea 4: 6: 'My people are destroyed for lack of knowledge.'[111] Two texts, in particular, seemed to her to provide a rationale for mobilizing

[106] Cobbe, 'Recollections', 289, 284. (The italics and exclamation mark are, of course, Cobbe's own commentary.)

[107] Boston Public Library, Boston, Massachusetts, Mary Carpenter Papers, Ms. A.9.2, Vol. 22, No. 107, Mary Carpenter to Mrs Maria (Weston) Chapman, Boston, 31 October 1846.

[108] Carpenter, *Mary Carpenter*, 221, 237.

[109] See, for examples, Carpenter, *Our Convicts*, I, 87; Carpenter, *Juvenile Delinquents*, 369.

[110] Carpenter, *Red Lodge*, 3.

[111] Carpenter, *Reformatory Schools*, 55; Carpenter, *Mary Carpenter*, 115, 211.

Christians to help her in her work for the education, care, and reformation of needy or disruptive children. The first was Jesus' promise in Matthew 25: 40 that what one did to aid 'the least of these' would be accredited as having been done 'unto me'. The second is Jesus' statement in Luke 19: 10 that he had 'come to seek and to save that which was lost.'[112] Another text to which she would return in the hope that it could be truly said of her as well was Mark 14: 8: 'She hath done what she could.'[113]

Mary Carpenter was so confident in Scripture and her ability to understand and proclaim it that she even repeatedly consented to preach sermons. When visiting a prison on the Continent, she delivered a Sunday sermon in French in a prison chapel. Her text was the parable of the Prodigal Son. This sermon was so well received that copies were produced which were illustrated with a portrait of 'the preacher'.[114] Her personal advice to one of the prisoners there was 'to commune with the Heavenly Father, with the help of the Scriptures, and to study the life of the loving Saviour'.[115] As for her trip to North America, in Hartford, Connecticut, all the churches in town combined together so that her Sunday evening sermon in the largest church building was the only worship service offered that night.[116] (The centrality of the Scriptures for Mary Carpenter is markedly on display in her perspective on what was New York City's leading attraction: 'The chief novelty was the Bible House'.)[117] Although she spoke without a manuscript, the full text of her Sunday sermon at the Church of the Messiah, Montreal, was taken down and published. A perfect distillation of her biblical rationale for her reforming efforts, it begins, 'My Friends, Since our blessed Lord came especially to *seek out* and to save those who were lost', and ends with 'Inasmuch as ye did it unto the least of these ye did it unto me.'[118] A whole string of texts are cited in-between, including the parable of the Prodigal Son.

Morning and Evening Mediations, Mary Carpenter's first book, provided a window into her inner, spiritual life. This was granted once again in her last

---

[112] For example, these oft-cited texts both appear prominently in her *Juvenile Delinquents*: Carpenter, *Juvenile Delinquents*, 382, xxxix.

[113] Carpenter, *Mary Carpenter*, 292, 294, 384.

[114] Carpenter, *Mary Carpenter*, 314.

[115] Carpenter, *Mary Carpenter*, 317.

[116] Carpenter, *Mary Carpenter*, 321.

[117] Carpenter, *Mary Carpenter*, 322. (It was an institution for the efficient, mass printing of Bibles.)

[118] Carpenter, *Duty of Society*, 3, 12.

book, *Voices of the Spirit and Spirit Pictures*, which she was arranging to have printed at the time of her death, and which was published posthumously in that same year. Intended for private circulation in her own circle of personal contacts, it was a collection of a lifetime's worth of poems she had written, as well as some prose reflections. In contrast to her *Meditations*, Carpenter was no longer primarily doing the work of a compiler: these pieces were all her own compositions. Moreover, *Voices of the Spirit* was not a religious or devotional book: it was simply an intimate, personal book. Therefore, one finds in this collection poems with themes such as 'A December Sunrise', 'Venus, the Morning Star', 'The Meeting of Le Verrier and Adams, Discoverers of a new Planet', 'Reply of the Romans to Horace', and 'Wanderings of the Otter from Otterton to the Sea'.[119] There are even the obligatory poems on the moon and moonlight. Many of the poems mark an occasion—often the death of someone she loved or admired—but also joyful events such as birthdays. American reformers returning to their native land after a British tour prompted 'Farewell to Wm. Lloyd Garrison' and 'Farewell to Frederick Douglass'.[120] In other words, the biblical material in this collection simply finds its place as that which it naturally held in her entire life amidst the whole range of her sentiments, interests, affections, and concerns. So on to the biblical content. The titles of some of these poems are not only scriptural phrases, but for these (unlike her standard practice) quotation marks are added in order to underline their identity as Scripture, and sometimes the reference is helpfully provided: 'He shall give His Angels charge concerning thee, to bear thee up' [Psalm 91: 11–12], '"The Master is come and calleth for thee." John XI., 28', and '"Whether in the body, or out of the body I know not." 2 Cor. XII., 3'.[121] One poem's title is even literally just a reference: 'Jeremiah xxxii., 10' (a rather obscure verse, one might add).[122]

'Offerings from the Old World to the New, By Englishwomen' is an anti-slavery poem. As with a printed sermon, between the title and the poem there is a text written out (Carpenter's beloved proof-text, Matthew 25: 40). This poem opens with the biblical image of Mary Magdalene anointing Jesus' feet, and ends with an arresting inversion of biblical appropriations:

---

[119] Carpenter, *Voices*, 99, 100, 132, 12, 150.
[120] Carpenter, *Voices*, 120, 123.   [121] Carpenter, *Voices*, 155, 95, 97.
[122] Carpenter, *Voices*, 34.

> Land of our Pilgrim Fathers! Hear! O, hear!
> Grieve not their ashes by thy children's chains,
> Let not the slave-block shame the sacred soil
> Their prayers have hallowed! Wipe the Cain-mark off
> From thy degraded brow,—and then stand forth
> Before the world, a nation glorious, FREE![123]

Defenders of race slavery sometimes justified it by arguing that Africans were under the curse of Cain. Carpenter here boldly argues that it is rather white slave holders who are marked as bearing the collective guilt of murder.[124] 'Joy' likewise follows the sermon format, with Psalm 16: 11 as the text.[125] There is surely no need to illustrate the point that the verses of the poems often contain direct biblical quotations—even in poems that are not on a scriptural theme. An eccentrically biblicist trait is worth highlighting, however: Carpenter sometimes puts a biblical reference alongside a line of the poem as a kind of invitation to the reader to track it to its source. Her first sonnet on the Death of Rajah Rammohun Roy, for example, ends:

> 'Nations behold your God! rejoice—rejoice.'
> Is. xl.,9[126]

In the heart of 'Farewell to Frederick Douglass', on two separate and separated occasions, Carpenter cannot resist this impulse, annotating one poetic line with 'Is. lviii.' and another, 'Is. lxvi.'[127]

All sources agree that Mary Carpenter was a public, vocal, unapologetic, and unflinching Unitarian. When riled, she could let out indignant outbursts against bigoted evangelical or orthodox Christians. She gloried in the fact that English Unitarians did not submit to any articles of religion, proudly reporting to an American inquirer in 1846: 'No confessions or creeds of any kind are used in any of the Unitarian churches.'[128] The sacred writings, on the other hand, were absolutely central to her life, thought, piety, spiritual practice, writings, work, and reforming endeavours. They were the standard by which all theological beliefs must be judged. Even in

---

[123] Carpenter, *Voices*, 133–5.
[124] For slavery and the discourse of the mark of Cain, see Colin Kidd, *The Forging of Races: Race and Scripture in the Protestant Atlantic World, 1600–2000* (Cambridge: Cambridge University Press, 2006).
[125] Carpenter, *Voices*, 148.
[126] Carpenter, *Voices*, 61.   [127] Carpenter, *Voices*, 124.
[128] Carpenter, *Mary Carpenter*, 74–5.

1876, the last full year of her life, she dismissed a 'high Calvinistic sermon' she heard with the fatal observation that it was 'quite unscriptural'.[129] Frances Power Cobbe's view was not an objective one. Nevertheless, her summative impression as a freethinker can serve as a corrective to the general tendency to downplay the religious fervour and biblicist identity of many Victorian Unitarians: 'Had martyrdom been offered her, Mary Carpenter would have gone to the stake singing Psalms.'[130]

---

[129] Carpenter, *Mary Carpenter*, 361.   [130] Cobbe, 'Recollections', 298.

7

Quakers

Elizabeth Fry and 'Reading'

If someone in England today knows of any nineteenth-century Quaker, it would be a safe five-pound bet that it is the prison reformer Elizabeth Fry (1780–1845): a portrait of Fry is on the £5 note, making her the only woman beside the Queen whose image is on English money currently being printed (the only other woman who has ever been so honoured is another figure in this book, Florence Nightingale). Fry was an international celebrity in her own lifetime and almost certainly the most well-regarded British Quaker throughout the second half of the nineteenth century. In 1861, when Sir Morton Peto argued in the House of Commons for a new law that would have allowed the unbaptized to have a proper, churchyard burial he asked his fellow members if they thought that Elizabeth Fry did not deserve such treatment, indicating that she was the one Quaker whose name would elicit the most respect.[1] Fry is also an apt choice to represent the Society of Friends because she was a recorded Quaker minister. Being a woman makes her all the more representative as 'in the early Victorian period, woman ministers greatly outnumbered men'.[2] Moreover, Fry's Quaker ministry was far more prominent than that of most ministers in the denomination, even leaving aside her work as a social reformer: she was repeatedly commissioned by the Society of Friends to go on preaching tours, including to Ireland and continental Europe. Or, to take another example, Fry

---

[1] Timothy Larsen, *Friends of Religious Equality: Nonconformist Politics in Mid-Victorian England* (Milton Keynes: Paternoster Press, 2007), 55.
[2] Elizabeth Isichei, *Victorian Quakers* (Oxford: Oxford University Press, 1970), 94.

preached at a special meeting for Quaker youth at which some 2,000 people were present and 'hundreds went away who could not get in'—only the most eminent Quaker ministers received opportunities such as these.[3]

Given numerous hints in the existing scholarship, it seems likely that some might be uneasy about allowing Elizabeth Fry to represent nineteenth-century Quakers because she was an evangelical.[4] This concern, however, seems to be animated by what the Society of Friends became later, rather than what it was in Fry's day. Scholars have tended to exaggerate the theological diversity of mid-Victorian British Quakers, often by pointing to Friends in America where indeed the range of views was wider and differing camps were more substantial. The hegemony of evangelicalism was so strong in Britain, however, that the largest schismatic group broke away because its members wanted to be even more thoroughly evangelical and biblicist, the Beaconites (who tellingly referred to themselves as 'Evangelical Friends'). Elizabeth Isichei, in her very thorough study *Victorian Quakers*, reveals that there is simply no non-evangelical from this period who could represent the Quakers: 'All the eminent and "weighty" Friends of the mid-Victorian era were evangelicals.'[5] As to the one liberal schismatic group, it peaked at thirty attenders,[6] whereas Fry often ministered to more people than that at her household devotions! From the mid-1830s to the mid-1880s, evangelicalism not only thoroughly imbued the British Society of Friends, but there was literally no identifiable alternative within the denomination.

Furthermore, although it is accurate to identify Fry as an evangelical, it is interesting to observe that this was not her own self-descriptor. Indeed, the research for this study has not generated a single example of Fry self-identifying as an evangelical and the one example of her using this term about Quakers in the published version of her journal is negative: 'there is much stirring amongst Friends, arising from a considerable number taking apparently a much higher evangelical ground, than has generally been taken by the Society, bordering, I apprehend in a few, on Calvinism.'[7] (In line with the tradition of the Society, Fry was deeply anti-Calvinist.) Fry saw herself as

---

[3] *Memoir of the Life of Elizabeth Fry, with extracts from her journal and letters, by Two of Her Daughters* [Katharine Fry and Rachel Cresswell] (eds), 2 vols (London: Charles Gilpin, 1847), I, 486.

[4] For a definition and history of evangelicalism, see D. W. Bebbington, *Evangelicalism in Modern Britain: A History from the 1730s to the 1980s* (London: Unwin Hyman, 1989).

[5] Isichei, *Victorian Quakers*, 9.

[6] Isichei, *Victorian Quakers*, 44.

[7] *Memoir*, II, 157.

above the minor theological disputes and gradations that were in the Society in her day: 'neither on one side nor the other, but seeing the good of both'.[8] Instead of self-identifying as evangelical, her own category she described with terms such as 'plain and consistent Friends' or 'a decided Friend', speaking of herself thus: 'I am certainly a thorough Friend'.[9] The key distinction at the forefront of her mind, in other words, was not between evangelical Quakers and quietist or theological liberal ones, but rather between worldly, lax, or nominal Friends and fully observant, zealous, dedicated ones.

Elizabeth Gurney (to use her maiden name) was herself once a worldly and lax Friend. Both of her parents were Quakers from Quaker families. Her mother, Catherine, died when Elizabeth was twelve years old, leaving twelve children behind, of which Elizabeth was the fourth. Elizabeth's recollections of her mother centre upon her efforts to teach her children the Scriptures. Catherine read the Bible to her children in both the morning and evening as a devotional exercise and instructed the children individually during the day, 'particularly in the knowledge of the scriptures'.[10] Elizabeth recalled fondly walks together in their estate's verdant grounds while her mother would tell her about the Garden of Eden. On the other hand, Elizabeth also intimated that her mother told her Bible stories that disturbed and unsettled her such as the Almighty commanding Abraham to sacrifice his child. June Rose has rightly observed that the result of Elizabeth's childhood formation was that 'the Bible soaked into her being'.[11]

With Catherine's death, however, and perhaps the natural pull of a house full of teenagers and the headiness of living during revolutionary times, the family became increasingly worldly, keeping its identity as belonging to the Society of Friends while disregarding yet more Quaker plainness, seriousness, and doctrinal commitments for fashion, amusement, and free-thought. John, the widower father, was a wealthy merchant and banker, and the family lived at Earlham Hall, near Norwich. Earlham was a place of music and dancing and showy dresses which was far enough removed from Quaker austerity for Prince William Frederick to find it an entertaining place to frequent. Intellectually, Unitarianism, deism, and religiously sceptical ideas made inroads into the minds of members of the family, including Elizabeth herself. Her retrospective account was that beginning when she was fourteen years old: 'I had very sceptical or deistical principles. I seldom,

[8] *Memoir*, II, 189.   [9] *Memoir*, I, 94, 392; II, 109.
[10] *Memoir*, I, 4.   [11] June Rose, *Elizabeth Fry* (London: Macmillan, 1980), 4.

or never thought of religion.'[12] On 14 January 1798, Elizabeth observed in her journal: 'I don't feel any real religion; I should think those feelings impossible to obtain, for even if I thought all the Bible was true, I do not think I could make myself feel it'.[13] It is, of course, telling that she saw the veracity of Scripture as central to the question of religious faith or doubt. Four days later she wrote: 'I am now seventeen, and if some kind, and great circumstance does not happen to me, I shall have my talents devoured by moth and rust.'[14] Although she is a religious doubter, she nevertheless expresses her own sense of being at a loss in life in biblical language (a combination of the parable of the talents in Matthew 25 and Matthew 6: 19–20—both passages about failing to make one's life count as one ought).

The following month, however, her religious awakening began. It was initially triggered by the preaching of a visiting American Quaker minister, William Savery. The past, represented by her ostentatiously fashionable purple boots with scarlet laces, and the future, as evidenced by her tears in response to the sermon, collided. During the next year and a half Elizabeth would, with some fits and starts, learn to work out her inner spiritual renewal and now confident faith by conforming to the habits of strict and plain Friends. There are also a couple of intimations in her journal that she already suspected that the Almighty might call her to be a minister. Just a week after hearing Savery for the first time, it was arranged for her to go to London, a trip that she would have hitherto unequivocally embraced as leading to more diverting opportunities than usual, but which she now saw partially as a temptation. She resolved: 'Do not make dress a study, even in London. Read in the Bible, when I can'.[15] Already in that first year of her more earnest way of life, 1798, not only is Elizabeth reading the Bible regularly and memorizing key texts to nourish her own faith, but she was also finding ways to read the Bible aloud to those in need. She clearly believed that allowing people to hear Scripture was a valuable gift to give them. Here is an entry in her journal from June 1798 regarding a servant on his deathbed: 'I have been great part of this morning with poor Bob, who seems now dying. I read a long chapter in the New Testament to him' (an earlier entry reveals that reading the Bible to Bob began at her suggestion, not his).[16] Less than two weeks later, a journal entry speaks of her plan to

---

[12] *Memoir*, I, 45.   [13] *Memoir*, I, 24.   [14] *Memoir*, I, 24.
[15] *Memoir*, I, 36.   [16] *Memoir*, I, 49, 45.

'read in the Testament' to local poor children once a week: 'It might increase morality among the lower classes, if the Scriptures were oftener and better read to them.'[17] These impulses were the first fruits of a lifelong instinct that a good response to feelings of compassion for any group of people is to ensure that the Bible is read by them or to them.

In August 1800, Elizabeth Gurney married Joseph Fry, a Quaker businessman from a prosperous Quaker family. The great drama of her first year of marriage revolved around her efforts to institute the practice of household Bible reading as part of the morning routine. Such daily scriptural readings had been typical of the rhythm of a devout Quaker home in the seventeenth century, but during the eighteenth century it had largely lapsed. Fry was on the forefront of what turned out to be the strong recovery of this daily act of worship among faithful Friends in the nineteenth century.[18] (In 1829, the epistle of the London Yearly Meeting spoke of daily Bible reading both in private and 'in our families' as a normative expectation for British Quakers.[19]) Joseph apparently acquiesced to his wife's suggestion in principle, but did not exert himself to make it happen, especially as they had house guests—his elder brother, William, and an American Quaker minister, George Dilwyn. Elizabeth Fry felt the awkwardness of intimating to people whom they should show deference that they ought to be more observant, but the call of duty was greater. The breakfast party dispersed, but she was not at peace and made them reassemble. Fry began to read Psalm 46, but found herself too churned up to continue, and Joseph therefore completed the reading. The following day, 12 November 1800, her journal reports: 'I rather felt this morning it would have been right for me to read the Bible again, and stop George Dilwyn and Joseph reading something else.'[20] Her entry two days later is still taken up with how awkward this struggle is. The following day, however, Dilwyn had the kindness to tell her that he had found this new practice beneficial.

Henceforth, Fry would never let circumstances undermine this practice, but instead would observe it meticulously, indeed tenaciously, to the end of her days. Her attitude is captured in an annotation in her Bible. The Book of

---

[17] Memoir, I, 50.

[18] Roger H. Martin, 'Quakers, the Bible, and the British and Foreign Bible Society', Quaker History: The Bulletin of the Friends Historical Association, 85, 1 (Spring 1996), 14–16.

[19] The Epistle from the Yearly Meeting, Held in London . . . 1829 (Mount Pleasant, Ohio: Ohio Yearly Meeting, 1829), 8–9.

[20] Memoir, I, 96.

Acts tells the story of the apostle Paul being on a ship caught in such a severe and relentless storm that everyone was certain they would die. After a fourteen-day struggle in which the expectation of imminent doom meant that no one ate, Paul rallied the crew and other passengers with reassuring words and insisted that they take nourishment. Reading this dramatic tale, Fry's eye was caught by the incidental detail that Paul 'gave thanks to God in presence of them all' for the bread (Acts 27: 35), observing: 'He did not omit to return thanks even in this emergency'.[21] Never experiencing such extreme conditions herself, daily household devotions were certainly safe. Fry so far overcame her initial embarrassment regarding including house-guests in this practice that she came to see these Bible readings as a gift she had to offer others. Indeed, she would make every effort to arrange them even if she herself was the guest. The only record of her being thwarted in this is that when visiting her brother Daniel he would not allow her to lead his family in devotions.[22] Otherwise, she seemed to institute this practice wherever she went. On her tour of Scotland, for example, she would assemble everyone she could, including servants and even those not staying in the house—and this not only when a guest in a private home, but even when staying in an inn. She even did this on her continental tours—having hotel waiters and others follow along in a Bible in their own language, or doing the reading in the local language (Fry could conduct an entire service in French), or arranging for an interpreter.[23] Fireside Bible readings could inflate into something between a church service and a social event. Here, for example, is a report by Fry's niece and travelling companion about one such gathering:

> About 50 English came to our Reading in the evening. Our room was so small that we opened the large doors into our Aunt's bedroom to give more room....Many very gaily dressed people expressed to us their extreme interest in having heard our Aunt and anxiously enquired whether she would 'preach again' before leaving Brussels.[24]

And the fact that one would spend the whole day travelling was not an excuse to forego such duties but rather an opportunity to pursue them more

---

[21] British Library, London, Elizabeth Fry Papers, Annotated Bible, Add 73528.
[22] Rose, *Fry*, 163.
[23] Elizabeth Gurney, *Elizabeth Fry's Journeys on the Continent, 1840–1841* (London: John Lane, 1931), 45.
[24] Gurney, *Journeys*, 11.

diligently. Fry reported upon an 1838 journey to Aberdeen with her sister-in-law with whom she also shared the same name:

> These journeys are, I trust, not lost time; we have two Scripture readings daily in the carriage, and much instructive conversation; also, abundant time for that which is so important, the private reading of the Holy Scripture. This is very precious to dear Elizabeth Fry [Fry's sister-in-law], and I have thought it a privilege to note her reverent 'marking and learning' of these sacred truths of divine inspiration. Often does she lay down the Book, close her eyes, and wait upon Him, who hath the key of David to open and to seal the instruction of the sacred pages. Truly, it helps to explain how her 'profiting appears upon all,' when she is thus diligent and fervent, in 'meditating upon these things, and giving herself whole to them.' [1 Timothy 4: 15][25]

As to her own household, Fry eventually bore Joseph eleven children and this bountiful immediate family, together with the servants, formed the core of her daily Bible readings at home. Fry was so convinced that this practice was a vital source of spiritual enrichment and a primary way to deepen family unity and bonds, that once her children were grown and had families of their own (and had mostly left the Society of Friends for the Church of England) she instituted a monthly gathering for the extended family. What is striking about her announcement of this plan is that it was so focused on Bible reading that she did not even mention prayer.[26] Scholars tend to assume that Fry bullied people into enduring these exercises against their natural desires,[27] but her daughters report on the contrary that this monthly Bible reading was such a welcome event that the extended family was still continuing to meet in this way even years after their mother's death.

In as strong an illustration of the wider theme of 'a people of one book' as one could imagine, Elizabeth Fry referred to reading the Bible simply as 'reading' or, to express it the other way around, when she referred to 'reading' she meant the Bible. This usage is so pervasive there are literally over fifty examples of it in the excerpts from her journal and letters in the standard memoir. For Fry, 'reading' especially had the connotation of the Bible being read aloud with others, but she could use it merely to refer to private devotions as well. For example, she could make a note to herself: 'Plan to try for children. Boys sent to tutor, after our Reading. Little one with me till nearly ten o'clock'.[28] Here is a typical chronicle of her spiritual life:

[25] *Memoir*, II, 279.   [26] *Memoir*, II, 257–8.
[27] Rose, *Fry*, 65.   [28] *Memoir*, I, 190.

After reading, yesterday, I think I was too much off my watch, and did not keep that bridle over my tongue [James 1: 26], which is so important; too much disposed to bow the knee of my soul to mortals, rather than to the living God alone. In consequence, I felt this morning at reading, unwilling to take up the cross [Luke 9: 23].[29]

Or alternatively she might report that it seemed efficacious: 'In the morning we had a satisfactory reading with our children' or 'we also had a very satisfactory reading with the people at the inn.'[30] Fry wrote home to her children from a French hotel reassuring them that the daily routine had not been disrupted amidst such altered circumstances: 'After breakfast we read as usual'.[31] It should be kept in mind that 'a people of one book' is not intended literally. Fry wanted her children to receive a good general education, to study, for example, Britain's 'best poets' as well as modern languages.[32] Within a year of the first publication of Samuel Pepys's diary she had selected it for afternoon reading with the children.[33] She also made sure the women prisoners in Newgate had access not only to the Bible and other religious volumes, but also to a uniform set of forty-eight entertaining and informative books for general reading.[34] Nevertheless, for Fry, 'reading' meant the Bible, it was other literature that needed to be identified with qualifying words for the sake of clarity; thus, for example, she wrote about enjoying 'innocent and amusing reading' while on her sickbed.[35]

The Quaker ministry was unlike that of most other denominations: there was no formal training, it was not a paid position, and it was open to both men and women. Being silent together in the Lord's presence was the foundational act of Quaker corporate worship. In this silence, the Holy Spirit might inspire someone to speak. A person became a recorded minister by regularly speaking in this way and the community discerning that it was indeed the work, calling, and gifting of the Spirit. In other words, being a Quaker minister was something like being a prophet, and a Quaker sermon was somewhat akin to a prophetic utterance. In practice, these expectations necessitated a very high degree of biblical literacy and knowledge by ministers and would-be ministers. Isichei described Victorian Quaker preaching thus: 'It was characterized by a sing-song intonation, and the use of tradi-

---

[29] *Memoir*, I, 208.   [30] *Memoir*, II, 72, 256.   [31] *Memoir*, II, 260.
[32] *Memoir*, II, 146.   [33] *Memoir*, II, 7.
[34] Elizabeth Fry, *Observations on the Visiting, Superintending, and Government, of Female Prisoners*, second edition (London: John and Arthur Arch, 1827), 48.
[35] *Memoir*, I, 350.

tional phrases, usually biblical in origin, such as 'trying the fleece in the wet and the dry'. Some ministers, especially in the early stages of their careers, confined themselves almost entirely to strings of memorized texts.'[36] To put it another way, a prophecy is supposed to be a spontaneous utterance of the word of God; the word of God for Quakers was a category normed by the Scriptures and the expectation of extemporaneous inspiration ruled out not only using a manuscript or notes but even reading out texts from the Bible, resulting in a ministry that relied heavily on the impromptu stringing together of biblical phrases from a storehouse of passages known by heart.

It was in 1809 that Fry first yielded to the prompting of the Spirit to speak during an act of corporate worship. At her father's funeral, she uttered these words: 'Great and marvellous are Thy works, Lord God Almighty: just and true all Thy ways, Thou King of Saints; be pleased to receive our thanksgiving.' This is simply a quotation from Revelation 15: 3 with one phrase added on at the end. A Sunday or two just after this she felt a strong impulse to utter Psalm 31: 24 in the normal Quaker worship meeting in Norwich, but resisted it, justifying this act on the biblical grounds that Samuel needed to consult Eli first in order to discern the things of God. Her Eli was her uncle Joseph, whose advice to her consisted of his quoting 2 Corinthians 5: 7 at her ('walk by faith, not by sight'). Thus duly bucked up, during a meeting a few weeks later, Psalm 31: 24 once again 'came feelingly over' her, and this time she had the confidence to speak it out.[37]

In March 1811, Elizabeth Fry was formally acknowledged to be a Quaker minister. Throughout the rest of her life, her own descriptions of her sermons would standardly begin with—if not exclusively consist of—biblical quotations. A typical example is the following account of a sermon she gave after her brother Joseph had spoken at a meeting during their ministry tour in Scotland:

> it appeared as if I must follow him, and rise with these words, 'The sorrows of death compassed me about, the pains of hell gat hold upon me;' [Psalm 116: 3] then enlarging upon the feeling I had of the power of the enemy, and the absolute need there is to watch, to pray, and to flee unto to Christ, as our only and sure refuge and deliverer; I had to show that we might be tried and buffeted by Satan, as a further trial of faith and of patience, but that if we did not yield to him, it would only tend to refinement.[38]

---

[36] Isichei, *Victorian Quakers*, 95.   [37] *Memoir*, I, 150–1.   [38] *Memoir*, I, 330.

This whole summary is a string of biblical allusions, but it is clear from a series of examples that the phrase to 'rise with these words' was a Quaker way of saying 'the text for my sermon was'. Indeed, this translation was made at the time. Fry's ministry in one meeting was described by 'a lady who was present, not a Friend': 'then she rose, giving as a text, "Yield yourselves unto God, as those that are alive from the dead"'.[39] Fry even occasionally used this terminology herself. In her Bible, she wrote at Psalm 31: 24: 'The first text I ever preached in public.'[40] It is wholly fitting that Fry would describe the service of herself and all Quaker ministers as 'the ministry of the word'.[41]

Another Quaker distinctive related to prophetic preaching was the inner light, a conviction that believers could expect to be guided by the illumination of the Holy Spirit. Fry's inner light was a text prompter: 'The words that (I believe) have arisen for my encouragement, are these, "The Lord is my shepherd, I shall not want."' (Psalm 23: 1)[42] Fry's oft-repeated formula for the relationship between these two authorities was that the Almighty works in one's life by the Spirit through the Scriptures. For example, in a sermon in France delivered to a non-Quaker audience, Fry felt pressed to emphasize 'the point of the Lord Himself being our teacher, immediately by His Spirit, through the Holy Scriptures'.[43] While other Protestants often suspected that Quakers were less committed to the Bible than them, Friends saw themselves as more faithful to scripture than other Christians. For example, although not denying the doctrine itself, Quakers did not use the word 'Trinity' on the grounds of 'its not being found in the Bible'.[44] Fry likewise asserted that the Quaker objection to using the names of the days and months (which they therefore substituted numbers for) was 'more consistent with Scripture'.[45] If such practices made them look odd to outsiders, well, Fry reflected, they were called to be 'a peculiar people' (1 Peter 2: 9).[46] Fidelity to Scripture was a fundamental value for the Society of Friends. Isichei, for example, noted that the debate within the Society in the 1850s regarding whether or not first cousins could marry 'hinged largely round the precedent of the daughters of Zelophedad' (Numbers 36).[47] In an

---

[39] *Memoir*, II, 353–4.
[40] British Library, London, Elizabeth Fry Papers, Annotated Bible, Add 73528. Fry also once remarked, 'I rose with this text': *Memoir*, II, 116.
[41] *Memoir*, II, 188.   [42] *Memoir*, I, 174.   [43] *Memoir*, II, 330.
[44] *Memoir*, I, 13–14.   [45] *Memoir*, I, 413.   [46] *Memoir*, I, 5.
[47] Isichei, *Victorian Quakers*, 160.

experience disconcerting for her but indicative of the expectations of the denomination, a Friend once made a call on Fry to make sure that *she* was running a devout and disciplined Quaker home in which the children and servants had the benefit of regular Bible readings.[48]

Elizabeth Fry's effort to improve and reform the lives of the women prisoners at Newgate in London began in 1813. Intriguingly for the purpose at hand, it has been suggested that a prior effort might have awakened interest and thus led on eventually to this one: in 1806 the Bible Society and members of the Society of Friends worked to provide copies of the Scriptures for French prisoners in Newgate.[49] In order to pursue this work in a more organized and systematic way, in 1817 Fry founded an Association for the Improvement of the Female Prisoners in Newgate. The nature of the work is given in its founding statement that the association existed to:

> provide for the clothing, the instruction, and the employment of the women; to introduce them to a knowledge of the Holy Scriptures, and to form in them, as much as possible, those habits of order, sobriety and industry, which may render them docile and peaceable whilst in prison, and respectable when they leave it.[50]

As can be seen, the Bible was at the heart of this plan, and for Fry it was the magic ingredient in her internationally acclaimed recipe for prison reform. In effect, Fry instituted morning and evening household devotional Bible readings into prison life. A matron was appointed who ensured that this happened and when a lady from the association visited, one of her principal tasks was to 'read the scriptures to the female prisoners'.[51] Fry herself made a habit of doing the Friday morning Bible reading at Newgate. These became a sensation. The great and the good longed to come and see hardened criminals reduced to penitential tears by the power of God's word. As one might talk about a popular play, Sir James Williams was thrilled that a friend of his was able to procure 'me tickets for admission' to Fry's Newgate reading. He was not disappointed, and wrote for publication a dramatic account of the event as if it were a review of one of Charles Dickens's theatrical readings (to take a well-known example from later in the century)

---

[48] Rose, *Fry*, 54.
[49] Roger H. Martin, 'Quakers, the Bible, and the British and Foreign Bible Society', *Quaker History: The Bulletin of the Friends Historical Association*, 85, 1 (Spring 1996), 18–19.
[50] *Memoir*, I, 266.
[51] [Elizabeth Fry], *Sketch of the Origin and Results of Ladies' Prison Associations, with hints for the formation of Local Associations* (London: John and Arthur Arch, 1827), 49.

rather than a routine devotional exercise.[52] The guests became grander and grander: 'The American Ambassador wrote home to say that he had now seen the two greatest sights of London—St Paul's Cathedral, and Mrs Fry reading to the prisoners in Newgate.'[53] The culmination came in 1842 when Fry read the Bible to Newgate criminals while His Majesty the King of Prussia, Frederick William IV, looked on. Parisians were confident that the impact of Fry's readings should be attributed to her personality, charisma, and public-speaking techniques, and were therefore flummoxed when a decisive effect was had on the women in the prison of St Lazare at a reading Fry arranged when she visited it, despite the fact that a French woman did the actual reading and Fry addressed them through an interpreter. Those committed to Fry's way of seeing things trumpeted this experiment as proof that the active agent was 'the simple indwelling power of the word of God'.[54]

The centrality of these Bible readings in Fry's vision of prison reform work was highlighted when efforts were made to curb it in 1824. Some of the aldermen of the Goal Committee were influenced by the view that it was time to diminish the role of freelance, do-gooder ladies. They backed a proposal to have the Bible readings halted, replacing them with additional chapel services. Fry in her successful effort to resist this change, affirmed: 'this reading has we believe been of peculiar advantage to the poor Female prisoners under our care—of which we have had at different times and particularly lately several striking proofs.'[55] Her daughters accurately reported that when Fry gave evidence on prison reform to the Select Committee of the House of Lords in 1835 she stressed the importance of Bible reading 'far beyond all other topics'. Here is a portion of that evidence:

> I believe the effect of religious and other instruction is hardly to be calculated on; and I may further say, that notwithstanding the high estimation and reverence in which I held the Holy Scriptures before I went to the prisons, as believing them to be written by inspiration of God, and therefore calculated to produce the greatest good; I have seen (in reading the scriptures to those

---

[52] [Sir James Williams], *An hour in His Majesty's Gaol, of Newgate, on Friday the 22nd December, 1820*, second edition (London: J. Nisbett, n.d. [1830]), 5.

[53] Janet Whitney, *Elizabeth Fry: Quaker Heroine* (London: George G. Harrap, 1937), 235.

[54] *Memoir*, II, 265.

[55] Friends Historical Library, Swarthmore College, Swarthmore, Pennsylvania, Elizabeth Fry Papers, Elizabeth Fry to the Aldermen who constitute the Goal Committee, 9/1st Month 1824.

women) such a power attending them, and such an effect on the minds of the most reprobate, as I could not have conceived. If any one wants a confirmation of the truth of Christianity; let him go and read the scriptures in prisons to poor sinners; you there see, how the gospel is exactly adapted to the fallen condition of man. It has strongly confirmed my faith.[56]

Fry's Newgate work was made the template for prison reform in many other places. Everywhere Fry influenced prisons she emphasized Bible reading, even in countries with far different religious traditions and devotional practices such as Russia. When Fry first met the women of Bridewell prison in Glasgow and encouraged them to accept having their lives reorganized along the lines of Newgate, an observer noted, 'Her language was scriptural'.[57] Start as you mean to go on. These various local efforts eventually were united through an umbrella organization, the British Ladies' Society for the Reformation of Female Prisoners, Britain's first national women's organization of any kind. (Even its very name was reassuringly scriptural. Fry commented on Esther 1: 18: 'Ladies a bible term'.)[58] The Nottingham branch reported proudly: 'Portions of the scriptures are daily read amongst us'.[59] An Irish correspondent, by way of contrast, complained that a Protestant culture of Bible reading in the society at large was 'a great advantage', but they had to try their best to implement prison reforms without it in Catholic Ireland.[60] Fry also expanded her efforts to help women criminals whose sentence included transportation to New South Wales. She organized a gift parcel for each of these women which contained the most essential items they would need—with a copy of the Bible literally heading the list. Efforts were made to perpetuate the reformed Newgate model on these convict ships, not least the daily Bible readings. Fry herself would come to see the women off and would lead an embarkation Bible reading. John Kent, with the bemused cynicism of a modernist, remarked that Fry's decision on one such occasion to read Psalm 107 'at first sight looks like deliberate irony', apparently because he could not imagine someone who was being deported affirming that the Almighty is good and merciful.[61] Kent's assumption, however, belies the evidence that the women were often deeply affected by these readings. Indeed, on the very occasion Fry

---

[56] *Memoir*, II, 208.
[57] Susan Corder, *Life of Elizabeth Fry* (London: W. & F. G. Cash, 1853), 280.
[58] British Library, London, Elizabeth Fry Papers, Annotated Bible, Add 73528.
[59] Fry, *Sketch*, 29.   [60] Fry, *Sketch*, 34.
[61] John Kent, *Elizabeth Fry* (London: B. T. Batsford, 1962), 76.

read Psalm 107, the ship captain's daughter (who therefore did not even have the excuse of being emotionally vulnerable because it was a terrible and momentous day in her life) was so moved by Fry's simple reading of the Bible (the Quaker minister did not even comment on it or give a sermon) that she was still haunted by it twenty years later.[62] Indeed, the captain's daughter reported that Fry's unadorned Bible reading completely upstaged the speaker, whose address she had long forgot in its entirety—this orator being no less a personage than the eminent abolitionist William Wilber- force! Likewise, a man who heard her read Psalm 107 at Newgate asked her to come read it again at his deathbed, obviously not finding references to God's goodness ironic even in the face of such a daunting transportation.[63] Fry received a thank-you letter from a woman transported to New South Wales which was so infused with biblical references and quotations that it is natural to deduce that Bible readings sometimes did indeed make a favour- able impression that was more than transient.[64]

There are other ways in which Fry's measures for prison reform were deeply biblical. Both in the prisons and on the convict ships, Fry had the women organized into groups of twelve with a monitor in charge of each group. She never gives a range within which the size of the group should fit: her publications and comments on prison reform are riddled with her specification that twelve is the exact right number. Sometimes she intimates that the particular suitability of this number has been derived by empirical experience, but as she implemented it from the first and never varied it she could not have discovered inductively whether or not a group of ten might work even better.[65] The real source of this regulation therefore is in all likelihood the biblical significance of the number, most notably in the twelve tribes of Israel and Jesus' twelve disciples and then the twelve apostles. The twelve disciples is a particularly resonant model as the monitor then becomes the master who is teaching them the ways of God. And what is good for the prisoners is good for all: Fry herself founded the Newgate Association by gathering together exactly twelve ladies, and when she wrote up suggestions for founding local associations she could not resist including the number twelve as the quorum to aim at.[66]

[62] *Memoir*, II, 12.   [63] *Memoir*, II, 137.   [64] Corder, *Life*, 226–7.
[65] Fry, *Sketch*, 8 (stating that the very first groups were organized by twelve).
[66] Fry, *Observations*, 13.

The famous Rules that the Newgate women agreed to live by in order to reform their way of life together read at times almost like a church catechism, complete with footnoted proof texts:

VI. Swearing, or in any manner taking the *Sacred Name 'in vain,'—all bad words, immoral conversation, and indecent behavior, are to be especially avoided.

* See Exod. xx. 7, and 2 Tim. ii, 16.

VIII. The women are required to attend in the workroom every forenoon (except when the chapel is open for them), and occasionally in the evening, to hear a portion of the Holy Scriptures*

* See 2 Tim. iii. 16, 17.[67]

Her principles were also justified to prison reformers and authorities by proof texts. For example, she grounded her insistence that there should be absolutely no communication between male and female prisoners by quoting 1 Corinthians 15: 33.[68] As to the women's children who were in prison with them, it was resolved that 'the children be carefully and daily instructed in the Holy Scriptures, also taught spelling, reading...'[69] In other words, Bible instruction was primary: everything else was part of the 'also' clause. Finally, it should be observed that Fry heavily used biblical proof texts to motivate people to engage in prison reform. This can be illustrated through her *Observations on the Visiting, Superintending, and Government, of Female Prisoners.* The very first paragraph ends with a rousing call for her readers to become 'the faithful, humble, and devoted, followers of a crucified Lord, who went about DOING GOOD' (Acts 10: 38).[70] Ladies are rallied to join the work by reminding them of Hebrews 13: 16, but cautioned against adopting a haughty attitude in relationship to the prisoners through Romans 3: 23.[71] And so it goes on. Fry's *Sketch of the Origin and Results of Ladies' Prison Associations, with hints for the formation of Local Associations* made explicit what was perhaps the text underlying it all: Jesus' warning and promise in Matthew 25 that people would be distinguished on the Day of Judgment on the basis of whether or not they had visited in prison 'the least of these'.[72] Indeed, an allusion to this is arguably in the very name Fry used for the association: 'the British Ladies' Society for visiting prisons'.[73]

---

[67] Fry, *Sketch*, 54–5.   [68] Fry, *Observations*, 32.   [69] Fry, *Sketch*, 64.
[70] Fry, *Observations*, 2.   [71] Fry, *Observations*, 8, 21–2.   [72] Fry, *Sketch*, 51.
[73] Fry, *Observations*, 1.

The other great cause in Fry's life beside prison reform was the distribution of the Scriptures; and the other great society to which she was most
committed beside the British Ladies' Society for Visiting Prisons was the
British and Foreign Bible Society (commonly referred to as simply the
Bible Society), an organization which existed to increase and extend the
circulation of the Scriptures. Indeed, Fry's commitment to the Bible
Society preceded her prison work. Her daughters went so far as to say
that she was 'warmly interested in the Bible Society, from its commence-
ment [in 1804] to the close of her life'.[74] There is also the intriguing
possibility of another link (beside the one mentioned earlier regarding the
precedent of a Bible Society effort on behalf of the French prisoners of
Newgate) between the two. The nineteenth-century lives of Elizabeth Fry
do not name the founding members of the Newgate Association but
merely confine themselves to saying that they were all Quakers except
for one who was 'the wife of a clergyman'.[75] June Rose asserted that this
twelfth woman was a friend who lived nearby, Mrs Angelzaark.[76] More
recently, however, Annemieke van Drenth and Francisca de Haan have
identified her as Mrs Steinkopf, the wife of Dr Karl Steinkopf, the foreign
secretary of the Bible Society.[77] The present author has not found any
primary source evidence to use to adjudicate between these two claims,
but the more recent one is suggestive: it could indicate that Fry's natural
instinct was to draw upon the help of fellow Friends, but she knew that
obtaining copies of the Bible would be so important to her prison work
that she made an exception in order to gain a foundational tie to the Bible
Society. It is clear from extant primary sources that when Fry later had
another domestic, benevolent scheme that needed Bibles, Dr Steinkopf
was the route she used for approaching the Bible Society.[78] In any event,
Mrs Steinkopf certainly came to take a prominent place in the prison work,
being listed as the primary secretary of the Ladies' British Society—the

---

[74] *Memoir*, I, 174.   [75] Corder, *Life*, 225; *Memoir*, I, 266.   [76] Rose, *Fry*, 84.

[77] Annemieke van Drenth and Francisca de Haan, *The Rise of Caring Power: Elizabeth Fry and
Josephine Butler in Britain and the Netherlands* (Amsterdam: Amsterdam University Press, 1999), 56,
68. For Dr Karl Steinkopf, see Roger Steer, *Good News for the World: 200 Years of Making the Bible
Heard: the Story of the Bible Society* (Oxford: Monarch Books, 2004), 117–19.

[78] Friends Historical Library, Swarthmore College, Swarthmore, Pennsylvania, Elizabeth Fry
Papers, Elizabeth Fry to Dr Steinhopff, Bible Society House, London, 7/10 1824. (*Memoir*, I, 176,
in a third variant, spells the name 'Steinkoff'. I have used 'Steinkopf' as the modern sources I have
consulted agree on it.)

only office that was identified (and thus even Fry herself is not named as an officeholder).[79]

It is important to underline that the Bible Society was arguably the greatest cause that interested Friends in the first half of the nineteenth century—more perhaps even than the Abolition Society. The clergyman John Owen, who later would become the secretary of the Bible Society, candidly reminisced that he had been surprised when Quakers came to the 1804 meeting to found the Bible Society as he had imbibed the rumour that the Society of Friends de-emphasized the Scriptures in both theology and practice.[80] In fact, Quakers became a bulwark of the Bible Society, not only as members but also as financial contributors and officeholders. In an emphatic mark of official approbation, in 1833 the epistle of the London Yearly Meeting observed: 'We rejoice in the part which many of our members have taken in the general diffusion of the holy Scriptures'.[81] It was at the founding of the Norwich branch of the Bible Society in 1811 that a celebrated incident occurred in which Elizabeth Fry disconcerted and impressed a ministerial gathering held at the family seat of Earlham by being obedient to her own call and the prompting of the Spirit and prayed aloud. This meeting included not only Anglican clergymen, but Dr Steinkopf himself (who was a Lutheran minister). Quaker enthusiasm was such that her brother J. J. Gurney made the Norwich Bible Society the one which raised the most money of any of the British and Foreign Bible Society's seventy-six branches.

The Bible Society was always part of Fry's vision. Even when she was feeling somewhat incapacitated through low spirits, Fry recorded that she felt it was her duty to rouse herself to 'make a stir in our parish, about the Bible Society'.[82] Recurringly, one can glimpse the Bible Society and prison work side by side in Fry's life as her two chief benevolent causes. For example, she could report on the good that might come from her visit to the southern coast: 'We hope a Bible Society will be formed at Rye, in consequence of our visit, and a Prison Society at Dover.'[83] In 1840, Fry reported in a letter home to her family that she had taken the occasion of her interview with the Hanoverian Queen to admonish her regarding the royal

---

[79] Fry, *Sketch*, 66.

[80] Martin, 'Quakers', 13.

[81] *The Epistle from the Yearly Meeting, Held in London . . . 1833* (Mount Pleasant, Ohio: Ohio Yearly Meeting, 1833), 9.

[82] *Memoir*, I, 457.

[83] *Memoir*, II, 223.

family's duty 'to attend to and help in, Bible Societies, Prisons, &c.'[84] The overlapping of the two causes was such that Fry could even address the Ladies' British Society for Visiting Prisons on 'the great good the Bible Society had effected in Europe'.[85] Indeed, her interest in the Bible Society, if anything, only increased when she crossed the Channel. Fry's reaction to the grandeur of the Swiss Alps was to observe that these mountain people appeared to be cut off from the work of the Bible Society.[86] On the positive side, there was no more captivating continental conversation than to hear the Countess Reden recount her husband's thrilling exploits on behalf of the Bible Society's work in Silesia.[87]

The theme of 'a people of one book' is also reinforced by Fry's assumption that Bible reading, or even pointing people to particular texts of Scripture, stood above any sectarian strife or ecclesiastical disputes. She was delighted when an Anglican clergyman took it in hand to help her sisters out of their state of religious confusion by merely guiding them in Bible study without imposing any of his own views, maintaining this perspective in naïve gratitude when it just so happened that this encounter with the Scriptures resulted in them joining the Church of England.[88] Fry could not believe that the French press had reported that she had been distributing 'controversial tracts' when these publications were confined to texts of Scripture (it apparently seeming ludicrous to her that anyone could imagine that the translation or selection might be considered able to tilt matters toward certain sectarian positions).[89] When she gave evidence to a House of Commons Select Committee on prison reform, some members were clearly a little worried about handing over the religious instruction of people in the custody of the state to someone from a peculiar and controversial sect which was not by law established. Fry assured them, however, that she was only teaching the women 'the fundamental doctrines of Scripture'.[90] Fry gloried in the circulation of the Bible as the one cause that could unite people of diverse religious views who would not otherwise cooperate.[91] She made good on this herself by accepting an invitation to attend a Bible Society meeting held under the auspices of the navy and army, her resolute Quaker commitment to pacifism notwithstanding.[92]

[84] *Memoir*, II, 367.   [85] *Memoir*, II, 378.
[86] *Memoir*, II, 346.   [87] Gurney, *Journeys*, 171, 183.
[88] *Memoir*, I, 132–3.   [89] *Memoir*, II, 272.   [90] *Memoir*, I, 294.
[91] *Memoir*, I, 478.   [92] *Memoir*, II, 8.

The circulation of the Scriptures and Bible reading were a universal panacea for Elizabeth Fry: her heart never went out to any group without her practical response being this tonic. It was good for princesses as well as prisoners. Fry was on personal terms with most of the leading royal families of Europe. As she progressed from palace to palace in 1840, Fry actually received a letter from the Queen of Denmark complaining that the plain Friend had cut her from this royal tour! Already when Victoria was still a princess, Fry met her and called upon her to meditate on the Old Testament example of King Josiah, who came to the throne as a child and did what was right in the Lord's eyes.[93] That was a tentative, early effort: Fry became increasingly bold not only to give sovereigns specific texts which she thought were apt given their position, but also to turn a royal audience into a Bible reading. Thus we have records of the tears of the mighty as well as the lowly in response to the word of God as voiced by Elizabeth Fry. The Scriptures were essential for schoolchildren: she was particularly annoyed that the Dutch government, in an effort to maintain a stance of toleration for all its subjects whatever their religious convictions, had excluded Bible teaching from state schools.[94] The sick, of course, needed Bibles, and so Fry worked to get them into hospitals. Newlyweds needed the Scriptures, so a family Bible was Fry's standard wedding gift. She would notice sailors, wonder about their lives, and respond by organizing the distribution of Bibles to them.[95] When recovering her health on a seaside holiday at Brighton, she began to observe the isolated lives that members of the coastguard led. This resulted in an energetic, ambitious, and ultimately successful campaign to have the entire national force systematically supplied with Bibles.[96]

Fry's instinct that the Bible was good for whatever ailed humanity was so great that she habitually carried copies of the Bible, the New Testament, or Bible tracts to distribute to those who crossed her path in the course of the day. Indeed, she created a volume of biblical quotations herself and had it printed to be distributed personally: *Texts for Every Day in the Year; Principally Practical and Devotional.*[97] Originally compiled in 1830, she tellingly always referred to this as her 'text book'. It was essentially an aid to private

---

[93] *Memoir*, II, 126.   [94] Rose, *Fry*, 189.

[95] For just one example of this, see *Memoir*, II, 333.

[96] Friends Historical Library, Swarthmore College, Swarthmore, Pennsylvania, Elizabeth Fry Papers, Elizabeth Fry to Dr Steinhopff, Bible Society House, London, 7/10 1824.

[97] Elizabeth Fry, *Texts for Every Day in the Year; Principally Practical and Devotional* (New Bedford: Charles Taber & Co., 1859).

(as opposed to household) morning devotions. She hoped that a busy person would attempt to commit the assigned text to memory first thing in the morning and would then recall it during the midst of the duties of the day. Modern scholars have found this volume so uninteresting that it does not even appear in any of the bibliographies or notes of the twentieth-century biographies.[98] It was important to Fry herself, however. She distributed it liberally—literally thousands of copies—and even had a French edition printed as well. High-quality presentation versions were also produced as gifts for special occasions or recipients. One of these, given to a grandson, fell into the hands of a notorious character into whose home it unwittingly brought sweetness and light.[99] Fry was particularly zealous about distributing biblical and edifying literature on her continental trips and her niece reported that the text book was by far the most popular, well-received, and coveted of the tracts.[100] The future Prussian emperor read from one, the Queen of France was much pleased with hers, and the Queen of the Netherlands was so jealous of Princess Sophie's that she had a messenger go to Fry's hotel and beg for a copy for herself.[101]

The content of the text book is purely quotations from the Bible— usually two per day—given with each date of the year. Fry gave the date the Quaker way initially, but let clarity overrule purity by also including a parenthetical abbreviation of the month's name. Thus the first entry is for '1 Day. 1 Week. 1 Month. (Jan.) 1.' Quaker habits are reflected in other ways as well. Negatively, there is a complete disregard for the church year: even December 25 has as its text Psalm 5: 1–3 which is not remotely one of the numerous texts associated with Christmas. November 5's text is Matthew 5: 33–4 ('Swear not at all'), a text with literal import for Friends. April 27's text is Numbers 11: 29 ('Would God that all the Lord's people were prophets, and that the Lord would put his spirit upon them!')—a sentiment in accord with a Quaker view of the inner light and prophetic ministry. (In her own Bible, she wrote 'amen' by it.)[102] On a more personal note, August 1's passage is Revelation 15: 3–4—the text that she uttered as her first public ministry. Most of the quotations, however, are clearly simply meant to speak to people's hearts. 3 September, for example, has 'Remember not the

[98] Whitney, *Fry*; Kent, *Fry*; Rose, *Fry*.   [99] *Memoir*, II, 104–5.
[100] Gurney, *Journeys*, 23, 67.   [101] Gurney, *Journeys*, 120.
[102] British Library, London, Elizabeth Fry Papers, Annotated Bible, Add 73528.

sins of my youth' (Psalm 25: 6–7)—an apt prayer for both criminals and kings. 19 September offered hope to the women of Newgate: 'I the Lord have called thee . . . to bring out the prisoners from the prison, and them that sit in darkness out of the prison-house.' (Isaiah 42: 6–7). The selections range widely across the canon, but the Psalms loom very large, and to a lesser extent Isaiah—and Job and Lamentations recur more frequently than one would expect.

A particularly telling and neglected source is Fry's own Bible, which she was in the habit of annotating. As with Florence Nightingale's, it brings together in one place diverse interests, concerns, and conversations in her life and thought. It bears scant evidence that Fry read the Bible critically, however. There is certainly no awareness of or interest in issues of authorship, composition, and dating. Fry is completely accepting of the miraculous passages. One of the first verses from the New Testament to be discarded as an unhistorical embellishment is often Matthew 27: 52–3, which claims briefly and mysteriously that at the death of Christ some dead saints rose from their graves. Fry was so far from doubting this that she remarked: 'Proof that the dead are raised'.[103] As to the Old Testament, her comment on Elijah's supernatural ministry in 1 Kings 18 was: 'a wonderful answer to pray in the fire from heaven to destroy the sacrifice & in the return of rain!' Likewise, Joshua causing the sun to stand still prompted: 'A wonderful miracle!' A few notes are even apologetical in nature. 2 Chronicles 9 elicited a reference to an eighteenth-century travel narrative by James Bruce: 'Bruce says in his travels in Abyssinia that the visit paid Solomon by the Queen of Sheba is recorded in the records of their Queens.'

A few comments do betray some scepticism or at least confusion. God's apparently perpetual promise regarding Solomon's temple in 1 Kings 9: 3 is wrestled with: 'For ever in the Holy Scripture I think does not always mean from everlasting to everlasting but there was a condition there.' Likewise, Fry was somewhat uneasy as to the justice of the judgment pronounced on King Saul: 'Saul wanted the Lord's heart—but I do see that he was in too great a hurry to sacrifice.' Most of the texts she struggles with, however, are because, as it were, she wants to be more Christian than Scripture. Often these are in the Old Testament. For example, her summative statement at

---

[103] British Library, London, Elizabeth Fry Papers, Annotated Bible, Add 73528. (As the discussion that follows will all be from this source, it will not be necessary to continue to note it.)

the end of the book of Judges was: 'Too different to the Christian dispensation is where war is permitted.' Likewise here is Fry's comment on King
David's deathbed instructions that Shimei must be punished: 'Returning
evil for evil how different to the Christian dispensation.' The apparent
endorsement of corporal punishment for children in Proverbs 13: 24
evoked: 'I do not consider this means really a rod but suitable & seasonable
punishment.' This kind of reaction can even happen in the Gospels. Christ's
words in Luke 12: 49 that he had come to send fire on the earth occasioned
this reflection: 'No doubt our blessed Lord in one sense is the Prince of
Peace but He must here allude to religious differences & persecution which
have to much abounded in the Christian Church.' And Fry offered this
wishful-thinking gloss to the description of the heroine Rahab: 'Harlot here
means I am informed a keeper of a lodging House not a night woman.'

Some of the notes reflect Quaker distinctives or otherwise are justifica-
tions for Fry's views on various issues. Quaker pacifism is on display
throughout her Bible. For example, she found it significant that the notori-
ously sinful cities of Sodom and Gomorrah were named as part of the '1st
war we read of' (Genesis 14: 2). She also leaped upon any statement that
appeared to go against Calvinist doctrines. Many of her annotations on the
epistle to the Romans are a commentary on how not to read it in a Calvinist
manner. The Church of England is the target at Ephesians 1: 22: 'Christ the
only Head of the Church.' Those not committed to the Quaker practice of
silent worship would in all likelihood not be struck by 1 Kings 6: 7, but Fry
observed: 'Solemn silence preserved in building the Lords temple.' The fact
that the Society of Friends does not observe the sacraments is reflected in
various comments on baptism and the Lord's Supper. For example, at Acts
1:5 Fry wrote: 'He that believeth & is <u>baptised</u> shall be saved surely can
only allude to <u>this</u> baptism of the Holy Ghost.' A sprinkling of notes
throughout are about payments for priests or ministers and this seems to
be an area of ambiguity for her: the cumulative impression is that traditional
churches are indeed doing this wrong as Quakers believe, but there might
be more of a place for a proper way to pay ministers than Quakers practised.
A couple of notes observe the place of singing in corporate worship, rising
to a crescendo at James 5: 13: 'I think we as a Society miss it in <u>never</u> singing
Psalms'. (This is an example of wider evangelical practices influencing her
view of how the Society of Friends needed to change.) Fry often marked
those texts which give warrant to women in ministry. The reference to
Miriam the prophetess in Exodus 15: 20, for example, caused her to reflect:

'Women early made use of in the Church to speak.' Even Elizabeth's greeting to Mary is seen through the lens of 'Ministry of women'. The text most often used to exclude women from ministry, 1 Timothy 2: 12, has this annotation: 'It does not say not to prophesy or speak in the <u>name</u> of <u>the Lord</u>.' Positively, in addition to various texts about women prophesying, Fry's comments on women in ministry centre on the women disciples at the time of Christ's resurrection. All four gospels have comments about this. Mark 16: 9, for example, is annotated: 'Our Lord <u>first</u> appeared to women.' John 20: 17 has this comment: 'Mary sent by our Lord to tell of his resurrection. A woman employed by Him. She obeyed.'

More whimsically, Fry was in the habit of drinking wine daily. Her niece, noticing what went with them wherever they went on their continental trip, quipped that with her Bible and her bottles of wine Elizabeth Fry would be sufficiently fortified to 'travel over the Arabian deserts'.[104] Fry's annotations carry on a running refutation of teetotalism. I Chronicles 27: 27 is not a verse that has often attracted the attention of Bible readers, but Fry knowingly remarked: 'Care even over the wine-cellars.' 2 Chronicles 2: 10 prompted a bolder observation: 'Wine included as a necessary provision by the <u>wisest</u> man'. So to the very end of the canon it goes, with this agenda eccentrically being imported into Revelation 6: 6: 'The wine to be pre-served as valuable & useful.' Perhaps most telling of all, Romans 14: 21 asserts flatly that one should refrain from drinking wine if it would cause another to be offended or stumble. Fry's comment turns this injunction into one half of an equation that cancels itself out: 'We must on one hand be very careful not to offend a weak brother & on the other we must not unite in scruples that we think contrary to the will of God.'

To move from the polemical to the personal, Fry was criticized during her own lifetime (and sometimes thereafter) for allegedly neglecting her family to pursue roles in the public sphere. Her Bible, however, reveals that she was deeply and touchingly preoccupied with domestic relationships. Over and over again, what is incidentally revealed about family relationships in a narrative becomes the primary point she focuses upon—let alone her interest in more direct texts on this matter. Esau's expansion of his family by taking as an additional wife a daughter of Ishmael in an effort to compensate for his having previously married outside, as it were, has not usually impressed, but Fry wrote: 'Esaus care to please his father.' She was clearly struggling with

---

[104] Gurney, *Journeys*, 137.

her disappointment that her children again and again failed to choose a Friend as their marriage partner. Repeatedly, her motherly anxiety trumps her Quaker values when it comes to texts that call for capital punishment for rebellious children. Leviticus 20: 9, for example, elicits not 'So different in the Christian dispensation,' but rather 'Our duty to father & mother is inforced.' Deuteronomy 1: 31 is marked, 'So we must bare with our sons. 9/5 1837.' (The date indicates that she was worried that her sons would not respond positively to her appeal to have monthly extended family Bible readings.) A couple of chapters on, and thus perhaps she was reading in a sequence and was in the same period of anxiety, she wrote at Deuteronomy 4: 9: 'It is my desire to do it but I find it very difficult to teach these things to my sons & sons sons.' Rahab is indeed a hero: 'Saved herself and <u>her family</u>.' Fry reflects wistfully on 1 Samuel 8: 3: 'Too often the children follow not the devoted parent.' At Zechariah 8: 12, Fry recollects that when she was 'low' about her son Samuel's marriage (called here by his nickname 'Gurney'), 'as to temporal things—I opened out these verses'. This apparently means that she was not confident enough in his spiritual path to bless it, but she could still bless their marriage as to earthly prosperity. Luke 19: 9 prompted this earnest cry: 'May salvation come to my house!' Ruth 1: 8 elicits this word of approbation: 'So like my daughters in law.' The priestly blessing in Numbers 6 has this comment: 'Said to most of my children at or before their marriage.' This is but a fraction of such annotations.

As some of these comments have already revealed, Fry's remarks were occasionally explicitly autobiographical. It was not her standard practice to date an annotation, but she would sometimes do this if the text aligned with momentous circumstances in her life. The range of dates is 1836 through 1843. When the apostle Paul says he has been persecuted, Fry added: 'In degree my case in Ireland. 5th Mo. 1836.' Her note at 1 Timothy 4: 6 is: 'A text quoted to me by cousin Joseph Bevan before I spoke in the ministry— he wrote it in a letter and gave it me.' And so one could go on.

Probably the two most frequent types of comments made in Fry's Bible, however, are, firstly, ones that guide behaviour, thoughts, and dispositions and, secondly, ones that affirm that a text accords with one's own sentiments or experiences. As to the first, the observation that a particular text gives a 'lesson' or a 'hint' that one should heed—or prayers that one might come in line with the statement of the text—are generously strewn across her Bible. At the reconciliation of Jacob and Esau, she wrote: 'A striking lesson for brothers.' Here is her comment on 1 Samuel 8: 22: 'What a lesson not to choose for ourselves. The Almighty may yield to our wishes & the result may be bad.' Luke 4: 16 prompted: 'The example of our Lord to attend our place of worship on the Sabbath.' There are times when a comment can be paired with her life experience. For example, at 1 Samuel 19: 6 she wrote, 'The effect of rightly pleading one for another,' reminding one of a painful incident in her life when her undiplomatic pleas for a woman's death sentence to be commuted backfired. (Her advocacy for such prisoners is surely the context for her comment at Numbers 35: 30: 'One witness not enough to cause a man to die.') Often Fry is preaching to herself. At Proverbs 19: 20 she wrote: 'May I ever be willing to be instructed!' The apostle Paul's observation that it is hard to pursue both Christian ministry and family life is marked: 'A Hint for me!' Philippians 1: 14 elicited: 'a valuable hint for me when fatigued & almost overdone to murmur or faint by the way.' Although these comments are not belaboured here, it is important to realize that, for Elizabeth Fry, a main purpose of Scripture was to provide guidance for one's conduct.

The second major theme was the correspondence between life and text. Before focusing on her Bible, it will be beneficial to return to the general context of primary sources by Fry—and secondary ones about her. Twentieth-century scholars have been impatient with Fry's habit of expressing her own thoughts through biblical quotations. To take them in chronological order, Janet Whitney observed dismissively about Fry's journal: 'she fills pages with foggy scriptural language, common to many diarists of the period, which probably had a hypnotic, soothing effect on the spirit without exercising the mind'.[105] John Kent, also misguidedly assuming that biblical quotations obscure rather than reveal her inner life, complained that her journal was 'ridden with Evangelical cliché'.[106] June Rose, doing her best by her lights for her subject, observed in conclusion: 'Two hundred years after her birth, despite the sanctimonious clothing of her thought, she seems a brave and modern woman.'[107] Fry herself, however, found the Bible exciting precisely because it could so well locate and articulate her own feelings. She once reflected: 'How striking a proof of the truth of the Scriptures, and that of which they verify, is the way in which they speak to our individual experience.'[108] Fry frequently quoted a biblical text as expressing 'the language of my own soul', 'the language of my spirit', 'the

[105] Whitney, Fry, 189.   [106] Kent, Fry, 33.   [107] Rose, Fry, 204.
[108] Memoir, II, 48.

language of my heart', 'the feelings of my heart', or 'the acknowledgement of my heart'.[109] Such correspondences are frequently observed in Fry's Bible. To take an extreme example, five separate verses in Psalm 22 are each marked with the words: 'I may say this.' The book of Job recurs with notes that she too has experienced such states. In a particularly explicit statement of this theme, one note says: '26 Psalm Read to much comfort & edification feeling them the words of my heart expressed thus by the inspired David—Jersey 8.12.1836.'

In conclusion, to bring the general theme of 'reading' back to the fore, Elizabeth Fry often annotated her Bible so as to guide her choices in the public reading of Scripture. Sometimes she would just note that a chapter is 'excellent' or 'important' or the like: for example, Nehemiah 4 is headed 'Beautiful chap.' More explicitly, Leviticus 26 has: 'Chap. To read <u>aloud</u>.' Explicit in a different sense, Genesis 19, which contains one of the most sordid narratives in the whole Bible, is labelled: 'This chap not to be read <u>aloud</u>.' Specific audiences are also identified. In the book of Job, a note reads: '28th Chap. very striking the description of creation & wisdom good for young person.' Likewise, as to Proverbs: 'A most valuable chapter for youth is the 4th.' Romans 12 is: 'An important practical chapter for young persons to commit to memory.' Delightfully, 1 Corinthians 6, which addresses two issues: the scandal of lawsuits between church members and the scandal of sexual immoral behaviour by church members, is marked: 'For men.' As to Newgate, Psalm 81 is identified as 'for Prison reading'. The last part of Deuteronomy 17, on the other hand, is marked 'Directions for Kings' and 1 Chronicles 19 has a note which says 'A lesson for Kings not to listen to false accusers'—while these are apt summaries of these texts, Fry was a woman who did give biblical admonitions to kings. In 2 Corinthians comes this note: '4th Chap. for illness & affliction.' Whatever people's station or condition in life, Elizabeth Fry was confident that 'reading' would guide them—and perhaps even give words to the language of their heart.

---

[109] *Memoir*, I, 334, 347, 351, 353, 391, 435, 458, 482.

8

Agnostics

T. H. Huxley and Bibliolatry

A certain kind of Victorian gentleman was apt to take pride in having amassed a thorough, representative collection from the natural world—perhaps it was birds' eggs, or butterflies, or seashells. In 1869, a group of Victorian gentlemen executed a plan to collect specimens of Victorian gentlemen. It was called the Metaphysical Society—a sort of Kew Gardens for the range of religious and philosophical opinions which could be found amongst their peers.[1] The biologist Thomas Henry Huxley (1825–95) was a founding member. Despite the assumption of some others that he was merely a less colourful variety of atheist, Huxley discerned in himself a distinct species and, exercising the right of a discoverer, he named it, thereby coining the word 'agnosticism'. Huxley, therefore, is a uniquely fitting representative of agnostics. As he himself informed the editor of the *Agnostic Annual* for 1884: 'I have a sort of patent right in "Agnostic" (it is my trade mark).'[2] The term would catch on and became widely used—even fashionable. For example, another celebrated Victorian and member of the Metaphysical Society, the man of letters Leslie Stephen, articulated his own views in a work entitled *An Agnostic's Apology*.[3]

---

[1] Alan Willard Brown, *The Metaphysical Society: Victorian Minds in Crisis, 1869–1880* (New York: Octagon Books, 1973).

[2] Leonard Huxley, *Life and Letters of Thomas Henry Huxley*, 3 vols (London: Macmillan, 1908), III, 97.

[3] For Stephen's agnosticism, see Noel Annan, *Leslie Stephen: The Godless Victorian* (New York: Random House, 1984).

Throughout the decades, Huxley sincerely and strongly resisted being identified with atheism. He repeatedly objected to Charles Bradlaugh by name. G. J. Holyoake was a leader of popular freethought who also eschewed the atheist label. For himself, Holyoake chose instead the appellation of 'Secularist'. Huxley was grateful in 1873 when Holyoake defended his claim to be of a different species: 'I offer you my best thanks for your remonstrance against Conways connection of me with Bradlaugh & Co—for whom & all their ways & works I have a peculiar abhorrence.'[4] To be agnostic was to recognize and accept the limits of human knowledge:

> it is wrong for a man to say that he is certain of the objective truth of any proposition unless he can produce evidence which logically justifies that certainty. This is what Agnosticism asserts; and, in my opinion, it is all that is essential to Agnosticism.[5]

Atheists and materialists went astray on the left side of the path, as it were, just as orthodox Christians and spiritualists did on the right. Perhaps because the danger of confusion lay more in that leftward direction, Huxley would even make comments to the effect that he found the atheistic and materialistic positions even more distasteful than the other end of the spectrum. Both extremes, however, by providing people with unwarranted answers offered 'mental peace where there is no peace' (Jeremiah 6: 14); Huxley thought that rather than do that 'it is better to have a millstone tied round the neck and be thrown into the sea' (Mark 9: 42).[6] In short, for Huxley, the correct, agnostic position, given the current level of evidence, was neither to affirm nor to deny the existence of God.[7]

Huxley grew up as the youngest of a large family which was not in a financially sound position. Their father was the senior assistant master in a school that failed in Ealing. The family moved to Coventry when Huxley was around ten years old. Their father's humble post in a bank there did not improve the family fortunes. The family was Church of England and

[4] Co-operative College Archives, Holyoake House, Manchester, Holyoake Papers, 2178, T. H. Huxley to G. J. Holyoake, 2 August 1873. (He is referring to the popular freethinker Moncure Daniel Conway.)

[5] T. H. Huxley, *Essays Upon Some Controverted Questions* (London: Macmillan and Co., 1892), 450 [hereafter *Controverted*].

[6] Huxley, *Life*, III, 222.

[7] It has already been shown in Chapter 3 that Bradlaugh himself was careful to avoid defining atheism as denying the existence of God. Huxley, however, never credited Bradlaugh with evading this critique—presumably because he was not aware that he had.

Huxley's two years at the Ealing school—which had an evangelical ethos—was his only formal education as a boy. In his later polemic writings, Huxley sometimes emphasized the wrongheaded religious beliefs that were inculcated in him during his childhood: 'I was brought up in the strictest school of evangelical orthodoxy'.[8] Nevertheless, he also added on another occasion that he thought that the untenable religious beliefs he imbibed when young were also the experience of nine-tenths of his contemporaries.[9] In contrast to figures such as Bradlaugh, what is striking about Huxley's own autobiographical reflections is there is no particular religious authority figure or group of figures—whether parents, relations, teachers, or clergymen—that he resisted or that he formed his own identity by defying or debunking. Likewise there is no climactic crisis of faith—he seems to have shed the religious beliefs taught to him in childhood gradually and without any decisive moment of painful drama. Huxley's official autobiographical sketch is remarkably uninterested in his own religious history—ignoring both what he learned and the process of unlearning it.[10] For the purpose at hand, a telling bit of autobiographical reflection given elsewhere is Huxley's love of the Bible when 'a child of five or six years old':

> if Bible-reading is not accompanied by constraint and solemnity, as if it were a sacramental operation, I do not believe there is anything in which children take more pleasure. At least I know that some of the pleasantest recollections of my childhood are connected with the voluntary study of an ancient Bible which belonged to my grandmother. . . . What comes vividly back on my mind are remembrances of my delight in the histories of Joseph and David; and of my keen appreciation of the chivalrous kindness of Abraham in his dealing with Lot. Like a sudden flash there returns back upon me, my utter scorn of the pettifogging meanness of Jacob, and my sympathetic grief over the heartbreaking lamentation of the cheated Esau, 'Hast thou not a blessing for me also, O my father?' And I see, as in a cloud, pictures of the grand phantasmagoria of the Book of Revelation.[11]

As his own life story unfolds, it will become clear that Huxley was apt to tell it through the lens of biblical narratives.

Huxley's shedding of orthodox doctrines came both through his reading (Thomas Carlyle's *Sartor Resartus* was particularly influential) and, as Adrian

---

[8] Huxley, *Controverted*, 346.   [9] Huxley, *Controverted*, 20.

[10] T. H. Huxley, *Method and Results: Essays* (New York: D. Appleton and Company, 1896), 1–17.

[11] T. H. Huxley, *Science and Education: Essays*, Edition de Lure (New York: J. A. Hill and Company, 1904), 213.

Desmond has brilliantly shown, through the milieu of radical Dissent that he was exposed to in Coventry.[12] Huxley had two brothers-in-law who were in the medical profession and Huxley chose it for his own as well, securing a scholarship to Charing Cross Hospital. Even with this help, he could not afford to pursue the course all the way to obtaining his degree and in 1846 his constrained financial situation necessitated his joining the navy. Huxley thought he was being ignored if not thwarted by his official chief, Sir John Richardson, and began to grumble against him: 'But one day, as I was crossing the hospital square, Sir John stopped me, and heaped coals of fire on my head [Romans 12: 20] by telling me that he had tried to get me one of the resident appointments, much coveted by assistant-surgeons'.[13] Eventually Huxley was appointed assistant surgeon on a ship which went on a surveying expedition in the Asian Pacific, 1846–50. He wrote to his sister in 1846:

> Henceforward, like another Jonah, my dwelling-place will be the 'inwards' of the *Rattlesnake*, and upon the whole I really doubt whether Jonah was much worse accommodated, so far as room goes, than myself.[14]

Huxley's real ambition was not to be a medical doctor, but rather a man of science, and he had jumped at this trip as a way to make his scientific reputation. He was sending papers to England which presented his research and discoveries but, as with Sir John, he began to suspect, erroneously, that he was being ignored or thwarted. As he later reflected:

> During the four years of our absence, I sent home communication after communication to the 'Linnean Society,' with the same result as that obtained by Noah when he sent the raven out of his ark. Tired at last of hearing nothing about them, I determined to do or die, and in 1849 I drew up a more elaborate paper and forwarded it to the Royal Society. This was my dove, if I had only known it.[15]

Ashore in Sydney, he met, fell in love with, and became engaged to Henrietta Heathorn, whom he called Nettie. She was a devout Anglican Christian, who continued to attend church faithfully (along with their children) even after her husband had become one of the most famous critics

---

[12] Adrian Desmond, *Huxley: From Devil's Disciple to Evolution's High Priest* (London: Penguin, 1997). For a thought-provoking extrapolation of this insight, see Bernard Lightman, 'Interpreting Agnoticism as a Nonconformist Sect: T. H. Huxley's "New Reformation"', in Paul Wood (ed.), *Science and Dissent in England, 1688–1945* (Aldershot: Ashgate, 2004), 197–214.
[13] Huxley, *Method*, 11.   [14] Huxley, *Life*, I, 37.   [15] Huxley, *Method*, 13.

of Christian doctrine in Victorian society. In these early days of their relationship, Huxley candidly confessed to her his religious scepticism. This unsettled her and Huxley wrote her a letter in October 1847 in order to allay her concerns. Huxley argued that what is important is for people to form their opinions in the right way and to be 'truthful and earnest' and that of such matters of conviction 'the Almighty searcher of hearts can alone be the efficient judge'. He reassured her that he detested the kind of arrogant, iconoclast sceptics who 'exhibit their vain ingenuity for the mere purpose of puzzling and disturbing the faith of others'. Desmond recognized the importance of this letter and quoted it at length, but left off the ending, which is telling for the theme of this volume as Huxley skilfully used biblical language as a way of creating a soothing portrait of their future life together:

> In the mean time let nothing dispirit or sadden you. We have put our hands to the plough—let us not look back to the everlengthening furrows but forward to the Harvest—Confident in one another's love.[16]

In other words, he averred that they should follow Jesus' advice according to Luke's Gospel to not look back after putting one's hand to the plough (Luke 9: 62)—in this case, not to rethink their decision to pursue marriage.

As this letter to Nettie implicitly reveals, Huxley was in want of a word for his own religious stance. For some time to come he would make do with older, less satisfactory ones. In a letter in 1855 he referred to 'my pagan prejudice'.[17] In 1860, grieving at the death of his son, Huxley opened his heart to the clergyman Charles Kingsley and tried to describe his religious scepticism more fully and candidly than was his wont. He admitted that most people would be able to put a label to his views to their own satisfaction: 'I know right well that 99 out of 100 of my fellows would call me atheist, infidel, and all the other usual hard names.'[18] A couple of years later he referred to this correspondence as 'my heathen letters', and once again struggled with the fact that he did not see himself as of the same ilk as atheists, although it would seem he was doomed to be lumped together in the same category:

---

[16] Imperial College Archives, London, Huxley Papers, T. H. Huxley to Nettie Heathorn, 16–18 October 1847.
[17] Huxley, *Life*, I, 179.   18 Huxley, *Life*, I, 319.

I have never had the least sympathy with the a priori reasons against ortho-doxy, and I have by nature and disposition the greatest possible antipathy to all the atheistic and infidel school. Nevertheless, I know that I am, in spite of myself, exactly what the Christian world call, and, so far as I can see, are justified in calling, atheist and infidel.[19]

In the following year, 1864, in a letter to his sister he pleaded guilty to being 'a great heretic'.[20] 'Agnostic' would allow him to eschew all these labels—pagan, heathen, heretic, infidel, atheist—which essentially reflected how he looked when viewed from the position of others rather than from his own vantage point.

When Huxley returned to England at the end of the *Rattlesnake* expedition in 1850, he once again entered a period in which he felt ignored or thwarted. He was engaged to Nettie, whom he had left behind in Sydney, but he knew it would take years of hard graft before he would reach a position of sufficient financial security to be able to marry her. This goal was made more difficult by his determination to be a man of science—a profession that did not really exist yet as a way of making a living. He thought he was in danger of losing everything that mattered most in terms of his potential contribution to society, and he repeatedly cast this drama in biblical ways. In 1852, he confessed to Nettie: 'The spectre of a wasted life has passed before me—a vision of that servant who hid his talent in a napkin and buried it' (Luke 19: 11–27).[21] The following year he told her again that he must hold out against such self-betrayal:

> however painful our present separation may be, the spectacle of a man who had given up the cherished purpose of his life, the Esau who had sold his birthright for a mess of pottage and with it his self-respect, would before long years were over our heads be infinitely more painful.[22]

He failed to secure the university posts that he pursued during these years, but in 1854 finally found a steady place for himself to both pursue science and feed a family as a lecturer at the Government School of Mines in London. Nettie Heathorn and Tom Huxley had their Anglican church wedding in London in 1855. Through his research, discoveries, theories, and writings Huxley steadily emerged as one of the most gifted contributors to the field of natural history of his day. His fame was increased by his self-

---

[19] Huxley, *Life*, I, 346–7.   [20] Huxley, *Life*, I, 362.
[21] Huxley, *Life*, I, 121.   [22] Huxley, *Life*, I, 122.

imposed role from 1860 onwards as the defender of Darwinism. Already in 1851 Huxley had been elected a Fellow of the Royal Society, and his path was destined to be sprinkled with prestigious lectureships, presidencies of learned societies, medals, prizes, honorary doctorates, and other distinctions. He was eventually elected president of the Royal Society. His place of eminence was crowned in 1892 when he became a privy councillor (by taking an oath on a Bible).

Turning more from Huxley's life to his thought, the most obvious point to underline is that he habitually used biblical language and imagery in order to express his ideas. It would be wearisome to illustrate this at great length, but the cumulative effect of seeing it spread continually and thickly across a lifetime of his writings and recorded speech is powerful. The people he disagreed with in print were apt to be recast as biblical characters. The Duke of Argyll was Balaam. The Salvation Army's William Booth was Simon Magus. Auguste Comte was the prophet Samuel—or Moses. As to a clerical opponent:

> Things would assume more accurate proportions in Dr Wace's mind if he would kindly remember that it is just thirty years since ecclesiastical thunderbolts began to fly about my ears. I have had the 'Lion and the Bear' to deal with, and it is long since I got quite used to the threatening of episcopal Goliaths, whose crosiers were like unto a weaver's beam.[23]

Huxley told Darwin that he was determined to help financially a mutual friend of theirs who was sick 'even if I go like Nicodemus privily and by night to his bankers.'[24] He compared himself to Pilate. Writing to Herbert Spencer in 1888, Huxley playfully contrasted his own situation with that of Samson. When Huxley took to gardening as a hobby, he told J. D. Hooker in 1891 it was 'a Naboth's vineyard'.[25] A setback in this endeavour evoked a different biblical character: 'A lovely clematis in full flower, which I had spent hours in nailing up, has just died suddenly. I am more inconsolable than Jonah!'[26] Some of these allusions are more than a little obscure by today's standards: Huxley assumed a Victorian general readership would know what he meant by 'this supposed scientific Achitophel' or 'these scientific Sanballats'.[27]

[23] Huxley, *Controverted*, 408–9.   [24] Huxley, *Life*, II, 121.
[25] Huxley, *Life*, III, 197.   [26] Huxley, *Life*, III, 424.
[27] Huxley, *Controverted*, 321, 365.

This habit sometimes seemed to get a bit out of control. In his 'Evolution and Ethics: Prolegomena', Huxley referred to Haman and Mordecai merely by way of illustration, but became so overtaken by this material that he inserted the biblical passage in a footnote and observed how shrewdly it depicts human nature by way of a commentary on his text.[28] Later in 'Evolution and Ethics' Huxley incongruously expounded Buddhist and then Stoic thought through language lifted from the Christian Bible. Moreover, that essay begins by retelling the story of human civilization in natural history terms, but nonetheless using the language of the book of Genesis (it starts with a Garden of Eden, in which there is a serpent, and so on). In his letters, Huxley habitually, if not compulsively, expressed himself through biblical allusions. To take one random example, he reassured his sister that he had enough money to help her family in their distress with the words 'there is corn in Egypt' (Genesis 42: 2).[29] Scriptural words would slip even into technical, scientific comments. In an 1863 letter to Dr W. K. Parker, for example, Huxley wrote: 'I look upon the proposition opisthotis =turtle's "occipital externe"=Perch's Rocher (Cuvier) as the one thing needful [Luke 10: 42] to clear up the unity of structure of the bony cranium'.[30] Too much has been made of the encounter in 1860 between Huxley, as the defender of Darwinism, and Samuel Wilberforce, bishop of Oxford, as its critic, at the British Association. Huxley famously countered Wilberforce's flippancy with a high moral tone of indignation. Nevertheless, what generally goes unobserved is that Huxley's initial reaction was to quote Scripture, as he himself recalled:

> The Bishop began his speech, and to my astonishment very soon showed that he was so ignorant that he did not know how to manage his own case. My spirits rose proportionally, and when he turned to me with his insolent question, I said to Sir Benjamin, in an undertone, "The Lord hath delivered him into mine hands."' [Deuteronomy 3: 3][31]

To round off this point, here is an anecdote that Professor Jeffrey Parker told about Huxley:

> I was once grumbling to him about how hard it was to carry on the work of the laboratory through a long series of November fogs, 'when neither sun nor

---

[28] T. H. Huxley, *Evolution and Ethics and Other Essays* (London: Macmillan and Co., 1898), 29.
[29] Huxley, *Life*, I, 154.   [30] Huxley, *Life*, I, 353.   [31] Huxley, *Life*, I, 272.

stars in many days appeared.' 'Never mind, Parker,' he said, instantly capping my quotation, 'cast four anchors out of the stern and wish for day.' [Acts 27: 20–9][32]

It was agreed that Huxley had no gift for memorization, and there is no record that any contemporary of his ever thought of him as having an exceptional knowledge of Scripture. In other words, in a Victorian context, Huxley's ability to quote the Bible did not look particularly extraordinary.

On one level, especially in some of his letters with his friends or congenial professional contacts, Huxley's biblical quotations were clearly meant to be ironic or witty—to play off the incongruity of an agnostic drawing on a sacred text. This habit was so ingrained, however, that it cannot be reduced to this posture. For example, it continued when Huxley was as far from a playful mood as possible: when he was grief-stricken at the death on 20 November 1887 of his daughter, Marian. He wrote to J. D. Hooker on the very next day, telling him of his loss and notifying him that he would therefore be cancelling his immediate engagements: 'So I shall not be at the Society except in the spirit' (1 Corinthians 5: 3). A few days later, he wrote of Marian's last days to the religious sceptic, Edward Clodd: 'I suppose we ought to rejoice that the end has come, on the whole, so mercifully. But I find that even I, who knew better, hoped against hope' (Romans 4: 18).[33]

Having established Huxley's tendency to draw on Scripture, it is time now to journey into the way that the Bible shaped his thinking in more profound and structural ways. To begin at the periphery, most aligned to his playful, ironic mode is his persistent tendency to recast his opponents as the enemies of the people of God as presented in the Scriptures. This is particularly ironic as his enemies were so often Bible believers who saw themselves as members of God's chosen people. It has already been shown that he saw the clergyman, Dr Wace, as Goliath. Matthew Arnold so established the convention of referring to people one does not like as 'Philistines' that it is perhaps hard to observe how specific and scriptural this imagine is. Huxley certainly routinely referred to people on the wrong side of an issue with this appellation. To take a random example, in a letter to Darwin in 1865 Huxley advised him on how to act in the light of the

---

[32] Huxley, *Life*, III, 376.
[33] Huxley, *Life*, III, 44–5. When his son died in 1860, Huxley went so far as to write, 'I say heartily and without bitterness—Amen, so let it be'; a sentiment that would perhaps tempt some scholars to exhibit it as a textbook case of the oppressive nature of orthodox piety if it came from a more conventionally religious Victorian. Huxley, *Life*, I, 219.

Philistines.[34] A decade before Arnold had established 'Philistine' so firmly in the lexicon of the elite, Huxley was already in the habit of using 'Amalekites' in the same manner.[35] He had recourse to this usage throughout his adult life. For example, he wrote in an 1889 letter: 'I can't understand [the bishop of] Peterborough nohow. However, so far as the weakness of the flesh would permit me to abstain from smiting him and his brother Amalekite, I have tried.'[36] While Amalekites and Philistines are perennial names for Huxley's enemies, he would employ other variations as well. Charles Lyell commented on the proofs of Huxley's first book, *Man's Place in Nature* (1863). Huxley deferred to Lyell's advice that it would not be viewed as in the best taste for him to refer to his opponents as 'uncircumcized'.[37] Huxley once boasted that John Tyndall could hew his conservative Christian interlocutors 'to pieces before the Lord in Gilgal' (1 Samuel 15: 33).[38] In 1892, Huxley encouraged the secretary of the Royal Society after that body had been criticized with these words: 'Let not thine heart be vexed because of these sons of Belial.' ('Sons of Belial' being biblical parlance for those who do not know the Lord—see 1 Samuel 2: 12—once again, a rather inverted way for an agnostic to describe his opponents.)[39]

His religious scepticism notwithstanding, Huxley's instincts were often to appropriate the power of a biblical word or category rather than to attempt to replace or debunk it. It is now the norm to refer to the 'theory' of evolution, but Huxley—from his first encounter with Darwinism to the end of his life—standardly referred to it as a 'doctrine'. He used this language consistently both in his official, scientific writings and in his private correspondence: even when writing to Darwin himself he would refer to it as 'your doctrine'.[40] 'Sin' was a very real category for Huxley which he frequently evoked not only unironically, but even uncritically. Sounding very much like a pious evangelical, he testified penitently in dead earnest in 1860: 'I confess to my shame that few men have drunk deeper of all kinds of sin than I.'[41] Or, more generally, he observed that 'men of science . . . have our full share of original sin'.[42] Huxley even went so far as to appropriate rather than reject the category of miracles, affirming on behalf of the

---

[34] Huxley, *Life*, I, 387.   [35] Desmond, *Huxley*, 317.
[36] Huxley, *Life*, III, 108–9.   [37] Huxley, *Life*, I, 290.
[38] Desmond, *Huxley*, 364.   [39] Huxley, *Life*, III, 275.
[40] Huxley, *Life*, I, 253. For an example of his still using the language of 'the doctrine of evolution' in 1894, the year before his death, see Huxley, *Life*, III, 328.
[41] Huxley, *Life*, I, 290.   [42] Huxley, *Controverted*, 311.

scientific community: 'We have any quantity of genuine miracles of our own'.[43] Desmond has highlighted Huxley's 'goading talk of the "sin of faith"'.[44] It is true that Huxley sometimes condemned the category of faith, although he was often careful to define that he meant the wrong kind; and he was apt to attack it through biblical language, for example, arguing that 'faith, in this sense, is an abomination'.[45] Given his prominent identity as an agnostic, however, what is more intriguing is that 'faith' was frequently used as a positive category by Huxley throughout his adult life. He reassured Nettie, for example, by speaking of 'my faith in you'.[46] While too much weight ought perhaps not be put on what even a man of science says in his love letters, Huxley's published writings are sprinkled with references to his 'faith in the constancy of natural order', agnostics' 'perfect faith in logic', the 'faith which is born of knowledge', and the like.[47] Huxley even went so far as to speak of 'scientific faith' and of 'the agnostic faith, which if a man keep whole and undefiled, he shall not be ashamed to look the universe in the face' (as well as the 'agnostic confession').[48]

Thomas Huxley also shared the proof-texting habit of the Victorians—that is, the tendency to quote triumphantly a passage of Scripture that expressed or bolstered the point one was making. For example, he found warrant for rejecting the orthodox, Christian doctrine of creation *ex nihilo* in Jeremiah 4: 23.[49] He saw the disruption that the new knowledge he was advocating brought to the church as illustrating Jesus' teaching that old bottles cannot hold the new wine.[50] He used biblical texts to condemn the teachings and actions of Christian groups ranging from Roman Catholics to the Salvation Army—sounding like a Plymouth Brother, the latter's methods of conversion he denounced as contrary to the New Testament pattern.[51] Huxley averred that the agnostic method could be found in the verse: 'Try all things, hold fast by that which is good' (1 Thessalonians 5: 21).[52] A particularly telling example comes in Huxley's work *Physiography: An Introduction to*

---

[43] Huxley, *Controverted*, 256.   [44] Desmond, *Huxley*, p. xxi.

[45] Huxley, *Controverted*, 453.

[46] Imperial College Archives, London, Huxley Papers, T. H. Huxley to Nettie Heathorn, 27 November 1847.

[47] Huxley, *Controverted*, 306, 366; Huxley, *Evolution*, 8.

[48] Huxley, *Controverted*, 308, 362, 37.

[49] Huxley, *Controverted*, 120.

[50] He often referred to that text. See, for examples, T. H. Huxley, *Lay Sermons, Addresses, and Reviews* (London: Macmillan and Co., 1870), 305; T. H. Huxley, *Critiques and Addresses* (London: Macmillan and Co., 1873), 271–2.

[51] Huxley, *Evolution*, 191.   [52] Huxley, *Controverted*, 362.

the Study of Nature. This volume is not at all polemical in nature, but rather is simply a straightforward, scientific textbook. Nevertheless, Huxley was obviously thrilled to have a biblical text which articulated his argument on 'Evaporation' and therefore he ended the chapter of that title by gleefully quoting it: 'In the words of a wise man of old—"All the rivers run into the sea: yet the sea is not full; unto the place from whence the rivers come, thither they return again."' (Ecclesiastes 1: 7)[53]

To move to the heart of the argument, a dominant analytical tool in Huxley's thought was the deeply biblically infused category of 'idolatry'. This is curious as this category is typically only employed by someone who believes that they do know the one true God and understand what God is really like. Moreover, Huxley was strongly committed to the new discipline of anthropology. He even served as president of the Ethnological Society and helped it transition into the Royal Anthropological Institute. His preoccupation with denouncing the idolatrous is a mark of how comfortable Victorian anthropologists—even agnostic ones—were with biblical modes of thought; no anthropologist today would use the idolatry label. Huxley can be fittingly seen as akin to an Old Testament prophet railing against the idolatry of the nation. He critiqued almost anything and everything he opposed with this judgment. Roman Catholics were idolaters. If one travelled in southern Europe, Huxley assured the readers of the *Nineteenth Century*, 'the essence' of the old 'pagan idolatry' was still on display.[54] In a private letter from Rome he was even more forthright: 'It is the festa of St Peter's chair . . . I am possessed with a desire to arise and slay the whole brood of idolaters'.[55] The Oxford Movement fell under the same judgment: the Anglo-Catholics were corrupting England with 'an effete and idolatrous sacerdotalism' (the passage also condemns them through a proof text, the words of 'the Master' in Mark 7: 4, a critique which elided Huxley's critical point often insisted upon elsewhere that there is no warrant to assume that Jesus of Nazareth ever said what is recorded in the Gospels).[56] The more thoroughgoing claim, of course, was that Christianity in general was idolatrous—and the God of the Bible was an idol. Huxley's essay, 'The Evolution of Theology: An Anthropological Study', patiently makes the case that

---

[53] T. H. Huxley, *Physiography: An Introduction to the Study of Nature* (London: Macmillan and Co., 1891), 74.
[54] Huxley, *Controverted*, 312–13.   [55] Huxley, *Life*, II, 391.
[56] Huxley, *Controverted*, 411.

the people of Israel as revealed in the biblical books of Judges and 1 and 2 Samuel had no more worthy a view of God than Polynesian idolaters. To take just a couple of fragments of this arresting attempt to level down:

> If the pulling of the string to call the attention of the god seems as absurd to us as it appears to have done to the worthy missionary, who tells us of the practice, it should be recollected that the high priest of Jahveh [Jehovah] was ordered to wear a garment fringed with golden bells.
>
> The Tongans also believed in a mode of divination (essentially similar to the casting of lots) by the twirling of a cocoa-nut.[57]

More bluntly in private conversation, Huxley would baldly declare that Jehovah was no greater a conception of the divine than Zeus or Moloch.[58]

This is just to begin to see the utility of this category in Huxley's mind. Huxley claimed to want religion without theology; therefore, one might imagine that Positivism was made to order. Nevertheless, he railed against it. It was 'M. Comte's new idol'. Huxley dubbed it the 'new Anthropolatry' as a way of voicing his prophetic verdict that it made an idol of 'Humanity'.[59] Huxley had found his way out of orthodoxy with the help of the writings of Thomas Carlyle, but he came to see Carlyle as tainted in the same way: 'The other sect (to which I belong)' look upon 'hero-worship as no better than any other idolatry'.[60] Even Herbert Spencer's 'Unknown' was condemned: 'The tendency to idolatry in the human mind is so strong.'[61] Indeed. Sparing no one, Huxley confessed that modern science falls victim to this critique as well. Terms such as 'law, and force, and ether' often function as 'dogmatic idols'.[62] In a more penitent or winsome mood, he could even allow himself to seem to be included: 'Most of us are idolators, and ascribe divine powers to the abstractions "Force," "Gravity," "Vitality," which our own brains have created.'[63]

In this context, Huxley frequently condemned the orthodox view of Scripture as bibliolatry and its holders as bibliolaters. Unlike 'Anthropolatry' this was no neologism of his own but, on the other hand—whatever was or was not intended by others who used this term—Huxley meant it literally. Much of his public advocacy was a holy war against 'the powerful arm of Bibliolatry'.[64] Matthew Arnold was a cobelligerent in this cause and Huxley

---

[57] Huxley, *Controverted*, 173, 181.
[58] Huxley, *Life*, III, 400.   [59] Huxley, *Controverted*, 371–6.
[60] Huxley, *Life*, I, 407.   [61] Huxley, *Life*, III, 291.
[62] Huxley, *Controverted*, 208.   [63] Huxley, *Life*, II, 358.
[64] T. H. Huxley, *Darwiniana: Essays* (New York: D. Appleton and Company, 1893), 56.

wrote to him in 1870, grumbling about their common foe: 'These people are for the most part mere idolaters with a Bible-fetish'.[65] Nor was this mere private posturing; in high prophetic mode, Huxley thundered in print:

> the green bay tree of bibliolatry flourishes as it did sixty years ago. And, as in those good old times, whoso refuses to offer incense to the idol is held to be guilty of 'a dishonour to God,' imperilling his salvation.[66]

(The green bay tree is a biblical image for the prosperity of the wicked—see Psalm 37: 35). The stark, unadorned version of this thought was perhaps even more devastating: 'it is clear that the biblical idol must go the way of all other idols'.[67] This target became so central to Huxley's work that when, in 1891, he was compiling a huge volume of all his recent writings he was sceptical of a plan to have it translated into French on the grounds that it would not be relevant as he assumed the French public 'knows little about Bibliolatry'.[68]

It is quite possible that even the very word 'agnosticism' is a biblical allusion. Certainly, it has been asserted that Scripture was behind it from the Victorian age to the present.[69] In his explanation of how he coined the term, Huxley recalled that he had been influenced by Sir William Hamilton's essay 'On the Philosophy of the Unconditioned' (1829). In it, Hamilton declared that the 'last and highest consecration of all true religion' is the *Agnosto Theo* (the Unknown God) for whom there was an altar in Athens and, according to Acts 17: 23, which the apostle Paul used as an acceptable bit of religious thought from which to begin his discourse.[70] Another key piece of evidence supporting this biblical influence on the derivation of 'agnostic' comes from Richard Holt Hutton, the editor of the *Spectator*. Hutton was at the private meeting in 1869 at which Huxley first

[65] Huxley, *Life*, II, 11.

[66] Huxley, *Controverted*, 21.

[67] T. H. Huxley, *Science and Hebrew Tradition: Essays* (New York: D. Appleton and Company, 1910), p. x.

[68] Huxley, *Life*, III, 203.

[69] For a Victorian example, see Henry Webster Parker, *The Agnostic Gospel: A Review of Huxley on the Bible; with Related Essays* (New York: John B. Alden, 1896), 2. For a recent example of this claim, see Tod E. Jones, *The Broad Church: A Biography of a Movement* (Lanham, Maryland: Lexington Books, 2003), 198.

[70] William Hamilton, *Discussions on Philosophy and Literature* (New York: Harper & Brothers, 1861), 22. Around the turn of the century, Thomas Hardy wrote a poem entitled, 'Agnosto Theo'. Also along these lines, Huxley prided himself on plain-speaking, as did many Victorian sceptics (a notable example is Leslie Stephen's *Essays on Free Thinking and Plain Speaking*), and this self-description is probably of biblical derivation as well (see 2 Corinthians 3: 12).

introduced the word and Hutton was the first person to use it in print. In 1870, Hutton wrote an article on Huxley in which he spoke of his 'favourite "agnostic" creeds, and the altar on which he has more than once professed to lay his offerings—that inscribed "to the Unknown God"'.[71] The exploration of Huxley's patterns of thinking regarding idolatry that has already been presented strengthens the case for this derivation. Essentially, the apostle Paul was saying that all the other Athenian gods were false gods, but the admission of not knowing what God is like—this agnostic view— was the only one that was not hopelessly idolatrous. This perspective is underlined by Huxley's concession that Spinoza's God was sufficiently underdetermined to be acceptable: 'God so conceived is one that only a very great fool would deny'.[72] Denying the existence of *any* God was precisely, in Huxley's mind, what distinguished atheism and agnosticism but even an agnostic was still free to discern that some reputed God was really just an idol and to denounce it as such.

The world of popular atheism was particularly disappointed that Thomas Huxley could and would sometimes commend Bible reading in glowing terms. According to Huxley, just because the Bible was often treated in an idolatrous manner, did not mean that it is not a highly admirable book in its own terms. He insisted that the Scriptures should not be relied upon for historical and scientific accuracy, but he would sometimes remind his more iconoclastic readers that this was also true of *Hamlet* and *Macbeth*. He even went so far as to observe that the sick and suffering gain more real help from a Bible woman than a man of science.[73] Huxley therefore could sometimes reposition himself as a defender of the Bible: 'the New Testament books are not responsible for the doctrine invented by the Churches that they are anything but ordinary historical documents.'[74] Compulsory state education for English children was enacted into law in 1870. Local boards needed to be elected in order to oversee this new venture, and Huxley agreed to be a candidate for the London School Board. He also wrote an article, 'The School Boards: What They Can Do, and What They May Do', which was

---

[71] Bernard Lightman, 'Huxley and Scientific Agnosticism: the strange history of a failed rhetorical stategy', *British Journal for the History of Science*, 35 (2002), 271–89 (here 276). Huxley claimed that an influence was that his neologism was 'suggestively antithetic to the "gnostic" of Church history': Huxley, *Controverted*, 356. This too arguably had a biblical prompt. In good agnostic fashion, Huxley would use against theology the text which warned against 'gnosis falsely so called' (1 Timothy 6: 20): Huxley, *Science and Education*, 209.

[72] Huxley, *Controverted*, 230.

[73] Huxley, *Life*, II, 43–4.   [74] Huxley, *Controverted*, 414.

published in the *Contemporary Review* in 1870. To the bewilderment of friend and foe alike, Huxley insisted that the Bible must be included in the core curriculum. He even went so far as to claim that he would rather his own children had such an education rather than a purely secular one—even if it meant that additional erroneously theological ideas were lumped in as well as part of a wider, orthodox religious education agenda. He certainly made sure his own children read the Bible, he observed. (He also gave his nephew a Bible as a present.)[75] This led Huxley into extolling the virtues of the Scriptures:

> I must confess I have been no less seriously perplexed to know by what practical measures the religious feeling, which is the essential basis of conduct, was to be kept up, in the present utterly chaotic state of opinion on these matters, without the use of the Bible. . . . Take the Bible as a whole; make the severest deductions which fair criticism can dictate for shortcomings and positive errors; eliminate, as a sensible lay-teacher would do, if left to himself, all that it is not desirable for children to occupy themselves with; and there still remains in this old literature a vast residuum of moral beauty and grandeur. And then consider the great historical fact that, for three centuries, this book has been woven into the life of all that is best and noblest in English history; that it has become the national epic of Britain, and is as familiar to noble and simple, from John-o'-Groat's House to Land's End . . .[76]

Atheist activists were so grieved by this that even after Huxley's death they were either still fuming angrily about it or attempting to deny that he sincerely held or, if it was conceded that he did at the time, continued to hold, this view. Bradlaugh's own daughter, in her biography of her father, took the fuming approach.[77] Another example is Robertson's *A History of Freethought in the Nineteenth Century*: its knowing statement, 'He won his election', invites the reader to assume that the school-board essay did not reflect Huxley's real beliefs, but rather was just a cynical attempt to garner votes. Robertson also claimed that Huxley himself ultimately recognized that he had made a false step in this matter.[78] In truth, however, although Huxley was well aware that some of his most fervent supporters were

---

[75] Desmond, *Huxley*, 403.   [76] Huxley, *Critiques*, 51.

[77] Hypatia Bradlaugh Bonner, *Charles Bradlaugh*, 2 vols (London: T. Fisher Unwin, 1895), II, 128.

[78] J. M. Robertson, *A History of Freethought in the Nineteenth Century* (London: Watts & Co., 1929), 391–2.

disappointed in him for this stance, he went out of his way to reaffirm his commitment to it right to the end of his life. To begin at the beginning, however, in a private letter dated 20 February 1871, Huxley told another member of the board that although his stance had evoked the 'disgust' of 'our liberal colleagues': 'I mean to stick to what I said in the "Contemporary" and act accordingly'.[79] Huxley voted with the successful majority which resolved as to the core curriculum:

> in infants' schools there should be the Bible, reading, writing, arithmetic, object lessons of a simple character . . . In junior and senior schools the subjects of instruction were divided into two classes, essential and discretionary, the essentials being the Bible, and the principles of religion and morality, reading, writing, and arithmetic, English grammar and composition, elementary geography, and elementary social economy, the history of England . . .[80]

It is hard to imagine a more fitting illustration of the theme that the Victorians were people of one book than this resolution, which gives primacy of place to the Bible even before reading, writing, and arithmetic—not to mention the additional fact that it was willingly agreed to by the father of agnosticism.[81]

A decade later, in a private letter to Edward Clodd, the author of a critical and unorthodox life of Jesus, Huxley reaffirmed his school-board stance, while admitting that his friends assumed he was either a hypocrite or a fool. Huxley argued on this occasion that the Bible was great literature and he would not see the masses deprived of it.[82] Another decade on, in 1892, Huxley not only insisted in print that he still believed what he said in praise of the Bible in the school-board essay, but he even added to it fresh and more extravagant claims:

---

[79] American Philosophical Society, Philadelphia, Pennsylvania, Huxley Papers, B 981, T. H. Huxley to George Dixon, 20 February 1871. Huxley added, however: 'But whatever resolution is carried involving Bible reading I shall move as an amendment that "a selection from the Bible" be used. As a French friend of mine observed the stories of "Madam Potiphar et les demoiselles Lot" are not edifying for children.' Huxley failed in his attempt to get the London School Board to bowdlerize the Bible.

[80] Huxley, *Life*, II, 38.

[81] Another marker of Victorian culture is given in the speculation of Huxley's biographer-son on why Huxley's book *Lay Sermons, Addresses, and Reviews*—a collection of pieces on themes such as 'On the Study of Zoology' and 'Geological Reform'—sold so well: it was because it had the alluring word 'sermon' in the title! Huxley, *Life*, II, 11.

[82] Huxley, *Life*, II, 273–4.

I may add yet another claim of the Bible to the respect and the attention of a democratic age. Throughout the history of the western world, the Scriptures, Jewish and Christian, have been the great instigators of revolt against the worst forms of clerical and political despotism. The Bible has been the *Magna Charta* of the poor and the oppressed . . . the Bible is the most democratic book in the world. . . . I do not say that even the highest biblical ideal is exclusive of others or needs no supplement. But I believe that the human race is not yet, and possibly may never be, in a position to dispense with it.[83]

Less than a year before his death, Huxley defiantly pronounced yet again that he did not repent 'in the least' of the stance he took in favour of requiring Bible teaching in state schools.[84]

In the mid-1880s Huxley abandoned scientific research and embarked on a late, second career as a biblical critic. While this has never been stated so baldly before, it is well documented. Huxley's colleague Michael Foster made it very clear that Huxley lost his appetite for scientific investigation, and it is therefore worth quoting his comments at length:

there was something working within him which made his hand, when turned to anatomical science, so heavy that he could not lift it. Not even that which was so strong within him, the duty of fulfilling a promise, could bring him to work. In his room at South Kensington, where for a quarter of a century he had laboured with such brilliant effect, there lay on his working table for months, indeed for years, partly dissected specimens of the rare and little studied marine animal, Spirula, of which he had promised to contribute an account to the Reports of the 'Challenger' Expedition, and hard by lay the already engraved plates; there was still wanted nothing more than some further investigation and the working out of the results. But it seemed as if some hidden hands were always being stretched out to keep him from the task . . .[85]

Huxley handed off the Spirula work to another man of science to finish, and instead threw himself into a plan to make 'Working-Men's Lectures on the Bible' which was 'constantly before Huxley's mind' right up to his death.[86] Eventually, Huxley actually gave away his books on biology, while avidly accumulating biblical studies volumes instead. He confessed to a scientific correspondent that he would like to give him some helpful insights but 'in truth I am getting rusty in science—from disuse.'[87]

---

[83] Huxley, *Controverted*, 52–3.
[84] Huxley, *Life*, III, 336.   [85] Huxley, *Life*, II, 113–14.
[86] Huxley, *Life*, III, 279–80.   [87] Huxley, *Life*, III, 172.

In contrast, as Desmond put it, 'Biblical criticism became Huxley's *cheval de bataille*'.[88] Already in August 1884 Huxley admitted: 'I am principally occupied in studying the Gospels.'[89] Biblical studies would dominate his reading, writing, and the projects he planned from 1885 till his death a decade later. His most ambitious projects, including the biblical lectures for the working classes, never were completed, but Huxley did produce an extraordinary stream of essays in the period 1885–91, most of which were published in the *Nineteenth Century*. Huxley explained to Holyoake that his goal in these writings was to educate 'the public mind'.[90] In order to do this, Huxley's articles plunge into learned, technical questions of biblical criticism and interpretation. Some of the titles of the essays make this apparent, but this generalization is true even for the ones that do not. This is the period in which Huxley expounded publicly and fully what he meant by 'agnosticism', especially in what ended up being a trilogy: 'Agnosticism', 'Agnosticism: A Rejoinder', and 'Agnosticism and Christianity'. These titles would be apt to cause someone today to assume that they would be philosophical discourses—probably with a heavy dose of epistemology. 'Agnosticism', however, the very essay in which Huxley explains how he came to coin the term, has at its heart an exploration of the synoptic problem in Gospel studies. 'Agnosticism: A Rejoinder' is even more largely taken up with biblical criticism, including the theory of Markan priority. 'Agnosticism and Christianity' continues a running exploration of the demonology of the New Testament.

And those are some of the essays that do not signal in their titles that they are addressing scriptural themes. One has to read these articles to grasp completely the full-blooded revelling in details that marks Huxley's efforts—often with an original harnessing of the latest biological knowledge with the most recent German biblical criticism. Gladstone thought he could find the progressive order of the creation of different categories of living things given in the book of Genesis in evolutionary history, but seemingly insurmountable problems ensue, Huxley insisted, when one tries to decide in which category bats belonged. Related concerns led on to an exegetical discussion about what species the Hebrew words do and do not refer to that

---

[88] Desmond, *Huxley*, 571.
[89] Huxley, *Life*, II, 362.
[90] Co-operative College Archives, Holyoake House, Manchester, Holyoake Papers, 3293, T. H. Huxley to G. J. Holyoake, 1 April 1891.

were translated in the Authorized Version as 'creeping things'. The veracity of the Gospels is put in a different light once one has patiently digested Eginhard's chronicles of Charlemagne's court. All the stray bits of evidence which might indicate the precise geographical location of Gardara are exhaustively sifted; while the actual Gospel narrative of the Gadarene swine involves grave legal questions that have been hitherto inadequately addressed—surely only the owner can sublet pig property to demons. Those who insist that Noah's flood is historical have not sufficiently taken into account 'holes bored by Miocene mollusks in the cliffs east and west of Cairo'.[91] And so it goes on.[92] Huxley then compiled these occasional pieces in a 625-page volume entitled *Essays Upon Some Controverted Questions* (1892). Desmond has observed regarding it: 'Ironically, after a life of science, his biggest book was of Biblical criticism.'[93]

One running argument in these essays should be particularly highlighted. Huxley astutely and forcefully presses home the question of the demonology of the New Testament—this is the real point of his focus on the Gadarene swine narrative (the fact that he could not resist being sidetracked by Victorian sensibilities into the issue of property rights only served to dissipate it). Still, by sheer tenacity—by returning to the point over and over again—Huxley forced his readers to attend to his argument. Huxley insisted that orthodox Christians were caught on the horns of a dilemma. If they accepted the biblical world view on demons then they doomed themselves and—as far as it was in their influence—humankind, to be forever trapped in a primitive, pre-scientific, and therefore erroneous and exploded view of reality. Theology would be thwarting the advance of knowledge: it would be a textbook example of the war between science and theology— Huxley's favourite way to structure the encounter between these two areas of thought.[94] If, on the other hand, orthodox Christians admitted that Jesus,

[91] Huxley, *Controverted*, 618.

[92] Huxley had made forays into this kind of work earlier, arguing, for example, that those who believed in the Garden of Eden had not taken into account the chalk deposits by the river Euphrates: Huxley, *Lay Sermons*, 215.

[93] Desmond, *Huxley*, 592–3. Huxley carried on his biblical reflections in some of the prefaces of the volumes of his *Collected Essays*. For example, Huxley's preface to *Science and Hebrew Tradition*, which is dated 9 October 1893, is entirely devoted to adding to and recapitulating some of his arguments about the Bible: Huxley, *Science and Hebrew Tradition*, pp. v–xiv.

[94] For the construction of the war metaphor for the relationship between faith and science, see James R. Moore, *The Post-Darwinian Controversies: A study of the Protestant struggle to come to terms with Darwin in Great Britain and America, 1870–1900* (Cambridge: Cambridge University Press, 1979).

the apostles, and the biblical authors believed that some people's afflictions were caused by demonic possession, but we now know better, Huxley would then insist that this concession destroyed the authority of the Bible as a source of revelation. If the Scriptures are wrong about this aspect of the spiritual realm, it is illogical to assume that they provide insights about any spiritual realities, he maintained. Despite the cogency of this argument, many Christians perhaps satisfied themselves with just an ill-defined sense that demons were less central to their view of Christianity, Christ, and the Bible than Huxley insisted they ought to be. Indeed, it is curious to observe that demons were often on Huxley's mind throughout his adult life. His letters are replete from youth to old age with statements that he is personally oppressed by some devil or possessed by some demon or tempted by Satan. A series of biblical texts featuring demons recur in his writings with remarkable frequency. For example, Jesus' observation that when a demon is cast out of a person, it might eventually be replaced by seven worse ones was an analogy which Huxley found to have utility in manifold contexts. In 1870, for example—that is, fifteen years before he took a learned interest in biblical demonology—Huxley explained to Darwin that Pusey had consented for Darwin to receive an honorary doctorate from Oxford University 'in order to keep out seven devils worse than that first'.[95] More substantively, Huxley insisted that his Romanes lecture on 'Evolution and Ethics' was really a sermon expounding the truth of the scriptural text which declares that Satan is 'the Prince of this world' (John 12: 31).[96] That lecture included an example of the kind of rather cumbersome and inelegant biblically based demonic analogy toward which Huxley's mind would gravitate: 'The beneficent demon, doubt, whose name is Legion and who dwells amongst the tombs of old faiths, enters into mankind and thenceforth refuses to be cast out.'[97] Huxley wrote to Nettie during their long engagement to explain that 'my demon says work! work! you shall not even love unless you work.'[98] So he went on year after year explaining his ailments, trials, motivations, and compulsions till his final illness which began with what he described at the time as 'the influenza demon'.[99]

[95] Huxley, *Life*, II, 14.   [96] Huxley, *Life*, III, 299.
[97] Huxley, *Evolution and Ethics*, 56.   [98] Huxley, *Life*, II, 14.
[99] Huxley, *Life*, III, 357.

Part of what made Huxley's engagement with the Scriptures so distinctive is that he had an alternative canon within the canon. Christians almost invariably have parts of the Bible that they think are more central than others. They therefore sometimes can take more calmly critiques of other parts of the canon in the quiet conviction that the main citadel is safe. For many Christians this inner canon has been the Gospels but for Huxley, by way of contrast, this was the part of the Bible that he most emphasized was untenable. He also, of course, exposed the problems with accepting the authority of the early books of the Old Testament, especially the book of Genesis (as well as his careful exploration of the primitive theological worldview assumed in Judges and 1 and 2 Samuel). Rather than challenge the contents of the Bible across the board in this way, however, Huxley found an alternative high point and citadel in the Hebrew prophets. Did they not also call their generation to forsake idolatry and pursue an ethical life? This was Huxley's idea of religion. Christianity, on the other hand, he saw as a declension from the spiritual level reached by the Old Testament prophets.[100] Huxley's favourite prophet was Micah and he found his own religious position best encapsulated in Micah 6: 8: 'He hath shewed thee, O man, what is good; and what doth the Lord require of thee, but to do justly, and to love mercy, and to walk humbly with thy God?' Here at last was the impregnable rock of Holy Scripture:

> If any so-called religion takes away from this great saying of Micah, I think it wantonly mutilates, while, if it adds thereto, I think it obscures, the perfect ideal of religion. But what extent of knowledge, what acuteness of scientific criticism, can touch this, if any one possessed of knowledge, or acuteness, could be absurd enough to make the attempt? Will the progress of research prove that justice is worthless and mercy hateful...?[101]

To the extent that Huxley adhered to a traditional faith it was 'the living body of the ethical ideal of prophetic Israel'.[102] Or more simply: 'the only religion that appeals to me is prophetic Judaism'.[103]

If influenza ever was exorcized from Huxley's body it was only to have it replaced by demons seven times worse—bronchitis and then a heart attack. He died on 29 June 1895. The scripture-filled Anglican burial service was read at his funeral. Nettie survived him and she wrote the inscription for his

---

[100] See, for example, Huxley, *Science and Hebrew Tradition*, p. xi.
[101] Huxley, *Controverted*, 95–6.   [102] Huxley, *Controverted*, 581.
[103] Huxley, *Life*, III, 272.

gravestone. It was a simple three-line poem. The central line was a scriptural text, Psalm 127: 2. This poem expresses uncertainty on the question of the immortality of the soul. Therefore, fittingly, the final word on Huxley is a medley of the Bible and an agnostic point of view:

> Be not afraid, ye waiting hearts that weep;
> For still He giveth His belovéd sleep,
> And if an endless sleep He wills, so best.[104]

---

[104] Huxley, *Life*, III, 363. Huxley had been careful to observe: 'I neither deny nor affirm the immortality of man.' Huxley, *Life*, I, 314.

9

Evangelical Anglicans

Josephine Butler and the Word of God

Josephine Butler (1828–1906) was a leading advocate for women's rights. Her enduring reputation is rightly first and foremost as an eminent Victorian feminist. While the word 'feminist' was not in general use in the nineteenth century, it is standard in the current scholarship to apply it to figures from that time period, with Butler being a prime example.[1] Butler herself did use a phrase that many might assume only came later, denouncing 'the double standard' in which women were judged more harshly than men for having extramarital sexual intercourse.[2] Specifically, Butler is most famous for leading the campaign against the Contagious Diseases Acts. Under these acts, women suspected of being prostitutes in certain towns where sailors disembarked or soldiers were garrisoned could be forced to undergo a painful and humiliating medical inspection for venereal disease. If a woman refused, she could be summarily imprisoned. If she passed the inspection, she essentially became listed (whether she wanted to be or not) as a prostitute in good standing with, as it were, a royal seal of approval on her marketable goods. Butler opposed these acts on forthrightly feminist grounds. Why were only women inspected and not men who were no less

---

[1] See, for example, Barbara Caine, *Victorian Feminists* (Oxford: Oxford University Press, 1992). A distinction has recently been advanced between Elizabeth Fry and Josephine Butler on this point: 'Fry was a pioneer of the women's movement, whereas Butler was a feminist.' Annemieke van Drenth and Francisca de Haan, *The Rise of Caring Power: Elizabeth Fry and Josephine Butler in Britain and the Netherlands* (Amsterdam: Amsterdam University Press, 1999), 20.

[2] Josephine E. Butler, *The Hour Before Dawn: An Appeal to Men*, second edition (London: Trübner & Co., 1882), 70.

the cause of the spread of venereal diseases? Why were women being treated as guilty without a trial when no such violation of the rights of men would be tolerated? How dare the government assume that an army of exploited women in the degraded position of being officially certified sex slaves was in the national interest? And so on, until the indignation of the public was so aroused that the acts were repealed.

For this study of the Bible and Victorians across the religious and irreligious spectrum, Butler's identity as an evangelical Anglican is central. Helen Mathers has convincingly presented Butler as 'a devout Anglican Evangelical', and this pioneering work has been generally accepted and built upon by scholars subsequently.[3] Nevertheless, as Butler's faith—and even more so, her presentation of it—is complicated, and as Lisa Severine Nolland has recently reflected that it 'seems to me that Mathers identifies Josephine too closely with Evangelicalism', it is worth going over some of this ground again.[4] Nolland's comment itself should not be over-read. Her book fully acknowledges that Butler's faith was profoundly evangelical in many ways. Indeed, Nolland's study was published in a monograph series entitled *Studies in Evangelical History and Thought*. Nolland's primary concern seems to be to respect the fact that Butler did not self-identify as an evangelical. This reticence, however, must be placed in context. Butler loathed religious labels and categories as apt to convey unwanted connotations. An obvious example is Butler's statement in her biography of her husband, the Reverend Canon George Butler, DD, that he should be thought of as more of a layman than a clergyman.[5] The rest of the biography reveals how pre-eminently fulfiling his ministerial calling became to George's desires, priorities, and identity; Butler's comment should not be taken literally but rather as a manifestation of her anxiety that people might impose negative stereotypes about clergymen upon her beloved husband. Butler even went so far once as to deny she was an Anglican!—this despite the fact that she

---

[3] Helen Mathers, 'The Evangelical Spirituality of a Victorian Feminist: Josephine Butler, 1828–1906', *Journal of Ecclesiastical History*, 52, 2 (April 2001), 282–312 (here 282). For examples of other scholars accepting this work, see Amanda W. Benckhuysen, 'Reading between the Lines: Josephine Butler's Socially Conscious Commentary on Hagar', in Christiana de Groot and Marion Ann Taylor (eds), *Recovering Nineteenth-Century Women Interpreters of the Bible* (Atlanta: Society of Biblical Literature, 2007), 136; Jenny Daggers and Diana Neal (eds), *Sex, Gender, and Religion: Josephine Butler Revisited* (New York: Peter Lang, 2006), 15 [hereafter *Revisited*].

[4] Lisa Severine Nolland, *A Victorian Feminist Christian: Josephine Butler, the Prostitutes and God*, Studies in Evangelical History and Thought (Carlile: Paternoster, 2004), 18–19.

[5] Josephine E. Butler, *Recollections of George Butler* (Bristol: J. W. Arrowsmith, n.d. [1892]), 63.

was baptized and raised in the Church of England, married a clergyman, throughout her adult life habitually worshipped only in Anglican churches, and was duly buried in the Church of England. Moreover, her Anglican spirituality is readily apparent in other ways: her quotations from the Psalms were often from the *Book of Common Prayer* version; she would refer to events in the church calendar in a way that Methodists would not (for example, dating a letter 'St Barnabas Day'), and she drew heavily upon Anglican religious authors.[6] In other words, once again, Butler could not bear to think that she personally might be implicated by unfavourable views of the Church. For the purpose at hand, what is particularly interesting is that on the occasion when Butler rejected the Anglican label she did so by emphasizing instead her evangelical identity (albeit without using the word): 'I was brought up a Wesleyan...I imbibed from childhood the widest ideas of vital Christianity, only it *was* Christianity. I have not much sympathy with the *Church*.'[7] 'Vital Christianity' is an evangelical way of referring to an evangelical faith.[8] Other of Butler's statements make it clear she is here referring to 'the Church' merely as an institution, seeing the true church, by way of contrast, as an invisible, spiritual reality. Her exaggerated statement about her upbringing is based upon the fact that when she was little she had a nurse who would take her to meetings at the Wesleyan chapel which her Anglican father had provided for his Methodist tenants.

Her commitment to 'vital Christianity' meant that Butler insisted that she and her husband were above sects and church parties. Once again, this should not be misconstrued as meaning that they belonged equally well to any or all. In fact, throughout their adult lives they both repeatedly ex-pressed their visceral abhorrence of 'ritualism', that is, the Anglo-Catholic wing of the Church of England. When George Butler was at Oxford, he had heard with profit E. B. Pusey's lectures on the Minor Prophets, and he was always grateful for them throughout his life. This just goes to prove, however, the extent to which the Bible was a common denominator in Victorian society: it did not prevent the Butlers from using his very name as a label for the kind of Anglicanism that they despised. 'Puseyism', they

---

[6] Josephine E. Butler, *An Autobiographical Memoir*, ed. George W. Johnson and Lucy A. Johnson (Bristol: J. W. Arrowsmith, 1928), 32 (for the St Barnabas Day letter) [hereafter *Memoir*].

[7] Jane Jordan, *Josephine Butler* (London: Hambledon Continuum, 2007 [originally 2001]), 16.

[8] Pietism is generally considered the continental equivalent of evangelicalism and, on another occasion, Butler observed that Pietism was the Swiss 'word for vital Christianity': Josephine E. Butler, *Truth Before Everything* (London: Pewtress & Co., 1897), 21.

agreed, was 'repellent'.[9] Butler was generally impressed with Canon Scott Holland when she met him in 1881, but nevertheless grumbled that he had 'something of the Pusey subtlety which hinders men from grasping an idea clearly.'[10] Nor should Butler's appreciation of medieval mystics be misconstrued as unevangelical. Diana Neal has recently demonstrated that this fascination did not counteract Butler's anti-Catholicism.[11] Indeed, Butler's biography of Catharine of Siena explicitly re-imagined this Doctor of the Roman Catholic Church as a Protestant:

> There can be little doubt that, had she lived two centuries later, in the midst of the convulsion which rent Christendom, she would have stood firm on the side of evangelical truth, and joined her protest to that of the Reformers. We cannot doubt that she, who so feared and abhorred the temporal domination and worldly magnificence of the Church, would have hailed the time when the pride of ecclesiastical Rome should be laid low; and above all, that she would have rejoiced to see the word of God, unchained and free, taking wings, and flying to the ends of the earth, the priceless possession of the nations, bringing to each in their own tongue the glad tidings of salvation.[12]

The other possibility is that Butler might have been a liberal or Broad Church Anglican (and these two categories are not synonymous). George Butler certainly had Broad Church affinities, and he is probably best viewed as either in this camp or as an evangelical-Broad Church hybrid. As a student at Oxford, he quickly became a core member of what might be dubbed the Broad Church set. Benjamin Jowett himself invited George to join an exclusive club of twelve which also included Arthur Stanley and Matthew Arnold.[13] He never threw off this clique, but rather became lifelong friends with many of them. These relationships were so deep that George and Josephine named two of their three sons after friends who were

[9] Butler, *George Butler*, 63, 170.

[10] Margaret Burton (ed.), *Josephine Butler has her say about her contemporaries* (London: The Fawcett Library, n.d.), 17.

[11] Diana Neal, 'Josephine Butler: Flirting with the Catholic Other', in Daggers, *Revisited*, 155–71.

[12] Josephine E. Butler, *Catharine of Siena: A Biography*, fourth edition (London: Dyer Brothers, 1885), 239. Nor should it be imagined that this was a singular interest. Arthur T. Pierson, for example, was so prominent in the evangelical world that he was C. H. Spurgeon's successor at the Metropolitan Tabernacle and several of his articles were printed in *The Fundamentals*, the collection that helped to give 'fundamentalism' its name. Nevertheless, his publications include: Arthur T. Pierson, *Catharine of Siena, an ancient lay preacher; a story of sanctified womanhood and power in prayer* (London: Funk & Wangnalls, 1898).

[13] Butler, *George Butler*, 30–1. For a study of Broad Church Anglicanism that emphasizes the various figures associated with it, see Tod E. Jones, *The Broad Church: A Biography of a Movement* (Lanham, Maryland: Lexington Books, 2003).

also prominent Broad Churchmen: their oldest son was named after her father, and then their second one was christened Arthur Stanley (in honour of the friend who would become the Dean of Westminster), and their last one Charles Augustine Vaughan (after the Charles Vaughan who ultimately became the Dean of Llandaff).[14] George's impressive social world contained many of Britain's most prominent liberal Anglicans or even post-Christian thinkers including F. D. Maurice, Charles Kingsley, Sir James Stephen, John Ruskin, Max Müller, Goldwin Smith, Dante Rossetti, Francis Galton (his brother-in-law), Arthur Clough, and J. A. Froude. George explicitly desired the broadest of broad churches: 'I hope some church of the future will find room within its borders for such people as H. Martineau, Francis Newman, J. S. Mill, and others. They are far too good to be left out in the cold.'[15] On the other hand, it is not at all clear that George was himself a liberal Anglican: there is no evidence that he ever rejected a traditional Christian doctrine such as substitutionary atonement or the unique inspiration, authority, and truthfulness of the Bible or advocated reformulating one in line with modern sensibilities. Many of his letters are deeply evangelical in tone and his ministry at Dilston parish church was so evangelical that Wesleyans started to attend again. It should also be noted that George's circle of friends included prominent evangelicals as well such as Francis Close, the staunchly evangelical Dean of Carlisle. George also struck up a close relationship with Josephine's cousin, the eminent evangelical Baptist minister Charles Birrell, and he was interested in the ministry of the American evangelical Holiness preachers Hannah Whitall Smith and her husband Robert Pearsall Smith.[16]

This wider social world clearly sometimes made Josephine Butler, who was more decidedly evangelical, uneasy. She rather pathetically claimed that George's lifelong, close friendship with J. A. Froude was entirely based on a common interest in fly fishing.[17] Butler recurringly spoke out against a sceptical tendency and it seems clear that she had in mind not just loss-of-faith figures such as Froude but also liberal Anglicans.[18] Here, for

---

[14] Jordan, *Butler*, 39, 50.

[15] Butler, *George Butler*, 227 (George Butler to Josephine Butler, 1 January 1870).

[16] Northumberland Record Office, Gosforth, Newcastle upon Tyne, Josephine Butler Papers, Spiritual Diaries: entry 14 September 1874. I am grateful to Dr Helen Mathers for providing me with her typescript of this source.

[17] Butler, *George Butler*, 264.

[18] Northumberland Record Office, Gosforth, Newcastle upon Tyne, Josephine Butler Papers, undated item entitled, '"To the Greeks foolishness". To a Sceptic'.

example, is her analysis of the men she and George knew when they lived in Oxford early in their marriage:

> A certain scepticism on many of the gravest questions had followed as a reaction on the era of Tractarianism, and it appeared to be very difficult for a man simply to assert his belief in anything. In some men this timidity, or self-imposed reticence, as to expressing any positive belief, or even asserting a simple fact, seemed to take the form of mental disease.[19]

Mathers decided that Butler was a 'liberal Evangelical', but even this is not an easy judgment to make.[20] The primary evidence for her liberal side is her declaration in 1903 that she did not believe in eternal punishment. As will be shown, however, this same document also shows Butler to hold conservative evangelical views on other subjects, as do other writings of hers. It would therefore seem best to refer to her evangelicalism without attempting a modifier.

David Bebbington's definition of evangelicalism is the standard one.[21] It identifies four hallmark characteristics of evangelicals: conversionism, activism, biblicism, and crucicentrism (an emphasis upon Christ's atoning work on the cross).[22] Butler demonstrated a strong, lifelong commitment to all of these four traits, making her evangelical identity readily apparent.[23] Rather than elucidate this claim thematically, however, it would be more useful to transition to a presentation of her life and work, albeit one that will highlight both her commitment to the Bible and her exemplification of evangelical characteristics. Before doing so, however, it is worth adding a few comments on the choice of Butler for this study. While the notion of anyone being 'representative' is problematic, Butler's religious writings and judgments were sufficiently distinctive blends of her own to make it even more so in her case. Nevertheless, if asked to name a Victorian evangelical Anglican woman, it is likely that most religious historians of the period

---

[19] Butler, *George Butler*, 95.   [20] Mathers, 'Evangelical Spirituality', 284.

[21] For documentation of this claim, see Timothy Larsen, 'The Reception Given *Evangelicalism in Modern Britain* since its Publication in 1989', in Michael A. G. Haykin and Kenneth J. Stewart (eds), *The Emergence of Evangelicalism: Exploring Historical Continuities* (Nottingham: Apollos, 2008), 21–36.

[22] D. W. Bebbington, *Evangelicalism in Modern Britain: A History from the 1730s to the 1980s* (London: Unwin Hyman, 1989), 1–17.

[23] Building on the Bebbington quadrilateral, I have attempted a fuller definition of evangelicalism. Butler thoroughly and completely fits this definition as well: Timothy Larsen, 'Defining and Locating Evangelicalism', in Timothy Larsen and Daniel J. Treier (eds), *The Cambridge Companion to Evangelical Theology* (Cambridge: Cambridge University Press, 2007), 1–14.

would name Josephine Butler. Moreover, as Bebbington has convincingly shown that evangelicals are biblicist by definition, there is no need to worry that choosing Butler has skewed the picture of evangelical Anglicanism toward biblicism.

Josephine Grey (to use her maiden name) was the seventh child of John and Hannah Grey. Hannah was raised in the Moravian Church. John Grey was an influential land agent and the cousin of Earl Grey, the Whig prime minister. He was also a very sound evangelical Anglican. As a young man, he had a serious illness which prompted an evangelical spiritual awakening that manifested itself in frequent and intense private Bible reading.[24] It is emblematic of his deep commitment to the Scriptures throughout his adult life that John Grey's first public speech was on behalf of the Bible Society.[25] Josephine claimed that when she and her siblings thought of their father a prominent childhood memory was of his reading the Bible aloud to them. Resolutely opposed to slavery, John Grey instilled in his daughter an evangelical activism which equated serving God with campaigning against injustice. One of his favourite verses was Isaiah 58: 6: 'Is not this the fast I have chosen? to loose the bands of wickedness, to undo the heavy burdens, and to let the oppressed go free, and that ye break every yoke?'[26] He also instilled in her a permanent conviction that a profound, ongoing attentiveness to the contents of the Bible was central to a life of Christian devotion.

Josephine grew up in the family's large house at Dilston, Northumberland. As has already been noted, John Grey's sense of vital Christianity meant that he was a supporter of Methodists and other evangelicals outside the Church of England—and happy for his daughter to experience their forms of worship. At the age of 74, Butler was more struck by the vital Christianity she experienced in her childhood in more demonstrative evangelical circles than Anglican ones. She remembered 'a wonderful revival' under the leadership of a Methodist preacher whom her parents welcomed when he came into their area.[27] She recalled going to 'delightful' Methodist camp meetings. She had an Irvingite governess and even boasted that she had experienced the charismatic worship of that community and

---

[24] Josephine E. Butler, *Memoir of John Grey of Dilston* (Edinburgh: Edmonston and Douglas, 1869), 18–19.
[25] Butler, *George Butler*, 27.   [26] Butler, *George Butler*, 48–9.
[27] Liverpool, University of Liverpool Library, Josephine Butler Papers, JB1/1 1902/03/16 (1), Josephine Butler to Maurice Gregory, 16 March 1902.

defended it in principle (while coyly conceding that she was not very attracted by it at the time). Most telling of all, Josephine recalled a dramatic moment when she witnessed as a child the supernatural power of the sword of the Word of God when wielded by a faith-filled evangelical:

> An incident occurred which impressed me much. My mother had been ill, and got up one night and took what she believed was her prescribed dose of medicine. It was a strong dose of prussic acid! She spoke staggered to that governess I spoke of, who took her to her heart and with perfect calm repeated to her the words 'and if they drink any deadly thing it shall not hurt them', (the words of our Lord recorded in the last chapter of Mark[)] and just before his ascension He said, 'these signs shall follow them that believe' (not 'them that believe during the first 100 years from my departure from earth,' but apparently meant for all time.) My mother became sick and vomitted up the poison, and she felt very little inconvenience.[28]

Throughout her life, Josephine believed in divine healing and that God answers prayer, and she would often assert these convictions in deliberate defiance of scepticism.[29] More broadly, one of her primary approaches to the Bible was to see it as a book of divine promises.

Butler recollected that her own spiritual conversion took place at the age of seventeen. It began with an existential and emotional time of crying out to God that lasted some months. She articulated this most personal of experiences through two biblical narratives, Jacob's wrestling with God, and Jesus' prayerful struggle in Gethsemane:

> For one long year of darkness the trouble of heart and brain urged me to lay all this at the door of the God, whose name I had learned was Love. I dreaded Him—I fled from Him—until grace was given me to arise and wrestle, as Jacob did, with the mysterious Presence, who must either slay or pronounce deliverance.... Looking back, it seems to me the end must have been defeat and death had not the Saviour imparted to the child wrestler something of the virtue of His own midnight agony, when in Gethsemane His sweat fell like great drops of blood to the ground.[30]

---

[28] Liverpool, University of Liverpool Library, Josephine Butler Papers, JB1/1 1902/03/16 (1), Josephine Butler to Maurice Gregory, 16 March 1902.

[29] She recounts, for example, how her prayer of faith based on the 'promises of God in scripture' led to George's recovery in 1886: Butler, *Memoir*, 143–4. For her defiance of scepticism regarding the power of prayer, see Josephine E. Butler, *Sursum Corda; Annual Address to the Ladies' National Association* (Liverpool: T. Brakell, 1871), 27–9.

[30] Butler, *Memoir*, 11–12.

In a classic evangelical manner, Butler confessed that Christ saved her from her sins, filling her with inexpressible contentment. She also added that her spiritual history was therefore no different from that of a converted prostitute—they were both just sinners who had been set free by Jesus.

Josephine Grey met George Butler in 1850, when he was a tutor at the University of Durham. Even during their courtship, their ardour was biblically charged. He wrote to her in 1851:

> But though I have 'wandered out of the way in the wilderness,' I do not despair of taking possession of the promised land. You say you can do little for me. Will it be little, Josephine, if urged by your encouragement and example, I put off the works of darkness and put on the armour of light? Blessings from the Giver of all blessings fall upon you for the joy you have given to me, for the new life to which you have called me![31]

They were wed in 1852 and spent the first five years of their marriage in Oxford, where George pursued various duties related to the university including being a public examiner and eventually founding a private hall. He was also ordained during this period. Butler was dismayed by the attitudes and opinions of typical Oxford men, and given her less extensive education and training in debate and their sexist assumption that women did not have anything to add to intellectual discussions, she found her social life beyond her marriage largely frustrating. Part of this clash was between her heartfelt evangelical spirituality and the academic detachment and scepticism of the dons. Butler was shocked and grieved when she thought she had established a point by quoting the words of Christ as recorded in the Gospels, only to receive the callous retort: 'But you surely don't imagine that we regard as of any authority the grounds upon which you base your belief?'[32] Butler's knowledge of the Bible, however, bolstered her sense of self-esteem. When Francis Palgrave let slip that he did not recall having heard of Damascus before, it was her turn to be withering: 'There is an ancient book which has been translated into English, and can be had at most book-shops, called "The Bible," where I believe he could find some mention made of the place.'[33] Mostly, however, she was relieved when all these clever, impervious guests finally went home, and she and George could renew their biblical faith through household devotions: 'And then in

---

[31] Butler, *Memoir*, 16. (There are, at the very least, six distinct biblical allusions in those four sentences.)

[32] Butler, *George Butler*, 98. [33] Butler, *George Butler*, 78.

the evenings, when our friends had gone, we read together the words of Life, and were able to bring many earthly notions and theories to the test of what the Holy One and the Just said and did.'[34] Her private, unpublished spiritual diary from her last year in Oxford reveals how much she was drawing on and prioritizing Scripture. The first entry, from February 1856, recounts an experience of divine encouragement: 'Precious words of Scripture came pouring into my soul with a sort of unbidden violence, unsolicited by any act of my will. They seemed spoken to me by Jesus.' In this same entry, she correlates her experience to that of a biblical character (a woman traditionally thought, including by Butler, to have been a reclaimed prostitute): 'He met me, and called me by my name, as when He called "Mary" in the garden.'[35] The last dated entry from her Oxford life is from 8 December 1856. In it, Butler makes spiritual resolutions, with the Bible given the place of pre-eminence:

> 1st. Not to form a scheme or plan of holy living of my own, so much as to be simply guided by the Word of God, reading it daily with prayer that God would reveal to me there the secret of that life which I believe is attainable, but which I have never yet attained to. 'Receive I pray thee, the law from his mouth, and lay up his words in thine heart.' (Job 22: 22)[36]

It is worth rounding off George's career and life as a whole at this point—and their family life together—before focusing in on Butler's activism and writings. It was determined that the Oxford climate was contributing to Butler's deteriorating health and so a move was deemed essential. In 1857, George took the position of vice-principal of Cheltenham College. In 1865, he became principal of Liverpool College. After he retired, he was appointed a canon of Winchester Cathedral in 1882. He died on 14 March 1890. The Butlers had four children, three sons and a daughter. Not only were there morning and evening Bible readings as part of daily household devotions, but the Scriptures are pervasive even in the glimpses that have survived of the family at play. During an Easter holiday, George amused the children with his riddle: 'What part of the Scriptures do two young ladies fulfil when kissing each other?' Answer: 'They do unto one another what

---

[34] Butler, *George Butler*, 102.

[35] Northumberland Record Office, Gosforth, Newcastle upon Tyne, Josephine Butler Papers, Spiritual Diaries: entry Thursday [no calendar day] February 1856.

[36] Northumberland Record Office, Gosforth, Newcastle upon Tyne, Josephine Butler Papers, Spiritual Diaries: entry 8 December 1856.

they would have men do to them.' (Luke 6: 31)[37] One Christmas Eve, the family entertainment included a charade enactment of Jael assassinating Sisera by hammering a tent peg into his head while he was sleeping.[38]

George instinctively recommended passages of Scripture when he wanted to encourage someone.[39] Rebecca Jarrett, a Salvationist whose cooperation with William Stead's 'Maiden Tribute of Modern Babylon' journalistic investigation into sex trafficking led to her own arrest, was a friend of the Butlers. George was away during this crisis, but he wrote asking that Jarrett be informed of his recommendations of chapters of the Bible she should read.[40] George was a proficient student of the Old Testament in the original Hebrew. On one occasion during household devotions, after the English of a chapter was read out, George recited the Hebrew from memory. One of his innovations as principal of Liverpool College was to introduce a course in Hebrew.[41] As to the English Bible, he had almost the whole Psalter by heart. George's letters are infused with the earnest deployment of biblical quotations. When he came to Liverpool College, he made an immediate impression on the boys by expounding in his first address upon the Levitical wave offering. Butler, at any rate, depicted her husband as a man of one book:

> He was not, strictly speaking, much of a theologian, I suppose. He had little taste for controversial writings, but his Bible was his constant companion. Even in railway journeys—especially in his later years—he almost invariably carried a Bible in his little handbag, and would take it out to read during the journey. 'I find,' he wrote, 'that Biblical criticism is too apt to take the place of profitable reading. When I want to derive food and sustenance from the Word of God, I take no commentary, but shut myself up with the plain Word, and meditate on that.'[42]

Butler's narrative repeatedly emphasizes that George's commitment to the Bible became almost a monomania in his last illness. When he knew he did not have the strength to make it through the day, he would move the evening devotions up earlier so that he would not miss it. Although his mind became cloudy sometimes, it would clear when the Bible was read to him. In the end, he gave up on classical authors almost altogether and turned

---

[37] Jordan, *Butler*, 51.   [38] Jordan, *Butler*, 187.
[39] For his fortifying Butler with Scripture for her continental tour, see Butler, *George Butler*, 282.
[40] Jordan, *Butler*, 231.   [41] Butler, *George Butler*, 170.
[42] Butler, *George Butler*, 348.

'constantly to the Bible' instead.[43] There is no need to doubt the truthful-ness of this portrait but, even if it is inaccurate, it would still reinforce the point of this chapter by demonstrating that Butler herself believed that a saintly life should reflect this level of biblicism.

The defining tragedy of their lives happened to the Butlers in 1864. Their only daughter, Eva, just five years old, died after falling over a banister. Butler threw herself into evangelical activism as a way of combating the engulfing grief. As she poignantly put it: 'I became possessed with an irresistible desire to go forth and find some pain keener than my own'.[44] She also added wryly that, fortunately, misery was not hard to find in Liverpool. Butler went to the oakum-picking sheds—work for women so humble that only the most desperate were there and criminals were even sent there as part of their punishment. On her first day, Butler struck up a rapport with these women, and immediately tried to improve their lives by introducing them to Scripture: 'I proposed that they should learn a few verses to say to me on my next visit.'[45] A girl memorized John 14 and her recitation of it triggered an evangelical revival atmosphere with the women praying fervently with moaning and tears.

This led Butler on to working with desperate women of many different sorts. The most desperate of women were reduced to prostitution, but there was a final desperation even beyond that: what happened to a seriously ill or dying prostitute? Butler began to care for these women, even going so far as bringing them to live in the family home. This was essentially a version of the classic ministry goal of 'rescuing' prostitutes. It was also an expression of evangelical conversionism: Butler longed for these women to come to Jesus, have their sins forgiven, and be saved. As Jane Jordan has rightly observed, although Butler also fought for women's rights, she began by contending 'for their *souls*'.[46] Moreover, while it is convenient to present this aspect of Butler's work here, it should be borne in mind that she continued to pursue rescue work even when she was campaigning against the Contagious Dis-eases Acts. Among the first of these women was one whom Butler gave the pseudonym Marion.[47] In biblical language, Butler saw Marion as 'a kind of first-fruits of the harvest'.[48] Marion lived with them for three months before she died. She was converted so solidly during this period that Butler goes so

---

[43] Butler, *George Butler*, 476.   [44] Butler, *Memoir*, 43.
[45] Butler, *Memoir*, 44.   [46] Jordan, *Butler*, 82.
[47] Her real name was Mary Lomax: Jordan, *Butler*, 83.   [48] Butler, *Memoir*, 48.

far as to refer to her as a saint. Tellingly, Butler recounts that Marion was unfamiliar with the Bible upon her arrival, but studied it eagerly and perceptively, so that she 'mastered the New Testament'. As if to prove she had indeed made it all the way through that volume, Marion's last words came from the end of its final chapter: 'Oh, come quickly, Lord Jesus.' (Revelation 22: 20)[49] Butler published a whole series of conversion narratives of former prostitutes who came to Christ through her ministry. It is not surprising that a Methodist journal was glad to print them.[50] Scripture often plays a prominent role in these edifying tales. No one was beyond the grace of God. 'Margaret', for example, had presumably been reduced to infanticide. She was comforted when told that King Manasseh had murdered his own children, but he prayed to the Lord and was heard and forgiven.[51] Butler was outraged by the argument that prostitutes could not be reclaimed. She responded with buoyant faith: 'Yes, God can change hearts!'[52] She rattled callous and complacent men who denied the reclaimability of prostitutes by observing that fallen women wonder if their male clients could be redeemed: did they not participate in the same sin, but by living a double life—often even attending church—add the vilest hypocrisy to it?[53] Butler herself, however, had faith that even men driven by their lusts to the worse of offences could be reclaimed: 'I have seen dead men rising from their graves. I know the power of him who says, "Behold, I make all things new."' (Revelation 21: 5)[54] Nevertheless, in marked contrast to Huxley's assumptions about the untenability of such texts, Butler often saw lustful men through the accounts in the Gospels of demoniacs, and she was so insistent on this connection that it is not at all clear that she intended it only metaphorically.[55] In a rather elusive allegorical reading of a biblical text, Butler recommended to reclaimed men who wanted to make amends for their past actions that they should 'gather up the fragments that remain that

---

[49] Butler, *Memoir*, 48.

[50] For a study of these narratives, see Jane Jordan, '"Trophies of the Saviour": Josephine Butler's Biographical Sketches of Prostitutes', in *Daggers, Revisited*, 21–36. For an insightful, authoritative account of the origins of this genre, see D. Bruce Hindmarsh, *The Evangelical Conversion Narrative: Spiritual Autobiography in Early Modern England* (Oxford: Oxford University Press, 2005).

[51] Helen Mathers, '"'Tis Dishonor Done to *Me*": Self-Representation in the Writings of Josephine Butler', in *Daggers, Revisited*, 43–4 [hereafter 'Self-Representation'].

[52] Butler, *Sursum Corda*, 6.   [53] Butler, *Hour*, 33.   [54] Butler, *Hour*, 24.

[55] See, for example, Liverpool, University of Liverpool Library, Josephine Butler Papers, JB1/1 1902/03/16 (1), Josephine Butler to Maurice Gregory, 16 March 1902; see also, Butler, *Sursum Corda*, 12.

nothing be lost' (John 6: 12).[56] Throughout her life, Butler was wholeheart-
edly committed to the evangelical distinctive of conversionism. In 1902 she
was filled with hope that the world was on the brink of an unprecedented
spiritual revival: 'many will be swept into the Kingdom by this Pentecostal
tide, from all nations and from heathen lands, and there will be a harvest of
souls such as has never been gathered in yet.'[57]

It is often assumed that Josephine Butler is counted as a feminist because
of her opposition to the Contagious Diseases Acts, but it is actually the
opposite way around: Butler was invited to be an office holder in the Ladies
National Association for the Repeal of the Contagious Diseases Acts because
she was already prominent as an active feminist. Butler supported many, if
not all, of the efforts on behalf of the leading issues of women's rights of her
day: the rights of women to higher education, to vote, to preach, and the
movements against the Contagious Diseases Acts and for the Married
Women's Property Act. Already in 1866 she had signed J. S. Mill's petition
for women's suffrage. In 1867, Butler became the president of the North of
England Council for Promoting the Higher Education of Women, and this
cause prompted her first publication, *The Education and Employment of
Women* (1868).[58]

In the following year, she edited a feminist collection entitled *Woman's
Work and Woman's Culture*.[59] Other contributors included Frances Power
Cobbe and Julia Wedgwood, and a letter of support from Lucretia Mott, a
founding mother of American feminism, was also included. Butler herself
wrote a substantial introduction in which she presented the biblical case for
feminism. It is a mistake, she averred, to imagine that a statement or two
by the apostle Paul seeming to restrict women in ministry was the Bible's
main message on the subject, in the same way that the Bible's main
message is anti-slavery, certain passages that appear to tolerate it notwithstanding. The proof of this is that slaves have found the Bible a source of
liberation:

> so keen, and so dangerous to the minds of their masters, were the arguments
> which those poor negroes drew from the Scriptures (in spite of the sanction

---

[56] Butler, *Memoir*, 235. (The words are practical instructions regarding leftover food.)
[57] Liverpool, University of Liverpool Library, Josephine Butler Papers, JB1/1 1902/03/16 (1),
Josephine Butler to Maurice Gregory, 16 March 1902.
[58] Josephine E. Butler, *The Education and Employment of Women* (London: Macmillan, 1868).
[59] Josephine E. Butler (ed.), *Woman's Work and Woman's Culture* (London: Macmillan and Co.,
1869).

which on the surface and at first sight many parts of the Bible seem to give to slavery), that the masters found it convenient to forbid the reading of the Bible to their slaves.[60]

The apostle Paul was merely giving temporary instructions regarding women which were 'constrained by the circumstances of society' in the pagan Roman empire and therefore were 'for a given time' rather than permanent.[61] The everlasting teaching is to be found first and foremost in the life and words of Jesus of Nazareth, and these are completely egalitarian: 'the principle of the perfect equality of all human beings was announced by Him as the basis of social philosophy'.[62] Jesus was contemptuous of the attempt to enforce the penalty for adultery on the woman only. He was respectful to all women, even prostitutes. The Gospels reveal that the most important event in the history of the world, the resurrection of Christ, was first made known to women. Then as now, however, sexist men would not believe the testimony of women, but dismissed their report as 'idle tales' (Luke 24: 11).[63] In summary, Butler advanced her feminism, not by ignoring or challenging the Bible, but rather marshalling its support: 'I appeal to the open Book'.[64]

Butler reiterated this approach to the question of the Bible and feminism throughout her life. In her biography of Catharine of Siena, for example, she defended this medieval woman's public Christian ministry as the fruit of the unfolding of the 'teaching of Christ', despite the fact that it is in defiance of the apostle Paul's 'minute directions' which were 'wise and prudent, no doubt, for the state of society in which he lived'.[65] Pat Starkey has argued that Butler's biographies can be read as 'a brand of refracted autobiography—of self-making'.[66] While Starkey has in mind her books such as *Catharine of Siena*, this insight applies strikingly well to her obituary tribute for a contemporary of the same name, Catherine Booth. Butler's catalogue of the virtues of the mother of the Salvation Army reads like a self-portrait. On the point at hand, Butler wrote: 'On the question of the equality of the sexes, Mrs Booth was very firm.... She entered fearlessly into the never-ending controversy concerning the meaning of St Paul's supposed veto

---

[60] Butler, *Woman's Work*, pp. lv–lvi.   [61] Butler, *Woman's Work*, pp. xlix, liv.

[62] Butler, *Woman's Work*, p. lix.   [63] Butler, *Woman's Work*, p. lvi.

[64] Butler, *Woman's Work*, p. lvi.   [65] Butler, *Catharine*, 72–3.

[66] Pat Starkey, 'Saints, Virgins and Family Members: Exemplary Biographies? Josephine Butler as Biographer', in Daggers, *Revisited*, 136.

upon women preachers.'[67] Not incidentally, and again in a description that
could have been of herself, Butler also praised Booth for holding to a
conservative evangelical view of Scripture in the face of higher criticism
and liberal theology:

> To her the Bible was the Word of God. She felt a contempt for those educated
> people who tear that Word to pieces, or cast it aside, in order to meet the
> supposed exigencies of modern thought. She apparently herself found in it all
> that she required for her own needs and for her far-seeing plans for the
> progress of humanity. Apologies for the Almighty, and His recently discov-
> ered little blunders, excited her utmost contempt, her most withering scorn.[68]

Butler grounded women's ministry in the biblical freedom for women to
prophesy, and clearly saw herself as a prophetic voice. Many of her speeches
and writings were actually sermons. The American advocate for women's
suffrage, Elizabeth Cady Stanton, observed that Butler spoke to an audience
like a Methodist preacher at a camp meeting.[69] On at least one occasion,
Butler addressed a Sunday morning congregation. This was, of all places, in
a Calvinist church in Geneva, during a heated referendum campaign in 1896
regarding the state regulation of prostitution: 'All scruples about women
speaking in churches vanished like a slight cloud before the midday sun'.[70]
In 1880, when in Genoa, she also conceded to a request from a group of
men and women to preach to them about Jesus.[71]

   Butler's first mention of the cause of prostitutes is this comment in her
private spiritual diary, dated 18 April 1865: 'the poor women who are
driven as sheep to the slaughter, into the slave market of London; prisoners,
captives and exiles.'[72] It is emblematic that she used biblical language—and
language that is applied to Christ himself (Acts 8: 32–5). The Contagious
Diseases Acts were passed in the years 1864, 1866, 1868, and 1869, with their
intent and extent becoming wider and clearer with each one. In September

---

[67] Josephine Butler, 'Catherine Booth', *Contemporary Review*, 58 (November 1890), 638–54
(here 649).

[68] Butler, 'Catherine Booth', 644. Underlying her evangelical identity, it should also be noted
that Butler testified in other contexts that she had received spiritual strength from attending
Salvationist meetings and reading their writings: see, for example, Jordan, *Butler*, 209.

[69] Jordan, *Butler*, 115.

[70] Butler, *Memoir*, 165.

[71] Josephine E. Butler, *Personal Reminiscences of a Great Crusade*, second edition (London: Horace
Marshall & Son, 1898), 219–20.

[72] Northumberland Record Office, Gosforth, Newcastle upon Tyne, Josephine Butler Papers,
Spiritual Diaries: entry 18 April 1865.

1869, the National Association for the Repeal of the Contagious Diseases Acts was founded and immediately Josephine Butler began to wrestle with the question of whether it was her duty to be active in this cause. She knew that respectable society would punish her and her family if she publicly addressed such a taboo issue; not to mention the forceful, direct opposition she would receive from vested interests. Her journal entry recording this struggle began with a biblical quotation: 'Now is your hour, and the power of darkness.' (Luke 22: 53)[73] Butler decided she could not evade this call, however, and George backed her decision without being naïve regarding the cost they both would have to pay. At the end of the year a sensation was caused by a published protest against the acts signed by over a hundred notable women including Butler (and, of interest for this study as a whole, Florence Nightingale and Mary Carpenter). Butler quickly emerged as the most prominent leader of the opposition to the acts and, indeed, this cause made her famous.

It would be difficult to set a limit on the extent to which Butler pursued her attack on the Contagious Diseases Acts through biblical categories and language. Her first experience of physical danger because of this work came during a parliamentary election at Colchester in November 1870 in which a band of roughs was put up to intimidating the repeal advocates. Butler wrote an account of these menacing circumstances to her sons, explaining that she overcame her fear by quoting Psalm 91 (almost the whole of which she reproduced in the letter).[74] Butler's efforts for the cause bore fruit in a string of publications in 1871. She addressed the National Association on 3 July, announcing: 'If I were a preacher, I would choose for my text to-day, "The kingdoms of this world shall become the kingdoms of our God and of His Christ"' (Revelation 11: 15), which, of course, was a way of saying that her address was a kind of sermon expounding a biblical text.[75] Her main publication for that year was *The Constitution Violated: An Essay*. It was framed by the notion that the constitution ought to play the same role for the state as the Bible does for the Christian religion. This analogy collapses into one reality, however, as Butler rejects the Contagious Diseases Acts on the grounds that they support what is 'condemned by God's

---

[73] Butler, *Memoir*, 68.
[74] Butler, *Memoir*, 78–9.
[75] Josephine E. Butler, *Address Delivered at Croydon, July 3rd, 1871* (London: National Association, 1871), 4.

Word'.[76] She even goes so far as to provide scriptural warrant for civil disobedience: 'the question, "Shall we obey God or man?" is that which they are now called upon once more to answer.' (Acts 5: 29)[77] On 14 November, Butler gave the annual address to the Ladies' National Association. It is littered with biblical proof texts. To take a random example, the argument that men's sexual drive is such that they cannot maintain a state of celibacy or fidelity is invalid: does not the Bible testify that Elijah was both righteous and 'a "man of like passions" with the rest of his fellow men?' (James 5: 17)[78]

Britain was following the lead of various continental governments where the state regulation of prostitute was much more extensive, established, and entrenched, and therefore Butler decided to extend her campaign to other nations. Her mission began in December 1874 and, naturally, started with France. Her key addresses from this tour were published in 1875, in French and German, and then subsequently in Italian, Spanish, Dutch, Swedish, Norwegian, and Russian. An English version was not published until after Butler's death. Whatever the language, the title was a biblical quotation: 'The book which embodied her addresses was rightly called by the name of *The Voice of one crying in the wilderness, Prepare ye the way of the Lord.*' (Mark 1: 3)[79] Once again, proof-texting abounds. To continue with the same random example, here is her response on this occasion to the argument regarding men's allegedly unstoppable sexual needs:

> The true physiology of man is that which ought to be read into the words of the Apostle—'I have written unto you, young men, because ye are strong, and the word of God abideth in you, and ye have overcome the wicked one.' [1 John 2: 14] It is a good thing, and a wholesome thing, for a young man to be chaste, to be able to restrain his passions. Happy is the nation which possesses such young men in plenty.[80]

How ingrained this scriptural habit of discourse was for Butler may be measured by the fact that she also claimed that she was aware that some of her hearers were atheists and she was therefore refraining from using

---

[76] [Josephine E. Butler], *The Constitution Violated: An Essay* (Edinburgh: Edmonston and Douglas, 1871), 56.

[77] Butler, *Constitution*, 170.

[78] Butler, *Sursum Corda*, 6.

[79] Josephine E. Butler, *The Voice of One Crying in the Wilderness*, originally in French, trans. Osmund Airy (Bristol: J. W. Arrowsmith, 1913), 9.

[80] Butler, *Voice*, 63.

explicitly religious arguments![81] Moreover, it does seem that Butler's biblical quotations were rhetorically effective, even on the Continent. One of her most affecting moments related to the reality that respectable young women from the working classes could no longer move about unescorted at night—even just to go home after having been on an errand—for fear that they would be picked up by the police and recorded as a prostitute, thereby destroying their reputation:

> looking at the troubled and earnest faces all turned towards me, I could not refrain from uttering these words: 'The foxes have holes, and the birds of the air have their nests; but the honest workwoman of Paris has not where to lay her head.' [Matthew 8: 20] Many burst into tears, or hid their faces in their hands. In coming out from the meeting several poor girls came to me, their faces swollen with weeping, and said: 'Ah, Madam, how true those words were about the foxes!'[82]

It was part of Butler's strategy for advancing the repeal campaign to recast the entire debate regarding prostitution into scriptural language.[83] What exactly was the government regulating? She sought to expose the euphemistic terms employed by officials, denouncing them as from 'the father of lies' (John 8: 44).[84] Butler replaced them with biblical terms of abuse such as 'evil', 'abomination', and 'iniquity'. She spoke of 'those in authority who have established this "accursed thing" [Joshua 7: 1] among us'.[85] This is a particularly strong example of this inveterate habit of Butler's because this biblical phrase has been imported from a very different context (it refers to clothing, silver, and gold illicitly taken as the spoils of war). Butler was acutely aware that some of the girls and women working in brothels had been forced to do so: even though these brothels had government approval, they were nevertheless 'dark places of the earth wherein are the habitations of cruelty' (Psalm 74: 20).[86] And what precisely were the Contagious Diseases Acts? They were 'what the Hebrew prophet calls "a covenant with death" and "an agreement with hell."' (Isaiah 28: 15)[87] Butler longed for prostitutes to be treated with respect and sympathy, and she pursued this

---

[81] Butler, *Voice*, 43.   [82] Butler, *Personal*, 144–5.

[83] In a pioneering study, Alison Milbank observed that Butler constantly referred to Scripture 'in even the most official report': Alison Milbank, 'Josephine Butler: Christianity, feminism and social action', in Jim Obelkevich, Lyndal Roper, and Raphael Samuel (eds), *Disciplines of Faith: Studies in Religion, Politics and Patriarchy* (London: Routledge, 1987), 154–64 (here 156).

[84] Butler, *Personal*, 71, 124.   [85] Butler, *George Butler*, 223.

[86] Butler, *Hour*, 66.   [87] Butler, *Memoir*, 148; Butler, *Truth*, 5.

aim by referring to them with winsome scriptural words. One standard choice was 'outcast' (see, for example, Psalm 147: 2). Another one she used surprisingly often, however, is the rather cumbersome circumlocution 'a woman in the city, which was a sinner' (Luke 7: 37). Butler was convinced that its unwieldiness was more than compensated for by its import that Jesus himself did not shun or shame prostitutes, but rather treated them with sympathy and dignity. Thus, in *The Hour Before Dawn*, Butler would refer to 'certain "women in the city who are sinners"' as a general class, as well as tell a story about a specific person: 'She, once "a woman of the city and a sinner"...'[88] In her retrospective account of the campaign, Butler used both terms side by side: 'God has done me the great favour of allowing me in a manner to be, for these thirty years, the representative of the outcast, of "the woman of the city who was a sinner."'[89] Butler repeatedly went so far as to use scriptural language applied to Christ in traditional Christian teaching when referring to prostitutes, observing, in a particularly striking incidence, that they were those 'who have become the despised and rejected of men.' (Isaiah 53: 3)[90] Strategically deploying scriptural terms of praise and abuse, Butler could refer to prostitutes as 'God's redeemed ones' while at the same time condemning supporters of the Contagious Diseases Acts for their 'hardness of heart'.[91] Part of the social cost that the Butlers paid for their work in this campaign came from it being considered unseemly by many in their refined circle for a lady to speak of prostitution, especially in public. Butler countered that the Bible is in good taste: 'God gives us a phraseology, a pure and chaste and holy indignation, which makes it possible for us to go to the bottom of these things without offending the chastest ear.'[92]

Josephine Butler personally identified with a range of scriptural characters. It has already been observed that she viewed her advocacy work through the ministries of the biblical prophets generally and, specifically, John the Baptist, whose voice cried out in the wilderness. To this needs to be added, however, her sense of solidarity with the experience of the Virgin Mary. Scholars have often been struck by Butler's graphic statement that being called to oppose the Contagious Diseases Acts felt like being asked to

---

[88] Butler, *Hour*, 67, 90. Other scholars have noticed Butler's biblical terms for prostitutes as well. See, for example, Mathers, 'Self-Representation', 40–1; Jordan, *Butler*, 3.

[89] Butler, *Memoir*, 190.

[90] Josephine E. Butler, *The Lady of Shunem* (London: Horace Marshall & Son, n.d. [1894]), 91.

[91] Butler, *George Butler*, 219.   [92] Butler, *Memoir*, 153.

'run my heart against the naked sword which seemed to be held out', and that actually doing the work 'is like running one's breast upon knife points, always beginning afresh before the last wound is healed.'[93] Indeed, Jordan even used the second quotation as the title of a chapter in her biography.[94] Nevertheless, scholars have ignored the biblical allusion.[95] Butler was identifying with Mary who was prophetically warned about the cost of her divine mission: 'a sword shall pierce through thy own soul also' (Luke 2: 35). For Butler, Mary was the 'most solitary woman of the sword-pierced heart'.[96] Butler herself made this connection explicit:

> 'A sword shall pierce through thy own soul also, *that the thoughts of many hearts may be revealed.*' The sword-piercing of the heart of womanhood has been, and will continue to be, in an infinitely humble degree, the revealer of the thoughts of men. The sorrow of the holy mother of Christ, the woman of the sword-pierced heart, is still bearing fruit. In going from city to city on the continent of Europe, I have felt that I must needs meet this sword-thrust with open arms, and the promised result has followed.[97]

'The Victory' came in 1883 when the House of Commons voted to suspend the Contagious Diseases Acts. At this joyful culmination of her life's work, Butler's mind instinctively ran to biblical texts:

> Mr Fowler's face was beaming with joy and a kind of humble triumph. I thought of the words, 'Say unto Jerusalem that her warfare is accomplished.' [Isaiah 40: 2] . . . It was half-past one in the morning, and the stars were shining in a clear sky. I felt at that silent hour in the morning in the spirit of the Psalmist, who said, 'When the Lord turned the captivity of Zion we were like unto them that dream.' [Psalm 126: 1][98]

When the actual repeal was finally given the Queen's Assent, Butler's response was: 'So *that* abomination is dead & *buried*. Praise the Lord!'[99]

After the Contagious Diseases Acts had been repealed, Josephine Butler wrote works that addressed theological issues and expounded passages of Scripture. And so we turn to looking more directly at Butler as a biblical interpreter. Curiously, the most quoted remark on this subject is mistaken.

---

[93] Butler, *George Butler*, 218; Butler, *Memoir*, 105.
[94] Jordan, *Butler*, 146 (ch. 9).
[95] Even Nolland, who emphasizes Butler's Christianity, quotes these 'graphic expressions' without commenting on their biblical prompt: Nolland, *Victorian Feminist Christian*, 237.
[96] Butler, *Sursum Corda*, 30.   [97] Butler, *Memoir*, 233.
[98] Butler, *George Butler*, 394.   [99] Jordan, *Butler*, 237.

It is often claimed that John Henry Newman observed regarding Butler: 'She reads Scripture like a child and interprets it like an angel.' Lucretia A. Flammang was so pleased with this statement that she put it at the head of her article as an epigraph.[100] Even the recent collection of essays on Butler edited by Jenny Daggers and Diana Neal, boasts in its introduction that 'no less a churchman than John Henry Newman said of Butler...'[101] It is indicative of how unfamiliar with the religious history of nineteenth-century Britain most Butler scholars have been that they could imagine that Cardinal Newman would have said such a thing about an anti-Catholic and indeed anti-Anglo-Catholic evangelical Protestant laywoman. It was actually the cardinal's ultra-Protestant and then freethinking brother, Francis Newman, who made this statement.[102] Francis Newman had been a strong supporter of the campaign against the Contagious Diseases Acts. In her biography of Butler, E. Moberly Bell had attributed the quotation simply to 'Newman', and subsequent scholars have assumed she meant the Catholic convert.[103]

Beside this little, glittering red herring, Butler scholarship has generally ignored her biblical writings, the most substantial of which was her book *The Lady of Shunem* (1894). Butler's posthumously published memoir contains three extracts from it. The editors provided one sentence of context which described the book with the simple phrase, 'a series of Biblical studies'.[104] Bell, with an inaccuracy that seems to have been borne of personal dislike for spiritual literature, only mentions *The Lady of Shunem* in order to insist that its contents were not entitled to be called either a series or studies, and to warn readers off with the assertion that it is 'not an important book', before completing her comments with the 'Newman' quote that has so misdirected readers.[105] The definitive scholarly biography of Butler is Jane Jordan's 2001 study. Jordan never even mentions *The Lady of Shunem* in the main text or notes of this well-researched 350-page

---

[100] Lucretia A. Flammang, '"And Your Sons and Daughters Will Prophesy": The Voice and Vision of Josephine Butler', in Julie Melnyk (ed.), *Women's Theology in Nineteenth-Century Britain: Transfiguring the Faith of Their Fathers* (New York: Garland Publishing, 1998), 151–64 (here 151).

[101] Daggers, *Revisited*, 13.

[102] London, London Metropolitan University, The Women's Library, Josephine Butler Letters Collection, 3JBL/53/41, Elizabeth Pearson to the Office, 20 December 1898.

[103] E. Moberly Bell, *Josephine Butler: Flame of Fire* (London: Constable and Co., 1962), 209.

[104] Butler, *Memoir*, 158.

[105] Bell, *Butler*, 209.

biography—and this inattentiveness is underlined by the fact that, although this title did manage to make it into the bibliography, Shunem is mis-spelled.[106] Likewise, although the Daggers and Neal volume is focused on Butler's religious identity and thought, no chapter was included on Butler and the Bible and, remarkably, the list of her writings provided at the end found yet another way to misspell Shunem.[107] Fortunately, this neglect has started to change rapidly, albeit from a different direction. The determina-tive factor is not a newfound interest in her biblical writings by Butler scholars, but rather a newfound interest in Butler by biblical scholars. Marion Ann Taylor, a professor of Old Testament, is at the centre of a welcome, scholarly discovery of nineteenth-century women biblical inter-preters. An excerpt from *The Lady of Shunem* was included in an impressive anthology she co-edited which appeared in 2006, and then one of Taylor's research students, Amanda W. Benckhuysen, wrote an analysis of it for a volume that Taylor co-edited.[108]

The Lady of Shunem provides close readings of biblical passages which contain women characters who are distressed or marginalized. Butler de-monstrates God's love and care for these women and how they often ended up obtaining a larger place in God's purposes and greater manifestations of God's favour than their social status seemed to warrant in the eyes of those around them. It is a deeply evangelical book, offering faith-filled, encour-aging devotional readings. In direct contrast to the trend in liberal theology but in keeping with evangelical crucicentrism, Butler even went out of her way to defend substitutionary atonement.[109] She also proclaimed the doc-trine of justification by faith in a soundly evangelical manner.[110] *The Lady of Shunem* is also a volume that emphasizes gender equality. In a move that many assume was only a later theological development, Butler reminded readers in the introduction that God is not male, using as a divine title, 'the Great Father-Mother'.[111] The eponymous biblical character comes first in the series. Although her son had just died, the lady of Shunem answered a servant's question about the state of things with, 'It is well.' While many might assume she just wanted to speak to the prophet himself before revealing her woe, Butler presents this initial answer as an expression of

---

[106] Jordan, *Butler*, 348.   [107] Daggers, *Revisited*, 191.
[108] Marion Ann Taylor and Heather E. Weir (eds), *Let Her Speak for Herself: Nineteenth-Century Women Writing on Women in Genesis* (Waco, Texas: Baylor University Press, 2006), 234–42; Benckhuysen, 'Reading', 135–45.
[109] Butler, *Lady*, 131–2.   [110] Butler, *Lady*, 49.   [111] Butler, *Lady*, 3.

faith, and then applies it to her readers as they confidently come to Jesus in prayer when in trouble. Butler's concern for her own children, including their spiritual state, is evident, and this devotional is in some ways an effort to share spiritual strategies with other anxious mothers. The original and insightful heart of the book is centred upon Hagar, whom Butler presents as 'The Typical Outcast'.[112] 'Outcast', as has been mentioned, is one of her favourite code words for what other Victorians called 'fallen women', and 'typical' is being used here in the biblical interpretation sense of a 'type'.[113] Hagar reveals God's attitude towards all the nineteenth-century women whom some man has had sexual intercourse with and then thrown away to face destitution. Christians have been taught to feel the plight of the Prodigal Son, but the double standard means that 'the case of the lost daughter is sadder even than that of the lost son.'[114] While respectable Victorian society shuns such women, God, through this type, reveals extraordinary divine favour:

> Is it not a thought, a fact which should wake up the whole Christian world to a truer and clearer view of life as it is around us, that the first record of a direct communication from Jehovah to a woman is this of his meeting with the rejected Hagar, alone, in the wilderness? It was not with Sarah, the Princess, or any other woman, but with Hagar, the ill-used slave, that the God of heaven stopped to converse, and to whom he brought his supreme comfort and guidance. This fact has been to me a strength and consolation in confronting the most awful problem on earth . . . [115]

Butler goes on to discuss Rahab, who, though a prostitute, cared for her family and became a recipient and agent of salvation who is honoured in the New Testament as one of the 'heroes of faith'.[116] Butler briefly discusses other biblical women. Interestingly for this study as a whole, she also alludes respectfully to the account in Annie Besant's autobiography of how the illness of her daughter undermined her faith.[117] Although sympathetic to Besant's story, Butler's own experience was that the Bible could counteract

---

[112] Butler, *Lady*, 3.

[113] For this, see George P. Landow, *Victorian Types, Victorian Shadows: Biblical Typology in Victorian Literature, Art and Thought* (Boston: Routledge & Kegan Paul, 1980).

[114] Butler, *Lady*, 80. In a similar move, Butler observed that in the Old Testament idolaters sacrificed their sons to Moloch, but the nations in her day 'have caused armies of their daughters to pass through the fire': Josephine E. Butler, 'The Lovers of the Lost', *Contemporary Review*, 13 (January–March 1870), 16–40 (here 17).

[115] Butler, *Lady*, 82.   [116] Butler, *Lady*, 98–9.   [117] Butler, *Lady*, 120.

such an outcome: 'Through all the conflict, however his Word has sustained me'.[118]

Josephine Butler survived into the Edwardian age, and the other volume of hers that needs to be explored here is *'The Morning Cometh.' A Letter to My Children* (1903).[119] Scholars have ignored this as well: Jordan does not cite, let alone discuss it (*'The Morning Cometh'* rather forlornly appears in the section on Butler's writings in the index as the only title without a single page number after it); and it did not even make it into Bell's bibliography.[120] Scholars attentive to Butler's religious identity have been interested in the fact that, late in life, Butler announced that she did not believe in eternal punishment. This is the primary evidence that she was a 'liberal' evangelical. Nevertheless, scholars have learned this fact from her *Memoir*: her religious identity appears different when one actually reads through *'The Morning Cometh'*, the book where she made this announcement. It is true that denying eternal punishment was to depart from a conservative evangelical view of that subject. Moreover, Butler even expresses her approval of F. D. Maurice's liberal Anglican theologizing on this point, going so far as to call him 'a true teacher'.[121] One should not imagine, however, that an evangelical endorsing Maurice's view in 1903—over thirty years after his death—is the equivalent of having done so half a century earlier when it initially provoked controversy. Moreover, *'The Morning Cometh'* is a deeply evangelical book; and its resolute biblicism is particularly striking. The very title is a scriptural phrase (from Isaiah 21: 12), and the quotation marks are intended to draw attention to this. Far from challenging the teaching of Scripture, Butler insists that her rejection of eternal punishment is the result of rightly handling the word of truth: 'a flood of light has been poured upon the meanings of the sacred writings'. 'For many years,' she testified, 'the Bible has been my constant companion,' and now she has come to understand it better. Eternal punishment is rejected on the grounds that it is 'unscriptural'.[122] In a typically evangelical way of handling a perceived biblical difficulty, Butler blamed the fact that people have traditionally believed that some people will spend eternity in hell entirely on bad translations of the original Hebrew and Greek texts. Butler then goes on

---

[118] Butler, *Lady*, 136.

[119] 'Philalethes' [Josephine E. Butler], *'The Morning Cometh.' A Letter to My Children* (Newcastle upon Tyne: T. M. Grierson, 1903).

[120] Jordan, *Butler*, 359; Bell, *Butler*, 254.   [121] Butler, *Morning*, 25–6.

[122] Butler, *Morning*, 1–2.

to offer a careful biblical theology of the subject which draws upon numerous texts in both Testaments. Appendices tackle the meaning of specific biblical words that she argues have been mistranslated.

Extraordinarily, in the main text of 'The Morning Cometh', having dismissed eternal punishment, Butler goes on to defend a traditional, conservative evangelical doctrine of Scripture. She specifically rejects the higher criticism of the Bible, something that had been widely adopted even in evangelical circles by that date: indeed, it had come to be generally accepted among orthodox biblical scholars in the 1880s, and by 1903 it was being taught even in the ministerial training of Primitive Methodists.[123] In other words, if Butler's rejection of a traditional view of hell was in advance of many evangelicals, her doctrine of Scripture marked her as an evangelical of the old school. Butler complained that higher critics failed to grasp the vital aspect of the nature of Scripture: 'the Breath of God, which breathes throughout the whole'; instead, they turn the Bible into 'the dry bones of a dissected carcase.'[124] She provided a stoutly conservative argument for rejecting modern theories on the authorship and historicity of biblical documents:

> Have you observed with what frequency Christ Himself quoted the Scriptures, the book of Moses, as well as the Psalms and the Prophets? In that mysterious and awful encounter with the 'Prince of darkness,' in the desert, He answered and defeated that enemy by the authority of the Word of God. Again and again He replied, '*It is written.*' It cannot be imagined that He, who is Himself 'the truth,' based His teaching for all time on mere 'myths,' or doubtful historical traditions.[125]

Again, in line with the approach taken by conservative evangelicals, Butler asserted that the truly scientific and helpful scholars were not the higher critics, but rather archaeologists such as A. H. Layard whose work was providing evidence 'in confirmation of the Old Testament history'.[126] The main text ends with an articulation of her hopes that the great, end-time revival that would prepare the way for the second coming of Christ was underway.

---

[123] Timothy Larsen, 'A. S. Peake, the free churches, and modern biblical criticism', *Bulletin of the John Rylands University Library of Manchester*, 86, 3 (Autumn 2004), 23–53.

[124] Butler, *Morning*, 33, 36.   [125] Butler, *Morning*, 35.

[126] Butler, *Morning*, 37. For the role of archaeology in such debates, see Timothy Larsen, 'Austen Henry Layard's Nineveh: The Bible and Archaeology in Victorian Britain', *Journal of Religious History*, 33, 1 (March 2009), 66–81.

Butler's late letters reveal a strong commitment to the Bible and to evangelical doctrine and spirituality. In one to a friend, she predicted of *'The Morning Cometh'*, not that anyone would find it too liberal, but rather that 'the Higher Critics will scorn it, because it holds to the <u>whole</u> Bible as a Revelation from God.'[127] Freer to use strong language in private, she grumbled to her son about 'German critics tearing' the Scriptures 'to pieces, like dogs'.[128] Butler was increasingly proto-Pentecostal, enthusing about 'the latter rain', a great work of the Spirit dawning, the continuance of spiritual gifts, the *Tongues of Fire* newspaper, and the like.[129] People who assumed that England was 'going to the bad' were not taking into account the divine favour that came with being a people of one book: 'I think our God remembers that we are the "Land of the Bible," and have for a century past sent the divine Word into every land where there is a language into which it can be translated.'[130] She was particularly enamored by the Welsh revival.[131] One mark of its authenticity was the prominence given to Scripture: 'Whole chapters of Isaiah or the Psalms are repeated by young people without any book'.[132] These interests, of course, were markers of conservative rather than liberal evangelicalism.

Butler's sight was failing and, strikingly, she never referred to this without remarking on its mournful implications for Bible reading. Already in 1898 she had observed:

> I can feel for you perhaps the more keenly, because for some weeks after the Congress in London, something went wrong in my head, and my sight became dim. The greatest fear I had was lest I should not be able any more

---

[127] Liverpool, University of Liverpool Library, Josephine Butler Papers, JB1/1 1903/03/06 (1), Josephine Butler to Fanny Forsaith, 6 March 1903.
[128] Liverpool, University of Liverpool Library, Josephine Butler Papers, JB1/1 1903/03/02 (1), Josephine Butler to her son Stanley Butler, 2 March 1903.
[129] Liverpool, University of Liverpool Library, Josephine Butler Papers, JB1/1 1903/11/21 (1), Josephine Butler to Fanny Forsaith, 21 November 1903.
[130] Butler, *Memoir*, 252–3 (letter dated 26 December 1905).
[131] Liverpool, University of Liverpool Library, Josephine Butler Papers, JB1/1 1905/03/03 (1), Josephine Butler to Stanley Butler, 3 March 1905. For a recent study of the Welsh revival, see Dyfed Wyn Roberts (ed.), *Revival, Renewal, and the Holy Spirit*, Studies in Evangelical History and Thought (Milton Keynes: Paternoster, 2009).
[132] Liverpool, University of Liverpool Library, Josephine Butler Papers, JB1/1 1905/03/03 (1), Josephine Butler to Stanley Butler, 3 March 1905. In this letter, Butler comments on the book of Revelation in a way which at the very least skirts close to accepting some of the approaches of modern biblical criticism. This could be her liberal evangelical side on display. On the other hand, she is clearly trying to make the Bible and the faith seem attractive and defensible to an intelligently gifted, religiously wayward son who has been put off by conservative Christianity (and who has expressed enthusiasm for the Gospel of Thomas).

to read my Bible; and indeed it is only in the strongest light that I can do so. But mine is the gradual dimness of sight of old age—a trifle compared with the trial which has come upon you in 'mid career.'[133]

In 1904, she grumbled: 'My sight is failing so much that I cannot read anything almost, & there is no one to read to me,' going on to explain that she 'would so love' to read the new translation of the Septuagint Bible, 'but if it is not very large print I could not.'[134] Josephine Butler died on 30 December 1906. Her last report on her failing eyes came in February of that same year: 'My sight is dim,' she complained, but she was nevertheless grateful that she had not been deprived of the greatest advantage vision has to offer: 'I have the whole Bible printed in parts easy to hold & in large print, for old people.'[135]

[133] Butler, *Memoir*, 251
[134] Liverpool, University of Liverpool Library, Josephine Butler Papers, JB1/1 1904/04/05 (1), Josephine Butler to Fanny Forsaith, 5 April 1904.
[135] Liverpool, University of Liverpool Library, Josephine Butler Papers, JB1/1 1906/02/26 (1), Josephine Butler to Fanny Forsaith and Harriet Wooler, 26 February 1906.

10

Orthodox Old Dissent

C. H. Spurgeon and 'The Book'

Even many of his admirers thought that the Baptist preacher Charles Haddon Spurgeon (1834–92) had an awkward side. This was the combative, controversialist Spurgeon whose anger at an open foe would occasionally spill over into sustained fire at erstwhile allies that suspiciously were a few yards closer to the enemy's camp. Almost everyone regretted that the most spectacular of such incidents was still unresolved when Spurgeon's life was cut short by Bright's disease at the age of 58.[1] The Downgrade controversy in which Spurgeon attacked his own denomination because he detected that some of its ministers were sliding toward theological liberalism resulted in Spurgeon resigning from the Baptist Union in bitterness in October 1887. This rift notwithstanding, Spurgeon is a fitting representative figure. He was the most famous and most popular Baptist, not only in Britain, but in the entire world. The denomination as a whole had experienced considerable growth as a direct result of having Spurgeon in the camp,[2] and Spurgeon's own congregation was by far its largest. For almost his entire adult life Spurgeon's paramount stature in the Baptist Union was unrivalled. This was ritually recognized by his being asked year after year to deliver the sermon at its annual meeting. In 1881, he protested that it was unseemly for the Union never to offer this honour to

[1] Privately, Spurgeon insisted that it was the Downgrade controversy itself that was killing him. See, for example: Oxford, Regent's Park College Library, C. H. Spurgeon Papers, C. H. Spurgeon to Mr Jackson, 8 November 1883; C. H. Spurgeon to Mr Jackson, 4 February 1888.
[2] W. Y. Fullerton, *C. H. Spurgeon: A Biography* (London: William and Norgate, 1920), 320.

another minister, but the official reply unapologetically observed that this perpetual distinction was not thereby creating or promoting his pre-eminent status, but merely acknowledging it: 'The fact is, your position is unique.'[3] The disgruntled whined that Spurgeon was the Baptist pope. Neither side in the Downgrade controversy was willing to allow it to have the final word: Spurgeon's enduring representative place among British Baptists was symbolized by the president of the Baptist Union giving a tribute at his funeral.[4]

Indeed, it is fitting for C. H. Spurgeon to represent orthodox Old Dissent in general. Of the Protestant bodies outside the establishment that came down from the seventeenth century, two, the Unitarians and the Quakers, did not self-identify as 'orthodox', and the greater distinctiveness of these two denominations has been accounted for in separate chapters in this volume. The three Old Dissenting groups which did self-identify as orthodox were the Congregationalists (or Independents), the Baptists, and the minority of Presbyterians in England that had not adopted Unitarian views. Congregationalists and Baptists were practically fraternal twins, the formal difference between the two bodies being over issues of baptism (the former sprinkled infants, while the latter insisted on immersion and only after the candidate had personally made a confession of faith). On ecclesiology they were one. Spurgeon was proud to boast: 'I believe in the glorious principle of Independency.'[5] Beyond this general affinity, there are specific reasons why Spurgeon is an apt representative of a wider category that includes Congregationalists. To begin, Spurgeon was raised as a Congregationalist. Indeed, both his paternal grandfather (who Spurgeon lived with for some years when a boy and who was a major influence on his life) and his own father were Congregational ministers. Even after Spurgeon had become a convinced Baptist and was no longer living with relatives, he was content to become a member of a Congregational church.

When he first came to London as a very young and disconcertingly popular Baptist preacher, Spurgeon was sneered at in the press—and even attacked in print by a jealous Baptist minister. Weighty Congregational ministers such as Thomas Binney, Edwin Paxton Hood, and John Campbell,

---

[3] Susannah Spurgeon and J. W. Harrald (eds), *C. H. Spurgeon's Autobiography*, 4 vols (London: Passmore and Alabaster, 1897; facsimile reprint: Pasadena, Texas: Pilgrim Press, 1992), IV, 149–50 [hereafter *Autobiography*].

[4] Peter Shepherd, 'Spurgeon's Funeral', *Baptist Quarterly*, 41, 2 (April 2005), 72–9.

[5] *Autobiography*, I, 357.

however, defended him. As he settled in to his ministry, he regularly swapped pulpits with leading Congregational ministers such as Newman Hall and Joseph Parker, and delivered addresses for Congregational institutions such as the Congregational Home Missionary Society and Cheshunt College. He received significant support from prominent Congregational laymen including Samuel Morley and Apsley Pellatt; the latter even presided at the opening of the huge building designed to hold Spurgeon's enormous congregation, the Metropolitan Tabernacle. Perhaps the most famous Victorian Congregationalist, the explorer-missionary David Livingstone, not only came to hear Spurgeon preach, but carried with him in his African travels a copy of a Spurgeon sermon which he had annotated as 'very good'.[6] The closeness of Spurgeon's relationship with a popular Congregational evangelist from America, D. L. Moody, was symbolized by Spurgeon's widow giving Moody his pulpit Bible.[7] Most decisive of all, Spurgeon appointed a Congregationalist to be the master of the orphanage he founded, and another one to be the principal of his Pastors' College: there could be no more unequivocal proof that the Baptist preacher considered Congregational spirituality and theology very close to his own than that he would entrust the spiritual formation of children in his care and the training of ministers under his direction to the oversight of men from that denomination.

Spurgeon's affinity with orthodox Presbyterianism is also striking. The theological wells he drank deepest from were those of Presbyterian Puritans. He went so far as to educate his congregation in the faith through the Westminster catechism and he boasted that the students at his Pastors' College were formed in 'the old theology of the Westminster Assembly's Confession'.[8] Nor was this merely a historical debt. Spurgeon was delighted with the theological work of the American Presbyterian theologian, Charles Hodge, enthusing without qualification: 'With no writer do we more fully agree.'[9] Spurgeon considered Presbyterian-dominated Scotland as in a better spiritual state than England, and Presbyterian Scots, in turn, were enthusiastic about Spurgeon's ministry. Indeed, it would be fair to say that Spurgeon was for most of his adult life the most important champion of Calvinism in England. One of his closest friends was Robert Taylor, the

---

[6] *Autobiography*, II, 215.

[7] Patricia Stallings Kruppa, *Charles Haddon Spurgeon: A Preacher's Progress* (New York: Garland Publishing, 1982), 470.

[8] *Autobiography*, II, 150.

[9] C. H. Spurgeon, *Commenting and Commentaries* (London: Passmore & Alabaster, 1876), 178.

orthodox Presbyterian minister of Upper Norwood. In the last full year of his life, Spurgeon put forward a little 'local Fraternal Union' he had created as a model, in contrast to the Baptist Union, for a fellowship of truly theologically likeminded people. It was comprised of conservative, orthodox Baptists and Presbyterians.[10]

Moreover, this affinity extended beyond theology and fellowship to worship. Charles Greville went to hear Spurgeon and astutely observed in his memoirs: 'The service was like the Presbyterian: Psalms, prayers, expounding a Psalm, and a sermon.'[11] In defiance of the worship trends of his day, Spurgeon went so far in the purist Presbyterian direction as to ban instrumental accompaniment from the worship service—and emphasize the singing of the Psalter. Every winter Spurgeon relocated to Mentone, on the French Riviera, to attempt to renew his health and gain a break from his exhausting schedule. While there he worshipped habitually in a Presbyterian church. One of Spurgeon's last sermons before he became too ill to preach was an Exeter Hall meeting in support of Presbyterian missions.[12] Not least significantly, in his final illness Spurgeon entrusted his congregation—the largest Baptist one in the world—not to a Baptist minister, but rather to the American Presbyterian minister, Arthur Tappan Pierson. When the question was raised about whether or not it was appropriate for Dr Pierson to preside at communion, Spurgeon insisted that the Presbyterian minister certainly should and that he should be informed of who the culprit was if anyone else dared to object.[13] Spurgeon's final letters commend Pierson to the congregation over and over again. He wrote just a couple of weeks before his death about 'the rest of heart wh[ich] comes to me through knowing that you are all spiritually fed under the ministry of Dr Pierson.'[14] (To the American minister himself, Spurgeon good-naturedly offered a biblical pun: 'I trust that Mrs Pierson is not unhappy in the city of Gog, Magog and Fog.')[15] To round off this discussion, it is worth underlining in passing that

[10] *Sword and the Trowel* (1891), 446.

[11] Charles C. F. Greville, *Greville Memoirs (Third and Concluding Part): A Journal of the Reign of Queen Victoria from 1852 to 1860* (New York: D. Appleton and Company, 1887), 345.

[12] *Autobiography*, IV, 355.

[13] Charles Spurgeon (ed.), *The Letters of Charles Haddon Spurgeon* (London: Marshall Brothers, 1923), 120. (The editor is Charles Haddon Spurgeon's namesake son.)

[14] Spurgeon's College, London, C. H. Spurgeon Papers, C. H. Spurgeon to his congregation, 14 January 1892.

[15] Spurgeon, *Letters*, 202.

Spurgeon was glad to self-identify as a Dissenter: he was an active supporter of the Liberation Society, which sought the disestablishment of the Church of England, and he even won the praise of Annie Besant for defending Bradlaugh's right to sit in Parliament as an avowed atheist.[16] Spurgeon also, of course, gladly wore the label of orthodox, indeed he defiantly claimed to stand for 'old-fashioned orthodoxy'.[17]

It is not going too far even to enlist Spurgeon as a representative figure of his age. The only academic biography of Spurgeon takes as its overarching theme: 'Spurgeon as a representative Victorian'.[18] Spurgeon's popularity is difficult to overstate. By the time he reached his majority (that is, his twenty-first birthday), he was already the most popular preacher in Britain, a position he would not only retain for the rest of his life, but his reputation would continue to grow over the years. It is impossible to know how large a congregation he could have gathered if he had found a venue that would have held them all so that they could hear him. He eventually had his own built to accommodate just a portion of them—the Metropolitan Taber-nacle. As 6,000 people could be squeezed into it, it was larger than the Exeter Hall. He filled it on both Sunday mornings and evenings—with others often standing outside or going away disappointed—from its opening in 1861 till the end of his ministry thirty years later. While waiting for it to be built, his congregation rented for some time the Surrey Gardens Music Hall, and packed in 12,000 for each service. His largest ever audience was either at the Crystal Palace in 1857, where 23,654 were able to come within range of his voice, or at the Agricultural Hall, Islington, 1867, where estimates of the throng ranged as high as 25,000.[19] Wherever Spurgeon went it was the same. For example, 15,000 people applied for a ticket when he came to Liverpool in 1882, but most of them were disappointed as the venue could only hold 5,000.[20] Spurgeon's unpublished letters are heavy on notes of regret that he cannot fulfil the desires of seemingly every church, charity, and denomination in the land that he give them a boost by agreeing to speak at one of their meetings.[21] Everyone had to hear Spurgeon. Eminent Victorians from across the religious spectrum from Lord Shaftesbury to

---

[16] Kruppa, *Spurgeon*, 350.   [17] *Sword and the Trowel* (1888), 378.

[18] Kruppa, *Spurgeon*, 6.   [19] *Autobiography*, III, 95.   [20] Spurgeon, *Letters*, 83.

[21] For an early example of this, see Spurgeon's College, London, C. H. Spurgeon Papers, C. H. Spurgeon to an unidentified recipient, 22 May 1854. For a particularly apologetic one, see C. H. Spurgeon to an unidentified recipient, 8 September 1873.

Matthew Arnold to George Eliot came to see for themselves. For a season, John Ruskin was not just a curious observer, but a besotted follower; he even gave £115 toward the building of the Metropolitan Tabernacle.[22] At one service, over thirty members of Parliament were counted in the congregation, and Spurgeon's political guests at various services included Lord John Russell and H. H. Asquith. Some thought things had gone too far when even the sitting prime minister, W. E. Gladstone, came. Florence Nightingale shrewdly tried to enlist Spurgeon to seek recruits for her training programme for nurses. Naturally, she appealed to him in biblical language: 'The harvest is ready, but the labourers still are few.'[23] In a typical wish, a Scotsman said he longed to go to London before he died 'to see Madame Tussaud's and hear Mr Spurgeon'.[24] Had he been content with wanting merely to see Spurgeon he could save himself one of these stops as, of course, there was a Spurgeon waxwork at Madame Tussaud's. Spurgeon sermons were stocked by the railway newsagents in Scotland. One witness claimed to have stumbled into an isolated Scottish village in which the inhabitants did not recognize the names of either Gladstone or Disraeli, but would light up at the mention of Spurgeon. If that tale arouses suspicion, a study has been done of the *Saturday Review* from its founding in 1855 till its first editor retired in 1868 and it revealed that—despite being a review of politics and not of religion—this paper gave almost as much attention to Spurgeon as it did to either Disraeli or Gladstone.[25] Perhaps the ultimate tribute to his fame, Spurgeon was repeatedly stalked by murderous maniacs who were drawn to the famous. When he fell ill in 1891, his place in Victorian society as a whole was acknowledged by letters of sympathy— just to name a few such examples—from Gladstone, the Prince of Wales, the archbishop of Canterbury, and the Chief Rabbi.

Of course, he also had his detractors. A Strict Baptist minister who did not think the popular preacher was sufficiently Calvinist damningly re- marked that Spurgeon was 'a kind of person whom it would seem almost a cruelty to dislike. The same may be, with equal truth, said both of Dr Pusey and of Cardinal Wiseman.'[26] Likewise, from toward the other end of the ecclesiastical spectrum, when Bishop Wilberforce was asked if he

[22] Kruppa, *Spurgeon*, 126.   [23] *Autobiography*, IV, 178.   [24] Kruppa, *Spurgeon*, 246.
[25] Merle Mowbray Bevington, *The Saturday Review, 1855–1868: Representative Educated Opinion in Victorian England* (New York: Columbia University Press, 1941), 88.
[26] *Autobiography*, II, 38.

envied the Nonconformists for having Spurgeon in their camp, he retorted: 'Thou shalt not covet thy neighbour's ass.'[27] Nevertheless, such voices notwithstanding, it is not obvious where one could set a limit on just how popular Spurgeon was. He was easily the most popular preacher in the entire English-speaking world. Not content to receive the revised, printed version of the sermon a few weeks later, various attempts were made to have a reporter telegraph Spurgeon's weekly sermon to America and then have it printed in newspapers across the country that reached a million readers. It was said that every American going to England went with the ambition to see Shakespeare's tomb and Charles Haddon Spurgeon and that, when they returned, everyone enquired if they had seen the Queen and heard Spurgeon. Famous Americans who went to hear him preach when they came to England ranged from a former slave (Frederick Douglass) to a future president (James A. Garfield). Spurgeon's sermons were printed in newspapers in the Antipodes and because so many of the inhabitants were too distant from any minister to be able to attend a worship service regularly the English Baptist minister had an even more dominant impact in Australia and New Zealand. Nor does the English-speaking world set the limit. During his own lifetime, Spurgeon's sermons were translated into almost forty languages, including not only numerous European ones but also Middle Eastern (Arabic and Syriac) and African ('Congo' and 'Kaffir') and Asian (Bengali, Chinese, Hindi, Japanese, Tamil, and Urdu). The Antipodes were represented by Maori, and a Castilian translation was made for Argentina. One million copies of a translated collection of Spurgeon's sermons were circulated in Russia with the official approval of the Orthodox Church, making it quite possible that the pastor of the Metropolitan Tabernacle was the most popular living preacher in that vast country despite it being neither Protestant nor English-speaking.[28] An American minister published with an American press a biography of Spurgeon that had as its subtitle, 'The World's Great Preacher'.[29] While greatness can be judged on various

---

[27] Robert H. Ellison, *The Victorian Pulpit: Spoken and Written Sermons in Nineteenth-Century Britain* (Selinsgrove: Susquehanna University Press, 1998), 73.

[28] Mark Hopkins, *Nonconformity's Romantic Generation: Evangelical and Liberal Theologies in Victorian England*, Studies in Evangelical History and Thought (Milton Keynes: Paternoster, 2004), 155.

[29] Russell H. Conwell, *Life of Charles Haddon Spurgeon: The World's Great Preacher* (Philadelphia: Edgewood Publishing Company, 1892).

criteria and therefore is contestable, it is hard to imagine who would rival Spurgeon in his day for the title of the world's most popular preacher.

Before moving into the details of Spurgeon's life, work, and thought in relationship to the Scriptures, it is worth setting out a general theme that will recur: keenly aware that this conviction was under attack, Spurgeon resolutely insisted that the whole canon of the Bible was the Word of God and therefore it all ought to be encountered in sermons, corporate worship, and daily devotional reading. He never tired of reiterating this point. Here is a typical declaration: 'The Scriptures are as true in Genesis as in Revelation, and the five books of Moses are as inspired as the four Gospels.'[30] Or to put the matter more experientially: 'let the volume fall open as if by chance, and the reader will still discover the same singular majesty of manner.'[31] In an 1879 sermon he averred: 'every portion of God's word is given by inspiration, and is and must be profitable to you.'[32] The 'must' perhaps has a faint air of protesting too much. As will be shown, in practice, Spurgeon's actions in the light of this claim were mixed. At times, he would deliberately choose difficult texts in a way that was either a mark of bravery or foolhardiness, but he was also well aware that some texts might be more trouble than they were worth when he was trying to edify the faithful, and he would occasionally reflect on this—and act accordingly.

Spurgeon was an Essex lad, the son of a clerk whose lay preaching would eventually lead on to becoming a Congregational minister. For reasons that are not clear, Spurgeon was sent to live with his paternal grandparents for much of his childhood. This grandfather was the well-respected minister of the Independent chapel in Stambourne. Spurgeon's dominant recorded memories from his early years revolve around him being designated the Bible reader at household devotions when still 'a very small boy'.[33] When he was around ten years old the missionary Richard Knill visited and took an interest in his spiritual life, prophesying that Spurgeon would someday become a preacher. At the age of eighteen, by which time he was indeed a preacher, Spurgeon wrote to Knill to thank him, reminding him of who he was or how he had noticed him by remarking: 'I read at family prayer'.[34]

---

[30] C. H. Spurgeon, *The Treasury of David*, 7 vols (London: Passmore and Alabaster, 1908; originally 1869–85), VI, 325.

[31] C. H. Spurgeon, *The Clue of the Maze*, third edition (London: Passmore and Alabaster, 1892), 57.

[32] *Metropolitan Tabernacle Pulpit*, 25 (1879), 632.

[33] *Autobiography*, I, 17.   [34] Spurgeon, *Letters*, 187.

Spurgeon also offered as an amusing anecdote of his childhood how he interrupted a reading to ask his grandfather what could possibly be meant by a 'bottomless pit' (Revelation 9: 1). His grandfather insisted that he just keep reading, but Spurgeon had the power to choose the text and he retaliated by revisiting that part of the Bible every day: 'The process was successful, for it is by no means the most edifying thing in the world to hear the history of the Mother of Harlots, and the beast with seven heads, every morning in the week'.[35] Spurgeon insisted, 'I *can* bear witness that children can understand the Scriptures', but this anecdote and other memories show a certain ambivalence about experiencing certain parts of the Bible as a child. He recalled hearing 'long passages out of Daniel' and 'parts of the prophecy of Ezekiel' that were of no profit to him whatever.[36] As with the young Elizabeth Fry, some of what he read or heard was unsettling. He remembered the rushlight terrifying him as a sick child at night as 'it made me think of Nebuchadnezzar's burning fiery furnace.'[37] When Spurgeon created *The Interpreter*, a kind of family Bible for household devotions with selected passages, Revelation 9 was one of the excised chapters, indicating that he judged that children were not ready to get to the bottom of the bottomless pit.[38]

Spurgeon spent a year when he was around fourteen at an Anglican school in Maidstone. One of the clergymen there, acting as a devil's advocate to sharpen Spurgeon's theological reasoning, put forward the thesis that there was no biblical warrant for infant baptism and set him to disprove it. Instead, Spurgeon became convinced that only the Baptist position was scriptural and resolved that if he experienced conversion he would be baptized as a believer. He later reminisced proudly: 'I became a Baptist through reading the New Testament,—especially in the Greek'.[39] He waggishly told a gathering where Anglican clergymen and ministers from other paedobaptist denominations were present that when he is asked for a book that explains his distinctive view on baptism he always recommends the New Testament.[40] Spurgeon also asserted that somewhere in his early teen years he

---

[35] *Autobiography*, I, 17–18.　　[36] Spurgeon, *Commenting*, 22.

[37] *Autobiography*, I, 42–3.

[38] C. H. Spurgeon, *The Interpreter, or, Scripture for Family Worship, being selected passages of the Word of God for every morning and evening throughout the year, accompanied by a running comment and suitable hymns* (London: Passmore and Alabaster, n.d.).

[39] *Autobiography*, I, 150.

[40] C. H. Spurgeon, *Speeches at Home and Abroad* (London: Passmore & Alabaster, 1878), 18.

had experienced religious scepticism, but this must have been an internal struggle with little outward manifestations—and even he conceded that he was still simultaneously reading the Bible systematically. Spurgeon's spiritual new birth came on the morning of 6 January 1850. Intending to walk to another chapel, a snowstorm forced him to settle for a Primitive Methodist one. Before the sermon was over, Charles Haddon Spurgeon knew he had been saved. Spurgeon emphasized that the key to his conversion was the biblical text that this anonymous, humble, lay preacher proclaimed: 'Look unto me, and be ye saved, all the ends of the earth' (Isaiah 45: 22).[41]

Duly born again, Spurgeon's resulting spiritual exuberance manifested itself in engagement with the Scriptures. He wrote to his father a few weeks after his conversion: 'How beautiful is the Bible! I never loved it so before; it seems to me as necessary food.'[42] A few weeks later he reported to his mother that his appetite for this fare was greater than was practical: 'I should like to be always reading my Bible'.[43] By the middle of that year, it is apparent that this pursuit was scholarly as well as devotional: 'I am studying through Romans in the Greek, with Barnes, Doddridge, and Chalmers for my commentaries.'[44] These letters as a new convert are already marked by a tendency to speak in a biblical code. He hopes his father will receive 'the dew of Hermon', while his wish for his mother's birthday should be taken entirely as speaking of spiritual realities through biblical metaphors: 'May God give you a feast,—honey, wine, milk,—may you be satisfied with marrow and fatness'.[45] Parents are typically hungry for news of how an absent child is getting on, and Spurgeon did not deprive them of such details, confiding on one occasion that he feared he might 'be taken by the Philistines', but informing them triumphantly a couple of months later that he could now feel 'the warm air of Beulah'.[46] This positive report was confirmed in his private diary where he exalted that his soul was 'like the chariots of Ammi-nadib' (Song of Songs 6: 12).[47] Kruppa remarks that Spurgeon's use of scriptural 'erotic imagery' at this stage 'raises questions', noting that he was even willing to assume 'the submissive female role' in articulations of his relationship with Jesus. She suggests that this was sublimated adolescent sexual desires, but while allowance needs to be made for

[41] *Autobiography*, I, 105–8.   [42] Spurgeon, *Letters*, 13.   [43] Spurgeon, *Letters*, 16.
[44] *Autobiography*, I, 188.   [45] Spurgeon, *Letters*, 20, 31.
[46] Spurgeon, *Letters*, 16, 21.   [47] *Autobiography*, I, 131.

our heightened awareness of such realities, due compensation should also be made for our decreased familiarity with biblical language making it sound odder to us than it did to the Victorians. This language was not a passing teenage phase, but rather Spurgeon used it throughout his entire adult life. For example, when he was a 48-year-old man with a wife and children, Spurgeon was still enthusing about the 'wonderful sweetness' of being able to 'call Him our Husband'.[48] Indeed, he delighted in spiritualizing the erotic language of the Song of Songs, returning to that canonical book again and again throughout his ministry until he had accumulated an impressive total of sixty-three sermons with a main text from it.[49]

Spurgeon was baptized as a believer on 3 May 1850. A month later he was addressing Sunday school classes and had developed unofficial pastoral rounds in which he visited seventy people weekly. He delivered his first sermon to an adult congregation when he was sixteen. He began preaching for the Baptist congregation at Waterbeach (which was without a pastor) in October 1851 and his ministry for them was so well received that they were content for it to continue indefinitely. By the time Spurgeon was seventeen years old he was the settled minister there preaching at services that often gathered 450 people. Undoubtedly part of the reason that Waterbeach was willing to take this risk was because it was a poor congregation that could only pay a modest salary. Spurgeon wrote to his father insisting that he was economizing, but:

> I have bought several books, which I could not do without. This week I have purchased a good Septuagint, which is a Greek translation of the Old Testament; you will see it mentioned by commentators. This I did for two reasons—1. To improve my Greek. 2. To assist me in studying the Bible.[50]

Spurgeon seriously contemplated going to a Baptist college to gain formal ministerial training, but he felt providentially led to forsake such a plan. This guidance included an audible, mystical 'loud voice' which confined its advice entirely to quoting an apt text of scripture at him (Jeremiah 45: 5).[51]

---

[48] *Metropolitan Tabernacle Pulpit*, 44 (1898), 243. (Spurgeon's sermons were taken down in shorthand and thus this series continued long after his death. Spurgeon preached this sermon in 1883.)

[49] *A Complete Index to C. H. Spurgeon's Sermons, 1855–1917* (Pasadena, Texas: Pilgrim Publications, 1980).

[50] Spurgeon, *Letters*, 34–5.   [51] *Autobiography*, I, 242.

In 1853 New Park Street, Southwark, was still one of the most important Baptist chapels in England, but it was also on the decline and seemed threatened with a swift and deep descent if something was not done. The something that the congregation decided on was to call to occupy their pulpit a provincial nineteen-year-old who had not been to college but who did have a growing reputation as an effective preacher. Spurgeon used the honorarium from his first London sermon to buy biblical commentaries. The New Park Street congregation approved of Spurgeon and—still a teenager—he accepted a call to be their minister-on-trial. As has already been noted, he then had a meteoric rise to his permanent place as the most celebrated preacher in London, then in Britain—not stopping until he was widely acknowledged as 'the world's great preacher'. The youthful minister wanted a wife and set his eye on Susannah Thompson. He courted like a solid middle-class mid-Victorian—declaring his affections through a poem by Martin Tupper—and made love like a true Calvinist: 'God in His mercy showed me that you were indeed *elect*.'[52] She responded in kind by giving him Calvin's commentaries as a token of her ardour, and they married on 8 January 1856. Their only children—twin sons named Charles and Thomas—were born that autumn.

Spurgeon's reputation was built on his sermons. Simply put, his sermons moved people. As one eyewitness reported:

> While he was preaching I felt as if I was the only one in that great audience he was speaking to . . . I never was so touched with a sermon in my life. There in that audience of over 6,000, you could hear a pin drop, and see wet eyes. In fact, I could not restrain my tears, so exactly did he specify me.[53]

Innumerable people testified that a Spurgeon sermon prompted their conversion. Impressive tallies were compiled of conversions from a single sermon; sometimes even from a single copy of a single sermon circulating in some isolated community. His evangelistic powers were so strong that he gained a soul for heaven the day before his great Exeter Hall sermon when he was just testing the acoustics![54] There were endless reports that congregations without ministers simply had a layman read a Spurgeon sermon to the assembly. Nor was it uncommon for the ministers themselves—even Anglican clergymen—to choose to deliver a Spurgeon sermon rather than

[52] C. H. Spurgeon to Susannah Thompson, 11 January 1855: Spurgeon, *Letters*, 70.
[53] *Sword and the Trowel* (1886), 647.   [54] *Autobiography*, II, 239–40.

create an original one of their own. Once when Spurgeon was on holiday in the English countryside he attended a Methodist chapel, only to hear one of his own sermons preached back at him![55]

A key to the effectiveness of Spurgeon's sermons was undoubtedly the preacher's own holy earnestness. This, in turn, was fuelled by his deep and unwavering faith: he was a man of strong spiritual convictions whose passionate clarity and intensity could awaken conviction in others. Spurgeon himself insisted that the power behind his sermons was that of the word of God itself. From first to last, he could hardly address the subjects of either the Bible or preaching without averring that it was generally the text itself which was the key to a soul being won by a sermon. This was asserted on both a priori and a posteriori grounds. As to the latter, here is an example from a 1857 sermon, that is to say, from early in his ministry:

> I have marked, that if ever we have a conversion at any time, in ninety-nine cases out of a hundred, the conversion is traceable to the text, or to some Scripture quoted in the sermon, than to any trite or original saying of the preacher.[56]

As to the former, here is a comment from an address he gave in the last full year of his life: 'The Holy Spirit wrought your salvation through the Holy Scriptures. You trace your conversion, I am sure, to the Word of the Lord; for this alone is "perfect, converting the soul."' (Psalm 19: 7)[57]

Kruppa remarked, 'Rather curiously, his greatest problem in preparing a sermon was in finding a suitable text to expound.'[58] This is not at all curious, however, as Spurgeon really did think of his sermons as expositions of Scripture in which everything flowed out of and from the text. His standard sermon preparation began with this crucial task of selection. Once this was achieved, his wife, Susannah, would read aloud to him from commentaries that discussed it because, once again, he saw his task as unfolding the meaning of this portion of scripture. Spurgeon once observed, 'What are sermons but commentaries? At least, they ought so to be.'[59] When Spurgeon started including in his magazine, *The Sword and the Trowel*, an index of his published sermons, it was simply a textual index without identifying the title or the theme: the text was the theme in

---

[55] *Autobiography*, III, 337.   [56] *New Park Street Pulpit*, III (1857), 57–60.
[57] C. H. Spurgeon, *The Greatest Fight in the World* (New York: Funk & Wagnalls, 1891), 18.
[58] Kruppa, *Spurgeon*, 186.   [59] *Sword and the Trowel* (1866), 94.

Spurgeon's mind. Likewise, when Spurgeon published a four-volume set of sermon outlines to give bi-vocational preachers a helping hand with their sermon preparation, they were presented in canonical order beginning with Genesis and ending with Revelation.[60] He would concede that it was not inherently wrong to preach a topical sermon before driving home that what was really needed were expositional ones. Here is a typical appeal to the students at his Pastors' College: 'I am sure that no preaching will last so long, or build up a church so well, as the expository. . . . I cannot too earnestly assure you that if your ministries are to be lastingly useful you must be expositors. . . . Be masters of your Bibles'.[61] As to the whole canon, Spurgeon insisted on its utility in preaching. He delighted to confirm this by insisting that he had heard testimonies of conversions from the most un-likely of texts. One favourite anecdote was the story of a man who came to Christ through hearing a reading of a genealogical table![62] Spurgeon mod-elled this conviction up to a point, tackling many texts that less daring preachers would have avoided. On as sensitive an occasion as the death of Prince Albert, the Calvinist pastor charged forward unabashedly with a memorial sermon from Amos 3: 6: 'Shall there be evil in the city, and the Lord hath not done it?'[63] Still, Spurgeon had the sense not to defy Victorian propriety by expounding on the more unseemly scriptural narratives, and he was clearly aware that seeking out problem texts could be a route to ineffectual ministry. When he heard a sermon justifying the genocide of the Canaanites, although the preacher must be given full marks for textual bravery and theological conservatism, Spurgeon nevertheless fumed that it 'was as much adapted to convert a sinner, or to edify a saint, as Burke's Peerage, or Walker's Dictionary'.[64]

Not unrelated to his belief in the inherent power of God's word, Spurgeon was disconcertingly candid about eschewing any attempt at apologetics and confining himself exclusively to proclamation. In his very first volume of sermons, there was one simply entitled, 'The Bible'. In it, his hearers and readers were given fair warning about what his lifelong approach would be: 'How do you know that God wrote the book? That is just what I shall not

[60] C. H. Spurgeon, *My Sermon-Notes*, 4 vols (New York: Fleming H. Revell Company, n.d.; the preface is dated 1884).
[61] *Sword and the Trowel* (1874), 221.   [62] *New Park Street Pulpit*, III (1857), 62.
[63] *Autobiography*, III, 73.   [64] *Autobiography*, II, 369.

try to prove to you.'[65] In an 1882 sermon he informed his congregation flatly: 'A servant is not to justify his master's message, but to deliver it.'[66] Spurgeon once offered a kind of paradoxical anti-apologetic apologetic, musing that if he understood everything in the Bible then he would not believe it was from God.[67] Even in his most explicit attempt at apologetics, *The Clue of the Maze*, Spurgeon began with this disorientating disclaimer: 'The paragraphs of this little book are not supposed to be an argument.'[68] The Word did not need to be proven, but only proclaimed. Spurgeon told the Bible Society that believers should not attempt to defend the Scriptures, but only to expound and spread them: 'The answer to every objection against the Bible is the Bible.'[69]

As will become increasingly clear as this chapter unfolds, 'preaching the Word' (which was his standard phrase for delivering a sermon) was but one of the many ways in which Spurgeon expressed his commitment to the Bible. One that has been almost completely overlooked is his habit of reading and commenting upon a portion of Scripture as a discreet part of the worship service. This was a habitual aspect of his ministry in his own congregation, and he even pursued it when he was a guest preacher. For example, an account in the *Scottish Guardian* of a meeting where Spurgeon delivered a sermon when he was on a tour of that country in 1856 recorded that he had read and expounded Exodus 14 and then preached from Psalm 106.[70] Eventually, the printed sermons would state at the end the portion of Scripture read before the sermon, and ultimately Spurgeon's comments on the reading were printed as well. Sometimes this context is explicit in the sermon itself, as in one from 1885 where he observes in his opening remarks: 'As I said just now, in the reading of the chapter.'[71] Spurgeon repeatedly commended this custom to other ministers, arguing that otherwise they would not ground their congregation in the whole of Scripture, that it would give them an opportunity to clarify difficult passages that have been bewildering the faithful, and that it would creatively expand the possibilities in their own minds of suitable texts for their sermons.[72] Most remarkably, Spurgeon claimed that he spent more time in his study preparing for this separate exposition of a portion of Scripture than he did for the sermon

---

[65] *New Park Street Pulpit*, I (1855), 110.   [66] *Metropolitan Tabernacle Pulpit*, 28 (1882), 212.
[67] Hopkins, *Nonconformity's Romantic Generation*, 138.   [68] Spurgeon, *Clue*, 5.
[69] Spurgeon, *Speeches*, 17.   [70] *Autobiography*, II, 115.
[71] *Metropolitan Tabernacle Pulpit*, 31 (1885), 577.
[72] Spurgeon, *Treasury*, IV, p. iii.

itself.[73] Even if this was an exaggeration, it was one meant to underline how seriously he took the systematic presentation of the contents of the Bible to his congregation.

Another expression of Spurgeon's dedication to the Scriptures was his commitment to fostering a general culture of piety that was marked by daily personal and household Bible reading. In an early sermon he railed at his hearers: 'There is dust enough on some of your Bibles to write "damnation" with your fingers.'[74] The vast majority no doubt simply congratulated themselves on this charge not being applicable to them. In 1871 he tried again, this time accusing them of only reading God's word at daily family prayers and not privately as well.[75] Spurgeon claimed the Bible was for everyone, even insisting that scriptural knowledge could be instilled 'during the first months of a child's life', gesturing unconvincingly at the Moses birth narrative: apparently before there was 'Baby Mozart' there was baby Moses.[76] In this same sermon, Spurgeon goes on to claim that educators had discovered 'that children will learn to read out of the Bible better than from any other book'. This is another case of his ideologically driven wishes getting carried away. In *The Sword and the Trowel* Spurgeon gave an enthusiastic review of *The Story of the Bible from Genesis to Revelation told in Simple Language*—a book that would have no *raison d'être* if his previous claim was literally true.[77] More sensibly, the minister of the Metropolitan Tabernacle admonished in his 1859 pastoral letter: 'Let our youths and maidens study the Scriptures daily.'[78] And he did mean the word 'study' to be taken literally; Spurgeon specifically encouraged women to take up the challenge of learning biblical languages: 'Every member of our churches, who has a fair English education, should aim to acquire sufficient Greek to read the New Testament; we specially include in this exhortation our sisters in Christ.'[79]

Spurgeon offered practical assistance as well as admonitions by creating guides to daily Bible reading. The first of these appeared in 1865: *Morning by Morning: or, Daily Readings for the Family or the Closet*.[80] The main title is

---

[73] Spurgeon, *Commenting*, 24.   [74] *New Park Street Pulpit*, I (1855), 109–16.

[75] *Metropolitan Tabernacle Pulpit*, 17 (1871), 600.

[76] *Metropolitan Tabernacle Pulpit*, 31 (1885), 578.   [77] *Sword and the Trowel* (1888), 84.

[78] *Autobiography*, II, 306.   [79] *Sword and the Trowel* (1885), 431.

[80] C. H. Spurgeon, *Morning by Morning: or, Daily Readings for the Family or the Closet* (London: Passmore and Alabaster, 1865).

taken from Isaiah 50: 4. As to the subtitle, 'closet' is biblical language for a private, individual time of prayer (Matthew 6: 6), and thus Spurgeon was commending this volume as an aid to either personal or household devotions. As to the former, Spurgeon suggested that private morning devotions should be completed before meeting another human being; to go straight to work without doing this would be like neglecting to get dressed. The book is set out with a text and a reflection for every day of the year. As to the whole canon, already by the second sentence of the first entry (January 1), Spurgeon has his readers contemplating 'fierce Amalekites'.[81] Spurgeon insisted, however, that people must read 'the usual chapter as well', and use his book merely as a supplement to rather than a replacement for systematic reading of the whole Bible.[82] Inevitably, this volume was followed a few years later by *Evening by Evening: or, Readings at Eventide for the Family or the Closet*.[83] In the preface Spurgeon conceded that some households only find it possible to practice evening family devotions and not morning as well. He commended the volume for the range of its biblical material: 'We have striven to keep out of the common track, and hence we have used unusual texts, and have brought forward neglected subjects.'[84] More than making good on this feature, *Evening by Evening* includes the text, 'Let not one of them escape' (1 Kings 18: 40), the reflection being a spiritual reading for the whole family of God's desire for one to perpetrate a massacre.[85]

In 1873, Spurgeon compiled *The Interpreter, or, Scripture for Family Worship, being selected passages of the Word of God for every morning and evening throughout the year, accompanied by a running comment and suitable hymns*.[86] This was a very respectable volume in more than one sense. Made to look like a family Bible, it was a large, gilded and generally imposing and impressive volume. It was reported proudly that various aristocratic families were using it, and the inverse was undoubtedly true as well: it was too costly for poor households to have one. Respectable in another sense, it was essentially a bowdlerized Bible. Even inside its pages, it *looks* like a Bible with chapters

---

[81] Spurgeon, *Morning*, 1.   [82] Spurgeon, *Morning*, p. vii.

[83] C. H. Spurgeon, *Evening by Evening: or, Readings at Eventide for the Family or the Closet* (New York: Sheldon and Company, 1869).

[84] Spurgeon, *Evening*, p. viii.   [85] Spurgeon, *Evening*, 200.

[86] C. H. Spurgeon, *The Interpreter, or, Scripture for Family Worship, being selected passages of the Word of God for every morning and evening throughout the year, accompanied by a running comment and suitable hymns* (London: Passmore and Alabaster, n.d.).

set out in double columns with occasional, brief comments by Spurgeon discreetly interlaced in italics. Nevertheless, this is Spurgeon at his least adventurous, carefully excising problem passages. For example, even though Psalm 137 is only nine verses long, he discreetly cuts it off at verse six. Finally, it is also respectable in the sense of attentive to Victorian morality. For example, Spurgeon's comments on Joshua 2 are preoccupied with censuring Rahab for lying because it is wrong to tell a falsehood 'under any circumstances' despite the fact that her benevolent deception is not condemned by the biblical authors who refer to her in either Testament but rather they simply present her as a heroic woman of faith.[87] *The Interpreter* is laid out for daily household devotions with readings for the morning and evening of every day, although Spurgeon explicitly allows with alternative dates on each page for the possibility of families meeting only once a day and therefore taking two years to go through it. There are also a few additional readings for special circumstances such as 'For a Time of Trouble' or 'For a Wedding'. Bowdlerizing notwithstanding, Spurgeon's whole Bible commitment is on display by the predominantly canonical arrangement and flow of the readings. This concession to Scripture's own order is so strong that the entry for December 25 ends up being from Jude (a footnote suggests that those hoping for some Christmas cheer revisit the entry for August 14 where the nativity narrative in Luke 2 had landed in this canonical arrangement).

Finally, in 1888, Spurgeon compiled *The Cheque Book of the Bank of Faith. Being precious promises arranged for daily use with brief experimental comments.*[88] In the preface, he reflected that the trials of the Downgrade controversy had led him to need the consolation of Scripture more than ever. Even though the emphasis was on 'precious promises' and 'cheering Scriptures', the selection of texts was again daring. The entry for June 21 is on Jael assassinating Sisera by driving a nail in his head while he was sleeping. The reader is invited to hope that they too might be used to fulfil the Lord's purposes: 'Somebody may come to the house to-day, even as Sisera came to Jael's tent.'[89] This book is also arranged with a text and reflection for every day of the week. Spurgeon says explicitly that one is not to use it as

---

[87] Spurgeon, *Interpreter*, 157.
[88] C. H. Spurgeon, *The Cheque Book of the Bank of Faith. Being precious promises arranged for daily use with brief experimental comments* (London: Passmore and Alabaster, 1898; originally 1888).
[89] Spurgeon, *Cheque Book*, 173.

a substitute even for *Morning by Morning* or *Evening by Evening*, let alone 'the fuller meals'.[90] In theory, then, it may be supposed that the ideal was that one would read a chapter of Scripture and the entry from *Morning by Morning* in private at dawn before reading the daily portion from *The Interpreter* as a family before breakfast, sometime during the unsettling turmoil of the day one would pause to read the entry from *The Cheque Book*, and then one would read from the relevant section of *The Interpreter* with the household at dusk before retiring to read privately another chapter as well as the entry from *Evening by Evening*. If this was impractical, at least the desire for this ideal should be there: Spurgeon illustrated an admirable hunger to read Scripture often by referring to a man who when asked why he bathed twice a day replied: 'Because I cannot conveniently do it three times.'[91] In all these books Spurgeon even carefully made provision for leap day (29 February). It can also be added that Spurgeon compiled an annual almanac as well for which his wife selected the verses and this eventually led to the founding of a 'Text Union' comprised of people committed to memorizing the daily text.[92] That Spurgeon would make such books at all should not be taken for granted. As will be shown, he was an extremely busy man—and, although the evidence does not point toward this, if a sceptic were to assume that Spurgeon still might have coveted yet more wealth and fame, then his speaking and written sermons would have been easy and effective ways for him to have generated it. A major motivation was undoubtedly his strong assumption that Christians ought to be reading the Bible daily and his sense of duty as a pastor to assist them in their pursuit of this task.

Spurgeon once reflected that 'it is blessed to eat into the very soul of the Bible until, at last, you come to talk in Scriptural language, and your very style is fashioned upon Scripture',[93] and, by this standard, we may take him to have been a very blessed man indeed. Not content with his grandfather's 'pooh-pooh', Spurgeon would dismiss an erroneous view with 'Nay, verily, Jehovah-nissi!'[94] His admonitions, in particular, assumed a high level of biblical literacy, and become cryptic indeed without it. His advice to members of his congregation struggling during an economic depression

[90] Spurgeon, *Cheque Book*, p. vii.
[91] C. H. Spurgeon, *Feathers for Arrows, or Illustrations for Preachers and Teachers* (New York: Fleming H. Revell, 1870), 285–6.
[92] *Autobiography*, III, 306   [93] *Autobiography*, IV, 268.   [94] *Autobiography*, III, 58.

was a bolt from the blue: 'Do not run before the cloud.'[95] Other such abrupt, unexplained exhortations included 'be ye found with well-trimmed lamps and well-girt loins' and 'let us not be straitened in our bowels.'[96] Even when addressing the youth of the congregation, he would ask probing questions such as: 'Will the sacred rain leave some of you as dry as the mountains of Gilboa?'[97] Here was a manner of speech—indeed a life—fashioned by Scripture. Spurgeon wrote an entire book, *The Bible and the Newspaper*, illustrating how when he read news items he was prompted to meditate on scriptural texts.[98] When he was at Mentone, Spurgeon would even convince himself that he was seeing life as it was in biblical stories:

> I often fancy that I am looking out upon the Lake of Gennesaret, or walking at the foot of the Mount of Olives, or peering into the mysterious gloom of the Garden of Gethsemane. The narrow streets of the old town are such as Jesus traversed, these villages are such as He inhabited.[99]

One can safely assume that this tells us more about Spurgeon's biblically saturated imagination than it does about the French Riviera. Moreover, the Baptist preacher was literally surrounded by biblical passages while at Mentone as Susannah had lined his sitting room with a wallpaper border of scriptural texts.

Spurgeon gloried in the sole authority of the Bible in matters of faith and doctrine: 'our infallible standard lies in, "It is written." The Bible, the whole Bible, and nothing but the Bible, is our religion.'[100] His response to church practices that he found suspicious was: 'Plain proof texts are requested'.[101] Or again, 'To me one text of Scripture is worth seven years of argument.'[102] This standard had significant practical import from his decision to become a Baptist, to his refusal to be ordained, to his restructuring the congregation's leadership to include elders as well as deacons. This habit was so ingrained that Spurgeon had a tendency to overreach with it, sometimes, one suspects, in a deliberately playful manner, but in other cases in a risibly serious way. When he gave up shaving, for example, he announced that beards were 'scriptural', an absurd argument unless one also planned to take up wearing a

---

[95] *Metropolitan Tabernacle Pulpit*, 28 (1882), 208.   [96] *Autobiography*, II, 309; III, 157–8.
[97] Spurgeon, *Letters*, 178.
[98] C. H. Spurgeon, *The Bible and the Newspaper* (London: Passmore and Alabaster, 1880).
[99] *Autobiography*, IV, 219.   [100] *Metropolitan Tabernacle Pulpit*, 20 (1874), 698.
[101] *Metropolitan Tabernacle Pulpit*, 10 (1864), 540.   [102] *Sword and the Trowel* (1882), 163.

robe and sandals.[103] Evoking the events that lead up to the execution of John the Baptist, Spurgeon grounded his opposition to balls by observing: 'I remember that the first Baptist had his head danced off!'[104] Most bizarre of all was his apparently earnest rationale for eschewing the trend toward Gothic architecture when commissioning designs for the Metropolitan Tabernacle:

> The other sacred language is the Greek, and that is dear to every Christian's heart. Our fullest revelation of God's will is in that tongue; and so are our noblest names for Jesus. The standard of our faith is Greek; and this place is to be Grecian. I care not that many an idol temple has been built after the same fashion. Greek is the sacred tongue, and Greek is the Baptist's tongue; we may be beaten in our own version, sometimes; but in the Greek, never. Every Baptist place should be Grecian,—never Gothic.[105]

Part of what made Spurgeon such a phenomenon was his extraordinary capacity for work. Being the pastor of the largest congregation (at the very least) in the English-speaking or Protestant world, was just the beginning of his commitments. Many pastors find the most challenging time of their ministry is during a building campaign. Spurgeon often preached ten sermons a week as fundraisers for the Metropolitan Tabernacle and opened the largest place of worship in England debt-free in 1861 when he had only been a pastor of that congregation for less than seven years (and he himself was only twenty-seven). He declared at the opening ceremony:

> In the bottle which is to be placed under the stone, we have put no money,— for one good reason, that we have none to spare. We have not put news-papers, because, albeit we admire and love the liberty of the press, yet that is not so immediately concerned in this edifice. The articles placed under the stone are simply these:—the Bible, the Word of God, we put that as the foundation of our church. Upon this rock doth Christ build the ministration of His truth. WE know of nothing else as our standard.[106]

At this moment of triumph—out of the abundance of his full heart— Spurgeon exclaimed: 'Oh, that Jehovah-jireh may also be unto us Jehovah-shammah and Jehovah-shalom!'[107]

---

[103] C. H. Spurgeon, *Lectures to My Students*, First Series (London: Passmore and Alabaster, 1875), 134.

[104] *Autobiography*, III, 38.   [105] *Autobiography*, II, 327.

[106] *Autobiography*, II, 323.   [107] *Autobiography*, III, 11.

In 1856, Spurgeon founded the Pastors' College to train ministers. Its curriculum prioritized biblical studies. While wits dubbed it 'the Royal College of Spurgeons', the founder and faculty members tended to refer to it in biblical parlance as a 'school of the prophets'.[108] Once they received a call to a congregation, its graduates were apt to prefix their names with the scriptural word 'Pastor' rather than the conventional 'Reverend'. In 1866, Spurgeon founded the Colportage Association, which employed salesmen to increase the circulation throughout the country of Bibles and other Christian literature. The reports of the Colportage Association would tell tales like another charity might of the plight of people living rough: 'A family of eight persons without a Bible for two years'.[109] In 1865, Spurgeon founded a monthly magazine that he edited and largely wrote himself for the rest of his ministry, *The Sword and the Trowel*. The title, of course, was a biblical allusion (Nehemiah 4: 17–18). In 1867, he founded an orphanage. The core of Spurgeon's typical work week included four main services at the Tabernacle, at three of which he preached a publishable sermon; he would revise one sermon for publication every week and give a lecture at the Pastors' College, many of which were also published. He was always writing or editing some other book as well. Indeed, by the time of his death there were over 150 volumes with Spurgeon's name on the title page. This is not to mention the endless speaking he did for other churches and voluntary organizations (some of which were also published), his voluminous correspondence, and much more.

Spurgeon was a lifelong, unwavering opponent of modern biblical criticism, fuming that although its practitioners called it 'the higher criticism' he thought that 'the Profaner Cavilling' was more apt.[110] An incident in which a German ironclad sank after being struck by another vessel in the fleet during manoeuvres Spurgeon used to reassure his followers that German biblical criticism would also eventually self-destruct.[111] Spurgeon particularly excelled at condemning biblical criticism with scriptural imagery. A favourite one was that these critics were using 'the penknife of Jehudi upon the sacred roll' (Jeremiah 36: 23).[112] Scholars who claimed to have discerned that the book of Isaiah was composed of works from more than

---

[108] See, for example, an article by the principal, George Rogers, entitled, 'The Scripturalness of the Pastors' College', *Sword and Trowel* (1884), 307.

[109] *Sword and the Trowel* (1868), 467.   [110] *Sword and the Trowel* (1888), 378.

[111] Spurgeon, *Bible and Newspaper*, 146.   [112] *Sword and the Trowel* (1888), 206.

one author were accused of sawing the prophet asunder (Hebrews 11: 37).[113] The Baptist pastor was not fooled by the increasing tendency for biblical critics to strike a pious tone, countering dismissively: 'there is much pretence of the Jerusalem dialect, but their speech is half of Ashdod'.[114]

Spurgeon never wavered from his conviction that the entire Bible was the word of God, marked by plenary, verbal inspiration and therefore infallible and inerrant in its entirety in the original autographs. He taught this in season and out of season from the beginning of his ministry to the very end. In his first full year of ministry in London he proclaimed in a sermon on the Scriptures: 'each letter was penned with an Almighty finger; each word in it dropped from the everlasting lips, each sentence was dictated by the Holy Spirit.'[115] To take a random example from innumerable ones from his mature ministry, in 1886, Spurgeon declared: 'These words which we find in the Old and New Testaments are true. Free from error, certain, enduring, infallible.'[116] He was fond of referring to the whole canon from Genesis to Revelation in biblical parlance as 'that goodly land from Dan to Beersheba'.[117] The sword of the Lord which is the word of God he delighted to praise through David's comment on Goliath's sword that there was none like it (1 Samuel 21: 9).[118] Spurgeon was aware of the accusation of bibliolatry, but was defiant in the face of it.[119] Indeed, he seemed almost recklessly to court it, promising in a sermon entitled 'The Talking Book' that 'the Bible will love you', claiming on another occasion that like Jesus it also was an incarnation of the divine, and even going so far as to refer to the Bible as 'the god of books' and ascribe to it the attributes of being 'omniscient and omnipresent'.[120]

Outsiders to scripturally saturated spirituality often think of the point of the contents of the Bible for believers primarily in terms of issues of doctrine, morality, and behaviour, but for insiders a main feature of the Scriptures is that they are seen as a uniquely bountiful source of comfort, consolation, encouragement, divine promises, and emotional sentiments which correspond to their own. Spurgeon regularly encountered all these

---

[113] *Sword and the Trowel* (1884), 553.   [114] Spurgeon, *Greatest Fight*, 20.
[115] *New Park Street Pulpit*, I (1855), 110.   [116] Spurgeon, *Sermon-Notes*, IV, 395.
[117] Spurgeon, *Commenting*, 3.
[118] See, for examples, *Metropolitan Tabernacle Pulpit*, 20 (1874), 701; Spurgeon, *Treasury*, VI, 230.
[119] Spurgeon, *Sermon-Notes*, IV, 397.
[120] *Metropolitan Tabernacle Pulpit*, 17 (1871), 598; *Metropolitan Tabernacle Pulpit*, 34 (1888), 110; Spurgeon, *Clue*, 60, 66.

resources in the Bible and his attitude to it cannot be rightly grasped without
being aware of this. With the experience of a lifetime, Spurgeon observed in
his 'final manifesto': 'Within Scripture there is a balm for every wound, a
salve for every sore.'[121] He knew whereof he spoke. Susannah admitted
after his death that her husband had been permanently rattled by a tragedy
that happened early in his ministry, explaining that his eccentric behaviour
in certain circumstances thereafter was explicable once one was aware of
this. In 1856, when the congregation was renting the huge Surrey Gardens
Music Hall and still the crowds were greater than the capacity, a false cry of
'fire!' caused the packed audience to panic, resulting in numerous injuries
and seven deaths. Spurgeon was so prostrated by this terrible event that it
was thought he might never preach again. When he did return, he testified:
'The text I have selected is one that has comforted me, and, in a great
measure, enabled me to come here to-day'.[122] One of his last letters—
written to his congregation just two weeks before his death—tenderly
offered a particular text (Job 33: 27–8) to 'any very sad, down-cast, & self-
condemned ones among you'.[123] The conviction that the Bible expresses
one's own deepest feelings is particularly alien to many scholars today.
Novels and other works of fiction are routinely read as thoroughly—
however unintentionally—autobiographical, but most scholars seem to
have little faith that they will find significant clues about their subjects by
reading the sermons, devotional reflections, and biblical commentaries
which they wrote. Not so the Victorians. They thought of such writings
as highly intimate. In his own day, the pastor of the Metropolitan Tabernacle was not perceived to be striking a counterintuitive note when he
declared: 'Nothing ought to have the very soul and essence of a man in it so
much as a volume of his sermons.'[124] Spurgeon once received a letter from a
working man who hoped that the celebrated preacher would help him get
his manuscript published. The aspiring author reassured the great man that it
was not plagiarized: 'It is fully my own thoughts. Took from the Bible.'[125]
Just so.

Spurgeon's fight against biblical criticism must also be viewed through
this lens of Scripture's edifying and strengthening power: 'A gracious

---

[121] Spurgeon, *Greatest Fight*, 15.   [122] *Autobiography*, II, 214.
[123] Spurgeon's College, London, C. H. Spurgeon Papers, C. H. Spurgeon to his congregation,
14 January 1892.
[124] *Autobiography*, IV, 145.   [125] *Autobiography*, IV, 195.

woman bemoaned in my presence that a precious promise in Isaiah which had comforted her had been declared by her minister to be uninspired.'[126] Therefore, the nature and authority of the Bible was the primary issue for Spurgeon in the Downgrade controversy. Mark Hopkins, who has written the best scholarly account of that dispute, rightly listed scripture first as one of three doctrinal issues at stake (the others being the atonement and future punishment, both of which Spurgeon insisted could not be denied by anyone who accepted the truthfulness of the whole Bible).[127] Spurgeon's own words are even more emphatic: 'we believe the infallibility of Holy Scripture to be the centre of the conflict.'[128] Eventually, the most famous Baptist in the world gave up hope that 'the Baptist Union will obtain a Scriptural basis'. He revealed just how decisively he had decided to shake the dust off his feet in a bitter, private remark: 'Ephraim is given unto idols, let him alone.' (Hosea 4: 17)[129]

Spurgeon is standardly dismissed by scholars as having been a young fogey because of his rejection of biblical criticism. Kruppa especially advances this line of interpretation, dubbing him 'an intellectual captive of the past'.[130] In order to further this perspective she claimed that Spurgeon 'found little to approve of in the scriptural commentaries of his own time.'[131] This is an absurd statement based on the erroneous assumption that critical works were the primary commentaries of his time. Even a cursory look at Spurgeon's *Commenting and Commentaries* reveals that he approved of literally hundreds of commentaries from his own time from well-respected scholars as different from his own theological views as T. K. Cheyne, E. B. Pusey, B. F. Westcott, and J. B. Lightfoot. Even a commentary on as contested a book of the Bible as Isaiah by a leading German modern biblical critic, Heinrich Ewald, Spurgeon commended for having the capacity to heighten

---

[126] *Sword and the Trowel* (1887), 399.
[127] Hopkins, *Nonconformity's Romantic Generation*, 234
[128] *Sword and the Trowel* (1887), 366.
[129] Spurgeon's College, London, C. H. Spurgeon Papers, C. H. Spurgeon to Mr Harris, 2 May 1888. No less bitter, in another letter Spurgeon complained that what he could not bear was the betrayal of 'those who eat my bread' (Psalm 41: 9), a text that Spurgeon interpreted in *The Treasury of David* as referring to Judas to whom he is here presumably comparing graduates of the Pastors' College who sided with the Baptist Union: Oxford, Regent's Park College Library, C. H. Spurgeon Papers, C. H. Spurgeon to Mr Jackson, 11 February 1888. (Marked 'Private'.)
[130] Kruppa, *Spurgeon*, 6. Mark Hopkins insightfully critiques Kruppa for claiming inconsistently that Spurgeon is both representative of his times and a throwback: Hopkins, *Nonconformity's Romantic Generation*, 11.
[131] Kruppa, *Spurgeon*, 186.

one's appreciation of 'the poetic beauty of the book'.[132] Moreover, Willis
Glover has decisively shown that 'higher criticism did not get a foothold in
England until after 1880' and that the 'important transitional period' for the
acceptance of biblical criticism by Nonconformist scholars lasted until
1895.[133] It does not seem one could reasonably be too hard on Spurgeon
for failing to make a transition that did not begin until he had been in
ministry for over a quarter of a century and which was not completed by his
peers until several years after his death. As is even truer in the case of Pusey,
perhaps it is not so much that Spurgeon was being obscurantist as that
scholars are being anachronistic.

There is no more fitting illustration of the general theme of 'a people of
one book' than Spurgeon's habit of referring to the Bible in an etymologi-
cally apposite way as simply 'the Book'. He did this across the range of his
writings and in both his speeches and his sermons. Here, for example, is
Spurgeon in full flight preaching the Word:

> When the Book has wrestled with me; the Book has smitten me; the Book has
> comforted me; the Book has clasped my hand; the Book has warmed my
> heart. The Book weeps with me, and sings with me; it whispers to me, and it
> preaches to me; it maps my way, and holds my goings; it was to me the Young
> Man's Best Companion, and it is still my Morning and Evening Chaplain. It is
> a live Book: all over alive; from its first chapter to its last word it is full of
> strange, mystic vitality, which makes it have pre-eminence over every other
> writing for every living child of God.[134]

This usage is particularly prominent in *The Clue of the Maze* in which it is
even included in many of the very section titles including: The Book should
be examined; Effects of the Book; The Reading which the Book deserves;
Fulness of the Book; and Science and the Book one.[135]

And thus far has been left out of this account what is standardly referred to
as Spurgeon's *magnum opus*, his commentary on the Psalms, *The Treasury of
David*. A mammoth seven-volume work, it took him twenty-one years of
painstaking labour to complete it. In addition to his own exposition of all
one hundred and fifty psalms, Spurgeon also included a catena of quotations
from other expositors from across the centuries, as well as from literary

[132] Spurgeon, *Commenting*, 121.
[133] Willis B. Glover, *Evangelical Nonconformists and Higher Criticism in the Nineteenth Century*
(London: Independent Press, 1954), 36, 286.
[134] *Metropolitan Tabernacle Pulpit*, 34 (1888), 112.   [135] Spurgeon, *Clue*, 48, 49, 53, 60, 69.

authors whose thoughts illuminated the subject in hand. This gleaning was done entirely without consideration of the personal religious views of the authors: he quotes Pusey, Keble, and Newman; he quotes German higher critics such as Henrich Ewald and Wilhelm De Wette; he quotes an English Unitarian, J. R. Beard, other liberal Nonconformists such as Samuel Davidson and Thomas Toke Lynch, and liberal Anglicans including Thomas Arnold and A. P. Stanley; he quotes numerous Jewish texts and authors (including Moses Maimonides and Ibn Ezra); he quotes from medieval Catholic mystics (such as Bernard and Bonaventure). His literary authors include Voltaire, Volney, Bryon, Carlyle, Emerson, and Darwin. Spurgeon is again at his whole text bravest in *The Treasury of David*. He is unflinching when it comes to the imprecatory psalms, although he did confess regarding Psalm 109 that he sometimes thought that he never should have been able to handle it at all 'if it had not been for the Bulgarian massacres, which threw us into such a state of righteous indignation.'[136] As for Psalm 137, although he had felt a need to censor it for *The Interpreter*, in this work Spurgeon defiantly begins by pronouncing it 'one of the most charming compositions in the whole Book of Psalms'.[137] Eventually, he does make a concession to the sensibilities of the reader: 'The murder of innocent infants can never be sufficiently deplored, but...'[138] Still, many might think that this is a statement better ended with a full stop than followed by a 'but'. On a more positive note, Spurgeon particularly revels in the celebration of the Word of God that is the longest work in the psalter, Psalm 119. In addition to weightier matters, he included an amusing anecdote of a man who when asked what psalm he wanted read before his execution chose this one and was rewarded for his cunning by having the tardy word that he had been pardoned arrive before all of its 176 verses could be declaimed.[139] This exposition was so extensive and important to Spurgeon's view of the spiritual life that he had it published as a separate book entitled *The Golden Alphabet of the Praises of Holy Scripture* (1887).[140]

A biography of Spurgeon published in the year of his death claimed of *The Treasury of David*: 'No commentary on a single book of the Bible has in

---

[136] Spurgeon, *Treasury*, V, p. vi.   [137] Spurgeon, *Treasury*, VII, 198.
[138] Spurgeon, *Treasury*, VII, 202.   [139] Spurgeon, *Treasury*, VI, 4.
[140] C. H. Spurgeon, *The Golden Alphabet of the Praises of Holy Scripture, setting forth the believer's delight in the Word of the Lord: being a devotional commentary upon the one hundred and nineteenth psalm* (London: Passmore and Alabaster, 1898; originally 1887).

any age enjoyed such a circulation.'[141] When Spurgeon's autobiography was posthumously published in 1897 it was reported that 140,000 copies of *The Treasury of David* had been sold.[142] The statistics on Spurgeon's sales are indeed staggering. Already in 1885, he reported that *Morning by Morning* had sold over 100,000 copies.[143] His weekly sermons sold on average 25,000 copies. A single controversial one, 'Baptismal Regeneration', sold 350,000 copies in its first year.[144] Collectively, the sermons sold more than 56 million copies during the nineteenth century.[145] One could go on and on in this way: a volume that is not explored in this study at all, Spurgeon's countrified wisdom, *John Ploughman's Talk*, sold over 400,000 copies before the dawn of the twentieth century. Nor did Spurgeon's popularity die with his Queen sovereign. It was reported in 1982 that the sermons had sold another 50 million since 1900, and their popularity continues to this day.[146] A religious news magazine recently reported a claim that is, at the very least, plausible: 'In 2009, there are more writings in print by 19th-century Calvinist pastor Charles Haddon Spurgeon than by any other English-speaking author living or dead.'[147]

To return to *The Treasury of David*, once again it should not be taken for granted that Spurgeon would have ever written a biblical commentary at all, let alone one this time-consuming. Moreover, although it will not be examined here, Spurgeon even spent his last ailing days working on a commentary of Matthew which was published posthumously, *The Gospel of the Kingdom*.[148] Susannah called this New Testament commentary 'the tired worker's final labour of love for his Lord.'[149] These things are a reflection of his deep commitment to the genre—to the primacy of understanding and expounding the message of 'the Book'. Recall that he spent his first London honorarium to buy commentaries. Spurgeon's fatherly advice to his namesake son preparing to set out on the adventure of life was that he should endeavour to read 'right through' the weighty, multi-volume commentary on the whole Bible by Matthew Henry—'if you can before you are

---

[141] R. Shindler, *From the Usher's Desk to the Tabernacle Pulpit* (London: Passmore and Alabaster, 1892), 241.

[142] *Autobiography*, III, 313.　　　[143] *Sword and the Trowel* (1885), 378.

[144] Kruppa, *Spurgeon*, 270.　　　[145] Ellison, *Victorian Pulpit*, 47.

[146] Kruppa, *Spurgeon*, 236.　　　[147] *Christianity Today* (September 2009), 31.

[148] C. H. Spurgeon, *The Gospel of the Kingdom. A Popular Exposition of the Gospel According to Matthew* (London: Passmore and Alabaster, 1893).

[149] Spurgeon, *Gospel*, p. iii.

married'.[150] Spurgeon himself had a private library of over 12,000 volumes. A description of it begins: 'the volumes commence with Commentaries on Genesis, and continue in consecutive order, through the whole of the long side of the room, to the end of Revelation.' After this core, came ancillary sections such as 'miscellaneous literature for general reading'.[151] A father to many beside his own two sons, Spurgeon even published an assessment of the innumerable commentaries in existence for his students at the Pastors' College and the reading public in general, *Commenting and Commentaries*. He examined over 3,000 volumes in order to make this guide as useful as possible. It is disconcertingly blunt, replete with terse condemnations such as: 'A book of no importance'; 'A pile of paper, valuable to housemaids for lighting fires'; 'Mere platitudes. Paper spoiled'; and 'Confusing, eccentric and happily rare.'[152]

On the other hand, as has already been noted, Spurgeon goes out of his way in *Commenting and Commentaries* to extol the merits of works by his theological foes. To take just two examples, he says of a volume by the liberal Anglican A. P. Stanley: 'A fascinating book, which no one can read without being the better able to realize the scenes of Scripture history. The author's broad views are known and deplored: that he has equal breadth of learning we cheerfully admit.'[153] Likewise, Spurgeon was so opposed to the Catholic revival in the Church of England that he preached an entire sermon entitled, 'A Blow For Puseyism', but he nevertheless conceded: 'To Dr Pusey's work on Daniel all subsequent writers must be deeply indebted, however much they may differ from him in other departments of theological study.'[154] Therefore, the theme of 'a people of one book' is true in Spurgeon's life in another sense: he was most affirming of his theological opponents when he sensed a common commitment to the Bible. Spurgeon was quick to feel uneasy when pursuing united action with other ministers, but he was nevertheless a devoted supporter of the British and Foreign Bible Society even though it brought him into close cooperation with Anglican clergymen. Repeatedly, when addressing that body, he allowed himself to dream of a day when their common zeal for the Scriptures would melt away their theological and denominational differences: 'The

---

[150] Spurgeon, *Letters*, 82.   [151] *Autobiography*, IV, 288–90.
[152] Spurgeon, *Commenting*, 45, 48, 52, 108.   [153] Spurgeon, *Commenting*, 48.
[154] *Metropolitan Tabernacle Pulpit*, 11 (1865), 533–64; Spurgeon, *Commenting*, 128.

Bible is to be the end of all disunion.'[155] Spurgeon even went so far as to give full credit to a Roman Catholic priest that he heard preach in Brussels: 'if I had been handling his text, I must have treated it in the same way that he did, if I could have done it as well.'[156] When Canon Basil Wilberforce wanted to befriend Spurgeon he knew just the approach to take: 'Would it be possible for you to run down on Monday, March 6, and read the Bible to us at our quiet *home* Bible-reading?'[157] On more than one occasion Spurgeon reflected that he could respect and have fellowship with someone who agreed on the authority of 'the Book' even if they disagreed on whether or not particular doctrines were taught by it.[158] After all, the world's great preacher observed, 'A man of one Book—if that Book is the Bible—is a *man*, for he is a man of God.'[159]

[155] Spurgeon, *Speeches*, 14.   [156] *Autobiography*, II, 365.
[157] *Autobiography*, IV, 151.   [158] See, for example, *Sword and the Trowel* (1888), 205.
[159] *Metropolitan Tabernacle Pulpit*, 34 (1888), 120.

Conclusion

Spiritualism, Judaism, and the Brethren—A People of One Book

The original proposal for this project envisioned it as a two-volume work with additional chapters covering further varieties of religious traditions. The unequivocal response from Oxford University Press was that a two-volume work on the Bible and the Victorians was a commercial non-starter. Far from hankering after more chapters, most readers are no doubt more than content to have now arrived at the conclusion. I, in turn, having worked up substantive chapters on ten different traditions over the course of several years of my life, am quite ready to see this research project into print and move on to fresh pastures. Nevertheless, I do particularly regret the loss of three of the chapters that were cut in order to downsize this project to one volume: namely, those on Spiritualism, Judaism, and the (so-called Plymouth) Brethren. To compensate partially for this loss, I will briefly sketch here my working plans for those chapters. The reader should keep in mind, however, that these are research proposals and soundings rather than reports of research completed, and further study might well have changed their shape substantially. They are presented primarily as a way of gesturing at how the theme and scheme of this book could be extended, perhaps in subsequent work by other scholars.

Spiritualism

From the very beginning a chapter on Spiritualism had been at the core of my vision for this project. After all, Spiritualism is a quintessentially

Victorian tradition. Nevertheless, as I thought and thought about how one would actually go about creating such a chapter in line with the wider structure of this book I found myself repeatedly frustrated and checked. First, Spiritualism did not seem to offer figures who authored a pile of writings comparable in size to those presented in the other chapters. In particular, I found it hard to alight upon a suitable Spiritualist woman—one reason for this was awkward fits in terms of geographical identity, as the most prominent female Spiritualists in Britain seemed to have come from or gone on to other parts of the English-speaking world. Nevertheless, as so many scholars have been interested in Spiritualism in recent decades precisely because of the scope and opportunities it gave to women, it seemed perverse to choose a male figure to represent this tradition in a volume that has sought not to neglect the lives and thought of women.

   Another difficulty is that Spiritualism was generally held in tandem with one of the other identities already covered in this book. It is standard to divide the Victorian movement into two camps: Christian Spiritualism and Anti-Christian Spiritualism.[1] As to the former, there is a methodological problem with documenting a Christian Spiritualist's use of the Bible because it would not be easy to distinguish if it was a reflection of their Spiritualism or their dual identity as a liberal Anglican, a Catholic, a Unitarian or whatever other such commitment they might have maintained. Likewise, an Anti-Christian Spiritualist's comments on the Bible might better represent and derive from views articulated in this volume in the chapters on atheism or agnosticism rather than Spiritualist distinctives. The most prominent Anti-Christian Spiritualist, the London editor James Burns, told Charles Bradlaugh that he affirmed the distinctive views of Iconoclast's organization without reservation: 'I hold before me here the "Principles, Objects, and Rules" of the National Secular Society, and to the whole of these I am ready to subscribe in every iota. And I would say further, that there is no possible collision between these facts of psychology and the principles of Secularism.'[2] Having despaired of finding a suitable representative figure or pair of figures, I proposed that the Spiritualism

---

[1] Janet Oppenheim, *The Other World: Spiritualism and Psychical Research in England, 1850–1914* (Cambridge: Cambridge University Press, 1985), 63–110.

[2] Timothy Larsen, *Contested Christianity: The Political and Social Contexts of Victorian Theology* (Waco, Texas: Baylor University Press, 2004), 109–10; *Human Immortality Proved By Facts. Report of a Two Nights' Debate on Modern Spiritualism, between Mr C. Bradlaugh and Mr J. Burns* (London: Burns, n.d.; originally London, 1872), 47.

chapter would explore the contents of two journals: the oldest and most prominent one serving the movement, the *Spiritual Magazine*, which came to have Christian Spiritualist editors and even gained a subtitle for a while explaining that it 'incorporated the *Christian Spiritualist*'; and *Human Nature*, edited by the said James Burns, 'the principal spokesman for anti-Christian spiritualism in Britain throughout the second half of the nineteenth century'.[3] This chapter would therefore have broken with the pattern of representative figures followed in all the others, but this regrettable departure would have had the benefits of allowing in the voices of women who did not leave behind a large enough body of writings to sustain a full-length chapter on their thought, and to ensure at least that this material was being commended explicitly as by Spiritualists and for Spiritualists and not merely, for example, as the thoughts on the Bible of an Anglican who also happened to be a Spiritualist.

Gaining access to complete runs of either of these journals proved more difficult than I thought as well. I have, however, been able to examine the volume of the *Spiritual Magazine* for 1877. Before presenting the results of that sounding, however, it is worth noting some other Spiritualist titles as reflected in a bibliography published in the *Spiritual Magazine* in 1867, which I was able to obtain as a photocopy.[4] It would be tedious to list all the titles that have biblical connections, but a few of the more striking ones are worth highlighting. The sixth author in the list is someone writing under the pen name 'A Bible Spiritualist'. A completely anonymous work is listed under its title, *Spiritualism and the Bible*. Finally, in the section of 'works claiming to have been given by direct spiritual influence through human mediumship' comes one authored by Miss J. Fawcett with this intriguing title, *Ecce Homo: a Treatise upon the Nature and Personality of God, founded upon the Gospels of St Luke and St John*.

It is admittedly quite limiting to only look at the volume for 1877, but it is presented here simply because it was available for inspection and not because it was richer with biblical material than others. Moreover, it has the advantage of being a volume in which the editorship changed during the middle of the year. The initial editor was George Sexton, who had been a

---

[3] Oppenheim, *Other World*, 86. For Burns's biography, see Logie Barrow, *Independent Spirits: Spiritualism and English Plebeians, 1850–1910* (London: Routledge & Kegan Paul, 1986), especially 101–4; and *Medium and Daybreak*, Memorial Double Number, 22 March 1895, especially in the Supplement, 'A Biographical Sketch of James Burns', 1–9.

[4] *Spiritual Magazine*, n.s., II (1867), 366–84.

freethinking lecturer before his investigations of Spiritualism had helped to reawaken his Christian faith, and his successor was J. Enmore Jones, 'another well-known Christian spiritualist'.[5] The preface for the whole volume, written by Jones, begins:

> Fact and arguments are in this volume. The faith of many in verities of spirit-life and power, as registered in the New Testament, is confirmed by the modern facts that so aptly prove that the Lord God Almighty is the same yesterday—to-day and tomorrow. (Hebrews 13: 8)[6]

The very first article is essentially a sermon with the text (Matthew 16: 3) written out at its head, and numerous articles appear throughout the volume under both editors that follow this template. Indeed, the lead article in the next issue (February), not only had a text at its head (John 1: 23), but was even identified explicitly as a 'sermon' in its title.[7] In the March issue it was announced that Sexton would be stepping down as editor in order to found a new monthly journal, *The Bible and the Age*: 'It will deal largely with the important question of the relation of the Scriptures to the present time'.[8] There is an article entitled 'Shakespeare and the Bible' which, true to its name, simply documents biblical quotations and allusions in the Bard's plays and has no connection to Spiritualism.[9] Now under Jones's editorship, a lead article entitled 'Prophetic Power' makes the case in explicit defiance of modern biblical critics (the Old Testament scholar Samuel Davidson is quoted) that scriptural prophecies did indeed predict the future (and, by extension, amazing things can happen today as well).[10] Likewise, 'Universal Deluge' argues that the biblical flood as recorded in 'the Book of Facts' was not merely a local event, as some thinkers seeking to harmonize it with science had begun to assert. A note attached by the editor observes that his object in including the article is to increase people's confidence in the historicity of the Bible.[11] 'Music Stool Bowing to the Bible' is a news

[5] Oppenheim, *Other World*, 54. For Sexton, see Timothy Larsen, *Crisis of Doubt: Honest Faith in Nineteenth-Century England* (Oxford: Oxford University Press, 2008; paperback edition), 197–227. (For the paperback edition I was able to incorporate information on Sexton from a crucial, additional primary source.)

[6] *Spiritual Magazine*, 3rd series, III (1877), p. [i].

[7] *Spiritual Magazine*, 3rd series, III (1877), 49.

[8] *Spiritual Magazine*, 3rd series, III (1877), 137. (As far as I know, he never actually created a journal by that title.)

[9] *Spiritual Magazine*, 3rd series, III (1877), 140.

[10] *Spiritual Magazine*, 3rd series, III (1877), 193–4.

[11] *Spiritual Magazine*, 3rd series, III (1877), 216–18.

account of a séance led by D. D. Home at which a levitating piece of furniture took advantage of its newfound mobility to make obeisance to the family Bible.[12] Two different news items update readers on the progress of the biblical translation committee working on the Revised Version—again despite their being no Spiritualist connection.[13] Not only did Jones continue to include sermons with texts, but some of these now appeared with the text in the original Greek.[14] The lead article in the October issue was by 'A Scotch Minister' entitled 'Natural Law and New Testament Spiritualism'.[15] Finally, to round off this presentation of just the primary scriptural highlights from this volume of the *Spiritual Magazine*, 'Lawfulness of Spirit Communion' offered a biblical theology for Spiritualism that cited numerous texts.[16]

As to Anti-Christian Spiritualism, I was able to look briefly at a few volumes of *Human Nature* in the Cambridge University Library during a visit there, namely those for the years 1871–5. The first of these has numerous articles whose very titles are biblical quotations and whose contents explore scriptural material, but only a couple need to be presented here. First, Emma Hardinge contributed a 'spiritual' Ten Commandments 'given by the spirits through her hand the previous day'. Each commandment begins with 'Thou shalt' or 'Thou shalt not' and continues to employ Authorized Version language and phraseology throughout.[17] More substantively, there was a series spread over multiple issues and continuing into 1872 entitled 'The Myths of Antiquity', with each one of these substantive articles addressing a single character or event in the Old Testament including Jonah, Melchizedek, Jacob's Ladder, and Joseph. The one on 'Enoch' in the August 1872 issue was forced to be the last as the author died.[18] Rather than turning this setback into an opportunity to re-engage the interests of readers by introducing a series on a new theme, the editor replaced it in the very next issue with a series entitled 'The Spiritual Presences and Prophetic Characters of the Old Testament', again as the opening article for the issue, with 'Elijah' as the first instalment.[19] Elisha came next and turned out to be

---

[12] *Spiritual Magazine*, 3rd series, III (1877), 230.
[13] *Spiritual Magazine*, 3rd series, III (1877), 315, 563.
[14] *Spiritual Magazine*, 3rd series, III (1877), 357, 401.
[15] *Spiritual Magazine*, 3rd series, III (1877), 433–6.
[16] *Spiritual Magazine*, 3rd series, III (1877), 451–3.
[17] *Human Nature*, V (1871), 326–7.
[18] *Human Nature*, VI (1872), 337–40 (here 337).
[19] *Human Nature*, VI (1872), 385–91.

so engrossing that the treatment of this prophet was split into long articles spread over two issues, and so it went on.

Only twelve pages into the volume for 1873 comes an article entitled 'Clairvoyance and the Flood', which recounts insights from the American Anti-Christian Spiritualist medium, A. J. Davis, on the biblical Deluge.[20] There is also a long article which appeared in parts over several issues entitled 'God and Immortality: What Has Spiritualism to Say on the Subject?' It ends in an effusion of biblical language:

> When weary and fatigued with the labour and turmoil of earth, we approach the grave and lie down on the couch from which there is to be no more an uprising, how sweet the thought that we are entering into regions where 'the wicked cease from troubling and where the weary are at rest.' [Job 3: 17] The many mansions of the heavenly home [John 14: 2] then appear in view, and full of hope and of confidence in the future life, and trust in the paternal care of God, we are really able to exclaim with heartfelt truth, 'Oh Death, where is thy sting; oh grave, where is thy victory!' [1 Corinthians 15: 55][21]

'The Miracles of To-Day' argues that it is illogical for people to accept 'the miracles of Scripture' but to reject the reports of surprising events happening through mediums in their own day. In order to make this case, it rehearses numerous Bible stories, often quoting the text directly, and the drift of the piece is obviously not that one should be sceptical about both but rather that one should accept Spiritualism as well as the Bible.[22]

The first issue of *Human Nature* in 1874 included a long poem covering ten pages entitled, 'Jesus Christ'. It is filled not only with details taken from the Bible, but even actual quotations such as: 'What could it mean?—"Love ye your enemies, | Bless them that curse".'[23] Another poem is entitled 'The Bibles of the World'. It is essentially (if I have grasped it aright) a call to discover the truth behind various world religions, but it is telling that these teachings are described as 'Bibles'. A book entitled *Moses and Bacchus* not only received a favourable review, but readers of *Human Nature* were told they could purchase it at half price through the journal. The review commended modern biblical criticism, 'seeing that so little is known popularly of the nature and origin of the books called the Bible'.[24] The book's

---

[20] *Human Nature*, VII (1873), 12–13.　　　[21] *Human Nature*, VII (1873), 270.
[22] *Human Nature*, VII (1873), 425–6.
[23] *Human Nature*, VIII (1874), 15–24 (here 20).
[24] *Human Nature*, VIII (1874), 188–9 (here 188).

thesis is summarized: 'the legend of Moses must have been borrowed from that of Bacchus'. Reminiscent of Bradlaugh's work, 'The miraculous nature of the ten plagues inflicted upon Pharaoh's kingdom comes in for severe criticism.' 'A New Religion' again made the case that Spiritualist phenomena paralleled the accounts of miracles of the Bible and therefore one ought to accept the former as well as the latter.[25]

Moving on to 1875, extraordinarily, an article by the Bishop of Winchester which was entitled 'Inspiration' and was a defence of the divine origin of the Bible was reprinted in two parts.[26] It had been originally published in a volume of orthodox Christian apologetics, *Aids to Faith*. One can only speculate that this anti-Christian Spiritualist editor thought that it would interest his readers despite the fact that it was about Scripture and not Spiritualism. Further into the volume, however, an editorial note refers dismissively to 'the Jewish pamphlets now called the Bible'.[27] More substantively, there is a major article, 'Bibliolatry Illustrated by Jewish Deductions from the Scriptures'.[28] This is at least explicable in that it reflects better the editor's own view, but it is no less strange in being a departure from the ostensible Spiritualist theme of the journal in order to pursue the Victorian preoccupation with the Bible. Another piece again appropriates the Bible to the cause of Spiritualism, even using Spurgeon's beloved title of honour, 'the Book':

> The sacred record opens with the statement—that God, a Spirit, the fountain source of all power, intelligence, form, 'in the beginning created the heavens and the earth.' Here is the very basis and essence of Spiritualism, and the cardinal truth, on which is based the 'harmonial philosophy' so instructively elucidated in the works of Andrew Jackson Davis. Allow us here to observe that the Bible, instead of repressing philosophical speculation, sets all mankind an example in that highest of intellectual exercises by the bold postulate stated in the opening sentence of The Book. We have to look in quite another direction for the fetters that bind men's minds within the narrow limits of creeds and dogmas.[29]

'The Old Revelation and the New' is a detailed recounting of biblical history, with numerous footnotes giving the precise scriptural references.

---

[25] *Human Nature*, VIII (1874), 437–8.   [26] *Human Nature*, IX (1875), 27–37, 86–94.
[27] *Human Nature*, IX (1875), 144.   [28] *Human Nature*, IX (1875), 164–73.
[29] *Human Nature*, IX (1875), 240.

The argument is that the move from the Old Testament revelation to that in the New Testament was startling, but nevertheless a true unfolding of God's ongoing activity, and modern Spiritualism should also be seen in that light.[30] In other words, it is a biblical apologetic for Spiritualism. 'The Restitution of All Things' argues (as Josephine Butler later would) that eternal punishment is not taught in the Bible but rather that this is a misperception based on poor translations of the relevant Greek words.[31] Finally, a Gospel story is retold in the poem 'The Stilling of the Storm'.[32]

This brief excursus into Spiritualism is sufficient to demonstrate that this tradition was not an exception to the general Victorian engagement with Scripture. One senses that Spiritualists found real delight in reading old, familiar Bible stories in the new light of their own, reorienting experiences of remarkable phenomena.

Judaism

The plan for this chapter was to explore the life and works of Grace Aguilar (1816–47). She was born and spent most of her life in Hackney. She was a Sephardic Jew and her family was descended from Jews who had fled Spain during the Inquisition. Aguilar was educated at home. Her mother required her to study 'the Bible regularly; this was readily submitted to first as a task, but afterwards with much delight'.[33] Aguilar is primarily remembered as a novelist, the first Anglo-Jewish fiction writer to reach a wide audience. In her own day and in her enduring reputation, however, she has also always been well known as a writer on Judaism who advocated reforms from within and defended her faith from the pressures exerted from without by Christian thought. From the research I have done, I am confident that she is an apt choice for a representative figure—as well as a fascinating one. One of the practical problems I encountered, however, was an inability to gain access to a primary archival collection of unpublished materials by Aguilar.

The first of her major non-fiction works on her faith was *The Spirit of Judaism* (1842). First appearing across the Atlantic, it was edited by Isaac

---

[30] *Human Nature*, IX (1875), 369–79.   [31] *Human Nature*, IX (1875), 421.
[32] *Human Nature*, IX (1875), 454–7.
[33] 'Memoir of Grace Aguilar', in Grace Aguilar, *Home Influence: A Tale of Mothers and Daughters* (London: George Routledge & Sons, n.d.), p. xiii.

Lesser of Philadelphia and published in that city. The heart of the book is a multi-chapter exposition of Deuteronomy 6: 5: 'Thou shalt love the Lord thy God, with all thy heart, and with all thy soul, and with all thy might.' Throughout the book, Aguilar is preoccupied with commending the Bible to her co-religionists. As Jews in English-speaking countries did not usually know Hebrew, she insists that they should have no qualms about reading the Authorized Version: 'Mournfully they err, who thus preserve the English Bible from the hands and hearts of their children.'[34]

While not wishing to impose Christian categories on Jewish thought, as one of the purposes of this book is to see commonalities across diverse traditions it might be permissible to observe that Aguilar often criticized Judaism in ways parallel to Protestant critiques of medieval Catholic thought, and advocated reform, again to use a Protestant term, through the principle of *sola Scriptura*. If it is problematic for a scholar today to frame the matter in this way, it should also be observed that this active move of Aguilar's was also considered problematic at the time, and her editor, Isaac Lesser, engaged in a running dispute with her on it throughout the volume in disclaimer notes signed with his initials. *Sola Scriptura* is even proclaimed verbatim in the vernacular when Aguilar counsels Jews 'to look to the Bible alone for support and comfort in affliction, for the guidance and direction in every social, domestic, moral, and religious duty'.[35] (Lesser's note begins: 'The word *alone* strikes me as not quite proper...') In the chapter on the religious instruction of children and youths, Aguilar again declares: 'The Bible alone should be the guide to, and assistance in, this precious employment.'[36] The implication of many of Aguilar's comments (well understood by Lesser) is that wrongheaded traditions have crept into Judaism that need to be cleared away and this must be done by a return, *ad fontes* (again to use Protestant language), to the Bible.

In 1845 came Aguilar's *The Women of Israel: or Characters and Sketches from the Holy Scriptures and Jewish History, illustrative of the past history, present duties, and future destiny of the Hebrew females, as based on the Word of God*. It is essentially an application of the principle suggested in *The Spirit of Judaism*, the argument being that while misogynist statements may be found in Jewish tradition, the Bible itself is the only true authority for Judaism and

---

[34] Grace Aguilar, *The Spirit of Judaism* (Philadelphia: 1 Monroe Place, 1842), 53.
[35] Aguilar, *Spirit*, 104. [36] Aguilar, *Spirit*, 146.

it does not support the denigration of women. In this volume, Aguilar herself makes the parallel to Protestantism:

> We see no proofs of the humanising and elevating influence of Christianity, either on man or woman, till the reformation opened the BIBLE, the whole BIBLE, to the nations at large; when civilisation gradually followed. . . . if the degradation, mentally and morally, of the Hebrew female ever did become part of the Jewish law, it was when man was equally degraded, and the blessed word of God hid from him.[37]

Protestant countries are better places for Jews to live than Catholic or Orthodox ones precisely because of the free circulation of the Scriptures, Aguilar claims. The differences between the Jewish congregations of the Sephardim and the Ashkenazim could be overcome if Jews would 'only strive to become Hebrews as our Bibles teach'.[38] Indeed, while the doctrinal differences are irreconcilable, even Christians and Jews can respect one another if they only would remember that 'the SPIRIT of their widely differing creeds has exactly the same origin, the word of God'.[39]

Aguilar is eloquent on the devotional power of the Word of God:

> the Bible must become indeed the book of life to the female descendants of that nation whose earliest history it so vividly records; and be regarded, not as merely political or religious history, but as the voice of God speaking to each individual, giving strength to the weak, encouragement to the desponding, endurance to the patient, justice to the wronged, and consolation unspeakable as unmeasurable to the afflicted and the mourner.[40]

Aguilar also dismisses scepticism toward the truthfulness of Scripture. Another aim of the book is to counteract Christian interpretations of the 'Old Testament' (a term she often employs even when writing for Jews) in favour of Jewish ones.

A striking confirmation that the Victorians were a people of one book is that Aguilar repeatedly adopted language from the New Testament even when writing in defence of Judaism for a Jewish readership. This was presumably always done unconsciously as merely a trace of a shared,

---

[37] Grace Aguilar, *The Women of Israel: or Characters and Sketches from the Holy Scriptures and Jewish History, illustrative of the past history, present duties, and future destiny of the Hebrew females, as based on the Word of God*, new edition, 2 vols (London: Groomsbridge and Sons, 1865), I, 4.

[38] Aguilar, *Women of Israel*, II, 374.   [39] Aguilar, *Women of Israel*, II, 389.

[40] Aguilar, *Women of Israel*, I, 8.

wider Victorian culture. I was first alerted to this in an excerpt from the section on Sarah in *The Women of Israel* in an anthology in which the editors provided the reference in brackets: 'her laugh proves that even she was not exempt from the natural feelings of morality—the looking to human means and human possibilities alone; forgetting that with God all things are possible [Matthew 19: 26].'[41] I have not read very extensively in Aguilar's work, but even the bits I have read contain several additional examples. When recounting the 'mental darkness' of many Jews during the medieval period, Aguilar concedes: 'Individuals, there were, no doubt, who were Israelites indeed.'[42] This echoes Jesus' positive assessment of Nathanael, 'Behold an Israelite indeed' (John 1: 47). The *Women of Israel* crescendos to this admonition in the final paragraph: 'To the women of Israel, then, is entrusted the noble privilege of hastening "the great and glorious day of the Lord".'[43] The quotation is from Joel 2: 31, but the added notion of its being hastened comes from the exposition of this prophetic phrase in 2 Peter 3: 12. Aguilar repeatedly refers to children addressing their prayers to 'their Father who is in Heaven', which is, of course, how Jesus of Nazareth taught his disciples to pray (Matthew 6: 9).[44] An even more substantial echo of Jesus' Sermon on the Mount is the following: 'But surely this is a false estimate of the universal love that feeds the little birds of the air, and clothes the blossoms of the field' (Matthew 6: 26–30).[45]

The Jewish Faith: Its Spiritual Consolation, Moral Guidance, and Immortal Hope (1846) was a volume of Aguilar's shaped in an epistolary form as 'a series of letters answering the inquiries of youth'. It is deeply preoccupied with commending the Bible for the proper spiritual formation of a Jewish youth:

> Accustom yourself to feel that your morning and evening prayer are *not* complete, unless you commence, or conclude them, with one chapter of the Bible, or two or three Psalms: and you will so associate it with the pure and holy thoughts of God, which must accompany earnest prayer, that even as in times of difficulty and distress you fly to prayer, or in times of joy to praise, so

---

[41] Marion Ann Taylor and Heather E. Weir (eds), *Let Her Speak for Herself: Nineteenth-Century Women Writing on the Women of Genesis* (Waco, Texas: Baylor University Press, 2006), 131.
[42] Aguilar, *Women of Israel*, II, 364.   [43] Aguilar, *Women of Israel*, II, 397–8.
[44] Grace Aguilar, *Essays and Miscellanies* (Philadelphia: A. Hart, 1853), 135.
[45] Aguilar, *Essays*, 140.

will you equally seek your Bible secure of aid, sympathy, comfort, and love, which without it you dared not believe your God would give.[46]

Aguilar insists upon the inspiration of the entire Bible, and explicitly rejects challenges to the veracity of the Pentateuch based upon modern scientific findings. Indeed, she is so far from moving in the direction of modern biblical criticism that here is her reflection on the book of Job: 'Its elevated style seems to mark Moses as its author, and most probably during his sojourn with his father-in-law Jethro, in Midian.'[47]

The final text of Aguilar's that will be explored here is her posthumously published *Essays and Miscellanies*. In a full chapter, the opening section in the *Essays* would have given scope for presenting Jewish distinctives. The first five essays are all ones on the interpretation of specific biblical passages which have as their explicit aim refuting Christian readings of these texts. The first one is on Psalm 22 and in it Aguilar sets out a general, hermeneutical principle that will recur in other essays, remarking that after hearing a Christian interpretation of this psalm: 'I am more convinced in my own belief, because all that the Christian preaches, of portions of the Old Testament being typical of the sufferings of Christ, is to me clearly illustrative of my own loved nation.'[48] The second essay is focused on Genesis 1: 26 and argues against Christian attempts to find the doctrine of the Trinity in the Hebrew Scriptures (as William Cooke did). The third essay refutes the idea that Isaiah 7: 14 refers to the Virgin Birth of Jesus, and the fourth does the same for a Christological reading of Isaiah 53.

The fifth and by far the longest essay is on 'The Prophecies of Daniel'. As would E. B. Pusey, Aguilar accepts that the book of Daniel is divinely inspired and contains completely accurate predictive prophecy. She disagrees, however, on the identification of the world powers in the prophetic vision. Instead of having Christ's kingdom as the glorious *telos* of history, Aguilar scripts Protestants, Catholics, and Moslems in penultimate roles that are not always flattering. Here, for example, is her application of Daniel 7: 25 ('And he shall speak great words against the most High, and shall wear out the saints of the most High, and think to change times and laws'):

[46] Grace Aguilar, *The Jewish Faith: Its Spiritual Consolation, Moral Guidance, and Immortal Hope* (Philadelphia: 1227 Walnut Street, 1864), 143.

[47] Aguilar, *Jewish Faith*, 411.

[48] Aguilar, *Essays*, 21.

Christ completely altered the law of Moses; his followers attended not to the laws of the great prophet of Israel. They have changed not only laws but *times*. The Sabbath-day of the Jews is on Saturday, that of the Christians, Sunday; the Jews date their year either from the Creation or the Flood, the Christians from the birth of Christ. In the same way the principal day of worship peculiar to the Mahometans is Friday, and they date their year from the appearance of Mahomet.[49]

So, as we have seen throughout this volume—not least in the case of Lant Carpenter—an apologetic is advanced for one's own religious group primarily on exegetical grounds.

The second half of *Essays and Miscellanies* turns to the devotional life of Jews, and is largely comprised of prayers that Aguilar penned. Once again she sets out as normative the expectation that one would read the Bible every morning and every night.[50] She fears that Christians know their Bibles better than Jews and that this will lead them to be at a disadvantage when religious debates ensue: 'Even more necessary to us, in our scattered and forsaken state, is the Word of God, than to the Christian.'[51] In line with Spurgeon's thoughts on the matter, she insisted that 'a child of three or four is not too young' to listen to daily Bible readings.[52] She even put forward a plan for reading through the entire Old Testament in a year, by adding an extra (third) chapter on the Sabbath and also interlacing the Psalter as additional material: 'Only experience can tell the extent of comfort found in the simple act of perusing two chapters of the Word of our God every day (one when preparing for rest at night, and one in the morning).'[53]

This excursion into the works of Grace Aguilar has left completely unexplored her fictional works. A study of Aguilar by Michael Galchinsky, however, focuses on her story 'The Perez Family', which presents a heroic picture of the perpetuation of the Jewish faith through a long-suffering mother faithfully reading the Bible to her children. This story won Aguilar fame and 'unalloyed praise from middle-class Jews'.[54] Grace Aguilar died young due to a spinal disease. Her end was recorded in a scene remarkably similar to an account given earlier in this volume of Catherine Booth on her deathbed. Here is the dying Grace Aguilar:

---

[49] Aguilar, *Essays*, 91.   [50] Aguilar, *Essays*, 138.   [51] Aguilar, *Essays*, 147.
[52] Aguilar, *Essays*, 148.   [53] Aguilar, *Essays*, 161.
[54] Michael Galchinsky, *The Origin of the Modern Jewish Woman Writer: Romance and Reform in Victorian England* (Detroit: Wayne State University Press, 1996), especially 180–5 (here 185).

Speech had been a matter of difficulty for some time previous, her throat being greatly affected by her malady; but she had, in consequence, learned to use her fingers in the manner of the deaf and dumb, and almost the last time they moved, it was to spell upon them feebly, 'Though He slay me, yet will I trust in Him.' (Job 13: 15)[55]

The Brethren

This proposed chapter ended up on the cutting-room floor before I had done hardly any work on it. There is less to prove here, however, as it is generally observed in the secondary literature that the Brethren were biblicist so there is no need for me to try to convince the reader of this. Horton Davies, for example, in his massive study of *Worship and Theology in England*, discusses the Brethren along with several other groups founded in the nineteenth century including the Disciples of Christ and the Salvation Army, observing that they had certain characteristics in common: 'Each was marked, in the first place, by a strong Biblicism.'[56] While this point is not surprising in the sense that people have not generally assumed any different, it is telling in the context of the wider argument of this book: Victorians were such a people of one book that when they founded new sects or denominations they did so on the grounds that were even more committed to the Bible than the existing ones.

Brethren biblicism manifest itself in numerous ways—and this is not the place for an exploration of their distinctives—but one obvious area is nomenclature. Scholarship written by outsiders has usually referred to this group as 'the Plymouth Brethren', as the English port town was an important place of strength in the nascent movement. The faithful, however, do not use the qualifying term since 'brethren' is a scriptural word, but one cannot find an entry for 'Plymouth' in Cruden's concordance. In this biblicist way, numerous standard terms used by other Christians were replaced by ones the Brethren found to be more biblical. To take just one example, while other Christians spoke of 'the sacrament', 'the Eucharist',

[55] Aguilar, *Home Influence*, p. xvi.
[56] Horton Davies, *Worship and Theology in England*, 6 vols (Grand Rapids: Eerdmans, 1996), IV, 139. A recent, definitive history also speaks of 'Brethren biblicism': Tim Grass, *Gathering to His Name: The Story of Open Brethren in Britain and Ireland* (Milton Keynes: Paternoster, 2006), 173.

'Holy Communion', or 'the Lord's Supper', the Brethren revived a phrase from the book of Acts which had not been standardly used since and referred to 'the breaking of bread'.

My plan for this chapter was to have Emily Gosse (1806–57) as my representative figure. Gosse has been overshadowed by her son, the man of letters, Sir Edmund Gosse, and her husband, the man of science, Philip Gosse, FRS. The latter led a Brethren congregation and, although well respected for his work as a naturalist, was widely derided for his attempt to reconcile the veracity of the Bible with the findings of geology by arguing that the Almighty had created a mature earth that therefore gives the illusion of being much older than it is—complete with faux fossils. As for the son, Edmund—in the way that the Edwardians delighted to ridicule their Victorian forebears—wrote an exposé of his parents that became a minor literary classic, *Father and Son* (1907).

While the strict accuracy of Edmund's account has been challenged, it is worth rehearsing his presentation of his childhood. The distinctive religious identity of his parents, Edmund observes, was one in which the Bible pushed out seemingly everything else:

> My Father and Mother alike gradually, without violence, found themselves shut outside all Protestant communions, and at last they met only with a few extreme Calvinists, like themselves, on terms of what may almost be called negation—with no priest, no ritual, no festivals, no ornament of any kind, nothing but the Lord's Supper and the exposition of Holy Scripture drawing these austere spirits into any sort of cohesion. They called themselves 'the Brethren' . . . [57]

Father and Son is filled with statements on the centrality of the Bible for his parents. Two may serve as specimens: 'pleasure was found nowhere but in the Word of God, and to the endless discussion of the Scriptures each hurried when the day's work was over'; and 'My parents founded every action, every attitude, upon their interpretation of the Scriptures.'[58] Morning and evening household devotions Edmund recalled were 'extremely lengthy'. This, of course, was no substitute for private ones: 'I read the Bible every day, and at much length.'[59] When he would go for a walk with a friend, his father would set them a biblical text as a profitable

---

[57] Edmund Gosse, *Father and Son: A Study of Two Temperaments* (London: Penguin, 1989), 37. (He later confirms that they called the Lord's Supper, 'the Breaking of Bread', p. 116.)
[58] Gosse, *Father and Son*, 38, 43.   [59] Gosse, *Father and Son*, 73.

theme for their conversation. Emily Gosse, her son reminisced, held to the complete truthfulness of the Bible and endeavoured to live as though there was no historical gap between the world of the Scriptures and their own lives:

> In order to realize her condition of mind, it is necessary, I think, to accept the view that she had formed a definite conception of the absolute, unmodified and historical veracity, in its direct and obvious sense, of every statement contained within the covers of the Bible. For her, and for my Father, nothing was symbolic, nothing allegorical or allusive in any part of Scripture, except what was, in so many words, proffered as a parable or a picture. Pushing this to its extreme limit, and allowing nothing for the changes of scene or time or race, my parents read injunctions to the Corinthian converts without any suspicion that what was apposite in dealing with half-breed Achaian colonists of the first century might not exactly apply to respectable English men and women of the nineteenth.[60]

Father and Son is essentially a coming-of-age story and thus its climax is the son's break from his parents' faith. As the father senses that his son is leaving the prescribed path he attempts to steady him by having him promise that he would translate a portion of the Greek New Testament every morning: 'The great panacea was now, as always, the study of the Bible, and this my father never ceased to urge upon me.'[61] When Philip Gosse discovered that his son no longer believed in the authority of the Bible, he counted it a total loss, lamenting in a letter: 'We had, I found, no common ground.'[62] In *Father and Son*, Edmund presents his parents' faith as thoroughly old-fashioned—a throwback to the seventeenth century—and scholars have generally agreed with this interpretation for them and their co-religionists. An argument of this volume, however, is that Victorian studies can be refreshed by observing the extent to which the exact opposite interpretation is apt: Philip and Emily Gosse had left denominations rooted in past centuries in order to join the newest religious identity, the latest spiritual fad. Edmund himself tellingly recalled that the upstart Brethren assembly which his father led was a popular, growing congregation that attracted young people.

Emily Bowes (to use her maiden name) grew up in Devon as an Anglican. She was living in London when she joined a Brethren assembly in 1841.

---

[60] Gosse, *Father and Son*, 77–8.   [61] Gosse, *Father and Son*, 240.
[62] Gosse, *Father and Son*, 250.

She wrote to a cousin about her new religious identity, describing the Brethren as a group that took 'the Bible only as their rule of life'.[63] Later, Philip Gosse joined the congregation as well. They married in 1848 and continued to live in London. Edmund was their only child. In *Father and Son*, Edmund remarks that his mother was a celebrated figure. This distinction rested on her religious writings, particularly her tracts, more than seven million copies of which were apparently circulated.[64] Edmund reported that a half million copies were distributed of a single one with a particularly strong topical interest, 'The Guardsman of the Alma'.[65]

I have been able to examine a collection of Gosse's tracts. Most of them have a text at their head and therefore are to a certain extent in the genre of a sermonic biblical exposition. They are all narratives of true stories, Gosse insisted. Most of them are accounts of Gosse's own attempts to evangelize. They often end in conversions—not least deathbed ones—but others serve as warnings of people who put off their response to the gospel until it was too late. Still others record misguided answers to her spiritual questions which in turn enable Gosse to convey a lot of sound theology to her readers through her retorts. The tracts are littered with scriptural quotations and citations, and many discussions are settled by quoting a proof text. As her husband pointed out, the 'one principle' that Gosse most often proclaims in these tracts is that one should not trust in anything else but 'the naked Word of God'.[66] For example, in 'John Clarke: or, the ground of confidence', the eponymous character does not believe he is saved because he does not feel converted. She replies that feelings are no judge of such things. He asks, 'How else can I know it?' To which she replies, 'By BELIEVING GOD'S WORD' (the only phrase in capital letters in the whole tract).[67] 'Tom Fowler, the Boatman' tells of the spiritual fruit yielded from a plan 'to have an hour in the middle of the day to read God's Word' to a gathering of neighbours: 'Tom Fowler is not the only hardened sinner who has been reclaimed and converted through these simple meetings: and no wonder, for the Word of God is the appointed instrument by which sinners are

---

[63] Robert Boyd, *Emily Gosse: A Life of Faith and Works* (Bath: Olivet Books, 2004), 34.
[64] Boyd, *Gosse*, 45.   [65] Gosse, *Father and Son*, 54.
[66] Anna Shipton, *Tell Jesus: Recollections of Emily Gosse* (New York: Thomas Y. Crowell, n.d.), 143.
[67] P. H. Gosse and Emily Gosse, *Narrative Tracts* (London: Morgan and Scott, n.d.), III, 2. There are sixty tracts in this collection. The author is identified at the top of each one, and very few were written by her husband. The tracts are numbered and the pagination restarts with each one.

converted.'[68] Gosse's biblicism is so strong that her term for Christianity is 'the religion of the Bible'.[69] Several narratives recount Roman Catholics being converted by encountering the Scriptures directly despite the attempt of priests to prevent this. 'Mary Kelly's Letter', for example, is the story of an Irish servant girl who was given a Bible. It prompted her conversion, but she had to hide it from a priest who wanted to confiscate it. Her letter of gratitude included a donation to the Bible Society. 'The Power of the Word' offers anecdotes to confirm that: 'Many have been converted by reading God's Word, without any assistance from those who preach it.'[70] One of these is of a blind woman who hires a boy to read the Bible to her.

These are just a few highlights: there are many other scriptural dimensions to the tracts which could have been explored in a full chapter. I have also not examined any unpublished sources, though there are apparently archives which possess letters by Gosse and other items. Nor indeed have I seen a copy of her most substantial publication, though its title reveals that it would be of interest for this study: *Abraham and His Children, or, parental duties illustrated by scriptural examples*.[71] Gosse's poetry was recently republished and it is extraordinarily biblical, even by the standards of the Victorians.[72] The largest series of them are simply poetic presentations of the Psalter. The following psalms receive this treatment in individual poems: 22, 23, 24, 25, 63, 67, 106, 107, 120, 121, 123, 125, 131, 134, 146, and 150. Other poems also simply have a citation as their title: Genesis 22, Psalm 119: 27, Matthew 6: 19ff., Matthew 10: 37, Luke 6, II Corinthians 5: 8, Galatians 3: 9, and I Timothy 2: 1. Most of the rest of the poems have a biblical quotation for their title. Here are just a few examples: 'Walk by faith, and not by sight'; 'There is none upon earth I desire in comparison to thee', 'Suffer the little children to come unto me', and 'No man can serve two masters'. Of the rest, one of the longest is a retelling of a biblical narrative: 'Abraham's temptation'. 'Lines in an old Bible' is a kind of love poem for her copy of the Scriptures. Here is the middle verse:

> 'Twas in childhood my delight,
> 'Neath my pillow laid at night;

---

[68] Gosse, *Narrative Tracts*, IX, 1, 4.   [69] Gosse, *Narrative Tracts*, XXI, 3.
[70] Gosse, *Narrative Tracts*, XXX, 3.
[71] Emily Gosse, *Abraham and His Children, or, parental duties illustrated by scriptural examples* (London: Nisbett, 1855).
[72] Boyd, *Gosse*, 95–242.

> From its page my task I said,
> In it to my parents read.
> Thence I learnt in early youth,
> To revere the God of truth.[73]

Gosse's premature death came from breast cancer. She agreed to an experimental treatment which was of no help, but greatly increased her suffering. Her last words were 'the blood of the lamb' (Revelation 12: 11).[74]

A People of One Book

And so my work is done. *A People of One Book* has sought to display the diversity of the ways that Victorians thought about and interpreted the Scriptures, from Wiseman reading with the church, to Pusey reading with the early fathers, to Carpenter reading without the clouding of creeds and traditions, to Booth and Fry (in different ways) reading with the Spirit, to Bradlaugh and Huxley (in different ways) reading with scepticism. There is no need to drive home the unifying thesis of this study by way of conclusion as no one has ever doubted that the Bible had a prominent place in Victorian culture. The *raison d'être* of this book comes from encountering the remarkable extent to which this is true and the particular ways that it was manifest through the details that are presented in the case studies. Given the arresting power of such specifics, it invites an anticlimax to conclude with generalizations. Nevertheless, this risk notwithstanding, it is worth briefly identifying some common themes that have accumulated across these case studies or arisen from them. Still, far from gathering up all the common elements, these reflections are intended to be suggestive rather than exhaustive.

Victorians tended to be educated and raised in a way that immersed them in the Scriptures. All of the school work that we have from the atheist Charles Bradlaugh, for example, is explicitly biblical; Catherine Booth had read the sacred volume all the way through eight times by the age of twelve. Mary Carpenter ensured that the children in the care of her reformatory schools were given an education steeped in Scripture. The result of such a formation was that the Victorians thought and spoke in biblical words, phrases, and categories. This was not merely superficial, but often quite

---

[73] Boyd, *Gosse*, 156–7.   [74] Shipton, *Tell Jesus*, 150.

structural and profound. We have seen, for example, that even the agnostic
T. H. Huxley regularly assessed systems of thought through the biblical
category of idolatry. There was also a surprisingly widespread desire to
attempt to prove one's beliefs through the authority of Scripture. This
habit and method went well beyond predictable cases such as the systematic
theology of the Methodist William Cooke. Thus, although neither Catholics nor Unitarians are usually thought of as pursuing a proof-texting mode
of argument, Nicholas Wiseman's books include *The Real Presence of the
Body and Blood of Our Lord Jesus Christ in the Blessed Eucharist, Proved From
Scripture* and Lant Carpenter penned works such as *Comparative View of the
Scriptural Evidence for Unitarianism and Trinitarianism.* Expressions approxi-
mating the theological principle of 'one book', *sola Scriptura*, were surpris-
ingly widespread, encompassing not only Protestants ranging from
Unitarians and Quakers to Baptists and Methodists, but even the Anglo-
Catholic leader, E. B. Pusey, and the Jewish author, Grace Aguilar.

Contemporary scholarship—not least in the field of Victorian studies—
emphasizes the way that people read the Bible (and all texts) through their
own experience. This is a fruitful insight, but this study reminds us of the
extent to which the Victorians, conversely, endeavoured to read their own
experience through the lens of the Bible. There was a strong impulse to
understand one's life or situation by recasting it within the experience of a
specific biblical character or narrative: Florence Nightingale lived as though
the call of the Virgin Mary was her own, and even Annie Besant could find
no more fitting way to mark the significance of her decision to become an
atheist lecturer than to envision it as Isaiah's divine summons to the
prophetic ministry.

This study also underlines how general the expectation was that one
would read the Bible daily, with four times—private and household in both
the morning and the evening—being the ideal. It was striking to discover
how often the figures in this volume actually wrote or compiled aids to
daily Bible reading, most notably Mary Carpenter, Elizabeth Fry, and
C. H. Spurgeon. Likewise Grace Aguilar offered a scheme for reading the
Bible through in a year, and Catherine Booth's Salvation Army printed its
own guide. Even Florence Nightingale—who denied that the Bible was a
uniquely inspired book, criticized its contents as sometimes wrongheaded
and erroneous, and as an independent, single woman was quite free to
dispense with such devotions if she wished—faithfully and fervently read
the Scriptures as part of her daily routine.

Another theme of this study is that much has been overlooked or distorted by a preoccupation scholars have had with critical approaches to the Bible. Liberal Quakerism and liberal Unitarianism, for example, tend to get backdated so as to obscure how thoroughly biblical even these groups were in the middle decades of the nineteenth century. Likewise the rise of biblical criticism is so anticipated that figures who were typical of their times such as E. B. Pusey and C. H. Spurgeon are often painted as old-fashioned and obscurantist. As a corrective to this anticipatory haste to be out with the old and in with the new, it was revealing to observe how resistant to biblical criticism Josephine Butler—who is not usually thought of as behind the times—was even in the early twentieth century. Scholars focused on critical views of Scripture have neglected to observe that even a desire to write a hostile or iconoclastic work on the Bible is itself a tribute to the centrality of 'the book' for the Victorians. Charles Bradlaugh thought that being a good atheist leader meant learning Hebrew and making one's *magnum opus* a biblical commentary; T. H. Huxley introduced the notion of 'agnosticism' not by a philosophical discourse on epistemology but rather in articles that were mainly explorations of the synoptic problem in New Testament studies. It was seemingly impossible simply to ignore or sidestep the Bible—everyone felt they had to go through it, whether by deploying it as supporting their views and cause or by defying it in a sustained, resolute, and concerted way. Elizabeth Fry did not see the Bible and prison reform as two separate things; nor did Josephine Butler when it came to opposing the state regulation of prostitution; nor Catherine Booth when addressing urban deprivation; nor Mary Carpenter when it came to the reformation of juvenile delinquents. Florence Nightingale likewise assumed that Bible study should be a component in the proper training of nurses.

A related issue is that an interest in nineteenth-century critical biblical studies by scholars today has eclipsed devotional engagements with Scripture which were actually far more widespread. Moreover, despite contemporary academic work usually following a trail that implies this, such immediate, edifying encounters with the text by no means disappeared once biblical criticism had been widely accepted by scholars—or even ministers. One goal of this study has been to attend to such readings and the works that present them; to listen patiently to what the Victorians themselves found significant and compelling about the biblical text. When this is done it becomes abundantly clear that many, many Victorians experienced the Bible first and foremost as a richly abundant and life-giving source of spiritual comfort and divine promises. Still, whether it was so much their daily bread that it was to them simply 'reading'—or so repulsive that it could be dismissed in exasperation as 'this indictable book'—either way this intense, sustained engagement with this singular text across the whole spectrum of religious and sceptical beliefs reveals the Victorians to have been a people of one book.

Works Cited

PRIMARY SOURCES

Manuscripts

Catherine Booth Papers, British Library, London
Charles Bradlaugh Papers, Bishopsgate Institute, Bishopsgate Library, London
Josephine Butler Letters Collection, The Women's Library, London Metropolitan University, London
Josephine Butler Papers, Northumberland Record Office, Gosforth, Newcastle upon Tyne
Josephine Butler Papers, University of Liverpool, Liverpool
Mary Carpenter Papers, Boston Public Library, Boston, Massachusetts
Mary Carpenter Papers, Harris Manchester College, Oxford
William Cooke Papers, Methodist Archives, John Rylands University Library, Manchester
Elizabeth Fry Papers, British Library, London
Elizabeth Fry Papers, Friends Historical Library, Swarthmore College, Swarthmore, Pennsylvania
Holyoake Papers, Co-operative College Archives, Holyoake House, Manchester
T. H. Huxley Papers, American Philosophical Society, Philadelphia, Pennsylvania
T. H. Huxley Papers, Imperial College Archives, London
Frances Power Cobbe Papers, The Huntington Library, San Marino, California
E. B. Pusey Collection, Pusey House, Oxford
C. H. Spurgeon Papers, Regent's Park College Library, Oxford
C. H. Spurgeon Papers, Spurgeon's College, London
W. T. Stead Papers, Churchill Archives Centre, Churchill College, Cambridge
Nicholas Wiseman Papers, Ushaw College Archives, Ushaw College, Durham

Newspapers, Magazines, and Journals

Baptist Magazine
Christian Observer
Christian Remembrancer
Contemporary Review
Dublin Review
Ecclesiastic

Evangelical Magazine

Human Nature

Journal of Sacred Literature

London Quarterly Review

Medium and Daybreak

Methodist Times

Methodist New Connexion Magazine

Metropolitan Tabernacle Pulpit

Modern Review

New Park Street Pulpit

Primitive Methodist Magazine

Spiritual Magazine

Sword and the Trowel

Theological Review

Wesleyan Methodist Magazine

Contemporary Printed Material

Aguilar, Grace, *Essays and Miscellanies* (Philadelphia: A. Hart, 1853).

——— *Home Influence: A Tale of Mothers and Daughters* (London: George Routledge & Sons, n.d.).

——— *The Jewish Faith: Its Spiritual Consolation, Moral Guidance, and Immortal Hope* (Philadelphia: 1227 Walnut Street, 1864).

——— *The Spirit of Judaism* (Philadelphia: 1 Monroe Place, 1842).

——— *The Women of Israel: or Characters and Sketches from the Holy Scriptures and Jewish History, illustrative of the past history, present duties, and future destiny of the Hebrew females, as based on the Word of God*, new edn, 2 vols (London: Groomsbridge and Sons, 1865).

Apostolic Letter of Pope Pius IX; Pastoral Letter of Cardinal Wiseman; Lord John Russell's Letter to the Bishop of Durham (London: British Society for Promoting the Religious Principles of the Reformation, 1850).

Besant, Annie, *Autobiographical Sketches* (London: Freethought Publishing Company, 1885).

——— *God's Views on Marriage* (London: Freethought Publishing Company, 1890).

——— *Is the Bible Indictable? Being an enquiry whether the Bible comes within the ruling of the Lord Chief Justice as to Obscene Literature* (London: Freethought Publishing Company, n.d. [c.1877–8]).

——— *My Path to Atheism* (London: Freethought Publishing Company, 1885).

——— *Woman's Position according to the Bible* (London: Freethought Publishing Company, 1885).

Blakeney, Richard P., et al., *Popery: An Enemy of Scripture* (London: British Society for Promoting the Religious Principles of the Reformation, 1850).

Bonner, Hypatia Bradlaugh, *Charles Bradlaugh: His Life and Work*, 2nd edn, 2 vols (London: T. Fisher Unwin, 1895).

Booth, Bramwell, *On the Banks of the River; being a brief history of the last days on earth of Mrs. General Booth*, 2nd edn (London: The Salvation Army, 1900).

Booth, Catherine (as 'Mrs. Booth'), *Female Teaching: or, the Rev. A. A. Rees versus Mrs. Palmer*, 2nd edn, enlarged (London: G. J. Stevenson, 1861).

——— (as 'Mrs. Booth of The Salvation Army'), *Life and Death. Being reports of addresses delivered in London* (London: The Salvation Army, 1889).

——— *Papers on Aggressive Christianity* (London: The Salvation Army, 1891).

Bradlaugh, Charles, *The Autobiography of Mr. Bradlaugh. A Page of his Life* (London: Austin and Co., 1873).

——— *The Bible: What It Is* (London: Austin & Co., 1870).

——— *Genesis: Its Authorship and Authenticity*, 3rd edn (London: Freethought Publishing Company, 1882).

——— *God, Man, and the Bible. Three Nights' Discussion between Rev. Joseph Baylee, D.D., and Mr. C. Bradlaugh [then debating as 'Iconoclast'], on the 27th, 28th, and 29th June, 1860, at the Teutonic Hall, Liverpool* (London: Freethought Publishing Company, n.d.).

——— and Roberts, Robert, *Is the Bible divine? A six nights' discussion between Mr. Charles Bradlaugh . . . and Mr. Robert Roberts* (London: F. Pitman, 1876).

Burton, Margaret (ed.), *Josephine Butler Has Her Say about Her Contemporaries* (London: The Fawcett Library, n.d.).

Butler, Josephine E., *Address Delivered at Croydon, July 3rd, 1871* (London: National Association, 1871).

——— *An Autobiographical Memoir*, ed. George W. Johnson and Lucy A. Johnson (Bristol: J. W. Arrowsmith, 1928).

——— *Catharine of Siena: A Biography*, 4th edn (London: Dyer Brothers, 1885).

——— 'Catherine Booth', *Contemporary Review*, 58 (November 1890), 638–54.

[———] *The Constitution Violated: An Essay* (Edinburgh: Edmonston and Douglas, 1871).

——— *The Education and Employment of Women* (London: Macmillan, 1868).

——— *The Hour before Dawn: An Appeal to Men*, 2nd edn (London: Trübner & Co., 1882).

——— *The Lady of Shunem* (London: Horace Marshall & Son, n.d. [1894]).

——— 'The Lovers of the Lost', *Contemporary Review*, 13 (January–March 1870), 16–40.

——— *Memoir of John Grey of Dilston* (Edinburgh: Edmonston and Douglas, 1869).

[———] 'Philalethes', *'The Morning Cometh.' A Letter to My Children* (Newcastle-upon-Tyne: T. M. Grierson, 1903).

——— *Personal Reminiscences of a Great Crusade*, 2nd edn (London: Horace Marshall & Son, 1898).

Butler, Josephine E., *Recollections of George Butler* (Bristol: J. W. Arrowsmith, n.d. [1892]).

———*Sursum Corda; Annual Address to the Ladies' National Association* (Liverpool: T. Brakell, 1871).

———*Truth before Everything* (London: Pewtress & Co., 1897).

———*The Voice of One Crying in the Wilderness*, trans. Osmund Airy (Bristol: J. W. Arrowsmith, 1913).

Butler, Josephine E. (ed.), *Women's Work and Women's Culture* (London: Macmillan and Co., 1869).

Byron, Lord, *Hebrew Melodies* (London: John Murray, 1815).

Carpenter, J. Estlin, *The Bible in the Nineteenth Century* (London: Longmans, Green, and Co., 1903).

———*James Martineau: Theologian and Teacher* (London: Philip Green, 1905).

———*The Life and Work of Mary Carpenter* (London: Macmillan and Co., 1881).

Carpenter, Lant, *Comparative View of the Scriptural Evidence for Unitarianism and Trinitarianism*, 3rd edn (London: Rowland Hunter, 1823).

———*An Introductory Catechism* (Boston: Christian Register Office, 1828).

———*Unitarianism the Doctrine of the Gospel. A View of the Scriptural Grounds of Unitarianism; with an examination of all the expressions in the New Testament which are generally considered as supporting opposite doctrines*, 3rd edn (Bristol: Parsons and Browne, 1823 [facsimile by Kessinger Publishing's Legacy Reprints Series]).

———*An Apostolic Harmony of the Gospels*, 2nd edn (London: Longman, Orme, Brown, Green, and Longmans, 1838).

Carpenter, Mary, *The Duty of Society to the Criminal Classes; An Address Delivered in the Church of the Messiah, Montreal, on Sunday, July 6, 1873* (Montreal: Daniel Rose, 1873).

———*Juvenile Delinquents: Their Condition and Treatment* (Montclair, New Jersey: Patterson Smith, 1970 [reprint of 1853 edn]).

———*The Last Days in England of the Rajah Rammohun Roy* (London: Trübner & Co., 1866).

[———] *Morning and Evening Meditations, For Every Day in A Month* (Boston: Wm. Crosby and H. P. Nichols, 1847).

———*Our Convicts*, 2 vols (London: Longman, Green, Longman, Roberts & Green, 1864).

———*Reformatory Schools for the Children of the Perishing and Dangerous Classes and for Juvenile Offenders* (London: G. Gilpin, 1851 [facsimile reprint: London: Woburn Press, 1968]).

———*Six Months in India* (London: Longmans, Green, and Co., 1868).

———*Red Lodge Girls' Reformatory School, Bristol: Its History, Principles and Working* (Bristol: Arrowsmith, 1875).

———*Voices of the Spirit and Spirit Pictures*, 'For Private Circulation Only' (Bristol: I. Arrowsmith, 1877).

Carpenter, Russell Lant, *Memoirs of the Life of the Rev. Lant Carpenter, LL.D.* (Bristol: Philip and Evans, 1842).

——————*A Monotessaron: or, the gospel record of the life of Christ, combined into one narrative, on the basis of Dr. Carpenter's apostolic harmony* (London: E. T. Whitfield, 1851).

Clarke, Samuel, *The Scripture Doctrine of the Trinity* (London: James Knapton, 1712).

Cobbe, Frances Power, 'Personal Recollections of Mary Carpenter', *Modern Review*, 19, 2 (April 1880), 279–300.

——————*Life of Frances Power Cobbe, By Herself*, 2 vols (Boston: Houghton, Mifflin and Company, 1894).

Conwell, Russell H., *Life of Charles Haddon Spurgeon: The World's Great Preacher* (Philadelphia: Edgewood Publishing Company, 1892).

Cooke, William, *The Bible: Its Trials, and its Triumphs* (London: Hamilton, Adams, & Co., n.d.).

——————*A Catechism: embracing the most important doctrines of Christianity. Designed for the use of schools, families, and Bible classes* (London: Methodist New Connexion Book Room, new and enlarged edition, 1860).

——————*Christian Theology: Its Doctrines and Ordinances Explained and Defended* (London: Hamilton, Adams, and Co., 1869).

——————*Explanations of Difficult Portions of Holy Scripture, &c., in 565 Queries and Answers* (London: Henry Webber, 1866).

——————*The Fallacies of the Alleged Antiquity of Man Proved, and the Theory shown to be a Mere Speculation* (London: Hamilton, Adams, and Co., 1872).

——————*A Survey of the Unity, Harmony, and Growing Evidence of Sacred Truth* (London: Hamilton and Adams, 1874).

Corder, Susan, *Life of Elizabeth Fry* (London: W. & F. G. Cash, 1853).

St Cyril of Alexandria, *Commentary on the Gospel according to S. John*, trans. Philip Edward Pusey et al. (London: Rivingtons, 1874).

Desanctis, Luigi, *Popery, Puseyism, Jesuitism: described in a series of letters* (London: James, 1903).

Dickens, Charles, *The Life of Our Lord* (London: Associated Newspapers Ltd, 1934).

Discussion between Mr. Thomas Cooper and Mr. C. Bradlaugh [in 1864] (London: Freethought Publishing Company, 1888).

Driver, S. R., *The Book of Daniel, with introduction and notes* (Cambridge: Cambridge University Press, 1912).

The Epistle from the Yearly Meeting, Held in London . . . 1829 (Mount Pleasant, Ohio: Ohio Yearly Meeting, 1829).

Foote, G. W., *Bible and Beer* (London: Pioneer Press, 1912).

——————*The Bible Handbook for freethinkers and inquiring Christians* (London: Pioneer Press, 1912).

Fry, Elizabeth, *Observations on the Visiting, Superintending, and Government, of Female Prisoners*, 2nd edn (London: John and Arthur Arch, 1827).

——————*Texts for Every Day in the Year; Principally Practical and Devotional* (New Bedford: Charles Taber & Co., 1859).

[————] *Sketch of the Origin and Results of Ladies' Prison Associations, with hints for the formation of Local Associations* (London: John and Arthur Arch, 1827).

[Fry, Katherine and Cresswell, Rachel (eds)], *Memoir of the Life of Elizabeth Fry, with extracts from her journal and letters, by Two of Her Daughters*, 2 vols (London: Charles Gilpin, 1847).

Gibbs, Mary and Gibbs, Ellen, *The Bible References of John Ruskin* (London: George Allen, 1898).

Goodwin, Thomas, *Puseyism proved to be 'the number of the name' of the apocalyptic beast* (Dublin: W. Curry, 1843).

Gosse, Edmund, *Father and Son: A Study of Two Temperaments* (London: Penguin, 1989 [originally 1907]).

Gosse, Emily, *Abraham and His Children, or, parental duties illustrated by scriptural examples* (London: Nisbett, 1855).

Gosse, P. H. and Gosse, Emily, *Narrative Tracts* (London: Morgan and Scott, n.d.).

Greville, Charles C. F., *Greville Memoirs (Third and Concluding Part): A Journal of the Reign of Queen Victoria from 1852 to 1860* (New York: D. Appleton and Company, 1887).

Gurnell, R. M., *Popery and Puseyism, twin demons with one soul, or, ritualism unmasked* (London: Published at the Office of 'The Gospel Guide', 1867).

Hamilton, William, *Discussions on Philosophy and Literature* (New York: Harper & Brothers, 1861).

Hansard's Parliamentary Debates, 3rd series, vol. 253 (1880).

Hulme, Samuel, *Memoir of the Rev. William Cooke, D.D., Author of 'The Deity,' "Christian Theology," "Shekinah," &c.* (London: C. D. Ward, 1886).

Human Immortality Proved By Facts. Report of a Two Nights' Debate on Modern Spiritualism, between Mr. C. Bradlaugh and Mr. J. Burns [London, 1872] (London: Burns, n.d.).

Huxley, Leonard, *Life and Letters of Thomas Henry Huxley*, 3 vols (London: Macmillan, 1908).

Huxley, T. H., *Critiques and Addresses* (London: Macmillan and Co., 1873).

————*Darwiniana: Essays* (New York: D. Appleton and Company, 1893).

————*Essays Upon Some Controverted Questions* (London: Macmillan and Co., 1892).

————*Evolution and Ethics and Other Essays* (London: Macmillan and Co., 1898).

————*Lay Sermons, Addresses, and Reviews* (London: Macmillan and Co., 1870).

————*Method and Results: Essays* (New York: D. Appleton and Company, 1896).

————*Physiography: An Introduction to the Study of Nature* (London: Macmillan and Co., 1891).

————*Science and Education: Essays*, Edition de Lure, (New York: J. A. Hill and Company, 1904).

————*Science and Hebrew Tradition: Essays* (New York: D. Appleton and Company, 1910).

Keble, John, *The Psalter, or Psalms of David in English Verse* (Oxford: J. H. Parker, 1839).

[Kennedy, Benjamin Hall], *Rome or the Bible—which?* (Shrewsbury: John Davies, 1850).

Kenrick, John, *An Essay on Primaeval History* (London: B. Fellowes, 1846).

'Layman of the Established Church', *Puseyism, the School of the Infidels* (London: A. Miall, 1865).

Liddon, Henry Parry, *Life of Edward Bouverie Pusey: Doctor of Divinity; Canon of Christ Church; Regius Professor of Hebrew in the University of Oxford*, ed. J. O. Johnston and Robert J. Wilson, 3rd edn, 4 vols (London: Longmans, Green, and Co., 1893).

Martineau, James, *Essays, Philosophical and Theological* (Boston: William V. Spencer, 1860).

McDonald, Lynn (ed.), *The Collected Works of Florence Nightingale*, Vols 1–3 (Waterloo, Ontario: Wilfrid Laurier University Press, 2001–2).

McGee, James E., *Lives of Irishmen's Sons and their Descendants* (New York: J. A. McGee, 1874).

Memorials of Robert Spears, 1825–1899 (Belfast: Ulster Unitarian Christian Association, 1903).

Morris, John, *Puseyism Unmasked! or, the Great Protestant Principle of the Right of Private Judgment Defended, against the arrogant assumptions of the advocates of Puseyism: A Discourse*, 3rd edn (London: Paternoster Row, 1842).

Newman, John Henry, *Apologia pro Vita Sua*, ed. Ian Ker (London: Penguin, 1994 [originally 1864]).

Palfrey, John Gorham, *Harmony of the Gospels* (Boston: Gray and Bowen, 1831).

Parker, Henry W., *The Agnostic Gospel: A Review of Huxley on the Bible; with Related Essays* (New York: John B. Alden, 1896).

Pierson, Arthur T., *Catharine of Siena, an Ancient Lay Preacher; a Story of Sanctified Womanhood and the Power of Prayer* (London: Funk & Wagnalls, 1898).

Pusey E. B. (trans.), *The Confessions of S. Augustine* (*Library of the Fathers* 1) (Oxford: John Henry Parker, 1853).

——*Daniel the Prophet: Nine Lectures, delivered in the Divinity School of the University of Oxford, with copious notes* (Oxford: John Henry and James Parker, 1864).

——*Daniel the Prophet* (London: A. D. Innes, 1892).

——*The Minor Prophets, with a Commentary, Explanatory and Practical, and introductions to the several books*, 2 vols (New York: Funk & Wagnalls, 1885).

——*The Rule of Faith as maintained by the Fathers, and the Church of England, A Sermon preached before the University on the fifth Sunday after Epiphany 1851* (Oxford: James Parker, 1878).

——*Scriptural Views of Holy Baptism*, 4th edn, Tracts for the Times 67, Part 1 (London: Rivington, n.d. [original edition, 1835]).

Rabett, Reginald, *The Anti-Christ of Priesthood, or, the subversion of the system of Popery and Puseyism by the light and force of divine truth* (London: W. H. Dalton, 1844).

Robertson, F. W., *Expository Lectures on St Paul's Epistle to the Corinthians* (London: Smith, Elder and Co., 1859).

Rogers, George, 'The Scripturalness of the Pastors' College', *Sword and the Trowel* (1884), 307.

The Salvation Soldiers' Guide: Being a Bible Chapter for the Morning and Evening of Every Day in the Year, with Fragments for Mid-day Reading (London: The Salvation Army, 1883).

Scrivener, F. H. A., *A Plain Introduction to the Criticism of the New Testament*, ed. Revd Edward Miller, M.A., 4th edn, 2 vols (London: George Bell & Sons, 1894).

Shindler, R., *From the Usher's Desk to the Tabernacle Pulpit* (London: Passmore & Alabaster, 1892).

Shipton, Anna, *Tell Jesus: Recollections of Emily Gosse* (New York: Thomas Y. Crowell, n.d.).

Spurgeon, C. H., *The Bible and the Newspaper* (London: Passmore & Alabaster, 1880).

———*The Cheque Book of the Bank of Faith. Being precious promises arranged for daily use with brief experimental comments* (London: Passmore & Alabaster, 1898 [originally 1888]).

———*The Clue to the Maze*, 3rd edn (London: Passmore & Alabaster, 1892).

———*Commenting and Commentaries* (London: Passmore & Alabaster, 1876).

———*Evening by Evening: or, Readings at Eventide for the Family or the Closet* (New York: Sheldon and Company, 1869).

———*Feathers for Arrows, or Illustrations for Preachers and Teachers* (New York: Fleming H. Revell, 1870).

———*The Golden Alphabet of the Praises of Holy Scripture, setting forth the believer's delight in the Word of the Lord: being a devotional commentary upon the one hundred and nineteenth psalm* (London: Passmore & Alabaster, 1898 [originally 1887]).

———*The Gospel of the Kingdom. A Popular Exposition of the Gospel According to Matthew* (London: Passmore & Alabaster, 1893).

———*The Greatest Fight in the World* (New York: Funk & Wagnalls, 1891).

———*The Interpreter, or, Scripture for Family Worship, being selected passages of the Word of God for every morning and evening throughout the year, accompanied by a running comment and suitable hymns* (London: Passmore & Alabaster, n.d.).

———*Lectures to My Students*, 1st Series (London: Passmore & Alabaster, 1875).

———*Morning by Morning: or, Daily Readings for the Family or the Closet* (London: Passmore & Alabaster, 1865).

———*My Sermon-Notes*, 4 vols (New York: Fleming H. Revell Company, n.d. [1884]).

———*The Treasury of David*, 7 vols (London: Passmore & Alabaster, 1908 [originally 1869–85]).

———*Speeches at Home and Abroad* (London: Passmore & Alabaster, 1878).

Spurgeon, Charles (ed.), *The Letters of Charles Haddon Spurgeon* (London: Marshall Brothers, 1923).

Spurgeon, Susannah and Harrald, J. W. (eds), *C. H. Spurgeon's Autobiography*, 4 vols (London: Passmore & Alabaster, 1897 [facsimile reprint: Pasadena, Texas, Pilgrim's Press, 1992]).

Stanley, Arthur Penrhyn, *The Life and Correspondence of Thomas Arnold, D.D.* (New York: Charles Scribner's Sons, n.d. [originally 1844]).

Stevenson, George John, *Methodist Worthies: Characteristic Sketches of Methodist Preachers of the Several Denominations* (London: Thomas C. Jack, 1885).

Taylor, John, *The Scripture-doctrine of original sin proposed to free and candid examination* (London: J. Wilson, 1740).

Taylor, Robert, *The Diegesis: being a discovery of the origin, evidences, and early history of Christianity, never yet before or elsewhere so fully and faithfully set forth* (London: R. Carlile, 1829).

Ward, Wilfrid, *The Life and Times of Cardinal Wiseman*, 2 vols (London: Longmans, Green, and Co., 1897).

Ware, Jr, Henry, *The Life of the Saviour*, 7th edn (Boston: American Unitarian Association, 1873).

[Williams, Sir James], *An hour in His Majesty's Gaol, of Newgate, on Friday the 22nd December, 1820*, 2nd edn (London: J. Nisbett, n.d. [1830]).

Wiseman, Nicholas, *An Appeal to the Reason and Good Feeling of the English People on the Subject of the Catholic Hierarchy* (London: Thomas Richardson and Son, 1850).

——— *Essays on Various Subjects*, 3 vols (London: Charles Dolman, 1853).

——— *Horae Syriacae: seu commentationes et anecdota res vel litteras syriacas spectantia* (Rome: Francisci Bourliè, 1828).

——— *Lectures on the Principal Doctrines and Practices of the Catholic Church, delivered at St. Mary's Moorfields, during the Lent of 1836*, 2 vols (London: Joseph Booker, 1836).

——— *The Real Presence of the Body and Blood of Our Lord Jesus Christ in the Blessed Eucharist, Proved From Scripture*, new edn (Dublin: James Duffy and Co., n.d.).

SECONDARY SOURCES

Anger, Suzy, *Victorian Interpretation* (Ithaca: Cornell University Press, 2005).

Annan, Noel, *Leslie Stephen: The Godless Victorian* (New York: Random House, 1984).

Arnstein, Walter L., *The Bradlaugh Case: Atheism, Sex, and Politics among the Late Victorians* (Columbia, Missouri: University of Missouri Press, 1983).

Barbeau, Jeffrey W., *Coleridge, the Bible, and Religion* (Basingstoke and New York: Palgrave Macmillan, 2008).

Barrow, Logie, *Independent Spirits: Spiritualism and English Plebeians, 1850–1910* (London: Routledge & Kegan Paul, 1986).

Bebbington, D. W., *Evangelicalism in Modern Britain: A History from the 1730s to the 1980s* (London: Unwin Hyman, 1989).

Bell, E. Moberly, *Josephine Butler: Flame of Fire* (London: Constable and Co., 1962).

Bevington, Merle Mowbray, *The Saturday Review, 1855–1868: Representative Educated Opinion in Victorian England* (New York: Columbia University Press, 1941).

Booth-Tucker, F. de L., *The Life of Catherine Booth: The Mother of The Salvation Army*, 3rd edn, 2 vols (London: Salvationist Publishing, 1924).

Bostridge, Mark, *Florence Nightingale: The Making of An Icon* (New York: Farrar, Straus and Giroux, 2008).

Boyd, Robert, *Emily Gosse: A Life of Faith and Works* (Bath: Olivet Books, 2004).

Bronkhurst, Judith, *William Holman Hunt: A Catalogue Raisonné*, 2 vols (New Haven: Yale University Press for the Paul Mellon Centre for Studies in British Art, 2006).

Brown, Alan W., *The Metaphysical Society: Victorian Minds in Crisis, 1869–1880* (New York: Octagon Books, 1973).

Budd, Susan, *Varieties of Unbelief: Atheists and Agnostics in English Society, 1850–1960* (London: Heinemann, 1977).

Bullen, Donald A., *A Man of One Book? John Wesley's Interpretation of the Bible* (Milton Keynes: Paternoster, 2007).

Butler, Perry (ed.), *Pusey Rediscovered* (London: SPCK, 1983).

Caine, Barbara, *Victorian Feminists* (Oxford: Oxford University Press, 1992).

A Complete Index to C. H. Spurgeon's Sermons, 1855–1917 (Pasadena, Texas: Pilgrim Publications, 1980).

Calabria, Michael D. and Macrae, Janet A. (eds), *'Suggestions for Thought' by Florence Nightingale: Selections and Commentaries* (Philadelphia: University of Pennsylvania Press, 1994).

Cook, Edward, *The Life of Florence Nightingale*, 2 vols (London: Macmillan, 1913).

Currie, Robert, *Methodism Divided: A Study in the Sociology of Ecumenicalism* (London: Faber and Faber, 1968).

Daggers, Jenny and Neal, Diana (eds), *Sex, Gender, and Religion: Josephine Butler Revisited* (New York: Peter Lang, 2006).

Davies, Horton, *Worship and Theology in England: From Watts and Wesley to Martineau, 1690–1990*, Vol. IV (Grand Rapids, Michigan: Eerdmans, 1996 [originally 1961]).

Davies, Rupert, George, A. Raymond, and Rupp, Gordon (eds), *A History of the Methodist Church in Great Britain*, Vol. II (London: Epworth Press, 1978).

De Groot, Christiana and Taylor, Marion Ann (eds), *Recovering Nineteenth-Century Women Interpreters of the Bible* (Atlanta: Society of Biblical Literature, 2007).

Desmond, Adrian, *Huxley: From Devil's Disciple to Evolution's High Priest* (London: Penguin, 1997).

Elliott-Binns, L. E., *Religion in the Victorian Era* (London: Lutterworth Press, 1946).

Ellison, Robert H., *The Victorian Pulpit: Spoken and Written Sermons in Nineteenth-Century Britain* (Selinsgrove, Pennsylvania: Susquehanna University Press, 1998).

Faught, C. Brad, *The Oxford Movement: A Thematic History of the Tractarians and Their Times* (University Park, Pennsylvania: Pennsylvania State University Press, 2003).

Ferrell, Lori Anne, *The Bible and the People* (New Haven: Yale University Press, 2008).

Flammang, Lucretia A., '"And Your Sons and Daughters Will Prophesy": The Voice and Vision of Josephine Butler', in Julie Melnyk (ed.), *Women's Theology in Nineteenth-Century Britain: Transfiguring the Faith of Their Fathers* (New York: Farland Publishing, 1998), 151–64.

Forrester, David, *Young Doctor Pusey: A Study in Development* (London: Mowbray, 1989).

Fothergill, Brian, *Nicholas Wiseman* (New York: Doubleday, 1963).

Franklin, R. William, 'The Impact of Germany on the Anglican Catholic Revival in Nineteenth-Century Britain', *Anglican and Episcopal History*, 61, 4 (December 1992), 433–48.

Frye, Northrop, *The Great Code: The Bible and Literature* (New York: Harcourt Brace Jovanovich, 1982).

Fullerton, W. Y., *C. H. Spurgeon: A Biography* (London: William and Norgate, 1920).

Galchinsky, Michael, *The Origin of the Modern Jewish Woman Writer: Romance and Reform in Victorian England* (Detroit: Wayne State University Press, 1996).

Gardner, Phil, *The Lost Elementary Schools of Victorian England: The People's Education* (London: Croom Helm, 1984).

Garnett, Jane, 'Commercial ethics: a Victorian perspective on the practice of theory', in Roger Crisp and Christopher Cowton (eds), *Business Ethics: Perspectives on the Practice of Theory* (Oxford: Oxford University Press, 1998), 117–38.

George, Timothy, 'John Calvin: Comeback Kid', *Christianity Today* (September 2009), 31.

Giebelhausen, Michaela, *Painting the Bible: Representation and Belief in Mid-Victorian Britain* (Aldershot: Ashgate, 2006).

Glover, Willis B., *Evangelical Nonconformists and Higher Criticism in the Nineteenth Century* (London: Independent Press, 1954).

Grass, Tim, *Gathering to His Name: The Story of Open Brethren in Britain and Ireland* (Milton Keynes: Paternoster, 2006).

Green, Roger J. *Catherine Booth: A Biography of the Cofounder of The Salvation Army* (Grand Rapids, Michigan: Baker, 1996).

Grodzins, Dean, *American Heretic: Theodore Parker and Transcendentalism* (Chapel Hill, North Carolina: University of North Carolina Press, 2002).

Gurney, Elizabeth, *Elizabeth Fry's Journeys on the Continent, 1840–1841* (London: John Lane, 1931).

Hanna, Robert C. *The Dickens Christian Reader: A Collection of New Testament Teachings and Biblical References from the Works of Charles Dickens* (New York: AMS Press, 2000).

Hinchliff, Peter, *Benjamin Jowett and the Christian Religion* (Oxford: Clarendon Press, 1987).

Hindmarsh, D. Bruce, *The Evangelical Conversion Narrative: Spiritual Autobiography in Early Modern England* (Oxford: Oxford University Press, 2005).

Hopkins, Mark, *Nonconformity's Romantic Generation: Evangelical and Liberal Theologies in Victorian England*, Studies in Evangelical History and Thought (Milton Keynes: Paternoster, 2004).

Hoppen, K. Theodore, *The Mid-Victorian Generation: 1846–1886* (Oxford: Clarendon Press, 1998).

Howsam, Leslie, *Cheap Bibles: Nineteenth-Century Publishing and the British and Foreign Bible Society* (Cambridge: Cambridge University Press, 1991).

Isichei, Elizabeth, *Victorian Quakers* (Oxford: Oxford University Press, 1970).

Jiménez, Nilda (compiler), *The Bible and the Poetry of Christina Rossetti* (Westport, Connecticut: Greenwood Press, 1979).

Jones, Tod E., *The Broad Church: A Biography of a Movement* (Lanham, Maryland: Lexington Books, 2003).

Jordan, Jane, *Josephine Butler* (London: Hambledom Continuum, 2007 [originally 2001]).

Kent, John, *Elizabeth Fry* (London: B. T. Batsford, 1962).

Kidd, Colin, *The Forging of Races: Race and Scripture in the Protestant Atlantic World, 1600–2000* (Cambridge: Cambridge University Press, 2006).

Knight, Mark and Mason, Emma, *Nineteenth-Century Religion and Literature: An Introduction* (Oxford: Oxford University Press, 2006).

Kruppa, Patricia Stallings, *Charles Haddon Spurgeon: A Preacher's Progress* (New York: Garland Publishing, 1982).

Landow, George P., *Victorian Types, Victorian Shadows: Biblical Typology in Victorian Literature, Art and Thought* (Boston: Routledge & Kegan Paul, 1980).

Larsen, Timothy, 'A. S. Peake, the Free Churches, and Modern Biblical Criticism', *Bulletin of the John Rylands University Library of Manchester*, 86, 3 (Autumn 2004), 23–53.

——'Austen Henry Layard's Nineveh: The Bible and Archaeology in Victorian Britain', *Journal of Religious History*, 33, 1 (March 2009), 66–81.

——'Charles Bradlaugh, Militant Unbelief, and the Civil Rights of Atheists', in Caroline Litzenberger and Eileen Groth Lyon (eds), *The Human Tradition in Modern Britain* (Lanham, Maryland: Rowman and Littlefield, 2006), 127–38.

——'Christina Rossetti, the Decalogue, and Biblical Interpretation', *Zeitschrift für Neuere Theologiegeschichte*, 16, 1 (2009), 21–36.

——*Contested Christianity: The Political and Social Contexts of Victorian Theology* (Waco, Texas: Baylor University Press, 2004).

——*Crisis of Doubt: Honest Faith in Nineteenth-Century England* (Oxford: Oxford University Press, 2008).

———'Defining and Locating Evangelicalism', in Timothy Larsen and Daniel J. Treier (eds), *The Cambridge Companion to Evangelical Theology* (Cambridge: Cambridge University Press, 2007), 1–14.

———'E. B. Pusey and Holy Scripture', *Journal of Theological Studies*, 60, 2 (October 2009), 490–526.

———*Friends of Religious Equality: Nonconformist Politics in Mid-Victorian England* (Woodbridge, Suffolk: Boydell, 1999; Milton Keynes: Paternoster Press, 2007).

———'John William Colenso', in Jeffrey P. Greenman and Timothy Larsen (eds), *Reading Romans through the Centuries: From the Early Church to Karl Barth* (Grand Rapids, Michigan: Brazos Press, 2005), 187–204.

———'Joseph Barker and Popular Biblical Criticism in the Nineteenth Century', *Bulletin of the John Rylands University Library of Manchester*, 82, 1 (Spring 2000), 115–34.

———'The Reception Given *Evangelicalism in Modern Britain* since its Publication in 1989', in Michael A. G. Haykin and Kenneth J. Stewart (eds), *The Emergence of Evangelicalism: Exploring Historical Continuities* (Nottingham: Apollos, 2008), 21–36.

Larson, Janet L., *Dickens and the Broken Scripture* (Athens, Georgia: University of Georgia Press, 1985).

Lemon, Rebecca, et al. (eds), *The Blackwell Companion to the Bible in English Literature* (Chichester: Wiley-Blackwell, 2009).

Lightman, Bernard, 'Interpreting Agnosticism as a Nonconformist Sect: T. H. Huxley's "New Reformation"', in Paul Wood (ed.), *Science and Dissent in England, 1688–1945* (Aldershot: Ashgate, 2004).

———'Huxley and Scientific Agnosticism: The Strange History of a Failed Rhetorical Strategy', *British Journal for the History of Science*, 35 (2002), 271–89.

Livesley, Alan, 'Regius Professor of Hebrew', in Perry Butler (ed.), *Pusey Rediscovered* (London: SPCK, 1983), 71–118.

Manton, Jo, *Mary Carpenter and the Children of the Streets* (London: Heinemann, 1976).

Martin, Roger H., 'Quakers, the Bible, and the British and Foreign Bible Society', *Quaker History: The Bulletin of the Friends Historical Association*, 85, 1 (Spring 1996), 14–16.

Mathers, Helen, 'The Evangelical Spirituality of a Victorian Feminist: Josephine Butler, 1828–1906', *Journal of Ecclesiastical History*, 52, 2 (April 2001), 282–312.

Matthew, H. C. G., 'Edward Bouverie Pusey: From Scholar to Tractarian', *Journal of Theological Studies*, n.s., 32, 1 (April 1981), 101–24.

———and Harrison, Brian (eds), *Oxford Dictionary of National Biography* (Oxford: Oxford University Press, 2004).

Milbank, Alison, 'Josephine Butler: Christianity, Feminism and Social Action,' in Jim Obelkevich, Lyndal Roper, and Raphael Samuel (eds), *Disciplines of Faith: Studies in Religion, Politics and Patriarchy* (London: Routledge, 1987).

Moore, James R., *The Post-Darwinian Controversies: A Study of the Protestant Struggle to Come to Terms with Darwin in Great Britain and America, 1870–1900* (Cambridge: Cambridge University Press, 1979).

Nash, David, *Blasphemy in Modern Britain: 1789 to the Present* (Aldershot: Ashgate, 1999).

Nolland, Lisa Severine, *A Victorian Feminist Christian: Josephine Butler, the Prostitutes and God*, Studies in Evangelical History and Thought (Carlisle: Paternoster, 2004).

Oppenheim, Janet, *The Other World: Spiritualism and Psychical Research in England, 1850–1914* (Cambridge: Cambridge University Press, 1985).

Prothero, Rowland E., *The Life and Correspondence of Arthur Penrhyn Stanley, D.D.*, 2 vols (London: John Murray, 1894).

Roberts, Dyfed Wyn (ed.), *Revival, Renewal, and the Holy Spirit*, Studies in Evangelical History and Thought (Milton Keynes: Paternoster, 2009).

Robertson, J. M., *A History of Freethought in the Nineteenth Century* (London: Watts & Co., 1929).

Rogerson, John, *Old Testament Criticism in the Nineteenth Century: England and Germany* (London: SPCK, 1984).

Rose, Jonathan, *The Intellectual Life of the British Working Classes* (New Haven: Yale University Press, 2001).

Rose, June, *Elizabeth Fry* (London: Macmillan, 1980).

Royle, Edward, *Victorian Infidels: The Origins of the British Secularist Movement 1791–1866* (Manchester: Manchester University Press, 1974).

Sandall, Robert, *The History of the Salvation Army, Volume 1: 1865– 1878*, 5 vols (London: Thomas Nelson and Sons Ltd, 1947).

Schiefen, Richard J., *Nicholas Wiseman and the Transformation of English Catholicism* (Shepherdtown, West Virginia: Patmos Press, 1984).

Schoepflin, Rennie B., 'Myth 14. That the Church Denounced Anesthesia in Childbirth on Biblical Grounds', in Ronald L. Numbers (ed.), *Galileo Goes to Jail and Other Myths about Science and Religion* (Cambridge, Massachusetts: Harvard University Press, 2009).

Shea, Victor and Whitla, William (eds), *'Essays and Reviews': The 1860 Text and Its Reading* (Charlottesville, Virginia: University of Virginia Press, 2000).

Sheehan, Jonathan, *The Enlightenment Bible: Translation, Scholarship, Culture* (Princeton: Princeton University Press, 2005).

Shelley, Bryan, *Shelley and Scripture: The Interpreting Angel* (Oxford: Clarendon Press, 1994).

Shepherd, Peter, 'Spurgeon's Funeral', *Baptist Quarterly*, 41, 2 (April 2005), 72–9.

Smith, F. B., *Florence Nightingale: Reputation and Power* (New York: St Martin's Press, 1982).

Steer, Roger, *Good News for the World: 200 Years of Making the Bible Heard: The Story of the Bible Society* (Oxford: Monarch Books, 2004).

Stephen, Sir Leslie (ed.), *Dictionary of National Biography* (Oxford: Oxford University Press, 1921–2).

Sugirtharajah, R. S., *The Bible and Empire: Postcolonial Explorations* (Cambridge: Cambridge University Press, 2005).

Taylor, Anne, *Annie Besant: A Biography* (Oxford: Oxford University Press, 1992).

Taylor, Marion Ann and Weir, Heather E. (eds), *Let Her Speak for Herself: Nineteenth-Century Women Writing on Women in Genesis* (Waco, Texas: Baylor University Press, 2006).

Tribe, David, *President Charles Bradlaugh, M.P.* (London: Elek Books, 1971).

Van Drenth, Annemieke and Haan, Francisca de, *The Rise of Caring Power: Elizabeth Fry and Josephine Butler in Britain and the Netherlands* (Amsterdam: Amsterdam University Press, 1999).

Walker, Pamela J., *Pulling the Devil's Kingdom Down: The Salvation Army in Victorian Britain* (Berkeley: University of California Press, 2001).

Webb, R. K., 'The Limits of Religious Liberty: Theology and Criticism in Nineteenth-Century England', in Richard J. Helmstadter (ed.), *Freedom and Religion in the Nineteenth Century* (Stanford: Stanford University Press, 1997), 120–49.

Webb, Val, *Florence Nightingale: The Making of a Radical Theologian* (St Louis: Chalice Press, 2002).

Whitney, Janet, *Elizabeth Fry: Quaker Heroine* (London: George G. Harrap, 1937).

Wigmore-Beddoes, Dennis G., *Yesterday's Radicals: A Study of the Affinity between Unitarianism and Broad Church Anglicanism in the Nineteenth Century* (Cambridge: James Clarke, 1971).

Wilbur, Earl Morse, *A History of Unitarianism: In Transylvania, England, and America* (Boston: Beacon Press, 1945).

Wolffe, John, *The Protestant Crusade in Great Britain, 1829–1860* (Oxford: Clarendon Press, 1991).

Woodward, E. L., *The Age of Reform: 1815–1870* (Oxford: Clarendon Press, 1938).

Zemka, Sue, *Victorian Testaments: The Bible, Christology, and Literary Authority in Early-Nineteenth-Century British Culture* (Stanford: Stanford University Press, 1997).

Index

Synoptic problem 147, 157, 213, 297
Synoptics 77
Syria 134
Syriac 47, 48, 53, 54, 253
Syro-Chaldaic 48, 54

Tanchuma 40
Taylor, John 149
Taylor, Marion Ann 241
Taylor, Robert 71, 72, 84, 249
Tertullian 37
Theist 140, 141
Theodore of Mopsuestia 38
Theodoret 38
Theosophical Society 74, 81
Theosophist(s) 80, 81
Theosophy 82
Thessalonians, biblical books of 1 and 2 71, 106, 205
Thirty-Nine Articles 33, 151
Tholuck, Friedrich August 15, 48
Thompson, Susannah, see Spurgeon, Susannah
Timothy, biblical books of 1 and 2 101, 163, 175, 183, 191, 192, 209, 294
Tischendorf, Constantin von 59
Titus, biblical book of 21, 150
Tractarian(s) 20, 24, 32, 41, 46, 75
Tractarianism 11, 20, 36, 224
Tregelles, S. P. 59
Tribe, David 83
Trinitarian(s) 60, 124, 151
Trinitarianism 148, 151, 153, 296
Trinity 60, 93, 95, 124, 137, 149, 156, 178, 288
Trinity College (Cambridge) 115
Trinity College (Dublin) 75
Trinity College (Oxford) 64
Tübingen school 97
Tuckerman, Joseph 142, 154
Tupper, Martin 258
Turton, Thomas 55, 56
Tyler, Henry 73
Tyndall, John 204

Unitarian(s) 6, 33, 95, 114, 115, 123, 137–67, 248, 273, 278, 296
Unitarian Fund for Promoting Unitarianism 149

Unitarianism 115, 137–67, 171, 296, 297
Universalist 123
University of Durham 227
Unorthodox 114, 115, 119, 137, 211
Unorthodoxy 64, 115
Upper Norwood 250
Ushaw College, see St Cuthbert's College (Ushaw)
Ushaw 46, 47
Ussher, James 98, 148

Vaughan, Charles 223
Victoria, Queen 137, 147, 169, 187, 253, 274
Victorians 1, 2, 3, 6, 8, 38, 51, 55, 72, 108, 113, 117, 135, 138, 205, 211, 220, 242, 251, 257, 270, 277, 286, 290, 295, 296, 297, 298
Victorian 1, 2, 3, 4, 5, 6, 7, 8, 9, 12, 19, 23, 41, 43, 47, 50, 52, 55, 68, 82, 83, 88, 90, 95, 98, 109, 110, 113, 114, 115, 135, 137, 138, 142, 157, 161, 162, 167, 169, 170, 176, 195, 199, 201, 203, 206, 208, 214, 219, 221, 224, 242, 249, 252, 260, 264, 278, 283, 284, 287, 291, 292, 295, 296
Virgil 94
Virgin Birth 71, 124, 131, 152, 288
Volney, C. F. 273
Voltaire 273

Wace, Henry 201, 203
Wales 252
Ward, Wilfrid 43, 47, 58
Ware, Henry, Jr 148, 155, 156
Watson, Richard 155
Wedgwood, Julia 232
Wesley, John 1
Wesleyan(s) 35, 36, 89, 90, 91, 92, 101, 103, 221, 223
Westcott, B. F. 271
Westminster Assembly 249
Westminster catechism 249
Westminster Confession 249
Westminster 44, 56, 65, 223
White, Blanco 45, 142
Wieseler, Karl 29
Wigmore-Beddoes, Dennis C. 138, 145